Changing
College Classrooms

Diane F. Halpern and Associates

*Foreword by Lee R. Kerschner
and Jacquelyn Ann K. Kegley*

Changing
College Classrooms

*New Teaching and Learning Strategies
for an Increasingly Complex World*

 Jossey-Bass Publishers
San Francisco

47.00

Substantial discounts on bulk quantities of Jossey-Bass books are available to corporations, professional associations, and other organizations. For details and discount information, contact the special sales department at Jossey-Bass Inc., Publishers. (415) 433-1740; Fax (415) 433-0499.

For international orders, please contact your local Paramount Publishing International office.

Library of Congress Cataloging-in-Publication Data

Changing college classrooms : new teaching and learning strategies for an increasingly complex world / Diane F. Halpern, and associates.
    p. cm. — (The Jossey-Bass higher and adult education series)
    Includes bibliographical references and index.
    ISBN 1-55542-643-3
    1. College teaching. 2. Learning. I. Halpern, Diane F.
  II. Series.
  LB2331.C4543 1994
  378.1'25—dc20   93-43163
                                                                CIP

FIRST EDITION
HB Printing   10 9 8 7 6 5 4 3 2   *Code 9435*

Contents

Foreword   xiii
Lee R. Kerschner, Jacquelyn Ann K. Kegley

Preface   xv

The Editor   xix

The Contributors   xxi

1. Rethinking College Instruction for a Changing
   World   1
   Diane F. Halpern

   **Part One: Instructional Strategies
   That Promote Active Learning**   **11**

2. Inquiry as a Tool in Critical Thinking   13
   Alison King

3. Using Examples to Teach Concepts   39
   Betsy Newell Decyk

4. Fostering Creativity Through Problem Solving   64
   Cris E. Guenter

5. Cooperative Learning in the Classroom   74
   *James L. Cooper, Pamela Robinson,
   Molly McKinney*

6. Questioning Techniques for the Active
   Classroom   93
   C. Bobbi Hansen

   **Part Two: Developing
   Multicultural Understanding**   **107**

7. Cultural Diversity and Curricular Coherence   109
   Bernard Goldstein

8. Experiential Approaches to Enhancing Cultural
   Awareness   128
   Ellen N. Junn

9. Unmasking the Myths of Racism   165
   Gale S. Auletta, Terry Jones

10. Strategies for Teaching in a Multicultural
    Environment   175
    Elliott Robert Barkan

    **Part Three: Teaching With
    and About New Technologies**   **189**

11. Using the Internet for Teaching, Learning, and
    Research   191
    Craig Blurton

12. Enhancing Learning with Interactive Video   213
    Penelope Semrau, Barbara A. Boyer

13. Hypermedia as an Instructional Resource   230
    Patricia A. Backer, Joseph K. Yabu

14. Software Ethics: Teaching by Example   254
    *Ralph H. Miller, Joyce Kupsh,
    Carol Larson Jones*

    **Part Four: Assessing Teaching
    Effectiveness and Learning Outcomes**   **269**

15. Using Assessment to Develop a Culture of
    Evidence   271
    Ralph A. Wolff, Olita D. Harris

16. How Classroom Assessment Can Improve
    Teaching and Learning 289
       Susan G. Nummedal

17. Student Portfolios as an Assessment Tool 306
       Mary Kay Crouch, Sheryl I. Fontaine

18. Assessment's Role in Strengthening the Core
    Curriculum 329
       James L. Ratcliff

19. Closing Thoughts: Creating a New Scholarship
    of College Teaching 349
       Diane F. Halpern

    Name Index 353

    Subject Index 359

Foreword

For years a loud chorus of voices has been telling of the death of higher education in the United States and identifying the villain as the American university professor. *Changing College Classrooms* dispels the myth of a self-interested, isolated, unconcerned faculty who display arrogance, disdain, and disrespect for students, teaching, and the classroom. Here faculty members and others involved with undergraduate education demonstrate a keen awareness of and concern for student learning and development. They advocate a classroom environment that is a genuine learning community dealing with significant moral and social issues of concern to individuals and society, and "communicative reason" as a model for teaching and research.

This book is an exciting and highly useful addition to the literature on higher education and teaching. It provides concrete information and suggestions for the improvement of teaching, student learning, and the whole educational process. It is written by highly skilled and dedicated teachers of a college population representative of the new multidiverse student body.

Unlike the stereotype of the erudite professor "belaboring tiny slivers of knowledge, utterly without redeeming social value" and producing scholarship cloaked in "stupefying, inscrutable jargon" (C. Sykes, *Profscam* [Washington D.C.: Regnery Gateway, 1988], p. 6), the contributors of this volume are engaged in both applied research with social value and research on teaching and learning. They believe that teaching is *the top priority* of the university and a vocation with clear ethical and fiduciary demands and responsibilities, and they realize that the educational system must be responsive to both student and community needs.

Changing College Classrooms helps faculty and administrators tackle the task of providing students with empowering skills, such as creative, critical, cooperative problem solving, as well as helping them meet the needs of multidiverse student populations. The chapters that follow show how to provide a relevant and coherent multicultural curriculum and make multicultural awareness come alive in the classroom and in students' lives. Concern is also shown for giving students the ability to use technology effectively and the means to critically assess and understand the limitations of technological innovations. Counter to the charge that faculty rely on the complexity of teaching assessment in order to avoid accountability, the faculty who speak here deal openly, concretely, and effectively with the assessment of teaching effectiveness and learning outcomes.

We know that there are those who teach with pride and genuine commitment to excellence and to student development and learning. This book is for you, and we believe that you will find it supportive of your work and enlightening to your task.

January 1994
Lee R. Kerschner
President, California State University
Stanislaus, California

Former Senior Vice Chancellor for Academic Affairs, CSU
Past Co-Chair, Advisory Board,
CSU Institute for Teaching and Learning

Jacquelyn Ann K. Kegley
Professor of Philosophy, California State University
Bakersfield, California

CSU Outstanding Professor for 1987–1988
Past and Present Co-Chair, Advisory Board,
CSU Institute for Teaching and Learning

Preface

College is a time and place for change. Students invest four prime years of their lives and staggering amounts of money in the belief that college will change them in ways that will help them become productive, thoughtful citizens who can succeed in a rapidly changing world. The public has an implicit trust that colleges create, advance, and transmit knowledge and, in the process, that the participants are altered in beneficial ways. This hope for higher education was eloquently expressed by Sheldon Hackney, chair of the National Endowment for the Humanities, in his testimony at his Senate confirmation hearings: "Every human experience is enhanced by higher levels of knowledge" (*Chronicle of Higher Education,* July 21, 1993, p. B4).

As we approach a new millennium, we need educated, thinking adults more than ever. Although the future has always been uncharted and unknown, the threats and opportunities have never been so great. What can we do to provide college students with the knowledge, skills, and abilities to overcome the threats and capitalize on the opportunities? In other words, how can we change college classrooms so that students are prepared for a changing world? This volume was written to provide direction for those struggling with this question, for all the stakeholders in higher education: students and their families; faculty and administrators; state and national legislative bodies; and agencies and organizations concerned with education, employment, and the economy.

Overview of the Contents

This book is divided into four parts. Chapter One gives an overview of the issues addressed and provides a rationale and framework for the rest of the book. In this chapter, I coin the term *teachism* as a label for the antiteaching prejudice that is pervasive in and destructive to higher education. I then list ways for moving teaching ahead. Chapters Two through Six in Part One address the crucial question of how thinking and learning can be enhanced so that new ways of learning will promote new ways of understanding—deeper and more comprehensive understanding than that demonstrated when students parrot facts, resort to empty slogans, or accept information without critical thought.

In Part Two, Chapters Seven through Ten focus on the increasingly diverse composition of college campuses that were formerly mostly populated with white males. The changing nature of the student body and the world points to the need for sensitivity toward those different than ourselves. Providing students with a basis for understanding and appreciating a wide range of personal and cultural differences is a critically important goal, and the contributors of these chapters devote serious attention to teaching and learning issues in a multicultural environment.

One of the primary forces driving the changes on campus is the exponential growth of technology, which is the theme of Part Three. Technology now allows us to instantly communicate with anyone in virtually any corner of the world. Once the greatest promoter of literacy, the invention of movable type, is now being usurped by the development of hypermedia, CD-Roms, interactive video, and the like. Chapters Eleven through Fourteen address ways to use this new technology to enhance teaching and learning.

Chapters Fifteen through Eighteen in Part Four consider some of the ways we determine how and if students are learning what we want them to learn. The only way we can know if students have become more cooperative, more knowledgeable, less prejudiced, or more skilled is by assessing cognitive and emotional growth over the college years. The contributors of these chapters present an overview of the issues involved in the assessment of learning outcomes. Finally, in Chapter Nineteen I "have the last word" and invite readers to reflect and act on the immense challenge of the changing college classroom.

Acknowledgments

I have been very fortunate in having so many fine colleagues who believe that the future of America lies in its most precious commodity — educated, thinking adults — and that the best way to ensure the future is by providing the best education possible for our college students. *Changing College Classrooms,* which is dedicated to this ideal, came to fruition because of the efforts of the wonderful staff at the California State University's Institute for Teaching and Learning, especially Helen Roberts, and the many reviewers who volunteered their time to read chapters and provide guidance in the crafting of its contents. These include: Julie LeMay Abner, Milton Clark, DeShea Rushing-McCauley, and Rodney Simard, in the English Department at California State University, San Bernadino; Susan Nummedal, in the Psychology Department at California State University, Long Beach; Kathleen Mitkika, at the Institute for Teaching and Learning; Daniel Martinez, in the Institutional Research Department at San Bernardino Valley College; Oliva Espin, in the Women's Studies Department at San Diego State University; and Ann M. Johns, in the Linguistics Department at California State University, San Diego. I especially thank Joanne Gainen at Santa Clara University for her insightful comments on an earlier draft of this book. My thanks to all of these individuals and also to several anonymous reviewers for their hard work and for believing that we can make positive changes in teaching and learning in college classrooms. Like all of the contributors to this edited volume, as well as the faculty, administrators, and others who care enough about college students to read this book, you are the real heroes of this story.

I also wish to express my sincere appreciation to the chapter contributors. All of their profits generated from the sale of this book will be donated to the California State University System to be used to change our college classrooms in ways that will help prepare our students for the new millennium.

January 1994   Diane F. Halpern
                                                 San Bernardino, California

The Editor

DIANE F. HALPERN is professor of psychology at California State University, San Bernardino. She earned her B.A. degree (1969) from the University of Pennsylvania, her M.A. degree (1972) from Temple University, and a second M.A. degree (1977) and her Ph.D. degree (1979) from the University of Cincinnati, all in psychology. Before joining the faculty at California State University, San Bernardino, she was a lecturer at the University of California, Riverside.

Halpern is the recipient of many awards for her teaching and research, including the California State University's State-Wide Outstanding Professor award, the Outstanding Alumna award from the University of Cincinnati, the Silver Medal award from the Council for the Advancement and Support of Education, and the G. Stanley Hall Lecture award from the American Psychological Association. She is the author or editor of several books in the area of cognition and instruction: *Thought and Knowledge: An Introduction to Critical Thinking* (2nd ed., 1989), *Sex Differences in Cognitive Abilities* (2nd ed., 1992), *Enhancing Thinking Skills in the Sciences and Mathematics* (1992), and *Student Outcomes Assessment: What Institutions Stand to Gain* (1987). Halpern is the guest coeditor, with Susan Nummedal, of a special issue of the journal *Teaching of Psychology* titled "Psychologists Teach Critical Thinking" (1994). She has received a Fulbright award to teach critical thinking at Moscow State University in Russia, where she plans to work with government officials on reforming higher education. She has also worked as a visiting professor at the Instituto Technologico y de Estudios Superiores in Monterrey, Mexico.

Halpern's most recent work is with the U.S. Department of Education's Project 2000, for which she is consulting on a plan to implement the higher-education goal of increasing the proportion of college graduates who can think critically.

The Contributors

GALE S. AULETTA is professor of communication and co-director of the Center for the Study of Intercultural Relations at California State University, Hayward. She received her B.A. degree (1968) from California State University, Hayward, and her M.A. (1970) and Ph.D. (1978) degrees from the University of California, Los Angeles, in speech communication. She publishes, receives grants, and consults in the areas of intercultural communication and integrating multicultural perspectives into higher education. She is the corecipient of the Woman of the Year award for the California State University, 1988.

PATRICIA A. BACKER is assistant professor of industrial technology at San Jose State University. She received her B.S. degree (1977) from Rutgers University in chemical engineering, her M.A. and M.S. degrees (1982) from Tennessee Temple University in education, and her M.A. (1986) and Ph.D. degrees (1987) from Ohio State University in neurocognition. At San Jose State University she is primarily responsible for the course titled Documentation and Communication Systems, for which she has developed hypermedia instructional modules. She serves on the editorial board of the *Journal of Industrial Technology* and has worked as a research associate for the Army Research Institute.

ELLIOTT ROBERT BARKAN is professor of history and ethnic studies at California State University, San Bernardino, and has been a visiting Fulbright professor at the University of Trondheim, Norway, for 1992–93. He received his B.A. degree (1962) from Queens College and his Ph.D. degree (1969) from Harvard University in history. His principal areas of research for the past two decades have been comparative ethnicity and immigration and naturalization patterns in the United States. He has also long advocated curricular reforms to integrate multiculturalism and gender. Barkan's publications include *California's New Americans: A Manual for Analyzing History with Computers* (1988), *Asian and Pacific Islander Migration to the United States: A Model of New Global Patterns* (1992), and *The Quest Continues: The Immigrant in American Society, 1920s–1990s* (1993).

CRAIG BLURTON is associate director of the NASA Classroom of the Future Project at Wheeling Jesuit College. He received his B.A. (1974), M.A. (1976), and Ph.D. (1985) degrees from Arizona State University in education, with an emphasis in elementary science education. Until recently, Blurton was an associate professor of education at California State University, San Bernardino, and served as the acting director of instructional technology at the California State University Chancellor's Office.

BARBARA A. BOYER is chair of the art department and professor of art education at California State University, Los Angeles. She received her B.S. degree (1958) from the University of New York in art education and fine arts, her M.A. degree (1968) from San Jose State University in educational administration, and her Ph.D. degree (1980) from the University of Oregon in art education. Her research concentration is cultural and technological influences on learning about art. Boyer has been chair of the L.A. County Art Education Council and president of the United States Society for Education in Art. Recently she was recognized as Outstanding Higher Education Art Educator by the California Art Education Association and the National Art Education Association. She has lectured extensively on cultural literacy and visual learning in technology both nationally and internationally.

JAMES L. COOPER is professor of graduate education at California State University, Dominguez Hills. He received his B.A. degree (1967) from the University of Michigan in psychology, and his M.A. (1969) and Ph.D. (1976) degrees from the University of Iowa in experimental psychology and educational psychology, respectively. His research interests include college teaching effectiveness and cooperative learning. Cooper is coordinator of the International Association for the Study of Cooperation in Education. He is also the director of the Network for Cooperative Learning in Higher Education and editor of the newsletter *Cooperative Learning and College Teaching*.

MARY KAY CROUCH is assistant professor of English, coordinator of the Developmental Writing Program, and director of the Teaching Associate Program at California State University, Fullerton. She teaches graduate courses in writing theory and practice and undergraduate courses in writing, grammar analysis, and detective fiction. She also conducts workshops in the teaching and evaluation of writing for teachers of English as a second language (ESL) students across the curriculum. She received her B.A. degree (1964) from Southern Illinois University in English, her M.A. degree (1978) from California State University, Long Beach, in English, and her Ph.D. degree (1988) from the University of Southern California in English. Crouch's publications include essays on the writing conference, developmental issues in training teaching assistants, and the influence of Vietnamese women on their family literacy practices.

BETSY NEWELL DECYK has been a lecturer in philosophy at California State University, Long Beach, for nine years. She received her B.A. degree (1970) from Mount Holyoke College in philosophy, magna cum laude, and her M.A. (1974) and Ph.D. degrees (1981) from Claremont Graduate School in philosophy. Decyk is recognized as an outstanding teacher of philosophy and has won the Special Recognition for Teaching award from the Student Philosophy Association at California State University, Long Beach, in 1990 and in 1986. Her works include a video, *Exampling* (1991), and "Solving by Resolving: Negotiation as Problem-Solving" in the *APA Newsletter on Teaching Philosophy* (Summer 1987).

SHERYL I. FONTAINE is assistant professor of English and Writing Center coordinator at California State University, Fullerton. She received her B.A. degree (1977) from Saint Lawrence University and her Ph.D. degree (1984) from the University of California, San Diego, in English. Fontaine teaches graduate and undergraduate courses on writing, the teaching and tutoring of writing, and contemporary poetry. She has published essays on the topics of academic discourse, writing program administration, and the displinary evolution of composition. She has also edited *Nothing Begins with N: New Investigations of Freewriting* (with Peter Elbow and Pat Belanoff, 1991) and *Writing Ourselves into the Story: Unheard Voices from Composition Studies* (with Susan Hunter, 1993).

BERNARD GOLDSTEIN is a member of the Board of Trustees of the California State University and professor of biology at San Francisco State University. He received his B.A. (1962) and M.A. (1964) degrees from California State University, San Francisco, in biology, and his Ph.D. degree (1968) from the University of California, Davis, in zoology. He served as the chair of the CSU statewide Academic Senate from 1984 through 1987 and has authored numerous publications in zoology, human sexuality, and the assessment of quality in undergraduate institutions.

CRIS E. GUENTER is associate professor of fine arts/curriculum and instruction at California State University, Chico. She received her B.F.A. (1976) and B.S. (1976) degrees from Pennsylvania State University in art and art education, respectively, and her M.A.T. (1983) and Ed.D. (1985) degrees from the University of Wyoming in painting and graphics and educational foundations, respectively. She has made many presentations on creativity and arts education at the state, national, and international levels and is also a practicing artist who exhibits her paintings, prints, and photographs at national exhibitions.

C. BOBBI HANSEN teaches in the College of Education at the University of San Diego. She received her B.S. degree (1967) from the University of Indiana in education, her M.S. degree (1972) from the University of Wisconsin, Madison, in education, and her Ed.D. degree (1980) from the University of Southern California in education. She has presented numerous papers at state and national conferences on topics such as thinking skills, metacognition, problem solving, and cooperative learning.

OLITA D. HARRIS is associate professor of social work and associate dean of undergraduate studies at California State University, San Diego. She received her B.A. degree (1967) from Rocky Mountain College, Billings, Montana, in biology and sociology, and her M.S.W. (1969) and Ph.D. (1977) degrees from the University of Denver in social work. Her past publications, presentations, and current research focus on student outcomes assessment and curriculum development.

CAROL LARSON JONES is associate professor in the Management and Human Resources Department in the College of Business Administration at California State Polytechnic University, Pomona. She teaches managerial communications and administrative management at both the graduate and undergraduate levels. She received her B.S. degree (1968) from San Jose State University in business, her M.B.A. degree (1970) from Golden State University, and her Ed.D. degree (1980) from the University of Northern Colorado in business teaching. Jones is past state president of the California Business Education Association. She is currently completing research in the areas of group writing, collaborative writing, and telecommuting. She recently returned from Swaziland, Africa, where she conducted research for a *Women in Development* monograph.

TERRY JONES is professor of sociology and social services, vice president of the California Faculty Association, and co-director of the center for the Study of Intercultural Relations at California State University, Hayward. He received his B.A. degree (1964) from Idaho State University in sociology, and his M.S.W. (1971) and Ph.D. (1974) degrees from the University of California, Berkeley, in social work. He publishes, receives grants, and consults in the areas of race and racism, criminal justice, and the sociology of sports. He is the recipient of the Human Rights Award from the California Faculty Association, 1991, and was voted Outstanding Professor in 1990.

ELLEN N. JUNN is associate professor in the Department of Child Development at California State University, Fullerton. She is also educational equity coordinator for the School of Human Development and Community Services. She received her B.A. degree (1979) from the University of Michigan, Ann Arbor, and her M.A. (1982) and Ph.D. (1984) degrees from Princeton University, all in psychology. Junn was selected through the California Association for the Education of Young Children to serve as one of twelve public policy interns for California.

ALISON KING is professor of education at California State University, San Marcos. She received her B.A. (1966) and M.A. (1976) degrees from California State University, Fullerton, in psychology and educational psychology, respectively, and her Ph.D. degree (1981) from the University of California, Riverside, in education. She has taught at California State University, San Bernardino, and also held a professorship at Chapman University in Orange, California, where she earned the position of Wang Research Fellow. King's research areas are cognitive strategies, critical thinking, and cooperative learning.

JOYCE KUPSH is professor in the Operations Management Department in the College of Business Administration at California State Polytechnic University, Pomona. She received her B.A. (1957) and M.S. (1961) degrees from Emporia State University and her Ed.D. degree (1975) from Arizona State University, Tempe, all in business. Kupsh teaches presentations and ergonomics at both the graduate and undergraduate levels and is director of the Presentation Design Center. She has conducted seminars throughout the United States and Canada, written numerous magazine and journal articles, and authored a number of textbooks. Her most recent book is *How to Create High-Impact Presentations* (1993).

MOLLY McKINNEY is a graduate student in the Education Department at Chapman University. She received her B.A. degree (1991) from California State University, Dominguez Hills, in behavioral sciences and is working toward an M.A. degree in education.

RALPH H. MILLER is professor in and chair of the Operations Management Department in the College of Business Administration at California State Polytechnic University, Pomona. He received his B.A. degree (1967) from the University of California, Berkeley, his M.A. degree (1969) from San Jose State University, and his Ph.D. degree (1979) from Claremont Graduate School, all in applied statistics and quantitative methods. Miller has received several teaching awards from the students in the College of Business Administration and has been elected to membership in Phi Kappa Phi, Delta Mu Delta, Psi Chi, Blue Key, and Golden Key National Honor Societies. He is a member of the Decision Sciences Institute, the Institute of Management Science, the American Association for the Advancement of Science, and the American Psychological Association.

SUSAN G. NUMMEDAL is professor of psychology and director of faculty development at California State University, Long Beach. She received her B.A. degree (1964) from the University of California in political science and her Ph.D. degree (1970) from the University of Minnesota in educational psychology. Nummedal has published several articles on critical thinking, improving student learning, student outcomes assessment, and classroom assessment.

JAMES L. RATCLIFF is professor of higher education and director of the Center for the Study of Higher Education at Pennsylvania State University. He received his B.A. degree (1968) from Utah State University in history, and his M.A. (1972) and Ph.D. (1976) degrees from Washington State University in higher education. He is executive director of the National Center of Postsecondary Teaching, Learning, and Assessment and editor of the *Journal of General Education*.

PAMELA ROBINSON is a part-time lecturer on psychology at California State University, Dominguez Hills. She received her B.A. (1991) from California State University, Dominguez Hills, in psychology, and her M.A. (1993) in psychology from California State University, Fullerton.

PENELOPE SEMRAU is professor of instructional technology in the School of Education at California State University, Los Angeles. She received her B.S. degree (1972) from the University of Wisconsin and her M.S. degree (1980) from Illinois State University in art education, and her Ph.D. (1987) from the Ohio State University in art education and computer graphics. Semrau has an extensive background of working with K–12 educators and has taught in the public schools. Her professional focus is the design, development, evaluation, and integration of newer technological media such as videodiscs, CD-ROMs, hypermedia, and telecommunications into the educational curriculum. She has authored and coauthored numerous articles in scholarly publications and several books on the subject of technology. She is the principal author for a textbook entitled *Interactive Video in Education* (1994), which she coauthored with Barbara Boyer.

RALPH A. WOLFF is associate executive director of the Accrediting Commission for Senior Colleges and Universities of the Western Association of Schools and Colleges, a position he has held since 1981. He received his B.A. degree (1968) from Tufts University and his J.D. (1971) from the National Law Center, George Washington University. From 1986 to 1988 he coordinated a comprehensive rewriting of the commission's accrediting standards, including significant revisions to standards dealing with academic freedom, general education, the meaning of the doctoral degree, assessment, and diversity. Since adoption of these new standards, he has been responsible for developing WASC policies on assessment. Prior to joining the commission staff, Wolff was on the law faculty of the University of Dayton Law School. Previously, he was a founder of the Antioch School of Law and associate provost of Antioch College and dean of the Graduate School of Education.

JOSEPH K. YABU is associate professor of industrial technology at San Jose State University, where he is primarily responsible for the design and drawing area. He received his B.A. (1964) and his M.A. (1972) degrees from the University of Maryland in industrial education, and his Ph.D. degree (1994) from the University of Maryland in industrial education and sociology.

Changing
College Classrooms

Rethinking College Instruction for a Changing World

Diane F. Halpern

The times are changing. More than in any other segment of society, change is felt most sharply on college campuses, where young and older adults come together to prepare themselves for a changing world and to develop their skills and talents so that they can influence the direction of that change. The college experience is a critical stage in adult development because the students who sit in today's college classrooms are the future workers and leaders who will make important decisions about national and international defense, conservation of natural resources, revitalization of the economy, use of nuclear energy, and other aspects of our lives. They will search for cures for debilitating diseases such as cancer, heart disease, and AIDS; they will seek solutions to such societal ills as poverty, prejudice, homelessness, child abuse, loneliness, and crime; they will develop new food sources to relieve world hunger; they will create artworks so that the human condition can be examined, uplifted, and improved. The list of tasks before them is virtually endless.

Responding to and Directing Change

As we approach the new millennium, the multiplicity of technological and social changes we must deal with is truly staggering.

Many college students will end up working at jobs that don't exist today. It seems safe to predict that technologies will change in ways that not even science fiction writers can imagine. Looking back over just the fifteen years since I completed graduate school, I am reminded that the few computers that were in use when I was in college were mammoth mainframes that took up most of a large room. I recall a time, which seems to me to be not so very long ago, when the long-range plan for a large university was to add 8 K of memory to its mainframe. Today I am writing this chapter on a tiny notebook-size portable computer that is more powerful than the computer that served an entire large university only a short time ago.

Students in college now will face changes and advances in the workplace and in the world at large that we cannot even guess at today. It is thus more important than ever to switch from an emphasis on rote knowledge of content, which is quickly outdated, to an emphasis on the processes of thinking, learning, and questioning. This switch from content to process is required by the massive changes in what college students need to know and need to be able to do when they leave school if they are to succeed at a time when the only certainty is the rapidly accelerating rate of change.

College students are also changing. More than half of all college students in North America are now female, a substantial shift in the composition of student populations over the last decade. There are also increasing numbers of students from ethnic minorities and recent immigrant groups, resulting in a change, quite literally, in the complexion of higher education. Hawaii and California are already "majority-minority" states in which groups that used to be called minorities now make up over 50 percent of the population. Arizona, New Mexico, and Texas will soon join the ranks of their more westerly neighbors in terms of their ethnic makeup, with numerous other states rapidly moving toward increasing diversity in their populations.

As the gap between the haves and have-nots in society continues to grow, it is even more important that colleges in all sections of North America attract and retain more students from underrepresented ethnic groups. The enrollment of large numbers of students from minority groups that have been traditionally underrepresented means that colleges have to respond with changes in the way they teach and in what they teach. An increasing proportion of students are not native English speakers; many bring different traditions with them and offer opportunities for the expression of diverse viewpoints that were not available with a more homogeneous student body. This greater variety of cultures in classrooms also brings with it new occasions for misunderstanding and prejudice unless traditional assumptions about cultural differences and minority groups also change.

North America's "new" student groups want to learn about their own cultural backgrounds and group contributions, while the "old" student groups would benefit from learning more about other cultures. The beauty, accomplishments, and atrocities could be brought to light more fully for many cultures. We can all learn here. We need to prepare students to become global citizens, which requires a curriculum that reflects worldwide contributions to knowledge and that applies knowledge to worldwide situations. All of the academic disciplines must respond in new ways to the changing composition of the student body and to the need to be multiculturally literate. There can never again be a course on "world history" (like the one I had in high school) that covers only the European tradition. Similarly, world literature courses must encompass the globe in the material that is included, and psychology must become the psychology of all people, not just the study of a narrow subset of society. The natural sciences must find ways to appeal to females and students of color, or we will face a future with a serious shortage of scientists, engineers, and mathematicians (National Science Foundation, 1989). Schools of business and law must become increasingly international in their focus as the world shrinks around them. The changing nature of North American society and of the world can revitalize the college curriculum and create a vast array of exciting possibilities, if we plan and prepare appropriately.

Changing technologies and demographics require that the way teaching and learning are achieved must also change. Rural groups that used to be isolated can now participate in urban experiences via electronic networks, down links, and other innovations that make distant learning possible. International classrooms can be formed on a moment's notice, with students from varied socioeconomic backgrounds and geographical locations communicating as equal partners, teachers, and learners. Active learning can be encouraged with interactive video technology, cooperative learning experiences, and student self-assessments of what has been learned.

The time has also come to establish a "culture of evidence," an ethic in which information is gathered and examined for the purpose of improving the teaching and learning process. Assessment of student outcomes is needed so that college faculty can determine what works and to ensure that those constituencies who are paying the bills are getting a quality product for their investment. This is an exciting time in higher education, and the themes addressed in this volume offer a wealth of empirical evidence for answering fundamental questions about educational reform. What needs to be done to realize these reforms? How can we move college teaching ahead?

Combatting Teachism and Other Prejudices

If a visitor from another planet were to land in North America and learn about the vast changes that are occurring on college campuses, it would surely be impressed with the enormity and importance of providing a high-quality education to our future leaders. Here in the shadow of the atomic bomb, we have the ability to destroy all life on earth or, conversely, to work cooperatively and eradicate many of society's greatest ills. The choices and outcomes will depend on the ethics, values, skills, and knowledge of the young adults we are currently educating. Surely this alien visitor would conclude that college teaching must be one of the most desirable and prestigious jobs to which anyone could aspire. The alien would be wrong.

Of the many obstacles to moving teaching ahead, the anti-teaching prejudice that pervades higher education is the most pernicious. This prejudice is particularly deleterious because it confers second-class citizenship on professors who work "too hard" on their teaching. University professors are rewarded for visible and easily quantifiable activities such as publishing, making presentations at scholarly conferences and societies, receiving grants, consulting with private industry, or engaging in other activities that bring money into our cash-strapped campuses.

All professors know the rules for "getting ahead" in their profession. Wagner and Sternberg (1985), two psychologists well known for their work in intelligence, wrote about this aspect of "practical intelligence." They defined *practical intelligence* as intelligence relevant to one's everyday life. It is this intelligence that is necessary for success in one's chosen field.

Successful people presumably have a great deal of practical intelligence. This is what makes them successful. Practical intelligence for a salesperson in a high-fashion store would include, for example, knowledge about what shades and fabrics are currently in vogue, and practical intelligence for a waiter would include being able to remember what each patron ordered and knowing how to stack a serving tray so that the food doesn't fall off. The underlying idea is that smart people know what they need to know and know how to solve problems that will help them succeed in their profession.

What about practical intelligence for a college professor? What does the smart professor need to know? This is one area of practical knowledge that Wagner and Sternberg investigated. They listed a variety of common work-related activities for professors. They then had three groups of subjects — professors, graduate students, and undergraduates — rate the relative importance of each activity, given the time constraints that faculty all live under and the fact that not every worthwhile activity can be accomplished. The results showed clearly that the professors had a very different view from the other two groups about which activities were important and which were not. The professors knew that their income, status, and job security depended on their success in activities that were only tangentially related to their roles as teachers — activities such as writing grants and publishing narrow, esoteric manuscripts.

Of course, preparing grant proposals and writing scholarly articles are valuable endeavors that should enrich a professor's ability to teach in a subject area. The "teach or publish" dichotomy is false, because many fine professors can do both well, and new definitions of *scholarship* have been proposed that include research in teaching (see, for example, Boyer, 1990). But it is also true that time and effort are limited commodities, and when most rewards accrue to one-half of the teach-publish equation, the professor who is "practically intelligent" will know where to put her or his efforts. For professors, increased prestige, income, and job security are associated with activities that are not directly related to teaching.

Asking who created the state of affairs such that teaching is denigrated while other aspects of the professorial role are exalted is like asking who created prejudice. It is no secret that a professor's prestige is inversely related to how much he or she teaches. Thus, one of the most important things that we can do to improve the quality of postsecondary education is improve the status of college teaching. Faculty at low-prestige "teaching universities" have heavy teaching loads, whereas professors at prestigious research universities rarely teach at all. According to this prestige pecking order, the professor at the top of the heap is the one who never sees a student. This hierarchy is made painfully clear to professors from "teaching universities" whenever they reveal their place of employment to professors from universities that are identified as "research universities."

The relationship between teaching and compensation was the focus of a recent study by the National Center for Education Statistics (National Center on Postsecondary Teaching, Learning, and Assessment, 1993). Results from a large national sample of colleges and universities showed an inverse relationship between the amount of time tenure-track full-time faculty spend on teaching and instruction and their salary. That is, the more time professors spent in instruction-related activities, the less money they earned.

Ratings of university quality are based on such variables as the number of faculty publications, the Scholastic Aptitude Test scores of entering freshmen, and the amount of money received in grants. The quality of the teaching or of student learning is seldom, if ever, considered in these ratings. At many universities with excellent reputations, students sit crammed into lecture halls with seven hundred or more classmates, where they are taught by graduate students and tested with multiple-choice exams graded by a computer. In many instances it is possible to obtain a bachelor's degree without ever speaking to a professor. Few of these students or their families would consider enrolling at a teaching university, because that would mean a serious loss of status. The message is clear: what happens in the classroom is nowhere near as important as the more traditional indicators of educational quality—indicators that are unrelated to the quality of the education.

The language we use reflects these lop-sided standards. The very term *teaching load* evokes an image of a massive weight hanging around one's neck. If faculty members have been good, they can get release time from teaching so that they can pursue the important work of research. I have never heard of anyone getting release time from research so that she can work on improving her teaching. These attitudes are as deeply ingrained in our profession as other types of prejudice are ingrained in American society.

Prestige is also stratified within teaching loads. Graduate courses are more prestigious than undergraduate ones, and, for those who do teach undergraduates, upper-division courses are more prestigious than lower-division courses. Other responsibilities, such as advising and directing student activities, which are critically important to students, are valued even less than what happens in the classroom.

I have labeled these elitist attitudes *teachism,* and I believe that the effects are as pernicious as those of the other "isms"—racism, sexism, anti-Semitism, and ageism, to name a few. And while we may not like these attitudes, it serves no purpose to pretend that they don't exist. Unfortunately, there are no organizations like the National Association for the Advancement of Colored People or the American Association of Retired Persons to fight against teachism. It is largely a silent prejudice, which makes it all the more difficult to fight.

Improving Teaching at the College Level

If we are serious about improving undergraduate education, we must enhance the rewards that accrue to those who provide excellence in teaching in higher education. Here are some suggestions for eliminating teachism and placing more emphasis on the education portion of higher education:

1. *Reward good teaching with something more tangible than words.* Of course it is difficult to assess and reward teaching quality. It is far easier to count someone's number of publications than it is to quantify teaching skills, which is why many departments weight publications more heavily than teaching excellence in their retention and tenure decisions. But the assessment of teaching is not an impossible task. It is no more difficult to measure teaching than it is to measure many other constructs in psychology and other disciplines—constructs such as personality, locus of control, depression, and anxiety. The task is difficult, but not insurmountable.

2. *Create endowed professorships for excellence in teaching.* The general public, the business community, and alumni can be persuaded to provide the money needed for such endowed professorships. Education has been in the news a great deal lately, and now is a good time to seek outside funding for initiatives that enhance education. Many constituencies have a stake in higher education. We need to give the same status to outstanding teachers as we do to outstanding researchers and administrators.

3. *Highlight and publicize teaching excellence.* If your institution values good teaching, make this commitment part of your advertising campaign. Put it on your brochures, tell it to prospective students, and use it to recruit new faculty.

4. *Set up teaching assistance centers on every campus so that faculty members who care about their teaching can learn to be even better.* Encourage periodic lunches and other meetings where faculty can get together to discuss teaching. Few faculty members were ever taught how to teach, but it's never too late to learn. Improving what happens in college classrooms should be a career-long activity. Even the best teachers can always get better.

5. *Make publishing in teaching journals and writing textbooks*

a recognized and regularized component of the retention and tenure process.
Be sure that the tenure message includes a strong positive statement about making a contribution to teaching in one's field.
The message must be sent that faculty members should be contributing to the body of knowledge about teaching in their substantive area, which is at least as important as original research
in the discipline.

6. *Provide release time for course-related activities, such as planning a new course or establishing a laboratory for use with a course or
upgrading skills that are needed in teaching.* Administrators need to
use whatever perquisites are available to assist professors who
are working on their teaching. These "perks" include giving
faculty who have made a strong commitment to teaching a better choice of classes or teaching schedules. By most standards,
these are meager perks, but I have known departments that have
shed blood over far less.

7. *Provide nonevaluative peer and "expert" reviews of teaching.*
Many campuses have a system of peer review as part of the retention and promotion process. Faculty members need to be provided with information that they can use to improve in a manner separate from provision of evaluative feedback. We are all
more accepting of constructive feedback that is nonthreatening
than we are of feedback that has an important impact on our
careers.

8. *Institute some sort of teaching experience for all graduate students that includes information on how to teach effectively and feedback
from observations of actual teaching performance.* Departmental curriculum makes certain that students know the content matter
of their field, but schools must also be concerned with having
them develop skills in communicating that content matter. Very
few college professors received any formal instruction in how
to teach, yet they spend substantial portions of their working
day teaching others. This situation can be changed.

9. *Make research an integral part of college teaching, and be sure
to include classroom research (a topic discussed in several chapters in this
book).* All students should be involved in some aspect of the research experience. The skills required to formulate and execute
a research project are a necessary component of every under-

graduate's college experience. Teaching and research should not be considered as mutually exclusive. We can value them both and find ways in which they reinforce each other.

Conclusion

What I am calling for is a truly radical, systematic change in the way higher education does business. And change is difficult in higher education. It's been said that changing a university is a lot like moving a cemetery — you don't get a lot of help from the residents. But, change *is* possible if enough people care enough about teaching and learning at the college level.

Teaching can be a more valued component of the professor's role, without denigrating the importance of research. The following chapters are crammed with ways to improve college-level teaching and learning so that students graduate with the knowledge, skills, and abilities they will need for a changing world; but unless we change the "rules of the game" and act as though teaching is the most important contribution that professors can make to the future, the call for change will go unheeded. If higher education is to become a national priority, if we are serious about moving teaching ahead, it is time to put the rewards where our hearts and heads are. It's time to take college teaching seriously.

References

Boyer, E. L. *Scholarship Reconsidered: Priorities of the Professorate.* Princeton, N.J.: The Carnegie Foundation for the Advancement of Teaching, 1990.

National Center on Postsecondary Teaching, Learning, and Assessment. *Newsletter,* Winter 1993, *2,* 1–2, 4.

National Science Foundation. *Reports on the National Science Foundation Disciplinary Workshops on Undergraduate Education.* Washington, D.C.: National Source Foundation, 1989.

Wagner, R. K., and Sternberg, R. J. "Practical Intelligence in Real-World Pursuits: The Role of Tacit Knowledge." *Journal of Personality & Social Psychology,* 1985, *49,* 436–458.

PART ONE

Instructional Strategies That Promote Active Learning

Learning rarely, if ever, occurs passively. Cognitive psychologists and educators have come to recognize that "effective instruction focuses on the active involvement of students in their own learning, with opportunities for teacher and peer interactions that engage students' natural curiosity" (American Psychological Association, "Learner-Centered Psychological Principles: Guidelines for School Redesign and Reform [draft]." *The Psychology Teacher Network,* 1992, *2,* 5-12). The active and motivated nature of learning is not optimized in the "old" style of classrooms where students sit quietly, passively receiving the words of wisdom being professed by the lone instructor standing in front of the class. New ways of learning emphasize active questioning and cooperative group activities that keep students involved with the material they are learning. These themes are developed in this section, which focuses on new types of knowledge and better ways of learning it.

Alison King, in Chapter Two, provides many examples of the way in which the type of questions that instructors pose can promote critical thinking. She argues that what we ask students to *do* with the material they are learning will determine how they will think about it. In Chapter Three, Betsy Newell

Decyk examines the use of examples as a teaching and learning tool. She explains that the most typical example of a concept, the prototype, may bias students by emphasizing only those relationships that are found in typical examples. She describes a flexible way of teaching concepts with examples and demonstrates why students and their instructors need to consider examples that may not be the most typical of their category.

Education at all levels has frequently been criticized for stifling creativity. In Chapter Four, Cris E. Guenter discusses how to change this perception with the use of problem-solving assignments. The need to work cooperatively with others is another theme that is emerging as critically important for future leaders and other workers. James L. Cooper, Pamela Robinson, and Molly McKinney (Chapter Five) present a variety of techniques that can be used in any college classroom to provide students with cooperative learning experiences. In the final chapter in this section, Chapter Six, C. Bobbi Hansen brings together several of the themes addressed in the other chapters by showing how a variety of questioning techniques can promote critical and creative thinking and cooperative learning.

Chapter 2

Inquiry as a Tool
in Critical Thinking

Alison King

One thing that futurists (such as Naisbett and Aburdene, 1990; Toffler, 1990) agree on about life in the twenty-first century is that it will be even more complex than it is now. The number of decisions individuals will have to make about which career to pursue, how to use their leisure time, which consumer products to purchase, what political causes and candidates to support, how to manage their financial resources, and what to do in their personal relationships will increase dramatically, as will the number of variables impinging on those decisions and the number of options from which to choose. Making wise choices about what to believe and what to do requires the ability to think critically—that is, to analyze the arguments presented, make inferences, draw logical conclusions, and critically evaluate all relevant elements, as well as the possible consequences of each decision.

To complicate the issue, in the future, distinctions will become increasingly blurred between fact and opinion, between theory and belief, between what is real and what is simulated (Naisbitt and Aberdene, 1990; Toffler, 1990). The forms of simulated reality prevalent in current popular culture (for example, on television shows such as *Hard Copy* and *Unsolved Mysteries*, which blur the line between what actually happened and what we are led to think happened) will give way to new forms of simulated reality such as multisensual and interactive media, virtual reality, microcomputerized self-replicating biomechanical robots, and artificial creatures. These fields of study and the fast-growing sciences of genetic engineering, life extension, cryogenics, and other transhuman conditions will make it increasingly difficult to differentiate between artificial reality and the "real reality." Furthermore, whole new fields of information will emerge only to become obsolete within a few years (Toffler, 1990). Instant worldwide connectivity and communication software "agents" will pave the way for "virtual communities" where people interact on a regular basis without ever actually ("really") seeing, hearing, or touching each other (Elmer-Dewitt, 1992).

Thinking and Empowerment

In such a world it will be difficult for individuals to experience a sense of personal control, to know that they are making informed and free choices and that they are not being unduly influenced by others or manipulated by the way information has been presented to them or by whom. In short, it will become increasingly difficult for people to feel empowered in their lives. The ability to critically analyze issues that affect personal, social, and political decision making will distinguish those who feel in control of their lives from those who do not. In this respect, the ability to think critically can free people from the tyranny of the media, advertising, and the many other threats to personal choice with which they are bombarded daily. Thinking can be liberating because it empowers us to make our own decisions and thereby take control of our own lives.

Teaching can be a process of helping people to become personally empowered. Teaching students to think critically can enable them to take more control over both their own learning and their own destiny. When people are able to think carefully about issues and decisions, they are empowered to thoughtfully choose their own paths to follow—they become self-directed—rather than following others' directions. In deCharms's (1968) terms, they feel more like originators than pawns in other people's games. This sense of personal control or self-efficacy can be particularly lacking in disadvantaged and minority students, and when such students reach the university level, many are at risk academically (Wehlage and Rutter, 1986). Learning how to think critically can improve their academic performance, can help them gain control over their learning, and may even make the difference between dropping out of school and staying in (Wehlage and Rutter, 1986). Over time, the gains in personal autonomy and self-esteem resulting from learning how to approach life in a thoughtful manner can have a positive influence on the lives of all students; for "at risk" students in particular, such thinking-skills instruction can act as a social and political "equalizer." For all of us, becoming critical thinkers influences how we see the world, expands who we are, and changes the way in which we make choices and the impact those choices have on the quality of our lives.

It seems clear, then, that one of the major functions of our educational system should be to teach students to think critically — not just in the classroom, but in their daily lives. We can promote empowerment and autonomy by teaching them how to think. The U.S. government has become aware of the need to teach thinking at the university level and has taken an initial step in addressing this issue. In *America 2000: An Educational Strategy* (U.S. Department of Education, 1990), one of the main objectives identified for higher education is: "The proportion of college graduates who demonstrate an advanced ability to think critically, communicate effectively, and solve problems will increase substantially" (Goal 5: Objective 5).

Knowledge Construction

Much of what transpires in today's college classrooms is based on the outdated transmission model of teaching and learning: the professor lectures and the students take notes, read the text, memorize the material, and regurgitate it later on an exam. According to contemporary constructivist models of learning (for example, Resnick, 1987), knowledge cannot be transmitted from one person to another in such a passive manner. In the constructivist view, knowledge does not come packaged in books, in journals, on computer disks, or on tape recordings (or in professors' and students' heads) to be passed intact from one to another. Those things contain *information,* not knowledge. Rather, knowledge is a state of understanding and can exist only in the mind of the individual knower. As such, knowledge must be constructed by each individual through the process of trying to make sense of new information in terms of what that individual already knows.

From the constructivist perspective, when individuals are presented with new information, they use their own existing knowledge and previous experience to help them make sense of the new material. In particular, they make inferences, elaborate on the new information by adding details, and generate relationships between and among the new ideas and information already in memory—in short, they think critically about the new material (Brown and Campione, 1986; Brown, Bransford, Ferrara, and Campione, 1983; Thomas and Rohwer, 1986; Pressley and others, 1992; Wittrock, 1990). In effect, through this active process of constructing meaning for themselves, they generate new knowledge or modify their existing knowledge. To the extent that individuals engage in constructing new knowledge or reconstructing given information, rather than simply memorizing it, they gain a deeper understanding.

Information-processing theorists (for example, Mayer, 1981, 1984) argue that this process of reformulating given information or generating new information based on what is provided helps the individual build extensive cognitive structures connecting the new ideas together and linking them to what is already known. Such elaborated mental representations facilitate understanding and provide more cues for recall.

Thus, in the constructivist view of teaching and learning, learners think about new information in such a way that they transform that material in some manner, thereby constructing new knowledge. The practical implication of this perspective is that students need to be taught how to engage effectively in this knowledge construction process—that is, they need to be taught how to think critically.

A Model for Enhancing the Teaching
and Learning of Critical Thinking
in the College Classroom

Most university professors do not know how to teach critical thinking because they have never been provided with pedagogical methods for doing so. A major factor in this situation is that teachers tend to teach in the same way that they were taught (Kennedy, 1991), and most have been taught using a transmission model of teaching and learning based on the memorization of facts transmitted via lecture. But to be effective, professors need to do more than lecture. They must engage their students in active learning techniques — ways that help students construct knowledge rather than the professor simply transmitting information to them.

It is not surprising that college students do not know how to think — in many cases their professors have been doing their thinking for them. To promote student thinking, professors must stop lecturing all the time like a "sage on the stage" and learn to function as a "guide on the side" (King, 1993b). This is a considerable shift in roles for the professor, from being the one who has all of the answers and does most of the talking to being a facilitator who orchestrates the learning context, motivates students, provides resources, and poses questions to stimulate students to think up their own answers. How can a professor change from being a dispenser of information to a sparker of ideas? This shift can be achieved by focusing on asking instead of telling — questioning rather than lecturing.

Through the appropriate use of questions, instructors can help students to construct knowledge. Posing thought-provoking questions can prompt students to make connections between new information and what they already know and to integrate the ideas and topics that constitute a body of knowledge or discipline. They can then begin to view the concepts of a discipline not as discrete structures, but as integrated mental models. Similarly, effective questioning can help students to see links between a discipline and their daily lives and to see the interrelatedness of disciplines with each other.

The hallmark of a critical thinker is an inquiring mind.

Good thinkers are good questioners. A broad definition of critical thinking includes not only knowledge construction of the creation of meaning but also the ability to search for and use meaning (Beyer, 1987). Critical thinkers are constantly analyzing new situations, searching for complexity and ambiguity, looking for and making connections among aspects of a situation, speculating, searching for evidence, seeking links between a particular situation and their prior knowledge and experience. Good thinkers are always asking, "What does this mean?" "Is there another way to look at this?" "Why is this happening?" "What is the evidence for this?" and "How can I be sure?" Formulating questions such as these and using them to make meaning is what characterizes good thinking. Isidor Rabi, the 1944 Nobel Prize winner in physics, learned to be a questioner very early in life. He recalls that when he was a child, every day when he returned home from school his mother, instead of asking him what he had learned in school that day (as most other mothers did), asked him what good questions he had asked. Rabi claims that his mother's daily greeting on his return from school had a strong influence on the development of his inquiring mind.

The level of thinking that occurs in a college classroom is influenced by the level of questions asked. Particular questions can be used to activate the specific thinking processes and skills we wish students to engage in. For example, when questions are merely factual, only facts are recalled; however, when questions are at higher cognitive levels, requiring inferences and analysis, evaluation, and integration of information, critical thinking is more likely to occur. Unfortunately, research shows that fewer than 5 percent of teacher questions are high-level cognitive ones (Dillon, 1988; Kerry, 1987), which suggests that professors may not be asking the kinds of questions likely to induce critical thinking in their students. Furthermore, the frequency of student-generated questions in the classroom is very low, averaging .11 per hour per student in classrooms in several countries; of these, most are factual questions rather than high-level thought-provoking ones (Dillon, 1988; Kerry, 1987). Neither of these statistics is surprising, because most college professors have not been taught how to use questioning in the classroom.

What Needs to Be Taught and Learned

In terms of the skills and strategies of thinking that must be addressed during instruction, it is important to emphasize that critical thinking, problem solving, decision making, and creative thinking are not separate areas; rather they are all aspects of thoughtfulness, or sets of related and overlapping skills. Although there is no clear consensus on what constitutes critical thinking, most definitions of critical thinking in some way, directly or indirectly, address the skills of analyzing, inferring, synthesizing, application, evaluating, comparison-contrast, verifying, substantiating, explanation, and hypothesizing. In addition to learning these skills and how to use them in specific university courses and disciplines, students need to be able to transfer their critical thinking skills to other academic contexts and to learn to apply them to their everyday lives (personal choices, TV viewing, political decision making, consumer purchases, and so on).

But there is more to the teaching and learning of critical thinking than strategies and skills. Instruction for critical thinking should also address thinking dispositions, the languages of thinking, and metacognition (Perkins, 1992).

Thinking Dispositions

Having what Ennis (1986) and Baron (1988) call a disposition toward thinking, and what Langer (1989) refers to as mindfulness, involves possessing attitudes and beliefs that support good thinking. Such attitudes include openness to others' ideas and arguments, confidence in one's own ability to solve problems, curiosity, the desire to look for meaning in complex situations, and willingness to think adventurously (Baron, 1988; Ennis, 1986). Beliefs conducive to thoughtfulness include the ideas that thinking (rather than luck) can lead to the resolution of problems and that there is nothing inherently wrong with changing one's mind on an issue.

Unfortunately, learners can hold beliefs that hamper or even preclude a thoughtful approach to learning. For example, Shoenfeld (1985) found that students in his university mathe-

matics class generally believed that if one can't solve a math problem in ten minutes, one can't solve it at all. Such a belief flies
in the face of all that is known about the value that persistence
has played in most mathematical and scientific breakthroughs
throughout history. Students who adhere firmly to this belief
do not persist long in solving a math problem. Another belief
that can influence thinking has to do with entity learning versus
incremental learning. Students who come to class with a belief
in what Dweck and her colleagues (Dweck, 1986; Dweck and
Bempechat, 1980) refer to as *entity learning* — "you either get it
or you don't" — are hampered in their ability to make an effort
beyond a first try. However, students who view learning as
incremental — a belief that one slowly and incrementally acquires
understanding — hold an attitude that is more conducive to a
disposition toward thinking. Likewise, students who believe that
knowledge is a collection of facts will see learning as simply
memorization, a very different approach than is held by those
who believe that knowledge is idiosyncratically constructed by
the learner.

Obviously, certain teaching practices tend to foster such
beliefs and dispositions. For example, asking a question and accepting answers from those students who immediately volun-
teer communicates to students that the answer should be readily available without thinking. On the other hand, using what
Rowe (1974) refers to as "wait time," allowing ample time for
thinking between the time a question or problem is posed and
responses are taken, clearly says that quality thinking and problem solving takes time. Similarly, engaging students in active
learning activities in which they must construct their own knowledge can help dispel the notion that learning is simply memorization of facts.

Professors, too, need to adopt a disposition for thinking.
For example, professors who take the position that they are always teaching thinking, regardless of the course or subject matter, keep the focus in their classrooms on thinking; for them
the subject matter becomes the vehicle by which instructors engage their students in the thinking process. Campus debate about
whether critical thinking is best taught at the college level in

a separate course or integrated into all courses exemplifies two very different beliefs about thinking and transfer. Those who see thinking as appropriately addressed in stand-alone courses believe that there are such things as generic thinking skills, and they tend to believe that once students have learned those skills, transfer will be automatic—that is, when an appropriate context arises, whether in another discipline or in everyday life, students will automatically see the need to use a particular skill and will apply it. On the other hand, those who hold the position that all thinking skills (generic as well as specific ones) should be taught in context—in the specific situations or subject matter in which they are to be used—believe that transfer does not occur automatically. They teach their students when, where, and how, to apply certain skills and strategies.

Languages of Thinking

Languages of thinking refers to the verbal expressions used with respect to the process of thinking. Words and phrases such as *evidence, rebuttal, explanation, analogous to, hypothesis, compare and contrast, argument,* and *brainstorming* help instructors to structure their thinking and discussion (Perkins, 1992). These words help people think in terms of the concepts behind them and make it possible to reach a shared understanding based on common vocabulary. Such terms also lay the groundwork for working with students to establish and discuss standards of thinking, such as those presented by Paul (1986): clarity, logic, relevance, and consistency. Familiarity with the language of thinking makes it possible for students to assess their own thinking according to standards and criteria for thinking.

Metacognition

Metacognition is the awareness and self-regulation of one's own thinking and learning processes (Flavell, 1981). Cognition and metacognition differ in that *cognition* is the construction of meaning while *metacognition* is the deliberate monitoring and control of the cognitive processes used in that construction. Awareness of the purpose of a task, noticing one's attention level, selection of thinking and problem-solving strategies, self-correction of identified mistakes, deliberate use of strategies for learning and remembering, monitoring one's progress toward a goal — all are aspects of metacognition (Brown, Bransford, Ferrara, and Campione, 1983; Flavell, 1981).

Effective questioning can be used to teach the skills of critical thinking, the languages of thinking, dispositions toward thinking, and metacognitive skills. These uses of questioning are addressed throughout the rest of this chapter. Although professors can use effective questioning in their classes by learning how to pose thoughtful questions during lectures and discussion sessions, as well as on exams (see Chapter Six for a related discussion), the focus of this chapter is on ways of teaching students how to generate and answer their own thoughtful questions — and thereby facilitate their own growth in critical thinking.

Guided Student-Generated Questioning

Teaching students to ask their own questions can help them become more autonomous in their learning and assume more responsibility for meeting their learning needs. However, research has shown that when students are asked to generate questions on their own, they usually pose ones that require only recall of factual material rather than thought-provoking ones (Dillon, 1988; Flammer, 1981; Kerry, 1987; King, 1990). Because students do not spontaneously generate thoughtful questions, they need to be trained to do so.

King (1989, 1990, 1991b, 1992) has developed and tested an instructional procedure for successfully teaching university students to pose their own thought-provoking questions. Once learned, this procedure becomes a thinking strategy that students can use either on their own or in groups (King, 1989, 1991b). In using this procedure, the professor provides students with a set of generic questions or question starters such as "What are the strengths and weaknesses of . . . ?" and "What do you think would happen if . . . ?" These questions are effective in guiding knowledge construction because they serve as cognitive prompts to induce high-level thinking on the part of the students. Students use these *generic* questions to guide them in formulating their own specific questions pertaining to the material to be discussed. Exhibit 2.1 presents a number of such generic thought-provoking question stems that can be adapted for use by "filling in the blanks" with specific content relevant to the topic being covered (King, 1989, 1990, 1991b, 1992). The critical thinking processes these questions induce are also listed in Exhibit 2.1.

The question stems are based on the higher levels of Bloom's (1956) taxonomy of thinking—application, analysis, and evaluation—and are designed to teach the skills of critical thinking. Specifically, these stems are intended to stimulate students to generate applications (How would you use . . . to . . . ?), develop examples (What is a new example of . . . ?), analyze relationships (How does . . . affect . . . ?), explain concepts (Explain why . . .), activate and use relevant prior knowledge and experience (How does . . . tie in with what we have learned before?), make predictions and hypotheses (What do you think would happen if . . . ?), synthesize ideas into something new (What are some possible solutions for the problems of . . . ?), compare and contrast (How are . . . and . . . alike and different?), and evaluate (Which one is the best . . . and why?).

In the individual or *self*-questioning version of this strategy, students use the question stems to guide them in generating their own thought-provoking questions following a classroom lecture or assigned reading. Then they answer those questions fully as a way to study the material and prepare for exams.

The group version of this procedure, called *guided reciprocal peer questioning,* is an instructional technique for professors to implement in the classroom. Guided reciprocal peer questioning can be used in any subject area to facilitate thinking and learning about course material. After listening to a lecture or reading assigned material, students use the generic question stems and work independently to generate two or three questions based on the material. Next, in pairs or small groups, they engage in peer questioning, taking turns posing their questions

Exhibit 2.1. Guiding Thought-Provoking Questioning.

Generic Questions	Specific Thinking Skills Induced
What is a new example of . . . ?	Application
How could . . . be used to . . . ?	Application
What would happen if . . . ?	Prediction/hypothesizing
What are the implications of . . . ?	Analysis/inference
What are the strengths and weaknesses of . . . ?	Analysis/inference
What is . . . analogous to?	Identification and creation of analogies and metaphors
What do we already know about . . . ?	Activation of prior knowledge
How does . . . affect . . . ?	Analysis of relationship (cause-effect)
How does . . . tie in with what we learned before?	Activation of prior knowledge
Explain why . . .	Analysis
Explain how . . .	Analysis
What is the meaning of . . . ?	Analysis
Why is . . . important?	Analysis of significance
What is the difference between . . . and . . . ?	Comparison-contrast
How are . . . and . . . similar?	Comparison-contrast
How does . . . apply to everyday life?	Application — to the real world
What is the counterargument for . . . ?	Rebuttal argument
What is the best . . . , and why?	Evaluation and provision of evidence
What are some possible solutions to the problem of . . . ?	Synthesis of ideas
Compare . . . and . . . with regard to . . .	Comparison-contrast
What do you think causes . . . ? Why?	Analysis of relationship (cause-effect)
Do you agree or disagree with this statement: . . . ? What evidence is there to support your answer?	Evaluation and provision of evidence
How do you think . . . would see the issue of . . . ?	Taking other perspectives

to their partner or group and answering each other's questions in a reciprocal manner.

King (1993b) cites the example of an accounting professor who lectured to his principles of accounting class on the topic of "intangible assets" for twenty minutes, then stopped and, displaying a list of generic questions on an overhead projector, directed students to turn to their neighbors to form pairs or groups of three. Each student, working individually and using the generic questions as a guide, selected appropriate question starters and formulated two or three specific thought-provoking questions about intangible assets. The professor encouraged individuals to generate questions they themselves did not have answers to. The students generated such questions as "How do tangible assets and intangible assets differ and how are they similar?" "What would happen to the value of an intangible asset such as a secret recipe or formula if it became publicly known?" and "How does the tangibility/intangibility of an asset affect how you calculate its value?" Then, at a signal from the professor, the students met in their small groups and began asking and answering each other's questions. The students continued discussing the topic of intangible assets using their questions as a way of guiding their discussion until the professor indicated that the discussion time was over. He then brought the class together to share and discuss the inferences, examples, and explanations generated and to clarify any misunderstandings that might have emerged regarding the topic of intangible assets.

On some occasions a professor might lecture for a shorter time and then allow students to engage in reciprocal peer questioning and responding for only a few minutes. After the students had discussed what they have learned to that point, the professor would continue lecturing. This sequence might be repeated several times during one class session. This approach provides students with more opportunities for thinking and discussion. Metacognitively speaking, it also serves as a self-testing experience, giving students the chance to check their understanding of the topic before getting too far into the material.

At other times reciprocal peer questioning can be used prior to instruction. In such situations the students generate questions along the lines of "What do I already know about . . . ?" in order to activate their background knowledge about the topic to be covered. Such prelecture questions also promote thinking about how the new information relates to what the students have learned previously about the particular topic. In addition, students establish a purpose for listening to a lecture by asking each other such prelecture questions as "Why are we learning about . . . ?" Generating questions prior to the lecture may also provide students with an opportunity to ask prediction questions at the beginning of an instructional unit or to pose questions they would like to have answered during their study of a particular topic. In these ways prelecture student-generated questioning can promote students' high-level thinking about the lecture topic.

Guiding Knowledge Construction
Through Questioning

The generic question stems function to guide critical thinking and knowledge construction. Students have to think critically about the material just to be able to formulate relevant thought-provoking questions. Formulating high-level questions based on the presented content forces students to identify the main ideas presented and to think about how those ideas relate to each other and to the students' own prior knowledge and experience. Responding to others' (or their own) questions further extends such high-level thinking, because it forces students to explain concepts, defend their ideas, give examples, and in other ways show that they really understand (Cobb, 1988; Doise and Mugny, 1979).

When students think about course material in these ways (as opposed to simply memorizing information as presented), they process the ideas more thoroughly and construct extensive cognitive networks connecting the new ideas and linking them to what they already know (see Mayer's [1984] internal and external connections). Developing such cognitive representations of the new material facilitates understanding.

Metacognitive Aspects of
Student-Generated Questioning

It is important that the question-generation strategy not be used by students in a rote manner instead of a meaningful way. A rote use of the strategy might be simply using the first two question stems on the list rather than thoughtfully choosing stems to generate questions that are most suited to that student's particular learning needs, or asking and answering the questions in a rigid turn-taking manner, rather than engaging in a full discussion in which group members contribute multiple responses to one question, with each response building on the previous ones.

When students deliberately select particular question stems to guide their own questioning, they are using the strategy in a metacognitive way. They are mindfully guiding their own thinking based on their perceived learning needs. In addition to guiding cognitive processes in this way, the guided reciprocal peer questioning strategy functions in a second way at this level; it can be used for monitoring comprehension. When students ask and answer each other's questions, they are testing themselves to determine the extent to which they have thought about and actually comprehended the material presented. If students are unable to ask thought-provoking questions, they probably do not understand the ideas presented; similarly, inability to answer each other's questions indicates knowledge gaps or some other form of inadequate comprehension. Once students have flagged these deficits for themselves, they can look for remedies, such as filling in their gaps in information, correcting misunderstandings, and the like. In this way comprehension monitoring improves the accuracy of the students' constructed knowledge representations of the material presented.

Research Findings on the Effects of
Guided Reciprocal Peer Questioning

Results of research with this student-generated questioning approach shows that it improves higher-level thinking and learning for university students. In a series of studies King (1989, 1990, 1991b, 1992) compared guided reciprocal peer questioning with various other strategies for learning material presented in lecture format. In each of these studies, students were initially tested on their ability to understand a lecture by answering inference and recall questions on a presented lecture. Then students in the experimental condition were trained to generate thought-provoking questions using generic questions (such as those in Exhibit 2.1) to guide them. In each case, during the training and practice the generic questions were displayed for the students on prompt cards. Comparison group students were trained in other strategies. Then students in all conditions practiced their strategies in the context of several lectures. Following training and practice with their strategies, all students listened to a lecture on new material, then discussed the material in their groups without being reminded to use their questioning strategies and without access to their question prompts. Tape recordings of these sessions were analyzed for evidence of high-level thinking and questioning. Lecture comprehension tests were administered at this time and retention tests were given several days later.

Results of this series of studies indicate that university students who used the thought-provoking question stems to generate questions and answers on the material showed better recall and understanding of the lecture content than did students who studied the material independently (King, 1989), who engaged in small-group discussions on the material (King, 1989), who generated summaries of the material (King, 1992), who studied in small groups using student-generated questioning and answering without the guidance of the question stems (King, 1990), or who used guided questioning and answering with provided (but similar) thought-provoking questions (King, 1993a). Furthermore, analyses of the verbal interaction of the students, tape-recorded during their questioning and answering sessions, showed that those particular questions used by students in the guided questioning conditions elicited inferences, explanations, and other high-level thinking (King, 1990, 1991a, 1991b).

King concluded that the guided reciprocal peer questioning strategy is effective because the generic questions control the level of student thinking. More specifically, the high-level generic questions guide students to write thought-provoking questions specific to the material to be learned. Asking and answering those questions induces high-level thinking such as making inferences, comparing, evaluating, and explaining. Such critical thinking activity is likely to promote the building of accurate and effective representations of the presented material in long-term memory, leading to better understanding.

The Role of Student-Generated Explanations

When responding to a peer's high-level question, other students often must generate explanations and state them to the group. A number of recent studies have shown that the process of explaining something to someone else promotes learning (for example, King, 1990, 1991a, 1992; Webb, 1989). In particular, Webb's (1989) extensive research on interaction and learning in peer groups indicates that the students who learn the most are those who provide elaborated explanations to others in their group.

Explaining something to someone else often requires the explainer to think about the material in new ways, such as relating it to the questioner's prior knowledge or experience, translating it into terms familiar to the questioner, or generating new examples (Bargh and Schul, 1980). Engaging in these thinking activities forces the explainer to clarify concepts, elaborate on them, reorganize content, or in some manner reconceptualize the material. Therefore, in the guided reciprocal peer questioning procedure, asking and answering those particular questions is likely to reveal individuals' differing perspectives on ideas and issues. Questions such as "How do . . . and . . . differ?" "Do you agree or disagree with this statement: . . . ? What evidence is there to support your answer?" and "What do you think causes . . . ? Why?" are designed to deliberately raise different perspectives, inconsistencies, and misconceptions with students and may lead to the emergence of cognitive conflict. By inducing students to explain their

positions and defend them, such cognitive conflict may be resolved, resulting in better understanding. Defending one's position encourages individuals to clarify their own thinking, recon-
cile conflicting views, relate new concepts to what they already
know, and generally modify and restructure their own thinking (Bearison, 1982; Cobb, 1988; Doise and Mugny, 1979).
Thus, the guided reciprocal peer questioning strategy, which
forces students to explain material to each other and justify their
thinking, promotes these thinking activities.

From Questions to Explanations

It seems clear that explaining, especially self-explanation, can
be a powerful force for enhancing critical thinking in the classroom and that the guided reciprocal peer questioning strategy
is an effective way to elicit self-explanation from students (King,
1990, 1991b, 1992). Significantly, explaining can be taught
(King, in press; Miltz, 1971; Rosenshine, 1971), and the effectiveness of this sequence of questioning-explaining can be even
further enhanced by teaching students *how* to explain.

Gage and Berliner (1992) provide a method for giving
an explanation that includes identifying the elements, concepts,
or variables in the relationship that need to be explained; identifying the relationship between those elements; and showing
how that relationship is an instance of a general principle or
rule. Effective explanations often follow a rule-example-rule sequence (Rosenshine, 1971), in which a generalization is provided
followed by several examples, capped off with a restatement of
the rule, generalization, or principle. Good explanations also
make use of *explaining links* (Rosenshine, 1971) — links that are
captured by such words and phrases as *because, therefore, consequently,* and *in order to* — that tie clauses together and make it clear
that a relationship exists and what the nature of the relationship is (causal, comparative, and so on).

Research recently completed has shown that fifth graders'
use of the guided reciprocal peer questioning strategy can be
enhanced by teaching them how to generate explanatory responses to thoughtful questions (King, in press). When teaching

about explaining, it is useful to begin by differentiating between describing and explaining. Describing tells the "what" about something, whereas explaining tells the "why" or the "how" about it. The use of words such as *evidence, analyze, implications, evaluation, counterargument,* and *analogous* within the question stems can promote the use of this language of thinking in the responses generated and thereby increase the likelihood that those responses will be at a thoughtful level.

The College Classroom
as a Community of Learners

When all members of a college class (the professor as well as the students) are engaged in making thinking explicit and external in these ways, the classroom can begin to take on the appearance of a community of learners. Use of guided reciprocal peer questioning over time can promote the evolution of a learning community in which the professor and students are co-inquirers engaged in the co-construction of meaning, where everyone is a teacher and everyone is a learner. The sociocognitive context of guided reciprocal peer questioning requires students to put their thoughts into words to be shared and evaluated and built on by others; at the same time it supports the students in this process by providing models of appropriate thinking skills, strategies, and language for them to imitate. Such a learning community fosters a shared cognition and a shared responsibility for meaningful learning about the subject matter of the course. It also promotes and maintains a high level of critical thinking activity for each of its members.

Transfer of Thinking Skills

Getting students to transfer their thinking skills to new or different contexts on their own — spontaneously — is a constant challenge for all educators. Because thinking is usually contextbound, skills learned in one context or subject area do not normally transfer to another; for example, having good reasoning skills in mathematics does not mean a person will be a good reasoner in history or psychology. Such skills are said to be domain specific or contextbound and generally do not transfer to new contexts. General strategies, on the other hand, are more likely candidates for transfer (Perkins and Salomon, 1989). The guided reciprocal peer questioning strategy is a general critical thinking strategy. The guiding questions prompt inferences, application, comparison-contrast, analysis, and the like — skills used in all disciplines. Also, because the generic questions are content-free, they can be applied in any course, subject matter, or non-school context. Therefore, the guided reciprocal peer questioning strategy itself can be used to facilitate critical thinking in any subject area (in contrast to those strategies and skills that are domain specific); if used in all areas of the curriculum, this strategy would facilitate the transfer of thinking skills to new contexts and other subjects.

In research studies on the use of guided reciprocal peer questioning, indications of transfer have been encouraging. Students trained in guided questioning demonstrated transfer of the strategy when they used the critical thinking questions in small-group discussion of new course material (King, 1990, 1992) or in solving a novel problem with their partners (King, 1991a). In none of these cases were the students reminded to use their questioning strategies, nor did they receive their question prompt cards. Further, in those same studies, the students trained to ask critical thinking questions performed better than the other students on the posttreatment written tests of comprehension (King, 1990, 1992) or problem solving (King, 1991a) administered several days later. These latter findings indicate that the critical thinking questioning strategy that was learned and practiced in a small-group or dyadic context was internalized and later transferred to an individually completed task.

The generic critical thinking questions in Exhibit 2.1 can be used in any situation calling for thinking, whether in school or in everyday life. They can be used during television viewing to detect bias in news reports or to analyze commercial messages, they can be used at an art gallery to analyze sculptures and paintings, they can be used at an electronics store to decide which compact disc player to purchase, or they can be used in any other daily experiences.

When students and professors alike get into the habit of using these questions to guide their thinking and model how to do so with each other, they are exemplifying transfer of the strategy and at the same time supporting the notion of a community of learners working together to enhance each other's thinking and learning.

Empowerment

Guided reciprocal peer questioning can be a vehicle to promote what Perkins (as in Perkins, Allen, and Hafner, 1983) calls a critical epistemology, which he points out can lead to more reasoned decision making and can foster feelings of self-efficacy and empowerment. Perkins distinguishes between a make-sense epistemology and a critical epistemology (Perkins, Allen, and Hafner, 1983). In a make-sense epistemology, the criteria for the truth of a statement are that it seems to hang together and it fits with one's prior beliefs. By this definition even an assertion made without any reason or evidence to support it would be accepted as truth as long as it was congruent with one's beliefs. Perkins describes this make-sense epistemology as a default position—if something appears superficially to be self-evident, it makes sense, and there's no need to think any more about it. In a critical epistemology, on the other hand, it is not sufficient for the statement to hang together or match prior beliefs; one needs to examine the data and the reasoning for inconsistencies, take alternative perspectives, construct counterarguments, and look for bias and overgeneralization, all of which takes time and effort. But it is necessary to do so for a deeper understanding of the situation and to achieve more reasoned and informed decision making.

Students find it easier to go with the default make-sense approach to issues and then stop thinking. Without looking at the other side of the issue, and without trying to generate alternatives, how can they be sure that they have made a reasonable decision? We need to help our students become critical epistemologists. The guided reciprocal peer questioning strategy can foster a critical epistemology because it provides a structure for thinking about issues from many perspectives through analysis, comparison-contrast, application, inference, explanation, prediction, evaluation, and counterargument. When students make decisions from such a critical perspective, they know they understand the elements of the situation and have reached the best decision possible.

Perkins and his colleagues (Perkins, Faraday, and Bushey, 1991) point out that the meaning that we make in our lives is what constitutes our lives, and critical epistemologists construct for themselves qualitatively richer lives than do make-sense epistemologists. Their models of the world give them more perspective, more variety, and a greater sense of empowerment and control over their futures.

Conclusion

Guided reciprocal peer questioning can be a powerful and effective way to teach critical thinking in the college classroom. The thought-provoking questioning component can induce critical thinking, while the explanations generated and provided can clarify, refine, and extend that thinking. When professors teach their students how to ask thought-provoking questions and give explanations in response, they are likely to raise the level of thinking in their classrooms. When students learn to ask their own thought-provoking questions (both in and out of the classroom) and provide explanatory answers, they are well on the way to self-regulation of their learning. They are on the road to empowerment and are ready to embrace their futures.

References

Bargh, J. A., and Schul, Y. "On the Cognitive Benefits of Teaching." *Journal of Educational Psychology,* 1980, *72,* 593–604.

Baron, J. *Thinking and Deciding.* New York: Cambridge University Press, 1988.

Bearison, D. J. "New Directions in Studies of Social Interactions and Cognitive Growth." In F. C. Serafica (ed.), *Social-Cognitive Development in Context.* New York: Guilford, 1982.

Beyer, B. *Practical Strategies for the Teaching of Thinking.* Needham Heights, Mass.: Allyn & Bacon, 1987.

Bloom, B. S. (ed.). *Taxonomy of Educational Objectives: The Classification of Educational Goals.* Vol. 1: *Cognitive Domain.* New York: McKay, 1956.

Brown, A. L., Bransford, J. D., Ferrara, R. A., and Campione, J. C. "Learning, Remembering, and Understanding." In J. H. Flavell and E. M. Markman (eds.), *Handbook of Child Psychology,* Vol. II: *Cognitive Development.* New York: Wiley, 1983.

Brown, A. L., and Campione, J. C. "Psychological Theory and the Study of Learning Disabilities." *American Psychologist,* 1986, *41,* 1059–1068.

Cobb, P. "The Tensions Between Theories of Learning and Instruction in Mathematics Education." *Educational Psychologist,* 1988, *23,* 78–103.

deCharms, R. *Personal Causation: The Internal Determinants of Behavior.* San Diego, Calif.: Academic Press, 1968.

Dillon, J. T. *Questioning and Teaching: A Manual of Practice.* New York: Teachers College Press, 1988.

Doise, W., and Mugny, G. "Individual and Collective Conflicts of Centrations in Cognitive Development." *European Journal of Social Psychology,* 1979, *9,* 105–108.

Dweck, C. S. "Motivational Processes Affecting Learning." *American Psychologist,* 1986, *41,* 1040–1048.

Dweck, C. S., and Bempechat, J. "Children's Theories of Intelligence: Consequences for Learning." In S. G. Paris, G. M. Olson, and H. W. Stevenson (eds.), *Learning and Motivation in the Classroom.* Hillsdale, N.J.: Erlbaum, 1980.

Elmer-Dewitt, P. "Dream Machines," *Time,* Fall 1992 Special Issue: "Beyond the Year 2000," pp. 39–41.

Ennis, R. H. "A Taxonomy of Critical Thinking Dispositions and Abilities." In J. B. Baron and R. S. Sternberg (eds.), *Teaching Thinking Skills: Theory and Practice.* New York: W. H. Freeman, 1986.

Flammer, A. "Towards a Theory of Question Asking." *Psychological Research,* 1981, *43,* 407–420.

Flavell, J. H. "Cognitive Monitoring." In W. P. Dickson (ed.), *Children's Oral Communication Skills.* San Diego, Calif.: Academic Press, 1981.

Gage, N. L., and Berliner, D. C. *Educational Psychology*. Boston: Houghton Mifflin, 1992.

Kennedy, M. "Policy Issues in Teacher Education." *Phi Delta Kappan*, May 1991, 661–666.

Kerry, T. "Classroom Questions in England." *Questioning Exchange*, 1987, *1*(1), 32–33.

King, A. "Effects of Self-Questioning Training on College Students' Comprehension of Lectures." *Contemporary Educational Psychology*, 1989, *14*, 1–16.

King, A. "Enhancing Peer Interaction and Learning in the Classroom Through Reciprocal Questioning." *American Educational Research Journal*, 1990, *27*, 664–687.

King, A. "Effects of Training in Strategic Questioning on Children's Problem-Solving Performance." *Journal of Educational Psychology*, 1991a, *83*, 307–317.

King. A. "Improving Lecture Comprehension: Effects of a Metacognitive Strategy." *Applied Cognitive Psychology*, 1991b, *5*, 331–346.

King, A. "Comparison of Self-Questioning, Summarizing, and Notetaking-Review as Strategies for Learning from Lectures." *American Educational Research Journal*, 1992, *29*, 303–323.

King, A. "Autonomy and Question Asking: The Role of Personal Control in Guidant Student-Generated Questioning." Unpublished manuscript, 1993a.

King, A. "Making a Transition from 'Sage on the Stage' to 'Guide on the Side.'" *College Teaching*, 1993b, *41*, 30–35.

King, A. "Guiding Knowledge Construction in the Classroom: Effects of Teaching Children How to Question and How to Explain." *American Educational Research Journal*, in press.

Langer, E. J. *Mindfulness*. Reading, Mass.: Addison-Wesley, 1989.

Mayer, R. E. "The Psychology of How Novices Learn Computer Programming." *Computing Surveys*, 1981, *13*, 121–141.

Mayer, R. E. "Aids to Prose Comprehension." *Educational Psychologist*, 1984, *19*, 30–42.

Miltz, R. J. "Development and Evaluation of a Manual for Improving Teachers' Explanations." Unpublished doctoral dissertation, Stanford University, 1971.

Naisbett, J., and Aburdene, P. *Megatrends 2000: Ten New Directions for the 1990s.* New York: Morrow, 1990.

Paul, R. "Dialogical Thinking: Critical Thought Essential to the Acquisition of Rational Knowledge and Passions." In J. Baron and R. Sternberg (eds.), *Teaching Thinking Skills: Theory and Practice.* New York: W. H. Freeman, 1986.

Perkins, D. N. "Creating the Metacurriculum." Paper presented at the American Educational Research Association annual meeting, San Francisco, Calif., 1992.

Perkins, D. N., Allen, R., and Hafner, J. "Differences in Everyday Reasoning." In W. Maxwell (ed.), *Thinking: The Frontier Expands.* Hillsdale, N.J.: Erlbaum, 1983.

Perkins, D. N., Faraday, M., and Bushey, B. "Everyday Reasoning and the Roots of Intelligence." In J. F. Voss, D. N. Perkins, and J. W. Segal (eds.), *Informal Reasoning and Education.* Hillsdale, N.J.: Erlbaum, 1991.

Perkins, D. N., and Salomon, G. "Are Cognitive Skills Context-Bound?" *Educational Researcher,* 1989, *18,* 16–25.

Pressley, M., and others. "Encouraging Mindful Use of Prior Knowledge: Attempting to Construct Explanatory Answers Facilitates Learning." *Educational Psychologist,* 1992, *27,* 91–109.

Resnick, L. *Education and Learning to Think.* Washington, D.C.: National Academy Press, 1987.

Rosenshine, B. V. "Objectively Measured Behavioral Predictors of Effectiveness in Explaining." In J. D. Westbury and A. A. Bellack (eds.), *Research into Classroom Processes.* New York: Teachers College Press, 1971.

Rowe, M. B. "Wait Time and Rewards as Instructional Variables, Their Influence on Language, Logic, and Fate Control, Part I: Wait Time." *Journal of Research in Science Teaching,* 1974, *11,* 81–94.

Schoenfeld, A. H. *Mathematical Problem-Solving.* San Diego, Calif.: Academic Press, 1985.

Thomas, J. W., and Rohwer, W. D. "Academic Studying: The Role of Learning Strategies." *Educational Psychologist,* 1986, *21,* 19–41.

Toffler, A. *Powershift: Knowledge, Wealth, and Violence at the Edge of the 21st Century.* New York: Bantam, 1990.

U.S. Department of Education. *America 2000: An Educational Strategy*. Washington, D.C.: U.S. Government Printing Office, 1990.

Webb, N. M. "Peer Interaction and Learning in Small Groups." *International Journal of Educational Research*, 1989, *13*, 21–39.

Wehlage, G. G., and Rutter, R. A. "Dropping Out: How Much Do Schools Contribute to the Problem?" *Teachers College Record*, 1986, *87*, 37–58.

Wittrock, M. C. "Generative Processes of Comprehension." *Educational Psychologist*, 1990, *24*, 345–376.

Chapter 3

Using Examples
to Teach Concepts

Betsy Newell Decyk

Giving examples is one of the most powerful tools we have as teachers for clarifying concepts. Sometimes we are able to give a definition of a concept. In an English class we might offer a definition of *metaphor* such as this one from *Webster's Ninth New Collegiate Dictionary:* "a figure of speech in which a word or a phrase literally denoting one kind of object or idea is used in place of another to suggest a likeness or analogy." Chances are, however, that we would immediately add an example, just as the dictionary entry does: "as in drowning in money." Sometimes we are able to express a concept by means of a formula. In physics, for example, average velocity can be written as $v = d/t$. Yet in physics textbooks this formula is typically followed by an example to illustrate its application. Furthermore, sometimes concepts do not have, or do not appear to have, a precise formulation. The term *existentialism* in philosophy is an example of a concept without a single precise definition. In fact, Wittgenstein ([1953], 1968), a philosopher in this century, argued that many concepts may not be precisely defined. For such concepts we rely heavily on examples to indicate what the concepts mean. The use of examples is thus a natural, and often crucial, element in teaching.

39

We also expect students to be able to give examples. We may ask for examples when we are first introducing an idea to find out what the students already know about the topic. Moreover, in class discussions, on tests, and in written essays we often expect students to be able to support their ideas with examples. In each of these cases, we use their ability to give examples and the examples they give as measures of their understanding.

In short, examples are instructional workhorses: they carry a great deal of the burden of teaching and learning. They help us dig into ideas and plow the land of the abstract. They help us transport information and ideas from one person to another and from one context to another. One way to improve teaching and learning is to improve the examples we use so that they more effectively communicate difficult concepts.

Although examples are powerful, they can also be problematic. As professional educators we try to avoid the most common pitfalls, such as giving examples that are wrong or unclear. In this chapter, I call attention to a much more surprising pitfall: problems that can arise even when we use well-chosen, clear examples. Furthermore, I suggest a strategy of harnessing examples together in order to overcome the limitations of these paradigmatic cases.

My strategy of sequencing examples originally developed from teaching critical thinking. In California, courses in a variety of disciplines meet the state mandate for critical thinking. As a philosopher by training, my courses introduce students to critical thinking through the techniques of formal and informal logic. While historically my strategy of sequencing examples developed in this particular kind of course, it actually developed in response to my students, so in that sense it could have been sparked by a course with a different content. The basis for the systematic sequencing of examples came from two observations: (1) generation after generation of students were making similar mistakes, and (2) on semester evaluations students suggested that there should have been more homework and more examples while at the same time acknowledging that the workload in my class was already equal to or greater than the workload in their other classes. Why did each set of students tend to make the same mistakes? Why did they feel they needed more examples? Why were they asking for more work? Were (1) and (2) related? Thus, the students themselves in the critical thinking courses prompted me to think more critically about the examples and exercises I had been using.

Many of the examples that I use in this chapter come from logic, but I do not believe that the technique is limited to either logic or philosophy. I believe that we can all benefit from greater reflection about the examples that we use and that we can benefit, in particular, from developing example sequences for difficult concepts. I will stretch my examples as best I can to show how the technique can be applied, and I invite professional educators to pick up where I leave off, developing edifying example sequences for often misunderstood concepts in their own fields.

Paradigmatic Examples and Typicality Effects

As a beginning example, suppose that I am teaching a class about analogical arguments and, in particular, about the fallacy of false analogy. To introduce the idea of false analogy, I use the scene about witches from *Monty Python and the Holy Grail* ([1974], 1991) as an example. In this section of the film, the townspeople are eager to burn a woman as a witch, but the inspector is more careful and offers an argument first. The argument is built on a series of analogies. The first part can be paraphrased this way:

> Witches burn.
> Wood burns.
> Witches are like wood in that they burn.
> Therefore, witches are made of the same stuff as wood.

The conclusion is indisputably false, and students immediately grasp that something is quite wrong with the argument. This example is especially memorable because of its ridiculousness, and, when the film clip is actually shown to the class, it makes an audio/visual impact missing from the written text.

There are several dimensions to consider when comparing

the relative merit of examples. Some examples are funnier than others, some are more topical or more relevant than others, some are closer to the students' own experiences than others, some are more visual than others, and so on. When we are choosing examples to introduce and clarify new concepts and to illustrate points or distinctions, we need to consider these dimensions. Most important, however, we need to present first of all a paradigm, "an outstandingly clear example" (*Webster's Ninth New Collegiate Dictionary*). We do not always have to find one as memorable and as visual as the one from *Monty Python and the Holy Grail,* but students will understand the concept or distinction in question better if we give as a first example a paradigmatic case. The witches example is a good one in this respect as well, because it is clearly a false analogy.

Using a paradigmatic case as a first example is supported by recent research in cognitive psychology. Psychologists have found that when people are asked to give an example for a concept, the answers often exhibit what have been called "typicality effects." For instance, when people are asked to give an example of a bird, they name robins most often, and robins are considered more representative of the concept *bird* than other birds are. These sorts of results are actually surprising in the following way. The concept *bird* is a defined biological concept. This means that there are specific and specifiable necessary and sufficient conditions for something to be a bird: a bird is "any of a class (Aves) of warm-blooded vertebrates distinguished by having the body more or less completely covered with feathers and forelimbs modified as wings" (*Webster's Ninth New Collegiate Dictionary*). Because the definition of *bird* covers all birds equally, we might expect that each bird would be as good an example of a bird as any other bird. In terms of a definition of birds, all birds are equally birds, but in terms of our examples of birds there is an asymmetry: some birds serve as better examples of the concept *bird* than others do. Robins and other middle-sized land birds are considered the more typical, the more paradigmatic cases of birds.

In fact, this sort of asymmetry has been found to exist for many categories. As Rosch, one of the pioneers in this field, has written: "Perception of typicality differences is, in the first place, an empirical fact of people's judgments about category membership. It is by now a well-documented finding that subjects overwhelmingly agree in their judgments of how good an example or clear a case members are of a category, even for categories about whose boundaries they disagree" (Rosch, 1988, p. 316). Another point about paradigms is that there is no need to think that there is exactly one paradigm for each category, only that there are members of the category that are considered more representative, more typical, than others (Rosch, 1988).

In their book *Classroom Assessment Techniques* (1993), Angelo and Cross suggest short classroom exercises that can be used to gain immediate insight into the students' preparation for a class or into a teacher's effectiveness. Near the beginning of a semester, I give the following exercise, a modification of Angelo and Cross's Background Knowledge Probe (1993, pp. 121–125):

Give an example of each of the following:

1.	a bird	6.	a hero
2.	a color	7.	a heroic action
3.	a triangle (a picture is fine)	8.	a game
4.	a motor vehicle	9.	a philosopher
5.	a sentence	10.	a writer

When everyone is done, we start collecting the answers on the board. At first different answers appear, because if someone says *red* as an example of a color, that answer is not suggested again by someone else. However, when I make a second run through the lists, this time asking how many people put red as their example of a color, the students are surprised. Because they have worked on their example lists independently and come up with their own individual answers, they are astonished to find that many people answered the same way they did. The answers typically look like this:

1. bird: robin, sparrow, (sometimes) eagle
2. color: red or blue
3. triangle: equilateral

4. motor vehicle: car
5. sentence: a true, short simple statement
6. a hero: overwhelmingly Superman; runner-up Batman (the third choice is usually a fireman; however, during the semester of the Iraq war, the third most common answer was a soldier)
7. a heroic action: saving a life
8. a game: Monopoly
9. a philosopher: Socrates (Artistotle sometimes runs a close second)
10. a writer: Stephen King (when other writers are suggested, they are overwhelmingly male novelists)

By means of this simple exercise, students dramatically reveal to themselves the typicality effects discussed more abstractly in cognitive psychology, and they begin to realize that paradigmatic examples are at work for many of their concepts, even though they are unaware of it. This is our first reflection on examples.

The existence of typicality effects for many concepts can be empirically established. But why do they happen? Paradigms, the typical examples that emerge for a concept, seem to serve as a kind of mental shorthand in the sense that it is cognitively economical to have one or a few clear central examples for a concept than a whole range of examples. How can we use that idea to improve our teaching and learning? The existence of typicality effects is the justification for teachers to present the paradigmatic cases first: these clear cases will be the easiest to learn and remember.

Misconceptions, Stereotypes, and Lack of Transfer

The problem is that an example, even a paradigmatic one, carries with it more information than just what we intend for it to show. When we pick an example, we know what *we* mean by it, but often we do not realize what extra information might be carried along with it until we give a test. Then we may be very surprised at how the example has been misinterpreted or misunderstood.

One problem is that students make inferences from examples, and sometimes these inferences are unjustified generalizations. For example, students may come to believe on the basis of just the witch scene from *Monty Python and the Holy Grail* that all analogical arguments are bad and hence should never be used. To infer this would be a mistake, of course, because many analogical arguments are sound and have proven to be useful. Making an analogy between light and water waves in physics, for example, has historically provided scientists with many insights and continues to be helpful for students studying the dynamics of light. Thus, we need to watch for misconceptions that arise because of poor inferences from good examples.

Furthermore, paradigmatic examples run the risk of becoming stereotypical in ways that are unintended and also unquestioned. An equilateral triangle may indeed be the paradigm of a triangle, but it fails to include right triangles, because right triangles cannot be equilateral triangles. Important insights in geometry, like the Pythagorean theorem, will be lost if the paradigmatic equilateral triangle is thought of as the only example of a triangle. Similarly, Socrates may indeed be the paradigm of a philosopher in Western philosophy, but this paradigm carries assumptions about what philosophy is and how it should proceed. Should philosophy only proceed by means of the Socratic method of dialogical questioning? Even the analogy between light and water waves, so fruitful an analogy for many years, made it difficult in this century to accept a quantum mechanical view of light. Thus, the typical example may become a stereotypical example, "a standardized mental picture that is held in common by members of a particular group and that represents an oversimplified opinion, affective attitude, or uncritical judgment" (*Webster's Ninth New Collegiate Dictionary*).

A third problem is that examples that seem to be paradigms may not be paradigmatic on reflection. The use of Superman or some other superhero as a paradigm of a hero is suspect in just this sort of way. First of all, Superman has superhuman powers. When he jumps off a bridge to save the falling Lois

Lane, has he really risked anything? Furthermore, because he has special powers, does he also have special duties to use those powers? Finally, what kind of exemplar can Superman provide for our actions if we, unlike Superman, are limited to merely human powers? Superman may not be the right example to serve as the paradigm of a hero after all.

Finally, paradigmatic examples, especially when used singly as if they express all one needs to know about the concept in question, may hinder students from transferring the information to new contexts and differently posed problems. In teaching students to do truthtables in logic, for example, we typically use syllogisms as our paradigmatic examples of arguments. A syllogism is a very basic argument form that has exactly two premises and a conclusion. A surprising number of students each semester are then confused about how to do a truthtable for an argument with only one premise and a conclusion or, heaven forbid, an argument with more than two premises. These students have generalized that all arguments are syllogisms, rather than generalizing that the technique that applies to syllogisms applies to other kinds of arguments as well. The paradigm example of a syllogism, and the inference that all arguments have exactly this form, leaves them helpless to deal with other argument forms. Thus, paradigms can give rise to faulty generalizations and other misunderstandings. To paraphrase Wittgenstein, a paradigm can hold us captive. This insight is our second reflection on examples.

In philosophy, to clarify concepts and distinctions examples are often paired with counterexamples. Examples can be used to show the limits of a concept or show that a claim is false. If someone were to claim, "All winged creatures have feathers," then a robin would be an example that supports this claim. However, a butterfly would be a counterexample, because it is a winged creature that lacks feathers. Counterexamples are useful for finding the boundaries of a concept, what the concept does not include.

The technique of giving paradigmatic cases, while important as a starting place, can lead to unjustified generalizations, unwarranted stereotypes, misunderstandings, and transfer paralysis. Moreover, the technique of pairing these examples with counterexamples will not eliminate the problems with a paradigmatic case. A student could know that robins are birds and butterflies are not and still make the unjustified inference that all birds are red-breasted or that all birds are land birds. To overcome the problems presented by a paradigmatic case, we need to develop new strategies; one of these involves generating example sequences.

Sequencing Examples

If examples are instructional workhorses, the strategy I suggest is to harness them together to create teams of examples. I distinguish these example sequences from merely sampling. Although sampling also involves generating several examples, samples can be completely random. The strategy I use involves the intentional development of organized sequences of examples to highlight different features of the concept. By means of this strategy we can fill in more of the complexities of the concept and help clarify the boundaries of the concept.

The concept of a hero and the suggested paradigm of Superman are illuminating and fun for a class to pursue. After discussing whether Superman (or any other superhero) is really a hero, we can start to develop other examples of heroes. The next suggestions for heroes are usually firemen and soldiers— real people who risk their lives to save others. With this new class of examples, we have moved from fictional characters to real people and from superbeings to mortals. But firemen and soldiers have particular jobs. Is heroism connected to a kind of job? What about Lenny Scutnik, neither a fireman nor a soldier, who dove into the icy Potomac River to save a woman from a plane crash? In fact, some people argue that heroism must be an action beyond one's duty in one's job. If heroism is supererogatory—that is, an action done above and beyond the call of duty—firemen and soldiers may not be heroes after all, if their actions are just fulfilling their duty. With this nudge, students will begin to list people who have been heroic outside their jobs.

At this point, however, new lists of heroes are still primarily people who have risked their lives, like Lenny Scutnik. Do heroes have to risk their lives? This will generate another sequence of examples. Furthermore, the students are usually thinking of adult heroes. Can children be heroes? Here another list may grow. Often the heroes suggested are men. Can women be heroes? At this point some students claim that women can only be heroines. Others claim that women can indeed be heroes and that *heroine* means something different. This creates an interesting discussion of the concept *hero* and how it, and the language it is embedded in, might be changing. These questions, and the example sequences that they create, make us wonder whether using firemen or soldiers as our examples of heroes is really as paradigmatic as we thought. From this short lively discussion of example sequences, the concept *hero* gains a texture and a complexity that it did not have before.

A similar lively discussion develops around the concept of a writer. Why did students pick Stephen King? Are there other writers beside King? Are there writers who are not novelists? Are there writers who are not male? Are there writers from other races? Are there writers from other countries? Very quickly the students see the importance of questioning the paradigmatic case and begin to generate other sets of examples. The idea that we can, and often should, move beyond the typical, the paradigmatic examples, becomes our third reflection about examples.

Just what features of a paradigm should be explored depends to some extent on the concept, distinction, or point that is being clarified and the reason or reasons for clarifying it. In the example about the concept *hero,* some of the features I choose to investigate with the students are connected specifically to philosophical issues. The question of whether heroism is supererogatory, for example, is an issue in moral theory. In addition to these theory-specific explorations, however, there are also explorations that seem to be applicable to a wide range of paradigms. Questioning the gender or age that is implicit in the paradigms of a hero leads to more general considerations. Here are some of the general dimensions along which we can consider varying examples:

Some Possible Parameters for Varying Examples

Paradigm	Possible Extension
common	uncommon
familiar	unfamiliar
literal	analogical, metaphorical
simple	complex
isolated	in a context
artificially neat	realistically complicated
classroom example	real-world example
single discipline	other disciplines, interdisciplinary
dominant gender	other gender
dominant culture	multicultural
time placement	time placement
past	present, future
present	past, future
future	past, present

This list is not meant to be exhaustive, only suggestive of parameters to explore. Furthermore, not all of these dimensions will be applicable to every paradigm. Alone or in combinations, however, they can often provide starting points and vectors for example sequences. The following cases show some of the possibilities.

Often a paradigm relies not only on what is "outstandingly clear" but also on what is familiar. Perhaps robins are a paradigm for the concept *bird* for people in certain parts of the United States because of familiarity. The concept *bird* can be extended by asking about less familiar sorts of birds. How about penguins, ostriches, or emus? How about blue-footed boobies or Canadian geese? Once started, the example extension can continue in a number of different sequences.

The concept *bird* can also be explored in a different way by thinking about its nonliteral extensions. We actually have a number of expressions that describe people as being like birds: "crazy as a coot," "chicken," "turkey," "dodo," "vulture," "eagle-eyed," "eats like a bird," "peacock," "mad as a wet hen," "silly goose," "queer duck," "lame duck," and so on. Birds also provide a rich assortment of metaphors: owls for wisdom, hawks for war, doves for peace, and so on.

To take a different case, sometimes an example, particularly one given in a textbook, is too simple, too isolated or contextually independent, and too artificially neat. Examples are often given this way precisely because they are meant as paradigmatic cases, the "outstandingly clear" example. This happens in many different disciplines. In physics, for example, students are originally taught that the acceleration of gravity is a constant and that under the influence of gravity the distance a body travels as a function of time equals $1/2\ gt^2$. It turns out, however, that this formula is too simple and too artificially neat, for it is only approximately true near the surface of the earth. Discussing the simplicity of the formula and investigating other contexts and more complicated situations would help avoid some of the misconceptions that arise from the paradigm.

Another combination of dimensions is helpful for exploring and extending concepts such as *philosopher*. When students offer Socrates as their example of a philosopher, they have offered a philosopher from the past — in this case, the distant past. We might, therefore, ask about other philosophers, either not so distantly past or in the present. In identifying Socrates they have also given a paradigmatic philosopher in Western philosophy, so another line of exploration would involve philosophers from other cultures. Furthermore, in identifying Socrates they have also chosen a man, so one could begin to ask about whether there are or have been any women philosophers. In addition, as pointed out earlier, by picking Socrates as their paradigmatic example they may have explicitly or implicitly made assumptions about how philosophy should be done, and this may also be questioned and investigated.

Most concepts and distinctions involve a richness and a complexity that the paradigm case alone does not show. The production of organized sequences of examples provides a greater awareness of the diversity and detail included between the paradigmatic cases and the problematic boundary ones. This becomes our fourth reflection on examples.

Teaching Students to
Generate Example Sequences

Creating example sequences is not just a strategy for teachers to use; it is also a strategy for teachers to teach. It empowers students to become more reflective about the examples that are being used and enables them, on their own, to question the paradigm and to seek a richer understanding of the concept, distinction, or point at issue. It helps them learn to transfer information to next contexts and applications. In short, it encourages critical thinking about examples.

In introducing the notion of paradigms and the need for example sequences to students, I begin with Angelo and Cross's Background Knowledge Probe (1993). Of course, this approach may be varied to fit different disciplines. Those teaching physics, for example, may want to assess their students' paradigms for concepts such as *work* or *force*; anthropologists or sociologists may be interested in having a concept like *culture;* people in the arts may be curious about the paradigms people have of an artist or a composer.

After discussing this exercise, I teach the students to consciously create example sequences themselves. First I introduce them to the technique of brainstorming, which is a fast method for generating lots of ideas. The one ground rule of good brainstorming is that suggestions should be made without criticism. This allows people to be creative in their suggestions, without feeling that they will be disparaged. Learning how to brainstorm encourages students to think beyond the paradigmatic cases. For the concept *game,* for example, brainstorming may generate such additional examples as football, solitaire, tennis, poker, and soccer.

However, brainstorming usually generates samples, not sequences. A second technique, the example map, is a way to visually add organization into the random list that has been generated. (This is also a classroom assessment technique discussed by Angelo and Cross, 1993, pp. 197–202, although I used it before I read about it there.) Students individually, in groups, or together with me draw a diagram that places the examples we have collected into relationships with each other. Suggesting Monopoly as the paradigm for a game gives us the beginning of an example map that looks like the depiction in Figure 3.1.

Figure 3.1. A Beginning Example Map with Monopoly as the Paradigm.

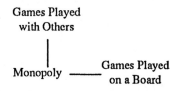

Additional organizational categories might include "games that are played with a ball" (football, soccer, tennis) and "games that are played with cards" (poker, solitaire). Mentioning solitaire may suggest a new category, "games that are played alone." In this way, the example map may grow like that shown in Figure 3.2. Obviously there will be overlap in these groupings, and some games will appear in more than one group. Soccer is a game played with a ball, and it is also played with others; solitaire and poker are both played with cards, but solitaire is played alone, while poker is played with others.

With organizational structures, these or others, in place, students may then think of additional examples. They may suggest kickball, volleyball, and handball as additional games played

Figure 3.2. An Example Map Showing More of the Categories for Games.

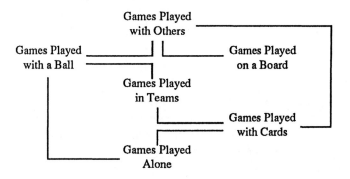

with balls, and Old Maid and Twenty-One as other games played with cards. The organizational structures may also help students think of new groupings of games that have not been suggested yet, like "games of chance" or "video games." With the help of an example map it is easy to explain example sequencing as an intentional strategy for developing examples to stretch beyond the paradigmatic cases. Here we can discuss parameters that have already been helpful in generating example sequences (games played with a ball, games played with cards, games played on a board, games played alone, games played with others, games of chance, video games, and so on). We can suggest other concept-specific parameters that might be helpful in thinking of additional example sequences (games that require referees or umpires, games played on grass surfaces, games that are played on courts, and so on). Or we might explore more general parameters, such as the ones mentioned earlier.

To illustrate this last point, all of the games that have been suggested so far are games that are played in the United States. What about games played primarily in other countries, such as go (Japan), cricket (Great Britain), bocce (Italy), or curling (Canada). Also, most of the games suggested are those played by older children or adults. What about games played with small children, such as pat-a-cake? Furthermore, the games suggested are all modern games. What about some games that were played in the past but are no longer played, or, at least no longer commonly played, such as rolling hoops, the Mayan ball game tarok, or the ancient Egyptian game of the dead?

By teaching the students to intentionally develop example sequences in this way, we make it possible for students to augment teacher- or textbook-generated examples with their own examples and example sequences. The teacher and the students become partners in trying to understand both the clarity and the limitations of paradigmatic cases. Together they can identify aspects of the paradigm that might have previously generated misconceptions, they can be on guard for the slippage from the typical to stereotypical, and they can appreciate the complexity present when concepts, seemingly clear in the paradigmatic cases, are applied in the real world.

Sequencing Exercises

Often the exercises developed for practice in various fields are also paradigmatic. Again, there is pedagogical sense to this. After all, we want our students to master the simpler, clearer, cleaner cases before they attempt the more complicated ones. However, paradigmatic exercises often create problems that are parallel to those of paradigmatic examples. Students tend to take the paradigmatic exercises as the only cases and then experience difficulty when they must apply information or newly acquired skills in a different or more sophisticated way. Sequencing exercises helps students transfer information or skills from a standard application to new applications.

Just as there are example sequences that can enrich the understanding of a concept, a distinction, or a point, there are exercise sequences that can enhance the transfer of applications from simple cases to more complex ones and from classroom cases to the real world. Exhibit 3.1 lists some of the parameters along which exercises may be extended to increase effective application of information and skills. Again, this list is not meant to be exhaustive of all the parameters along which it might be useful to vary exercises, but it is suggestive of additional ways in which we might encourage students to practice.

One of the parameters that I use regularly is the move from exercises that have a single, correct answer to exercises that have several correct answers. Often students seem to assume that there is only one correct answer to each problem. This idea has been reinforced by years of schooling, the kind of practice that has been expected, and experience with lots of multiple-choice exams, including college entrance examinations. Yet, it is an unjustified generalization. While it may be true that there is a single best answer for certain types of problems, it is not true for all problems.

Suppose that in teaching informal fallacies a professor (even me at an earlier age!) has introduced each informal fallacy with a separate, paradigmatic example. Suppose, further, that the exercises from the textbook also assume that the fallacies are completely separate from one another and that there

Exhibit 3.1. Parameters for Varying Exercises.

Exercise Paradigm	Extension
Answer relies on a single skill	Answer involves using multiple skills
Answer is simple	Answer is more complex
Answer relies on recent material	Answer involves using cumulative knowledge
Exercise has a single correct answer	Exercise has multiple correct answers
Exercise is similar to textual or classroom examples	Exercise goes beyond textual or classroom examples
Exercise asks for an example	Exercise asks for multiple examples or example sequences
Exercise asks for an example	Exercise asks for examples student would use to teach someone else
Exercise asks for examples similar to textual or classroom examples	Exercise asks for examples that go beyond textual or classroom examples: 1. Examples from other fields or disciplines 2. Examples from student's own interests or life 3. Examples from more complex situations
Exercise is teacher generated	Exercise is student generated

is one correct answer for each exercise (as indicated in the answer book). It would be natural for the students to assume, on the basis of the class presentation and their practice, that fallacies do not overlap. In reality, however, fallacies can, and often do, overlap. If students are unprepared for the possibility that a single passage might have multiple fallacies and hence multiple correct answers, it is not surprising that they find it difficult to pick out fallacies in more realistic settings, such as in newspapers, on television, and in everyday conversation. The paradigmatic presentation of fallacies and the accompanying paradigmatic exercises have failed to sufficiently prepare the students for the real complications of identifying fallacies.

It is a better strategy both to specify the paradigmatic cases of each fallacy and to give fewer paradigmatic examples, instead including ones in which the fallacies overlap. In a parallel fashion, it is a better strategy to sequence exercises so that they go from clear-cut cases that have a single correct answer to more complex cases that might have several correct answers, and finally to a mixture of these sorts of cases. This intentional sequencing of examples and exercises undercuts the assumption that every exercise has one correct answer and creates a critical thinking challenge that is more realistic.

Another kind of common exercise or test question asks for the student to give "an example." The directions can be made more specific, to yield more insight into whether the student has really understood the concept or distinction in question. For example, the question could ask for "a clear example." In this case the student is probably expected to give a paradigmatic example, or at least one that manifests the concept or distinction at hand. The question could be improved even further to ask for "a new clear example." In this case, the student must produce an example that is both appropriate and that has not been presented already in the class or the text. Both of these types of questions, although more specific, are asking for the clear case, the paradigmatic example.

Another way to change the question is to ask for not just an example but a range of examples or an organized sequence of examples to make the concept or distinction clear and to show its richness and variety. The production of multiple examples, rather than the single clear case, will give the professor a better idea of how well the student understands the concept and its various applications.

A third parameter that I have found extremely valuable is moving from exercises that ask for examples for the teacher to exercises that ask the students to produce examples in order to teach their fellow students. Students tend to produce different examples when they, themselves, are faced with the task of teaching. Furthermore, in trying their examples out they often discover that their examples, and even the concept or distinction at issue, may no longer be as clear to them as they once thought. Encouraging the students to be the teachers gives them a different responsibility for the material, a more active role in learning and understanding, and more "ownership," both of what they know and of what they do not know.

Finally, I am always concerned that the material my students are learning be applicable outside the classroom. For a writing assignment last spring the students were asked to apply example sequences to their own lives in the following way:

The Assignment:
Thinking part (does not have to be turned in): Think of a concept that has a paradigm that is troublesome or bothers you because it is misunderstood or tends to be used stereotypically. If you were going to use the technique of sequenced examples, what organized sequences would you develop to give people a more adequate understanding of the concept?

Written part (to be turned in): Write a thoughtful essay about this concept. The essay should identify the concept and its paradigm. The essay should also explain the problems with the paradigm and develop and discuss at least two different sequences of examples to provide a richer, more complete understanding of the concept.

Among the paradigms and stereotypes the students wrote about were American life as portrayed on television; cultural or racial stereotypes; the representation of women, especially the representation of women in commercials as young, blonde, and thin; the stereotypes of athletes as dumb and male; career stereotypes; and the gender stereotypes in Disney productions such as *The Little Mermaid* and *Beauty and the Beast*. This look into which paradigms bothered my students in their own lives and how the students could apply sequencing to overcome the paradigms was fascinating to me and rewarding for them. The papers were excellent, and many students later commented on the student evaluations that the assignment was extremely useful to them personally.

Teaching Sequencing Strategy to Teachers

In several different workshop sessions, I have had the opportunity to explain the strategy of sequencing examples and exercises to colleagues from diverse disciplines. Professors who have been puzzled about why students have misunderstood the "clear" examples they use now have an explanation for this phenomenon and a strategy for overcoming it. The workshops have generated a greater reflection about the examples we use in teaching and an energy for developing more effective examples and example sequences.

Some colleagues have raised questions about the strategy, however, and I would like to address those questions and allay their fears. One criticism has come from people who like to introduce students to a new concept by giving a definition. They worry that I am dispensing with definitions for concepts and just developing the understanding of a concept by means of examples. My point, instead, is that example sequences can be helpful whether or not one begins with definitions. The concept *triangle* is clearly a defined concept with necessary and sufficient conditions, and so is the concept *bird*. Even when the definition of *triangle* has been given and a paradigm triangle has been drawn, it is still helpful to students to show some of the variety of other triangles that come under the concept. Parallel remarks can be made about the concept *bird*. Even after one has given the biological definition of a bird and has given a paradigmatic case of a bird, it is helpful to show some of the variety of birds that are included under the concept. Where definitions are available for concepts, using them is fine. However, knowing the definition of a concept, or even the definition and a paradigm example, does not guarantee that one knows or appreciates the range or the complexity of the concept's application. This is exactly where example sequences can significantly add to the understanding of a concept.

For concepts that may not have definitions, generating example sequences will help students arrive at an understanding of the concepts. There may not be a definition of *game* that works for all games (Wittgenstein, [1953] 1968), and there may not be a definition of *hero* that will fit all cases of heroism. Generating organized sequences of examples for these concepts more adequately presents the diversity of cases than a single example can.

A different kind of comment about organized example sequences comes from the examples that I have used to explain the technique. For the most part, I have used the strategy to illustrate concepts that are already familiar to many students — concepts such as *bird, color,* and *triangle.* The Background Knowledge Probe that I use relies on this familiarity. But what about using example sequences for other kinds of concepts? Will the strategy work for unfamiliar concepts as well? (The people who ask this question are actually engaged in example sequencing: they are extending my examples to other kinds of cases.) I believe that it will.

In philosophy, many of the concepts that we use are what I call "mixed concepts." They are words that are commonly used in English but also have a different, more technical definition in philosophy. The word *argument* is like this. In common usage an argument can be a dispute or a disagreement, but in logic an argument is strictly a reasoned set of premises to a conclusion. In our original example from *Monty Python and the Holy Grail,* the townspeople and the inspector are having an argument (dispute) about whether a particular woman is a witch. However, the analogy to the conclusion that the woman is made of wood is an argument in the more technical sense, because reasons are given to support the conclusion. Making this distinction between the common and the technical uses of *argument* is important; otherwise students may confuse these two different meanings. While a paradigmatic case of an argument in terms of a dispute may be enough for students to recognize the distinction being drawn, example sequences are clearly important to convey the range of the more technical concept *argument.* This is a case where sequences are desperately needed to extend and enrich a concept that is new and unfamiliar. Example sequences for familiar concepts will provide insights about what has been typical or stereotypical in our understanding of a concept and what has been overlooked that needs to be regained. Example sequences for an unfamiliar or technical concept provide insight into the range of the concept from the beginning to help prevent misconceptions from taking hold at all.

Another objection that has been raised about generating

example sequences is that the technique is too time consuming. I have different answers to this criticism, depending on the basis of the complaint. First of all, it may be time consuming to generate sequences of examples, instead of relying on one or two paradigmatic cases to supposedly carry all the right information (and none of the wrong information), but it is also time consuming to straighten out conceptual misunderstandings after the fact (after one has read puzzling wrong answers on student exams, for example). In terms of teaching strategy, I prefer to anticipate and try to prevent some of the misconceptions that can occur. This does take time, but it is time well spent. Other fears about the time it takes to generate example sequences seem to have a different basis. Perhaps it sounds like I am advocating using this technique for every concept and distinction that we are trying to clarify. I agree, that would be too time consuming, but I am not advocating this approach. We need to exercise our professional judgment about which concepts are most troublesome and when sequences will be most beneficial. Being aware of the typical misunderstandings that occur, we can control the parameters we use to provide additional examples. In addition, if we teach our students to do example sequencing, they will also become responsible for questioning and extending concepts for their examples and can share the example sequences workload with us.

A final criticism is that sequencing examples may be a special technique for critical thinking as taught through logic but that it is not really important and it is not generally applicable to other fields. These are separable criticisms, but I would like to answer them together. To go outside the immediate examples of critical thinking and logic, we can show that concepts in moral philosophy are being reexamined. Recent work by French (1992), for example, illustrates how the paradigm of individual responsibility has so shaped people's notion of responsibility that they cannot deal adequately with new complications such as corporate responsibility. In response, French has developed a theory of corporate responsibility by extending the set of responsibility examples. Epistemological paradigms are also being questioned and new models are being suggested. Dennett (1991), for example, proposed that *self* is not a single or unified entity, but a collection of narratives (sequences of drafts?).

Going outside philosophy to literature, we can point to Calvino's book (1979), *If on a Winter's Night a Traveler,* in which Calvino uses two different sequences of chapters to explore and explode the traditional paradigm of a novel, or we can point to Lightman's novel (1993) *Einstein's Dreams,* which explores, through a set of short stories (a sequence of examples, if you will), how the life might be different in worlds in which time is different than the way we normally think of it (the paradigm). And in physics, Einstein himself had to break the traditional way of thinking about space and time in order to develop the theory of relativity. Kekulé, the chemist who discovered the structure of the benzene ring, had to be able to think about molecules folding back on themselves; biologists Watson and Crick had to be able to think a new model for molecules in order to unravel the mystery of the DNA strand; and the mathematician Mandelbrot was able to extend geometry by including fractals. In fact, Mandelbrot's description of his work is strikingly appropriate here:

> Why is geometry often described as "cold" and "dry"? One reason lies in its inability to describe the shape of a cloud, a mountain, a coastline, or a tree. Clouds are not spheres, mountains are not cones, coastlines are not circles, and bark is not smooth, nor does lightning travel in a straight line. More generally, I claim that many patterns of Nature are so irregular and fragmented that, compared with Euclid—a term used in this work to denote all of standard geometry— Nature exhibits not simply a higher degree but an altogether different level of complexity. . . . The existence of these patterns challenges us to study those forms that Euclid leaves aside as being "formless," to investigate the morphology of the "amorphous" [Mandelbrot, 1977, p. 1].

Individuals who have recognized the limits of a paradigm and have been able to think of new stories to tell, other examples to use, and different applications to make are a proud part of our epistemological heritage in many fields. It is not just logicians or philosophers who have been, or need to be, interested in identifying the problems with the paradigms that may be limiting our insight.

Conclusion

My earlier students who asked for more examples and more exercises made an important contribution to the education of my later students. Because my students now are aware of the power and problems of paradigm cases, they ask questions about the examples being used rather than just writing them down in their notebooks for future regurgitation. They specifically ask for more examples, and they will try out different examples themselves to see if they work. They make fewer "typical" mistakes, they have less trouble transferring information to new contexts, and they certainly are more engaged in their learning and more creative in their applications of ideas.

Thus, sequencing examples is a simple educational strategy that can improve our teaching and enrich the way our students learn. In a very real sense, clarity has been a paradigm for teaching, and it has had stereotypical influence, causing us to ignore conceptual complexity in the search for conceptual clarity. It is not that clarity is to be abandoned, but clarity alone, like most paradigms, is insufficient. Example sequences provide a way to introduce complexity and detail into the discussions of ideas and concepts. No longer will typical and stereotypical examples have the unquestioned authority that they once enjoyed. Paradigms will still present us with the "outstanding clear" example, but sequencing examples will allow us to explore a concept's richness and range. Clarity and complexity together will give us a more realistic, more applicable understanding of our disciplines, our fellow human beings, our experiences, and our world. I invite teachers and students to become partners in this exploration of complexity.

References

Angelo, T. A., and Cross, K. P. *Classroom Assessment Techniques: A Handbook for College Teachers.* (2nd ed.) San Francisco: Jossey-Bass, 1993.

Calvino, I. *If on a Winter's Night a Traveler.* San Diego, Calif.: Harcourt Brace Jovanovich, 1979.

Dennett, D. C. *Consciousness Explained.* Boston: Little, Brown, 1991.

French, P. A. *Responsibility Matters.* Lawrence: Kansas University Press, 1992.

Lightman, A. *Einstein's Dreams.* New York: Pantheon Books, 1993.

Mandelbrot, B. B. *The Fractal Geometry of Nature.* New York: W. H. Freeman, 1977.

Monty Python and the Holy Grail. National Film Company Limited, RCA/Columbia Pictures Home Video, 1991. Videotape. (Originally released 1974.)

Rosch, E. "Principles of Categorization." In A. Collins and E. E. Smith, *Readings in Cognitive Science: A Perspective from Psychology and Artificial Intelligence.* San Mateo, Calif.: Morgan Kaufmann, 1988.

Webster's Ninth New Collegiate Dictionary. Springfield, Mass.: Merriam-Webster, 1989.

Wittgenstein, L. *Philosophical Investigations.* (3rd ed.) New York: Macmillan, 1968. (Originally published 1953.)

Chapter 4

Fostering Creativity
Through Problem Solving

Cris E. Guenter

The twenty-first century will be a time of rapid technical, political, and social change, when creative solutions to both new and old problems will be needed more desperately and more often than ever. For this reason, college instructors are confronted with the problem of devising teaching techniques that will help students think and act more creatively. The instructor, too, needs to approach teaching in a more creative fashion. The greatest challenge for educators is to develop assignments that will provide students with the opportunity to solve problems creatively.

A problem-solving act is creative if it satisfies two criteria: (1) it provides a workable solution to the problem, and (2) most people could not or would not have arrived at the same solution. In other words, it must be a (relatively) novel solution. As Hayes (1978) points out, there is no "magic" or special gift of creativity that some people have and others do not. With appropriate prodding and motivation, everyone can be more creative: "Creative acts are instances of problem solving, but not all instances of problem solving are creative. The underlying psychological processes required for creative problem solving appear to be the same as those required for noncreative problem solving" (Hayes, 1978, p. 240).

Motivating Students for Creativity

In developing creative problem-solving assignments, teachers should consider the motivation that will be used to get students to work on the problems. Intrinsic and extrinsic motivation offer different means for reaching the outcome of any assignment. *Intrinsic* motivation — that is, the student's willingness to engage in the process without any external reward — offers the best avenue for generating creativity. "It appears that when people are primarily motivated to do some creative activity by their own interest in and enjoyment of that activity, they may be more creative than they are when primarily motivated by some goal imposed on them by others" (Amabile, 1983, p. 15). The problem with *extrinsic* motivation is that students stop working on the problem when the extrinsic reward is no longer available. By contrast, when the only rewards that accrue to the students are the joys of creating (that is, intrinsic or internal reward), they will persist at a task longer and the results will be more creative. Thus, creativity is enhanced best when students "own" the project that they are working on and when they are encouraged to complete the assignment because it is important for them. In particular, professors need to find ways to encourage intrinsic motivation in college classrooms where grades are often used as extrinsic motivators. We need to find ways to light a creative spark inside students so that they "own" a project or problem; then the drive to do well on the assignment will come more from a personal desire than from the need to accumulate three more credit units toward graduation. As Caine and Caine (1991, p. 134) have put it:

> Educators can generate much of the excitement and energy they desire by introducing creativity into the lives of their students and by supporting their desire to know. The practical consequence is that a student's desire to know more

about a subject is more important than a measure of performance at any point in time. That is why the setting of goals and the use of evaluation should not act to limit what a student can do or desires to do.

Providing basic information about the problem to be solved, outlining the expectations of the solution, and allowing time for exploring the possibilities are all needed to guide the creative process. Instructors need to convey the expectation that divergent thinking, or finding ways "around" a problem, is needed. They need to consider that more than one solution may be found. (This point is made eloquently by Decyk in Chapter Three.) Reciprocity must exist between creative and evaluative thinking, and students must respect deferred judgment, for divergent thinking to occur. Creative assignments often involve cooperative group work because working and discussing in groups generate different viewpoints that help establish a larger information base. With more information available, more connections — both obvious and remote — can be made. In this way, students can achieve a deeper and more connected understanding of the content of any course.

Techniques for Sparking Creativity

Teachers who wish to pursue creativity in their classrooms should present an assignment so that a general framework is evident, but not the exact solution. Challenging students to come up with three (or more) solutions often paves the way for involved and focused classroom discussions.

One way to keep creativity flowing is to show students how to SCAMPER: Substitute, Combine, Adapt, Magnify, Minify, Put to other uses, Eliminate, Rearrange, Reverse. This technique was first presented by Osborne in his book *Applied Imagination* (1957). It provides a starting point for students and teachers who don't know how to begin a creative flow of ideas. Students apply the SCAMPER action verbs to their thinking about the project or problem they are working on. This allows them to change perspectives and break out of mental sets so that a more creative combination of elements can emerge. Once the students understand the application of these terms, they can generate additional verbs that will help them change the way they think about a problem.

Another important point for college instructors is to learn to defer judgment until time for closure. Living with ambiguity is tricky, but it allows more information and ideas to float before criteria and final judgment sink most of them. As an instructor, it is important to be aware of "killer statements" (Amabile, 1989). Killer statements are remarks that cut an idea down before it has a chance to grow. Comments like, "We've tried that before," "We don't have the money to do that," and "That's ridiculous!" are examples. Killer statements are common and destructive.

Another way to get the creative juices flowing, especially when dealing with more than one subject, is to try forced associations. These were introduced by Parnes in his *Creativity Guidebook* (1967). With forced associations, students take two unrelated objects and make them relate in some manner. An example might be *ketchup* and *wheel*. A pair of students could be asked to design a machine that combines ketchup and wheels to improve our quality of life. The students could "SCAMPER" with the combination, sketch a few ideas, and share their results with the class. Risk taking, challenge, and problem solving are all addressed in assignments like this one.

Teaching for Creativity

Three essential components of the effort to teach for creativity are instructor characteristics, the classroom environment, and teaching strategies. These factors, combined with an understanding and appreciation of the creative abilities students bring with them to the classroom, are the foundation for an education that enhances creativity. Creativity in the classroom is encouraged when all three factors work together to provide a total experience in which creative expression is expected and encouraged.

Instructor Characteristics

An instructor who smiles and demonstrates a sense of humor is a key catalyst for creativity in the classroom. These characteristics are built-in creativity encouragers because they convey the message that risk is encouraged, and risk is inherent in any situation in which students need to make novel responses. Nonverbal messages — a medium of communication that is usually ignored in traditional sources — can convey the message that risk taking is welcome. Simply standing by the door and greeting students by name as they enter the room can help begin to establish this type of rapport. It is also important that the instructor be willing to relinquish control of the classroom by handing discussions and some of the decision making regarding the course over to the students. If the instructor believes that being in control all the time is necessary, then risk taking, spontaneity, and exploration by the students will be adversely affected.

Environmental Factors

The classroom environment can set the stage for creativity. Some simple environmental considerations such as the use of bright colors in the classroom, appropriate regulation of room temperature, and effective use of window space can help convey the message that creative thinking is welcome. The arrangement of tables and chairs in the classroom signals whether discussion is really encouraged. Arrangements that have students facing each other or that are all-inclusive, such as circles or similar groupings, encourage student interaction and class unity. Class content and curriculum (such as laboratory classes) often dictate certain layouts, but movement, space, and time are environmental factors that can influence a creative atmosphere. Students need to have personal space within the classroom and need to know that they may move about at certain times. This situation helps establish a sense of ownership and belonging that fosters creativity as process and product.

Instructional Strategies

Many instructional strategies can be used to foster creative expression. Here is a brief list of possibilities:

1. *Assignments that can involve another subject area or areas* provide opportunities for the stimulation of creativity while also providing a connection among the concepts being taught. In his book *Imagery and Creative Imagination,* Khatena (1984) explores and encourages the use of imagery in problem solving. Mental imagery is challenging for the instructor because it is "not directly observable and usually has to depend on self-reports," (Khatena, 1984, p. 8). For the instructor this means a bit of risk taking. Connections to other subject areas offer an assortment of images on both a concrete and abstract level for students. For example, a political cartoon might be used in an art class to make both an artistic and a political statement. The historical content for the cartoon would have to be researched and implemented appropriately for the student to get the most out of the interdisciplinary aspect of this assignment.

2. *Student journals* help develop self-discipline and creative expression and are useful in any discipline. The key task here is to generate questions that cause the student to reflect on the process, content, and outcomes of the learning experience. Using a "team" journal held in the reserve library or an "on-line journal" offers a novel twist for both students and instructor. Teacher recognition of ongoing student efforts is important for the journal to be effective.

3. *Games* are great for stimulating creative contributions to the classroom, especially when students have to devise a plan that will teach the subject matter. Class presentations of the developed games can become creative in themselves and offer necessary closure for the learning experience. Game content can be drawn from any subject matter.

4. *Contributions to class work using visual and performing arts* always stimulate interest and provide positive examples of the creative process and resulting product. For example, if the classroom material to be covered has any sort of background history (and virtually every academic discipline has a history), students

can recreate the historical information in a skit or play. The teacher or the students could come to school dressed as famous persons for a day and stay in character for all the day's activities.

Other possibilities can be generated by the students themselves as part of a creativity exercise in which they identify learning strategies that will help them think in novel ways about course content. When professors are mindful of the ways they are encouraging creativity in their students, they can make changes that will encourage students to think even more creatively. All will learn and thrive from this process.

An Example of a Creative Exercise

Exhibit 4.1 provides an example of a creative lesson I use in my graduate courses that incorporates the visual arts into any subject matter. The focus of the lesson is on the process and not the product, although the product will generate an ongoing discussion of the process. The lesson can take on many formats and is adaptable for use at any level and with any subject matter. In this project, students contribute to a mural, and as a group they construct the mural in one of many formats. The issue is not necessarily related to visual art so much as to equitable involvement and ownership of a problem-solving situation. The idea is for connections, both concrete and abstract, to be made. Fun and participation are by-products. An appropriate follow-up to this particular lesson would be to have the students construct their own group mural for a different concept taught in the course. This exercise allows the instructor to see the results of student thinking with a nonverbal medium and to identify the depth and richness of students' understanding.

Conclusion

Creative problem solving is best enhanced when students "own" the problem. Problem ownership creates intrinsic motivation, which has been found to be more effective in producing novel solutions than teacher-supplied or other forms of extrinsic motivation.

Exhibit 4.1. Piece Mural: A Lesson Utilizing Creative Thinking and Visual Art.

Grade Level: University student teachers
Time Frame: 45 minutes

Topic

Students each individually construct one piece of a group mural that features the art elements of line, shape, and color.

Component Objectives

Aesthetic Perception: Students will use art vocabulary for interpreting the art concepts of line, shape, color, and unity in a class discussion about the constructed piece mural.

Creative Expression: The student will design a drawing using thick black lines that connect the midpoints of a square and three designated colors.

Rationale

The visual arts can foster students' abilities to create, experience, analyze, and reorganize, thereby encouraging intuitive and emotional as well as verbal responses. Participation in an art experience opens avenues for creative self-expression and develops self-esteem in appreciating works of art. Negotiating ways to construct the mural and match appropriate combinations of color, line, and shape will heighten the creative awareness of each student and the class as a whole.

Strategy

A combination of guided discovery and cooperative groups will be used for this lesson.

Vocabulary

- *Mural*—A wall or ceiling painting painted directly on the surface or permanently fixed in place, large scale to match its setting.
- *Line*—The boundary between two shapes or areas; an identifiable path of a point moving in space. It can vary in width, direction, and length.
- *Shape*—A two-dimensional area or plane that may be organic or inorganic, free-form or geometric, open or closed, natural or of human origin.
- *Color*—Visual sensation dependent on the reflection or absorption of light from a surface (hue, value, and intensity being the primary characteristics).
- *Unity*—The big idea; a singleness of effect; reference of all elements of an artistic composition to a single main idea.
- *Midpoint*—Halfway, in the middle.

Procedure

Introduction

The challenge is to construct a mural. Each person will complete one piece of this mural. This task is nonthreatening yet offers a variety of solutions. All must participate to make the mural complete. Showing the required materials and how a completed piece fits with another completed piece stimulates interest and other possible solutions.

Exhibit 4.1. Piece Mural: A Lesson
Utilizing Creative Thinking and Visual Art, Cont'd.

Activity Sequence

1. Mark midpoints on the sides of square index cards. (Instructor may choose to do this ahead of time.)
2. Using thick black lines, draw a design that connects the midpoints. Make sure the thick black lines go off the edge of the cards at the midpoints. Simple, big lines and shapes work well.
3. Identify at least three color choices for students to use. Students may use more colors, but they must use those three colors to fill in the created shapes.
4. Have students write their names on the backs of the cards so that there is also personal accountability.
5. Make "paper donuts" from masking tape and place them on backs of the drawings.
6. Begin putting the piece mural together on a board. Decision making is required here. Lines, colors, and shapes will influence placement.

Closure

Group effort and discussion will determine the outcome of the mural. Mural can be redesigned by changing the placement of pieces.

Evaluation

Teacher observation and review of individual and group work will be the basis of evaluation for this lesson. Demonstrated use of line, shape, and color that helps unify the mural will be noted. Students' verbal comments regarding inferences of art content will also be noted.

Extensions

This lesson can be adapted for use from kindergarten through adult. It offers many possibilities for the creative teacher or student. It can be utilized in cross-curriculum lessons, such as natural science — How about a piece mural that depicts the four stages in the life cycle of a salmon? A history mural could depict the recent changes in the former Soviet Union. Psychologists could use this technique to have students show their interpretations of Freudian concepts such as the id, ego, and superego. Virtually any subject matter could be explored more creatively with group or individual murals. Professors may be surprised to see the sorts of visual depictions the students create to express their understanding of the course content.

Intrinsic motivation develops in college classrooms when the instructor, environment, and instructional strategies encourage risk-taking behaviors and meaningful involvement. Instructors in every discipline are encouraged to use games, cooperative projects, and other activities that foster active student participation as a way of developing intrinsically motivated students.

References

Amabile, T. M. *The Social Psychology of Creativity.* New York: Springer-Verlag, 1983.

Amabile, T. M. *Growing Up Creative.* New York: Crown, 1989.

Caine, R., and Caine, G. *Making Connections: Teaching and the Human Brain.* Alexandria, Va.: Association for Supervision and Curriculum Development, 1991.

Hayes, J. R. *Cognitive Psychology.* Homewood, Ill.: Dorsey Press, 1978.

Khatena, J. *Imagery and Creative Imagination.* Buffalo, N.Y.: Creative Education Foundation, 1984.

Osborne, A. F. *Applied Imagination.* New York: Charles Scribner's Sons, 1957.

Parnes, S. J. *Creative Behavior Guidebook.* New York: Charles Scribner's Sons, 1967.

Chapter 5

Cooperative Learning in the Classroom

James L. Cooper,
Pamela Robinson,
Molly McKinney

Cooperative learning is a structured, systematic instructional strategy in which small groups of students work together toward a common goal. Cooperative learning may be considered a subset of collaborative learning. Collaborative learning tends to encompass a variety of group learning experiences, such as peer tutoring, student-faculty research projects, short-term buzz groups, learning communities, and other techniques. This chapter gives the reader a brief overview of the major issues and concerns that instructors should consider in deciding whether to use cooperative learning in their courses. More detailed discussions of the issues described in each section may be obtained from the sources cited at the end of the chapter.

Preparation of this manuscript was made possible, in part, by a grant to Jim Cooper from the Fund for the Improvement of Postsecondary Education.
The authors thank Mimi Warshaw and Lyle Smith (California State University, Dominguez Hills) for reading earlier versions of the article.

Critical Features

Most forms of small-group instruction have a positive impact on students' attitudes (Slavin, 1983). However, certain elements of small-group instruction must be in place to ensure consistent effects on achievement. Two critical features often distinguish cooperative learning from other forms of small-group instruction: positive interdependence and individual accountability.

Positive interdependence is essential to fostering significant achievement gains. Structures must be built into the learning environment to ensure that all members of a cooperative learning team feel a sense of responsibility for their teammates. One way to promote this sense of responsibility is by providing materials that must be shared (materials interdependence). Another way to foster group cohesion is by assigning different members of each team a discrete amount of material to master and then share with teammates (task interdependence). Finally, a small part of each person's grade can depend on each member of the team improving his or her performance on course exams (goal interdependence).

A common complaint among those who use small-group instructional procedures is the inequitable distribution of work load across group participants. This problem is usually caused by giving students undifferentiated group grades for papers, presentations, and other course assignments. To combat this phenomenon, the second feature that often distinguishes cooperative learning from other collaborative learning techniques is the insistence on *individual accountability* in grading. Even though students work together in teams for some percentage of the in-class or out-of-class work, course grades are almost always exclusively determined by individually completed tests, papers, and other assessment procedures. Individual accountability helps decrease the sense of inequity perceived by many in traditional small-group procedures, where a significant percentage of the course grade is given to all members of a team, even when one or two of the team members have done most of the work. Forms of small-group instruction that do not contain the two features just described should be termed collaborative learning, not cooperative learning.

Four additional features are always characteristic of cooperative learning and are often used in other forms of collaborative learning as well. One such feature is *appropriate assignment to groups*. This grouping is usually heterogeneous in terms of race, sex, prior achievement, and other characteristics deemed appropriate by the instructor. Appropriate assignment of students to cooperative learning groups promotes improved attitudes toward persons of differing backgrounds, an issue of great concern in dealing with the student diversity that challenges many of our colleges and universities (Johnson and Johnson, 1989).

The *teacher as coach or facilitator* is another characteristic of cooperative and other forms of collaborative learning. Rather than functioning as an expert dispenser of information, as in the lecture format, the teacher is in a more collegial role, structuring the learning environment so that students are more interactive with one another and with the teacher. Students are expected to take more responsibility for their own learning than they would in traditional lecture and lecture/discussion formats.

An additional feature of cooperative learning is its *explicit attention to social skills*. In cooperative learning (and some other forms of collaborative learning) formal structures are designed to encourage such prosocial behaviors as active listening, cooperation, and respect for others. The simplest structure takes the form of stating certain specific prosocial behaviors as classroom expectations or requirements on the syllabus. A more complex structure is group processing, a technique in which each member of the group evaluates each teammate's behavior on specified criteria and reports his or her perceptions to the teacher or teammates for discussion or grading.

Finally, cooperative learning tends to emphasize *face-to-face problem solving*. Often this problem solving happens immediately after a lecture or reading, allowing students to elaborate on recently acquired information and to transfer this information into long-term memory. Fostering such metacognitive activity is consistent with what psychologists know about encouraging critical thinking and promoting lifelong learning.

Each of the six features of cooperative learning should be explicitly addressed by the instructor, no matter which form of small-group instruction is used.

History and Research
Base of Cooperative Learning

The roots of cooperative learning may be traced to John Dewey, who emphasized education as a vehicle for teaching citizens to live cooperatively in a social democracy. A second major figure in the history of cooperative learning is social psychologist Kurt Lewin, who in the 1930s and 1940s emphasized the importance of group dynamics in understanding the behavior of leaders and members of democratic groups. Morton Deutsch was a student of Lewin's at MIT who developed a theory of cooperation and competition based on Lewin's "field theory." More recently, David and Roger Johnson at the University of Minnesota, Shlomo Sharan at the University of Tel Aviv, and Robert Slavin at Johns Hopkins have been among the researcher/practitioners helping develop cooperative learning into one of the best-researched pedagogical approaches in education over the last thirty years, although almost all their work has been done in precollegiate settings.

In 1989 Johnson and Johnson surveyed 193 studies in which cooperative learning was compared to more traditional forms of instruction, using group productivity as an outcome measure. In over 50 percent of the cases, the cooperative learning approach was more effective than more traditional forms of instruction, while in 10 percent of the cases, competitive or individualistic approaches to instruction produced higher productivity. Regarding attitudes toward other people, Johnson and Johnson (1989) found that the cooperative learning approach produced greater interpersonal attraction in 60 percent of the comparisons and that competitive and individualistic approaches produced higher levels of interpersonal attraction in 3 percent of the cases.

Earlier the Johnsons and their colleagues (1981) published a meta-analysis of 122 studies of cooperative learning using academic achievement as the outcome measure. They found cooperation to be much more powerful in producing achievement than the other interaction patterns, and the results held for several subject areas and a range of age groups from elementary school through adult. These general findings have been replicated by a number of researchers looking at a variety of cognitive and attitudinal measures (Johnson and Johnson, 1989; Slavin, 1983). Analyses of cooperative learning's effect on critical thinking, self-esteem, racial/ethnic relations, prosocial behavior, and a variety of other measures have consistently demonstrated that cooperative learning is superior to more traditional forms of instruction in a majority of the cases and is rarely inferior to other forms of instruction. In other words, while cooperative learning is not always superior to other instructional approaches, it rarely has detrimental effects on student outcomes.

Unfortunately, relatively few well-controlled studies of cooperative learning have been conducted at the college level. In 1992 Smith and Conrad found 171 citations in the ERIC data base under the descriptor "Cooperative Learning and Higher Education." Almost all of these citations date from 1988 to 1992. Most were reports of practical applications of cooperative learning to specific disciplines rather than empirical comparisons of cooperative learning to other pedagogical approaches. However, Frierson (1986) found that nursing students at a predominantly black college who studied cooperatively for their state licensing exams passed their exams at a significantly higher rate than comparable students studying individually. Treisman (1986) found that African American students at the University of California, Berkeley, who worked cooperatively in enrichment sessions outside of class received calculus course grades over one letter grade higher than comparable African American students who did not use the enrichment programs. College attrition rates for African American students in the year-long program matched the Berkeley average for all students and were significantly lower for program participants than for comparable African American students not involved in the program.

Cooper and Mueck (1990) reported on over 1,000 students in cooperatively taught courses in nine different disciplines at a predominately minority, urban comprehensive university. Students were asked to compare their cooperative learning experiences with their experiences in courses taught using more traditional lecture and lecture/discussion classes. From 70 to 90 percent rated their cooperative learning experience as somewhat or significantly more positive on such variables as academic achievement, higher-level thinking skills, interest in subject matter, likelihood of attending class, time on task, ability to diagnose own knowledge of subject matter, amount of class time required to reach mastery, general class morale, and rapport with the teacher. Two of the highest-rated dimensions on these anonymously completed student evaluations were frequency and quality of student-student interactions and frequency and quality of student-teacher interactions.

Astin (1992) recently completed a study of over 200 colleges and universities to assess what factors make a difference in undergraduate education. After examining nearly 200 environmental variables, including a large number of curriculum factors, he concluded that student-student interaction and student-teacher interaction were by far the best predictors of positive student cognitive and attitudinal changes in the undergraduate experience. Curriculum arrangements seemed to have little effect on student outcomes. Based on this and related research, Astin has pressed for greater use of cooperative learning in college instruction.

Types of Cooperative Learning

According to Kagan (1992), there are over fifty forms of cooperative learning. Each has its appropriate application, depending on the nature of the student population and the type of educational outcome to be fostered. Ultimately, each teacher must decide which of the cooperative learning techniques to use and the relative amount of total in-class and out-of-class time devoted to cooperative learning. Listed here is a sampling of the forms of cooperative learning that have received the most empirical attention, beginning with the more teacher-centered and moving to more student-centered approaches.

1. *STAD (student teams achievement division).* In this cooperative learning technique, students receive information via lectures, films, readings, and so on, and then receive a worksheet to complete in teams of four. The teams, formed by the teacher, are typically heterogeneous, based on prior achievement, race,

sex, language background, and other factors determined by the instructor. The worksheets may contain case studies, problems to solve, or other tasks. Once all members have agreed that they have completed the task and mastered the skills assessed by the worksheet, the instructor is called over. In addition to verbally quizzing individual team members on how the worksheet problems were solved, the instructor may give one or all members of the team a quiz that must be completed individually by team members (individual accountability). The team is excused only if individual mastery of the content is assured. This is one of the most teacher-centered of the cooperative learning techniques, as the instructor often determines the members of individual teams and their roles within the teams, the nature of the learning materials, and most other elements of the instructional sequence.

2. *Jigsaw.* With this technique, the teacher assigns a different minitopic to each member of a team. The students research their assigned minitopics, then meet in expert groups with members of other teams assigned the same minitopic to discuss and refine their understanding of the subject. Team members then return to their original groups to teach the minitopics to the entire team.

3. *Constructive controversy (structured controversy).* Pairs within a four-person team are assigned different sides of an issue. Each pair researches one side of the topic (or a summary is provided by the teacher). The two pairs discuss the topic, not to win a debate but to adduce as much information on the topic as possible. Pairs then switch sides and develop arguments for the opposite side of the same issue.

4. *Group investigation.* Each team is assigned or selects a different topic within a rather general area. Students are given great freedom in determining how to organize their teams, conduct the research, and present their ideas to the total class. Often the class presentation is a brief play, a video or slide show, a demonstration, or some other type of performance. Even with this student-centered form of cooperative learning, however, the instructor grades the individual's contribution to the team project to prevent the dominator/freeloader phenomenon.

Instructors may mix and match these and the several

dozen other types of cooperative learning (see Kagan, 1992; Johnson, Johnson and Smith, 1991, for complete descriptions of many cooperative learning procedures). It is possible to modify the techniques for different student populations and academic disciplines. Note however, that all cooperative learning techniques must have the following features for most effective implementation: (1) a clear specification of the instructional goal or objective, (2) group work designed to promote some attitude, to teach something, or to give practice in performing a task, and (3) some form of individual student assessment to determine each individual's performance independent of the group work.

Fitting Cooperative Learning into Existing Teaching Styles

Susan Prescott of California State University, Dominguez Hills, has found that it is possible to begin experimenting with cooperative learning without implementing formal cooperative learning structures such as jigsaw and STAD. For example, if an instructor primarily uses a lecture format, she may consider adding the following as supplements to her current lesson. Before the lecture, she may establish a motivational hook to focus the students' attention on the content of the lecture. She may then take three to five minutes to pose a question or frame an issue that will be a focal point for the day. The teacher may have teams discuss the issue, take a position, or ask questions relating to the topic. During the lecture, the instructor can stop at critical points to actively involve the students. Research on student attention span suggests that breaking up the lecture every fifteen to twenty minutes will result in much higher time-on-task among students. For example, the professor might stop after fifteen minutes of lecturing on fairly technical information and ask pairs or teams of students to find an example of the concept(s) just presented or ask a question relating to the topic. (Refer to Chapter Three for excellent guidelines on sequencing examples.) A teacher might create an intentional error in a problem based on the fifteen-minute lecture and ask the groups to identify it. If the lecture has been procedural, students might be asked to compare notes to ensure that all procedural steps are understood by all students. Such breaks in the lecture need only take one to five minutes.

After the lecture, the instructor might organize a somewhat longer task to help students consolidate or practice the information just presented. Students can be asked to return to the questions they formulated at the start of the class and attempt to answer them. These questions and answers might be shared with individual teammates or with the entire class if time permits. Students might be asked to create a set of hypothetical test questions based on the lecture and then share those questions with the entire class. The instructor might even promise to use a sample of the test items created in class on actual tests. Teams may be asked to create compare/contrast charts, write explanatory captions of pictures given to them, or create a dialogue for a character in a play, film, or novel. Teams may simply be asked to solve a set of problems from a worksheet based on the content of the lecture. Many teachers have found that something as simple as a previously used test or an exercise from an instructor's textbook manual can provide highly interactive, metacognitive practice for students.

Activities such as those just described for enrichment of the lecture can be constructed for instructors who commonly use discussion methods and audio-visual materials. Cooperative learning activities can also be used before and after homework assignments. Prescott (1990) describes these techniques in more detail in the *Cooperative Learning and College Teaching* newsletter.

Tips on Implementation

Based on eight years of experience implementing cooperative learning at California State University, Dominguez Hills, and on conversations with practitioners around the country, we would like to offer the following tips to faculty who are considering use of cooperative learning in their classes.

1. *Start small.* Use cooperative learning in the class that you feel most confident about. If you do so, you will have a

better handle on the key points within the course that should serve as the focal points for cooperative learning activities. Also, if one of the cooperative learning activities fails or is completed in one-third of the anticipated class time, you will be able to say, "Good, that gives us time to preview the next unit of instruction." One surefire way to use cooperative learning is to review for a test. Cooper uses STAD to review for each unit test, and students commonly stay after the class to ask for additional sample problems and worksheets used during the review.

2. *Use cooperative learning with criterion-referenced grading.* Norm-referenced grading (grading on the curve) often explicitly encourages excessive competition for scarce resources (A's and B's). Almost all cooperative learning practitioners suggest absolute grading criteria in which all who achieve the prestated standard for a specific grade receive the commensurate grade.

3. *Make cooperative learning a small part of the total grade.* One instructor gives three bonus points for successful completion of twelve cooperative learning activities in his semester-long research methods class. If the cooperative learning activities are tied to important course objectives and help the students master individually completed tests and papers, little of the course grade need be tied to successful cooperative learning work. A few bonus points are enough to reward the students in these intrinsically motivating cooperative learning tasks.

4. *Introduce the technique well.* Clearly identify your rationale for using the technique. Indicate that there is a substantial research base for your experimenting with the technique. Clearly identify that, unlike other small-group techniques students may have experienced, course grades will depend almost entirely on individually graded tests and papers. In other words, if students help one another, they will not be putting their own grade in jeopardy.

5. *Structure the cooperative learning activities so that students must learn something, not do something.* If students know that they can complete a worksheet, then leave, that is what many will do. Develop a method to assess mastery of the content independent of the group work (such as individually completed quizzes) and communicate the ethic that the team's work is never done until

all members have mastered the skills that underlie the cooperative learning activity.

One technique used to reinforce the positive interdependence notion described earlier and to emphasize content mastery for all students is to give a one-minute quiz over the content of the worksheet. All students must pass the quiz at a high standard of mastery (often 100 percent) before any student may leave. Or, the instructor might have a randomly selected student take the brief quiz for all members of the team. If students fail to meet mastery, their teammates reteach the necessary skills for five or ten minutes. Then another quiz is administered.

6. *Clarity and organization are essential.* When asked to name the main cause of small-group failure, most teachers respond that students were not clear as to what the task was and how they should proceed in completing the assignment. At least initially, cooperative learning group tasks should be structured by the teacher. Students are less anxious about course content and grading when expectations are clearly delineated. This is true of all instructional approaches but is especially true in small-group work. Such structure may include specifying roles for each team member, setting time limits for each element of the task, making suggestions for getting started, describing what the final product for the day might look like, and so on. As students experience success and gain confidence in their abilities to work in teams, student control of many of these decisions may replace teacher control (Cooper and others, 1990).

Objections to Using Cooperative Learning

Many instructors are dissatisfied with their current teaching techniques, which they usually identify as lecture or lecture/discussion. Research by Karp and Yoels (1987) indicates that even in classes identified as discussion, three to five students dominate the discussion with the teacher. Thus, most teaching is characterized by a high degree of teacher control and student passivity and powerlessness. This creates an environment in which the teacher feels compelled to intellectually move the class from one level of skill to another. This burden of feeling totally responsible for such a daunting task is sometimes termed the Atlas complex. In cooperative learning, much of the responsibility for learning is explicitly placed on the student. However, handing over some of this control is a difficult change for many instructors to make. That is why we suggest that the change to cooperative learning be done in stages (see Implementation Tips).

Many instructors voice legitimate concerns or objections about adapting cooperative learning in their clasrooms. Here are the most common:

1. *"I can't cover as much content in my lectures."* It is certainly true that time spent in cooperative learning groups is time away from the lecture. Many of us feel that we already have too much content to teach in the forty to forty-five contact hours per term available in many courses. However, the information in our disciplines is only going to increase in amount and complexity. Because we cannot teach everything in any discipline, we must start teaching a more limited number of overarching concepts with wide-ranging applicability. Thus, we are covering less content via the lecture in our cooperative learning–taught classes. However, the retention rates for material that is presented in lecture and practiced in small groups is increased substantially. Courses taught using cooperative learning result in content being learned at a higher level of mastery and being retained longer relative to the case with more traditionally taught classes. Thus, the content is available for generalizing to new situations because it has been modeled, discussed, and critiqued in highly interactive small groups. Compare this cooperative form of learning difficult material with a more traditional procedure in which the student hears a lecture on a given topic, then memorizes as much of this content as possible for an exam given several weeks after the lecture (Johnson and Johnson, 1989).

2. *"I don't have time to prepare cooperative learning activities."* The first time an instructor converts a course to include cooperative learning activities, there is an additional time commitment involved. However, the power of cooperative learning is such that students become highly involved, even in such easily accessible material as old exams, exercises from instructor or student manuals, and simple problem sets. The pleasure of watching

students actively engage in solving the problems is so exciting that it makes whatever additional time is required for preparation seem like time well spent. Once the instructor becomes more skilled at identifying the major concepts within his or her courses, and observing what works and what doesn't in small groups, he or she becomes more interested in constructing materials that are more challenging, more exciting, and more tightly linked to his or her own course goals.

3. *"What happens when some people work and others don't?"* This objection is partially handled by making students individually accountable. Almost all the course grade in cooperative learning courses is still determined by individually completed tests, papers, and so on. To deal with a sandbagger who will not contribute, we suggest keeping close tabs on groups as they work. During cooperative learning class time, the instructor should remain in the classroom, moving from team to team, monitoring group progress. If there is a noncontributing group member, the instructor may take that person aside, outside of class, and attempt to remedy the problem. Failing this, the instructor may intervene within the group setting. Only if a student repeatedly and intentionally refuses to contribute to the group would we recommend dismissal from the group. This rarely happens, especially if the teacher states on the first day of the class and in the syllabus that all students are expected to participate in group activities.

Conclusion: The Future of Cooperative Learning in Higher Education

One can scarcely pick up a newspaper without reading another indictment of college teaching and learning. These reports (Association of American Colleges, 1985; Bok, 1986; Boyer, 1987; National Institute of Education, 1984) decry excessive passivity in the current teaching/learning process and call for greater involvement of students in their own learning.

Cooperative learning is a pedagogy with a record of over twenty-five years of success at the K–12 level. One task for research in higher education over the next decade should be to relate the efficacy of cooperative learning to the college classroom. Can the powerful effect of cooperative learning seen in hundreds of K–12 studies be replicated with college students? Research on the characteristics of college students and adult learners suggests that well-conceived cooperative learning techniques should be effective. If cooperative learning has a generally positive effect on achievement in the college classroom, is this effect differential? That is, does it work particularly well for some disciplines and courses? Does it work particularly well for certain types of students? Precollegiate research suggests that the answer to these questions may be yes. Perhaps cooperative learning is particularly useful for the at-risk student or for the student whose cultural background emphasizes cooperation rather than competition. With its emphasis on highly involving, informal contacts among students and between students and teachers, does cooperative learning have potential as a relatively cheap retention device, since it incorporates many of the dimensions recommended by leading retention researchers such as Noel and Tinto?

Research undertaken by Cooper and his colleagues at California State University, Dominguez Hills, is attempting to address several of these issues. They are looking at the effects of cooperative learning on a variety of outcomes measures, including Perry's "stages" of cognitive development, attrition in college, critical thinking, and other cognitive and attitudinal measures. More than 1,300 students taught in over thirty sections of undergraduate courses are serving as subjects for this study. Tinto and his colleagues at the National Center on Postsecondary Teaching, Learning, and Assessment (at Pennsylvania State University) are looking at the effects of cooperative learning and collaborative learning on a number of outcome measures. Smith and MacGregor at Evergreen State College have been exploring the impact of collaborative learning on various outcome measures for several years. David and Roger Johnson and Karl Smith at the University of Minnesota have recently expanded their study on the effects of cooperative learning on precollegiate populations to include college-level applications.

However, the classroom teacher may not wish to wait the

years it will take to develop unambiguous answers to the questions and issues described above. The data at both K–12 and college level indicate that cooperative learning is generally more effective than more traditional forms of instruction and is rarely less effective. In light of the importance of teamwork and cooperation in our society and the lack of instruction concerning these values in our current higher-education systems, some amount of cooperative learning instruction seems justified even if it is found to have relatively little impact on achievement, critical thinking, or other cognitive outcomes.

Many professional accrediting groups are calling for a commitment to teaching such values in their disciplines (including accounting, a discipline that is often unfairly stereotyped as being individualistic and competitive). The continuing unrest in our cities is a clear symptom that we, as a society, have a long way to go in meeting Dewey's goal of preparing our citizenry to function cooperatively in a social democracy.

Appendix: Resources

The following list of persons and groups doing work in cooperative learning and collaborative learning comes from *Collaborative Learning: A Sourcebook for Higher Education*. This book can be purchased for $23 by contacting the National Center on Postsecondary Teaching, Learning, and Assessment, Pennsylvania State University, 403 South Allen St., Suite 104, University Park, PA 16801-5252, 814-865-5917, FAX 814-865-3638, Bitnet NCTLA@PSUVM.

Network for Cooperative Learning
in Higher Education

Those wishing to find out more about cooperative learning in higher education may contact this network, which was started by Cooper and funded by a grant from the Fund for the Improvement of Postsecondary Education (FIPSE). In addition to sponsoring research on cooperative learning in higher education, the California State University, Dominguez Hills, program has a dissemination strand. Among the materials available from the network are articles and bibliographies concerning cooperative learning and college teaching. Many chapters in the bibliographies deal with discipline-specific applications of cooperative learning. The network also produces a newsletter published by New Forum Press that deals with applications of cooperative learning to higher education. In addition, Jim Cooper and his associates have written a fifty-five-page workbook on cooperative learning in the college classroom that can be purchased for $14 by contacting the California State University Foundation, California State University Institute for Teaching and Learning, Office of the Chancellor, 400 Golden Shore, Long Beach, CA 90802-4275. For materials on cooperative learning in higher education contact Jim Cooper, California State University, Dominguez Hills, HFA-B-316, 1000 E. Victoria St., Carson, CA 90747, 310-516-3961.

Collaboration in Undergraduate Education (CUE) Collaborative and Cooperative Learning Network

This network organizes the Collaborative Learning Action Community of the American Association for Higher Education (AAHE) and is a part of the National Collegiate Honors Council. Since 1983 CUE has sponsored various conferences and publications to promote the use of collaborative learning in undergraduate education. A bibliography on collaborative learning and additional information may be obtained by contacting Roberta Matthews, LaGuardia Community College, 31-10 Thompson Ave., Long Island City, NY 11101, 718-582-5443.

Cooperative Learning Center

The focus of this center is on research in cooperative learning, the structured use of interdependent team members, and individual accountability. Much of the work has been done at the K–12 level, but in recent years the researchers have turned their attention to cooperative learning at the college level. The center is a resource for materials, teacher training, and workshops on cooperative learning across the country. For more information contact David Johnson or Roger Johnson, University of Minnesota, 202 Pattee Hall, 150 Pillsbury Dr. SE, Minneapolis, MN 55455, 612-624-7031. The cooperative learning workbook published by Johnson, Johnson, and Smith (1991) can be purchased by contacting the Cooperative Learning Center.

New England Resource Center for Higher Education

This center serves private and public higher-education institutions within New England. Some of the specific interests and concerns of the center are the development of collaborative relationships within and among colleges and universities in New England, preparation and continuing professional development of administrators and faculty, and incentives for high-quality work. The resource center has a number of ongoing research projects, sponsors, conferences, and seminars for a wide range of professionals in higher education and publishes a newsletter, *The Academic Workplace*. For inclusion on the mailing list, contact Zelda Gamson, University of Massachusetts, Boston, Graduate College of Education, Harbor Campus — W/2/143, Boston, MA 02125-3393, 617-287-7740, FAX 617-287-7922.

Washington Center for Improving the Quality of Undergraduate Education

Established in 1985 as an interinstitutional consortium, the Washington Center focuses on low-cost, high-yield approaches to educational reform, emphasizing better utilization and sharing of existing resources through interinstitutional collaboration. The center, supported by the Washington State Legislature, includes forty-two participating institutions: all of the state's public four-year institutions and community colleges, and nine independent colleges. It supports and coordinates interinstitutional faculty exchanges, the development of interdisciplinary learning community programs, conferences, seminars, and technical assistance on effective approaches to teaching and learning (*Washington Center News,* 1991).

The center publishes the *Washington Center News,* an outstanding newsletter filled with reports of activities from various institutions in the state. To be included on their mailing list, write or call Barbara Leigh Smith or Jean MacGregor, The Evergreen State College, Olympia, WA 98505, 206-866-6000 ext. 6863.

References

Association of American Colleges. *Integrity in the Curriculum: A Report to the Academic Community.* (Project on Redefining the Meaning and Purpose of Baccalaureate Degrees.) Washington, D.C.: Association of American Colleges, 1985.

Astin, A. W. *What Matters in College? Four Critical Years.* San Francisco: Jossey-Bass, 1992.

Bok, D. *Higher Learning.* Cambridge, Mass.: Harvard University Press, 1986.

Boyer, E. L. *College: The Undergraduate Experience in America.* New York: HarperCollins, 1987.

Cooper, J., and Mueck, R. "Student Involvement in Learning: Cooperative Learning and College Instruction." *Journal on Excellence in College Teaching,* 1990, *1,* 68–76.

Cooper, J., and others. *Cooperative Learning and College Instruction: Effective Use of Student Learning Teams.* Long Beach: California State University Institute for Teaching and Learning, 1990.

Frierson, H. T. "Two Intervention Methods: Effects on Groups of Predominantly Black Nursing Students' Board Scores." *Journal of Educational Psychology,* 1986, *69,* 101–108.

Johnson, D. W., and Johnson, R. T. *Cooperation and Competition: Theory and Research.* Edina, Minn.: Interaction Book, 1989.

Johnson, D. W., Johnson, R. T., and Smith, K. A. *Active Learning: Cooperation in the College Classroom.* Edina, Minn.: Interaction Book, 1991.

Johnson, D. W., and others. "Effects of Cooperative, Competitive, and Individualistic Goal Structures on Achievement: A Meta-Analysis." *Psychological Bulletin,* 1981, *89,* 47–62.

Kagan, S. *Cooperative Learning.* San Juan Capistrano, Calif.: Resources for Teachers, 1992.

Karp, D., and Yoels, W. "The College Classroom: Some Observations on the Meanings of Students' Participation." *Sociology and Social Research,* 1987, *60,* 421–439.

National Institute for Education. *Involvement in Learning.* (Study Group on the Conditions of Excellence in Higher Education.) Washington, D.C.: National Institute for Education, 1984.

Prescott, S. "Fitting Cooperative Learning into Existing Teaching Styles. *Cooperative Learning and College Teaching,* Dec. 1990, pp. 5–6.

Slavin, R. E. "When Does Cooperative Learning Increase Student Achievement?" *Psychological Bulletin,* 1983, *94*(3), 429–445.

Smith, K., and Conrad, J. "Cooperative Learning: Theory and Practice." *The National Teaching and Learning Forum,* 1992, *1*(3), 8–11.

Treisman, P. U. "A Study of the Mathematics Performance of Black Students at the University of California, Berkeley." Unpublished doctoral dissertation, University of California, Berkeley, 1986.

Washington Center News, Fall 1991, p. 36.

Chapter 6

Questioning Techniques for the Active Classroom

C. *Bobbi Hansen*

The great humorist James Thurber focused on the importance of questions and answers when he remarked that it is better to ask some of the questions than it is to know all of the answers. Have you ever been disappointed in the answers that students give to the questions you ask in class? Do you want to understand the various types of questions available to you that encourage critical thought in your students? Do you want to learn how to interact with your students in a more dynamic way and to inspire more student-to-student dialogue? Do you want to learn how to probe students' thinking processes so that they become more reflective?

Some teachers seem to have a natural talent for asking the right question at precisely the right moment. In their classes one can almost hear the "Ah ha!" being murmured by a student for whom the "light just went on." I am reminded of Professor Kingsfield from the TV series *The Paper Chase*. He, most certainly, had the "gift" of asking good questions. The great majority of college professors, however, must work at developing their questioning skills. The aim of this chapter is to assist in that development. For a related discussion, see Chapter Two in this volume.

Phrasing Questions
and Probing the Responses

A vast literature base has accumulated on teacher questioning and its relationship to student learning (for example, King, 1992). The literature on teacher questioning has established that effective questioning contributes significantly to student learning (Brophy and Good, 1986; Wilen and Clegg, 1986). Two types of questioning practices that have been reviewed extensively are phrasing questions and probing the responses (Gall, 1987).

Being able to phrase questions properly is an important ingredient in effective questioning. Dantonio and Paradise (1988) state that clearly phrased questions: (1) contain words that are easily understood; (2) are stated simply, without cluttering the question with excess words or explanations; (3) focus students on the content; and (4) identify the specific thinking skills students are to use in answering the questions.

Perhaps the questioning behavior that elicits the highest quality responses from students is probing. Four types of probing questions are identified by Borg and others (1970):

1. Seeking further clarification (What do you mean?)
2. Increasing students' critical awareness (Why do you think that is so?)
3. Refocusing the students' response (How does this relate to . . . ?)
4. Prompting or giving clues (Let me get you started . . .)

In addition to using these research-based guides in questioning to obtain the desired student thinking outcomes, a skilled questioner needs to make decisions in at least two other critical areas: the type of question needed for desired thinking outcomes, and the type of student interaction needed for the desired engagement level.

Types of Questions

To assist in selecting appropriate questions, it may be useful for an instructor to first become acquainted with the many systems now in use for classifying questions (King, 1990, 1991). Among the more effective systems currently in use are Bloom's taxonomy of educational objectives, the Aschner-Gallagher question system, and Taba's instructional strategies. I will give a brief description of each system, along with examples of open-ended questions to assist instructors in making use of each question type in their own discipline.

Bloom's Taxonomy

Bloom's taxonomy of educational objectives (1956) is, perhaps, the best known of the models. It has certainly been the catalyst for much inquiry into teacher questioning practices. Bloom's classification system contains six levels of objectives: knowledge, comprehension, application, analysis, synthesis, and evaluation. The last four would be considered at a "higher" cognitive level than the first two, which represent a more factual understanding of the content. Many studies have shown that most instructors ask the preponderance of their questions at the knowledge or simple recall level, which is the lowest level of questioning in Bloom's taxonomy (Blosser, 1980; Daines, 1982; Gall, 1970). Examples of questions at each of Bloom's levels are provided in Exhibit 6.1.

Aschner-Gallagher's Question System

Aschner and Gallagher (1965) based their model on Guilford's structure of the intellect, a three-dimensional scheme for organizing thinking skills. The question types are memory, convergent thinking, divergent thinking, and evaluation. Memory questions require simple recall of information; convergent questions use supportive data for students to reach a response that is objectively correct or incorrect. Divergent questions may have many correct answers and often require the generation of original information. Finally, evaluative questions require students to make a judgment. Similar to the higher levels in Bloom's taxonomy, the last two question types require a more in-depth, critical response from students. Examples of questions based on Aschner-Gallagher's classification are provided in Exhibit 6.2.

**Exhibit 6.1. Using Bloom's Taxonomy:
Examples of Open-Ended Questions for Use Across Disciplines.**

Knowledge

List three important details from the assigned reading.

From the text, list all of the _____ that you can remember.

Define _____ .

Label the parts of _____ .

Comprehension

Explain what is meant by _____ .

Discuss the reasons that the author gives for _____ .

Paraphrase _____ .

Application

Illustrate how you could apply the _____ principle in your life.

Explain how you could (would) have solved the problem.

Put _____ in graph form.

Analysis

Analyze _____ from the perspective of _____ .

Simplify the _____ to its basic components.

Search through this _____ to find as many principles of _____ as
is possible.

Synthesis

Create a new _____ from the information given in this chapter.

Design a model of _____ using _____ principles.

Develop a plan for the improvement of _____ .

Formulate an innovative idea for _____ .

Evaluation

Decide which _____ is the best.

Judge the effectiveness of _____ .

Justify the actions of _____ .

Which solution would you choose? Justify your opinion.

**Exhibit 6.2. Using Ascher-Gallagher's Classifications:
Examples of Open-Ended Questions for Use Across Disciplines.**

Memory

Arrange the _____ in the correct sequence.

List all of the _____ that you can recall.

Identify the reasons the author gives for _____ .

Convergent Thinking

Based on the information in the text, which solution would be considered the most appropriate?

Analyze this example and tell me the governing principle.

Divergent Thinking

Quantity model: List all of the _____ .

How many ways can you come up with _____ ?

Viewpoint model: How would this look to a _____ ?

What would _____ mean from the viewpoint of _____ ?

Involvement model: How would you feel if you were _____ ?

You are a _____ . Describe how you feel.

Conscious self-deceit model: You have been given the power to _____ . How will you use it?

Suppose you were _____ . How would you solve _____ ?

Forced association model: How is _____ like _____ ?

Get ideas from _____ to improve _____ .

I only know about _____ . Explain _____ to me.

Reorganization model: What would happen if _____ were true?

Suppose _____ happened, what would be the consequences?

Evaluation

Decide which proposal is the best.

Prioritize the ideas from most important to least important.

Assess the effectiveness of the solution presented by other groups.

Questioning Processes

Questioning processes (Dantonio, 1990) are derived from the
work of Taba (1971) and Ehrenberg and Ehrenberg (1978). They
include ten thinking processes grouped into four categories:

1. *Gathering:* observing and recalling
2. *Sorting:* comparing, contrasting, and grouping
3. *Organizing:* labeling, classifying, and sequencing
4. *Interpreting:* inferring (causes, effects, qualities) and
   predicting

I am particularly partial to this system because, in my
opinion, it already categorizes the various purposes that the instructor might have for asking questions. All the instructor has
to do, then, is to select questions from the category that most
closely meets the identified instructional objective. Sample questions based on the model of questioning processes are provided
in Exhibit 6.3.

Types of Interactions

In addition to the questions themselves, instructors need to be
cognizant of the interaction and response patterns that occur
in their classrooms. As instructors, we desire to give each student an equal opportunity to respond to questions. Research
has shown, however, that we are not equitable in our questioning practices. We tend to call on students whom we perceive
to be "high achievers" more often than we call on students whom
we perceive to be "low achievers." Males get more response opportunities than females. Students sitting in the front rows get
recognized and called on more frequently than students who
sit in the back of the classroom (Brophy and Good, 1986).
These tendencies underline the need for us to pay attention to classroom dynamics. One way to counteract inequitable interaction patterns is to plan for them directly and not rely
on the chance interaction patterns of students who raise hands

**Exhibit 6.3. Using a Questioning Process Taxonomy:
Examples of Open-Ended Questions for Use Across Disciplines.**

Observing

What do you notice about _____?

What do you observe about _____?

Recalling

What do you recall about _____?

Tell me what you remember concerning _____?

Based on your reading, what did you find out about _____?

Comparing

How are _____ and _____ alike?

Compare _____ and _____.

Who (what) is similar to _____?

Contrasting

What are the differences between _____ and _____?

Tell me what discrepancy you noted concerning _____ and _____.

Grouping

How can we group these items?

Based on your reading, which of these could be grouped together because they are alike in some way?

Labeling

What are some appropriate names for this idea?

What terms can you think of to communicate the critical characteristics of this concept?

Classifying

Is this _____ an example of _____ (category)?

Which of the examples belongs in the _____ (label) group?

Find or create an example of _____ (concept label).

Sequencing

Rank the items from _____ (criterion) to _____ (criterion).

Place the following information in _____ (criterion) order.

What do you think is the first significant piece of information in this chapter?

Exhibit 6.3. Using a Questioning Process Taxonomy:
Examples of Open-Ended Questions for Use Across Disciplines, Cont'd.

Inferring

What are some causes of _____?

What are some effects of _____?

What do you think is true about _____?

Predicting

What do you think will solve the problem of _____?

What do you think will happen next in this situation?

What do you think will happen as a result of _____?

to be recognized. A number of strategies are available for guiding student responses.

Paired Responses

For many instructors, paired response techniques are the easiest to use, for they require no advance preparation. Instead of the instructor calling on a single student to answer a question, students respond to another student first, then responses are shared with the entire class. Using this slight alteration of the traditional single-student interaction pattern ensures that all students respond to all questions. Exhibit 6.4 presents a description of three paired response interactions.

Small-Group Interactions

Small-group (three, four, or five students) interactions may require more planning time for the instructor and more actual class time for the activity, but the payoff is increased student-to-student interest and motivation. You will recognize the links between posing questions to small groups and the types of collaborative learning activities that were discussed in Chapter Five by Cooper, Robinson, and McKinney. Several small-group strategies are outlined in Exhibit 6.5.

Exhibit 6.4. Paired Response Interactions.

Name of Strategy: Turn to Your Partner And . . . (Weaver and Cotrell, 1986)

Procedure: This is an informal technique to use throughout a lecture. Tell students to identify a "partner" sitting in close proximity. Lecture as usual, but pause every five or ten minutes and direct partners to discuss various points of lecture. You may occasionally ask partners to share their ideas with whole class.

Uses: This technique is best used with simple recall of factual information or to better understand the lecture.

Name of Strategy: Paired Partners: Think Aloud (Whimbey and Whimbey, 1975)

Procedure: This is used as a problem-solving strategy. Pair students and have them react to a point made in the lecture or in a reading. One partner thinks out loud while the other monitors with cues and questions. Then the partners reverse roles. Students share experience either in writing or in class discussion.

Uses: This approach is best used with material that requires students to clarify information and understand it from a personal perspective.

Name of Strategy: Think/Pair/Share (Lyman and McTighe, 1988)

Procedure: To maximize critical thinking and reflection, ask students a question and then have them pause and think. Use wait-time (approximately five seconds), then direct students to share their thoughts with one another.

Uses: This strategy is best used for information that requires judgment or evaluation.

Whole-Class Techniques

An instructor who desires to direct questions to the entire group can draw from several strategies that assist in gaining the attention and interest of all the students. Three such strategies are presented in Exhibit 6.6.

General Questioning Strategies to Enhance Student Responses

Perez and Strickland (1986) give the following suggestions to assist instructors in any discipline to have meaningful classroom discussions:

Exhibit 6.5. Small-Group Interactions.

Name of Strategy: Triads (Costa, 1986)

Procedure: Group students in threes and give them a task to complete or a question to answer. Including a third person adds more ideas to the discussion but still maintains a small-group feeling, where students feel safe in expressing their opinions.

Uses: Many instructors find triads the ideal group size for discussing textbook chapters. More students tend to read the textbook if they know they will be responsible to a small group of their peers for the content. It is difficult for a student to "hide" in a group of three. Many instructors find success in keeping the "textbook discussion team" together for the entire term in order to build trust and continuity.

Name of Strategy: 2–4–8: Tell/Retell (Fogarty and Opeka, 1988)

Procedure: Pair students and ask them a question. Then have the pairs form groups of eight, where the question is again discussed.

Uses: This is an ideal icebreaker to encourage sharing of personal information or personal reactions to the course material. Students enjoy this technique, and it encourages sharing with other classmates with whom they might not otherwise interact.

Name of Strategy: Jigsaw (Aronson, 1978)

Procedure: Assign students to groups of four to six. Divide the content to be studied and assign each student a segment to teach the other students (like a jigsaw puzzle, with each student having an essential piece). Each group of students is teaching the same content. At times you may regroup students to meet in "expert" groups of individuals who have been assigned the same topic. Expert groups allow students to gain clarity on their particular topic before they individually present it to their group.

Uses: This is a beautifully crafted teaching technique for gaining students' complete engagement in a subject, a point that was noted in Chapter Five by Cooper, Robinson, and McKinney. Most questions become student-to-student interactions, with the instructor sitting in on the various jigsaw groups to listen and to further clarify difficult content. Many instructors try this out for the first time by dividing up a chapter in a textbook into five equal parts and then assigning students to one of the five parts. Again, all teaching is accomplished by students within their small group. They do not give a whole-class presentation.

Name of Strategy: Group Investigation (Sharan and Sharan, 1976)

Procedure: Lead the class in brainstorming a list of provocative questions that pertain to the course and that they would like to investigate. Have students sign up in teams of four to six to investigate the answers. Give students class time

Exhibit 6.5. Small-Group Interactions, Cont'd.

to organize and to make decisions pertaining to the investigation (who is going to do what). In subsequent sessions, give groups some class time to communicate with each other. Set dates for groups to present their findings to the whole class.

Uses: This strategy uses the students' own curiosity about the course content. Questions are initiated by students, investigated by students, and presented by students. The instructor provides guidance, resources, and class time. The group investigation runs parallel to the instructor's teaching of the course.

Exhibit 6.6. Whole-Class Techniques.

Name of Strategy: Total Group Response (Fogarty and Bellanca, 1987)

Procedure: Have students respond to questions by standing (or sitting) in particular areas of the room. (Another version of this strategy is for students to form a "human graph" based on a question that the instructor poses.)

Uses: This is an especially effective strategy for opinion and evaluative questions. For example, you may inquire which of several economic policies the federal government should enact. Students then stand in a particular place in the classroom if they favor one policy and stand in another spot if they favor a different policy. Students may then confer with classmates who are standing with them and together construct a rationale for their opinion to share with the entire class.

Name of Strategy: Forced Response

Procedure: Have students sitting in a semicircle or circle each respond to a question you pose. Students are allowed to "pass" if they do not wish to respond. When the question has gone all around the circle, initiate "cross-talk," in which any individual may direct a comment or question to any other individual (or to the entire group). All students listen to each interchange and decide whether to make a contribution. When the conversation halts, you may pose a new question and begin the circle response again.

Uses: Students seem to enjoy this strategy because everyone is given equal status and is allowed to give his or her opinion on the topic. The "pass" option allows for individual safety in the group. This approach is also an effective means for developing class unity and cohesion because all students face each other in the seating arrangement and are allowed to hear all individual points of view on a topic.

1. Work to involve all students.
2. Allow extra time for ample exploration of ideas.
3. Ask probing questions if the students don't.
4. See that students provide data to support ideas and opinions.
5. Promote student-to-student interaction.
6. Provide control without inhibiting.
7. Wait for students to follow up first.
8. Avoid repeating or restating student contributions.
9. Avoid passing judgments that inhibit creativity and productivity.

Conclusion

Instructors who appreciate the power that good questions can bring to the classroom take time to construct questions with care and precision. For it is the questions themselves that become the catalysts for critical, reflective thinking. However, a good question is never *done*. It is, in a very real and profound sense, a new beginning.

References

Aronson, E. *The Jigsaw Classroom.* Newbury Park, Calif.: Sage, 1978.

Aschner, M. J., and Gallagher, J. J. *A System for Classifying Thought Processes in the Context of Verbal Interaction.* Urbana: Institute for Research on Exceptional Children, University of Illinois, 1965.

Bloom, B. S. *Taxonomy of Educational Objectives.* Vol. 1: *Cognitive Domain.* New York: McKay, 1956.

Blosser, P. E. *Review of Research: Teacher Questioning Behavior in Science Classrooms.* Columbus, Ohio: Educational Resources Information Center, 1980.

Borg, W., and others. *The Mini Course: A Microteaching Approach to Teacher Education.* Beverly Hills, Calif.: Collier-Macmillan, 1970.

Brophy, J., and Good, T. "Teacher Behavior and Student Achievement." In M. Wittrock (ed.), *Handbook of Research on Teaching.* New York: Macmillan, 1986.

Costa, A. *Teaching for Intelligent Behavior*. (3rd ed.) Unpublished syllabus, 1986.

Daines, D. *Teachers' Oral Questions and Subsequent Verbal Behavior of Teachers and Students*. Provo, Utah: Brigham Young University, 1982. (ED 225 979)

Dantonio, M. *How Can We Create Thinkers?* Bloomington, Ind.: National Educational Service, 1990.

Dantonio, M., and Paradise, L. V. "Teacher Question-Answer Strategy and the Cognitive Correspondence Between Teacher Questions and Learner Responses." *Journal of Research and Development in Education*, 1988, *21*, 71–76.

Ehrenberg, S. D., and Ehrenberg, L. M. *Building and Applying Strategies for Intellectual Competencies in Students (BASICS)*. Miami, Fla.: Institute for Curriculum and Instruction, 1978.

Fogarty, R., and Bellanca, J. *Patterns for Thinking — Patterns for Transfer*. Palatine, Ill.: Skylight, 1987.

Fogarty, R., and Opeka, K. *Start Them Thinking*. Palatine, Ill.: Skylight, 1988.

Gall, M. D. "The Use of Questions in Teaching." *Review of Educational Research*, 1970, *40*, 707–721.

Gall, M. D. "Review of Research on Questioning Techniques." In W. W. Wilen (ed.), *Questions, Questioning Techniques, and Effective Teaching*. Washington, D.C.: National Educational Association, 1987.

King, A. "Enhancing Peer Interaction and Learning in the Classroom Through Reciprocal Questioning." *American Educational Research Journal*, 1990, *27*, 664–687.

King, A. "Improving Lecture Comprehension: Effects of a Metacognitive Strategy." *Applied Cognitive Psychology*, 1991, *5*, 331–346.

King, A. "Promoting Active Learning and Collaborative Learning in Business Administration Classes." In T. J. Frecks (ed.), *Critical Thinking, Interactive Learning, and Technology: Reaching for Excellence in Business Administration*. New York: Anderson, 1992.

Lyman, F., and McTighe, J. "Cueing Thinking in the Classroom: The Promise of Theory-Embedded Tools." *Educational Leadership*, April 1988, p. 7.

Perez, S., and Strickland, E. "Teaching Children How to Discuss What They Read." *Reading Horizon,* 1986, *27,* 89–94.

Sharan, S., and Sharan, Y. *Small Group Teaching.* Englewood Cliffs, N.J.: Educational Testing Publications, 1976.

Taba, H. *Hilda Taba Teaching Strategies Program.* Miami, Fla.: Institute for Development, 1971.

Weaver, R., and Cotrell, H. "Using Interactive Images in the Lecture Hall." *Educational Horizons,* Summer 1986, *64,* 180–185.

Whimbey, A., and Whimbey, L. *Intelligence Can Be Taught.* New York: Innovative Science, 1975.

Wilen, W. W., and Clegg, A. "Effective Questions and Questioning: A Research Review." *Theory and Research in Social Education,* 1986, *14,* 153–161.

PART TWO

Developing
Multicultural Understanding

The curricular battlelines have been drawn on college campuses throughout North America and many other parts of the world. Many participants in higher education from both sides of the desk have questioned why the contributions of "dead white guys" dominate almost every academic discipline, with the corresponding exclusion of work by and about other types of people. With women now making up more than half of the enrollment in higher education, they, and many of their male colleagues, want to learn "herstory" in addition to his. Students of color, along with many of their paler counterparts, want to learn about those who went before them. But changing the college curriculum proceeds slowly, and the cry for change has often been met with resistance.

The chapters in this section provide a case for making the whole of the curriculum multicentric rather than adding a multicultural component to an existing group of courses. Many faculty senates and curriculum committees have debated whether the move toward a multicultural curriculum will destroy the unity or coherence of an undergraduate education. Bernard Goldstein addresses the diversity versus coherence dichotomy in Chapter Seven. He rejects the either-or argument in which coherence must be sacrificed for diversity and provides several examples and guidelines for maintaining a coherent curriculum and providing a multicentric perspective.

In Chapter Eight, Ellen N. Junn presents a broad array of guidelines and exercises to heighten students' appreciation and understanding of multicultural experiences and values. Gale S. Auletta and Terry Jones (Chapter Nine) take a different approach by contrasting common beliefs about racism and showing how these beliefs are quite disparate from the "facts" of racism. They suggest that this two-part model (beliefs and realities) serves as a framework for teaching students about racism and the perception of racism, which they argue is as important to acknowledge as actual racist acts and comments.

Finally, in Chapter Ten in this section, Elliott Robert Barkan provides a list of sixteen guidelines for effective multicultural teaching. Instructors who want to learn more about these issues or want to learn ways to make their own courses multicultural will find a treasure chest of information in these chapters.

Chapter 7

Cultural Diversity and Curricular Coherence

Bernard Goldstein

The United States has become one of the most culturally diverse countries in the world. This diversity has changed the nature of postsecondary education in America and brings with it both advantages and challenges for the academic community. The multicultural background and experience of students, faculty, and staff enriches the university's intellectual life and creates a unique learning environment.

Prior to the 1950s, a major objective of the U.S. educational system was to assimilate children into an "American" culture. The United States was seen as a huge "melting pot" where differences between cultures were melted away. Israel Zangwell said it first in his play "The Melting Pot": "The real American has not yet arrived. He is only in the Crucible, I tell you — he will be the fusion of all races, the coming superman." The melting pot concept is currently being replaced with the metaphor of a "tossed salad," where different cultures contribute to a national culture while simultaneously maintaining their distinct identity and character (Tiedt and Tiedt, 1990).

Multicultural education encompasses programs that critique ethnocentric or exclusionary educational practices and policies. Its intent is to foster understanding and respect for ethnic minorities (Tiedt and Tiedt, 1990). Multicultural perspectives infuse the educational process with relevant information concerning societal diversity. The debate about what students should learn and who should determine the curriculum is fundamental to all levels of education. Curriculum reform has had a long and tortuous history, and our educational system was and is resistant to the concept of multicultural education.

Changing Student Profiles

Overall, U.S. higher education enrollment has increased 400 percent during the past forty years, and student profiles and demographics have changed dramatically as well (Forrest, 1987). In particular, the numbers of women and ethnic minorities have increased significantly since 1983. For example, in the twenty-campus California State University system, the proportion of women increased from 34 to 54 percent between 1983 and 1989, African Americans increased by 7.4 percent, Asian Americans increased by 57.5 percent, and Mexican American and other Latino groups increased by 49.4 percent (California State University, 1992). One must also keep in mind that striking diversity exists even within ethnic groups. For example, Asian Americans include Laotians, Vietnamese, Cambodians, Pacific Islanders, Koreans, Asian Indians, Japanese, Chinese Americans, and Filipinos. Although many of these groups have been in America for generations, English is a second language for 60 percent of all Asian American students in the United States (Erickson and Strommer, 1991).

      The demographic changes are clear; change will be felt first in California, with aftershocks radiating throughout the other western, then the southern states, and then through much of the rest of the country. By the year 2000 one of three Californians will be Latino, one in seven will be Asian, three-fourths of California retirees will be white, and approximately 60 percent of California's work force will be persons of color. Similar estimates are projected for many other parts of the country. Lifelong education for all ethnic groups will be fundamental in stimulating future economic, scientific, and social advancement in the United States.

Cultural Diversity and Coherence

Considering the diversity of institutions and the constant pressure to respond to new knowledge and market demands, it is not surprising that curricula are always in a state of flux. The tension points are perennial (Carnegie Foundation, 1978). Should we emphasize synthesis or specialization, scholarship or training, choices or requirements, depth or breadth, understanding or skills, ethical commitment or ethical neutrality? These issues appear to shift one way or the other depending on current moods and are never fully resolved. This ongoing debate is what keeps academic senates and endless curriculum committee meetings alive and well.

Current challenges to higher education include teaching about diverse races and ethnic traditions, gender differences and similarities, the origin of sexual orientations, global economic and environmental perspectives, exchange among nations, and human dimensions of the educational enterprise (Toombs and Tierney, 1991). At one extreme is the view that we should emphasize the perspectives, history, and values of Western civilization; at the other is the concept that higher education should focus on the origins and history of selected ethnic groups (Western Association of Schools and Colleges, 1992).

In addition to multiculturalism, we are faced with a "knowledge revolution" and a concomitant shift to a renewed emphasis on critical thinking skills. Today's industries are looking for employees who are well trained in critical thinking, logical reasoning, and abstract thought. These skills are transferable from one career to another and are essential for lifelong learning. This renewed emphasis on thinking skills is seen in the report from the Coleman Commission: "[T]he basics of the twenty-first century include communication and higher-order problem-solving skills, and scientific and technological literacy — the thinking tools that allow us to understand the fast-changing world around us" (Carnegie Foundation, 1974, p. 268). More than ever, educators must see clearly the dual objective of education for living and education for making a living. It seems clear that increased knowledge of the multiple cultures that make up our population will be needed for both. In this context, higher education faces the opportunity to diversify the university curriculum, faculty, and students. At the forefront are issues of ethnicity, gender equity, sexual orientation, internationalism, ethics, conservation of natural resources, and social responsibility. How do we diversify the curriculum and yet maintain curricular coherence? How do we join a commitment to non-Western studies with a similar commitment to our shared Western heritage? How do we implement a culturally diverse curriculum and at the same time eliminate or protect against racist and sexist behavior?

The college curriculum is more than a collection of courses. It can be viewed as a conceptual framework that considers at least the following questions (Toombs and Tierney, 1991): What is the sum of knowledge of a discipline, profession, or area of study? What do students expect from their educational experiences? What does society expect in the area of student outcomes? Ernest Boyer (1986) identifies an "enriched major" as one that responds to three questions: What are the history, philosophy, and tradition of the field? What are the economic and social implications to be pursued? What are the moral and ethical issues within the field that need to be confronted? Answers to these questions are made richer with a good knowledge of diverse cultures.

Toombs and Tierney (1991) define a comprehensive curriculum as "an intentional design for learning negotiated by faculty in light of their specialized knowledge and in the context of social expectations and students' needs" (p. 21). In this definition the faculty have the primary responsibility for the learning plan, with social and cultural expectations central to the curriculum. The Association of American Colleges (1992) has defined several key elements of a strong curriculum, including clear and explicit goals, a focus on inquiry and analysis, a connection with other disciplines and fields, and an understanding of student needs.

Strong programs acknowledge and respect the expectations of students. This means that faculty must be aware of the variety of student characteristics. Faculty members responsible for strong programs are aware of demographic shifts and the benefits of engaging students from diverse backgrounds in teaching and learning. "All study is intended to break down the narrow certainties and provincial vision with which we are born" (Association of American Colleges, 1985, p. 5).

Cultural Diversity Issues on Campus

Many university curricula reflect the belief that intergroup understanding is fostered by exposing students to multicultural course content as part of general education requirements. These general education course components are often serviced by an ethnic studies department or school that can give the impression that other academic departments are "off the hook." Balance is needed to mainstream multicultural course content and to make cultural diversity an all-university goal. Some universities have developed a single required course focusing on cultural diversity. For example, Stanford University has developed a one-year course, "Culture, Ideas, Values," that must be taken by all incoming students. At other universities students may choose from a wide range of classes. Ohio State, for example, offers courses with such titles as "Biology of Human Diversity," "Women, Culture and Society," and "Ethnic Music in the United States." The educational impact of these programs and courses remains to be determined, because there is little research on the question of whether the goals of multicultural education have been achieved with these courses.

An inherent danger exists when a particular department or school is "*the* part" of the university responsible for a culturally diverse curriculum. A strong sense of proprietorship can develop that may discourage other departments from offering competing courses, which would inhibit the development of a well-balanced and representative "all-university" curriculum. An ethnic studies department or school could minimize this danger by providing faculty experts in multicultural teaching methods and multicultural research skills who could act as consultants to other departments.

While faculty members debate how to introduce diversity

into the curriculum, a diverse group of students and faculty are already in place, learning how to live together. New tensions arise as students, faculty, and administrators try to balance the rights of free speech and expression with the rights of those who feel that their equal protection rights are under siege (Grabmeier, 1991). The debate is about creating positive learning environments and responsibly exercising personal freedoms.

It would seem that the university has been forced to take over the challenging role of arbiter in this debate. Several universities have established written policies that vigorously protect members of the academy from harassment while honoring freedom of speech. Recent efforts to regulate the content of speech have been challenged in the courts because "fighting words" policies have often been ambiguous and too all-encompassing. Some of these policies have been contested on constitutional grounds, resulting in rescission by the institutions involved.

The clash between the right to free speech and the need to make college access equal to all groups is likely to escalate in the coming years as the move toward multiculturalism is met by a vocal, and sometimes hostile, backlash. Every member of the college community must prepare to deal with issues where these two basic rights come in conflict. The list of possible examples is virtually endless: What, if anything, should be done about racist statements in a student-run newspaper? Who should decide whether individuals who are avowed members of racist organizations should be allowed to speak on campus? Who pays for these speakers if they are allowed to present their views? If a speakers' series is an official university-sponsored event, is this implicit endorsement by the university of the speakers' comments? Can a professor espouse theories of racial superiority? What are the limits of academic freedom, and who should decide? These are thorny issues that all of the constituents of higher education will be facing. As these conflicts arise, it becomes clear that multicultural education is not an abstract concept. Knowledge of cultures other than one's own is needed in order to think critically about these and similar issues.

Information overload has become a serious problem for faculty as they struggle to deal not only with the growing literature on and controversy surrounding cultural diversity but also the knowledge explosion, the demand to understand different learning styles, and the pressure to include student outcomes assessment as a key part of the curriculum. Faculty are expected to keep up with new and improved teaching techniques and to perform research and public service. Many fields of scholarship have paid little attention to studies of women and minorities, and the shifting of gears today cannot be entirely smooth or graceful (Limerick, 1992). Adequate funding and released time are absolutely essential to support faculty as they engage in professional development activities designed to help them expand in these areas.

Although faculty of ethnic studies departments can and should be a vital link between themselves and faculty from other disciplines who are willing to learn about the fast-growing literature on cultural diversity, we cannot rely on volunteers for this critical undertaking. All of the faculty need to make a genuine commitment to multicultural education. This means confronting and working constructively with our own prejudices and stereotypical thinking patterns. A strong desire for equality is not enough; the entire faculty must become informed about social issues and the way prejudice and stereotypes have, consciously or unconsciously, affected their academic discipline. Faculty who mean well but who are uninformed cannot promote social justness in their classrooms.

Outcomes of a Multicultural Curriculum

Discussions about cultural diversity and curricular coherence often result in a debate over which strategy will best meet the twin goals of equity and quality. Faculty who favor development of a multicultural curriculum focus on equality and criteria that include race, gender, and sexual orientation. The curriculum is motivated by a concern for decency, social justice, and fairness so that students of different ethnic and racial backgrounds will be assured a better chance at professional school admission or lucrative careers after graduation (Fox-Genovese, 1991). A multicultural curriculum can help students develop a positive sense of identity and strong racial and ethnic pride. It aims at awareness of diversity and allows for dispelling of stereotypes (Tiedt and Tiedt, 1990).

On the other side, there is concern that using gender and race in making curricular decisions may undermine intellectual quality and academic tradition. In this view, a curriculum should emphasize traditional American values, individuality, free speech, and the unique characteristics of Western culture. Emphasis is on the value of "longstanding intellectual consensus about curricular content" (Eaton, 1992, p. 31). Some faculty with this view espouse development of a "true" multicultural curriculum that involves study of non-Western ideas in relation to, and not as a substitute for, the works of the Western world. Study would include the "best" that has been thought and said in other cultures in the form of "non-Western Classics" (D'Souza, 1991).

This conflict reveals profoundly different assumptions about the nature of society and the human condition. Is there an objective truth, or is all truth relative to time and culture? Do we have proof for the existence of reality, independent of our representations of reality? These differences can become the heart of the debate over a multicultural curriculum.

Multiculturalism in the Hard Sciences

Often the focus of the multicultural debate has been limited to a small part of general education or to one discipline—humanities, social science, or literature (Searle, 1990). To many faculty, the primary reason for teaching humanities is political—humanities has value primarily as a means of transforming society. The humanities are often seen as the heart of the liberal arts curriculum because of the intrinsic intellectual and aesthetic merits of the quality texts—Plato, Shakespeare, Dante, Darwin, and Conrad, for example (Searle, 1990). We can learn about power, politics, culture, and history from these authors. The addition of multicultural perspectives and great works from other cultures can broaden students' minds and sharpen their thinking.

The hard sciences are sometimes viewed as transcending the political power and multicultural influences found in humanities and social science because of the relative objectivity of the scientific method. Conventional wisdom holds that scientific fields with a strong and relatively objective knowledge base are relatively independent of political pressure. However, progress in science is intimately related to its philosophical and historical foundations. Personalities, social pressures, and cultural traditions also play major roles in the complex and circuitous routes of scientific discovery. Science itself is a metaphor for interrelatedness, and this metaphor can be used to explore general education in its broadest sense.

Science is not just a body of knowledge produced by a scientific method — it also consists of groups of people deciding on directions, collaborating on methods, and consulting on concepts. A scientist, after all, is a member of a community of understanding in a culture composed of diverse and often conflicting influences (Goldstein, 1989). Thus, there are no aspects of the curriculum or human knowledge that are free from social influences. These influences can be clearly seen in the field of biology, where "scientific" facts have often reflected common prejudices.

Model Indicators of Learning and
Multicultural Approaches in Biology

Biology, as a scientific field, provides good examples of how information about diverse cultures may be included in the curriculum to enhance the outcomes. Biology students develop cognitive skills, values, attitudes, laboratory skills, and techniques as they matriculate. A study by Peterson and Hayward (1989) shows that a clear consensus exists among 136 biology departments as to what biology students should know when they graduate. Biology students not only must have a basic knowledge of the field but must be skilled in observation, measurement, inquiry, problem solving, and critical thinking. They must appreciate objectivity, be open to new ideas, be able to work as a team member, develop respect for the maintenance of natural systems, and approach knowledge with skepticism. In addition, a wide range of laboratory activities from skill at microscopy to computer analysis is required. To achieve these outcomes, biologists employ several diverse teaching techniques that encourage "knowing" through memorization, "understanding" through the use of examples, and "thinking" by applying what one has learned.

Barriers to a minority student's pursuit of science include the degree of compatibility among the home, community, and school environments (Martinez and Ortiz de Montellano, 1988). Interventions involve exposure of students to culturally relevant science. The specific information, examples, and applications given in a general or introductory biology course can have multicultural derivations and can be made culturally relevant. The subjects of evolution, genetics, ethnobotany, herbal medicine, disease factors, and food chemistry can all be taught from a perspective that celebrates the accomplishments and knowledge of ethnically diverse cultures. Male and female scientists from various ethnic groups can be identified as role models.

Examples of Coherence and Diversity in the Biology Classroom

Following are several examples chosen from biology that show how even a "hard" science can provide a rich multicentric learning experience. In considering these examples, remember that the professor must be well informed about the content, alert to the presence of narrow, prejudicial views, and willing to confront racist, sexist, anti-Semitic, homophobic, and other uninformed and stereotypical comments and behaviors. If the professor is not adequately prepared, the lesson may turn into a confirmation of already held prejudices.

Cultural Universals. Several cultural universals can be discussed that reflect the social adaptation of individuals from a variety of societies. Regulations governing avoidance of incest, kinship relations, deference of children to parents, courage, self-control, and similar attributes are found universally throughout all human cultures (Laszlo, 1983). All societies show an "alliance" or "marriage" between male and female with some degree of mutual obligation, time commitment, sexual access, and social sanctions (Daly and Wilson, 1978). For all these topics to be pursued well, actual multicultural data are needed. Without solid data, these concepts can yield rehearsal of old, inaccurate, and unhelpful views.

One study by Inkeles (1983) surveyed 1,000 persons in each of six developing countries, including Chile, Israel, and India, to search for cross-national and transcultural findings that would reveal "not only a potential but . . . an actual psychic unity in humankind" (p. 16). The results identified four basic characteristics that appear to transcend cultural differences: being an informed citizen; having a marked sense of personal efficacy; being highly independent and autonomous; and being open to new ideas and experiences. It can be argued that these cultures are all in the process of development and that more established cultures would likely show a different set of characteristics. Students need to be aware that this is where data can foster an informed rather than a stereotypical explanation. Assumed differences may or may not actually be present.

Cultural Lag. The concept of a *cultural lag* is also useful for students to understand in the multicultural context. *Cultural lag* is defined as "a lag in values, beliefs, perceptions, and conceptions compared with the evolution of objective societal conditions" (Laszlo, 1983, p. 191). Examples include the antiscience attitudes and delegitimation of objectivity embraced by many people at a time of great scientific and technological advances. Belief in astrology, UFOs, paranormal events, and Lysenkoism are examples of this countervision. Cultural lag can be the focus of a stimulating classroom discussion.

Language and Genetics. A third topic of interest to general biology students is the evolution of language and its diversity. It is estimated that more than 700 million people around the world speak English as a primary or second language. However, this statistic is diminishing proportionately in the 1990s because of the population increase in third world countries where other languages are spoken (Holeton, 1992).

Language is vital to reinforcing social norms, but it can also be used to denigrate or devalue groups of people. The current debate about stereotypes provides many good examples for classroom discussions. Researchers have recently shown that a correlation exists between genetic traits and native languages throughout Europe, "giving a new twist to old disagreements about the origins and distribution of the first Indo-Europeans" (Hoppe, 1992, p. 117). European genetic traits clearly correlate with language patterns, and this evidence can be used to trace migrations in the early history of Europe. The principles of Mendelian genetics can be a focal point of these discussions.

Linguistic Gender and Ethnic Gaps. A forming consensus reveals that men and women may use different word meanings, inflections, and understandings when speaking to each other. For men the word *communication* often means to give information, whereas women interpret *communication* to mean "understanding" the other person. Men think they are weak if they discuss personal problems, whereas women feel that such discussions are necessary to establish close ties (Kaplan, 1992). These differences in menspeak-womenspeak are particularly challenging in professional-client or teacher-student discussions.

Various ethnic groups may be speaking past each other as well. The term *racism,* for example, has different meanings in different ethnic cultures. According to Blauner (1992), whites generally adhere to earlier definitions—"ideologies of white supremacy, bigotry, discriminatory behavior; African Americans prefer the newer meanings which locate racial hierarchy in society's economic and social structures and does not require prejudice or discrimination to reproduce inequality" (p. 221). (See Chapter Nine for a related discussion.) Discussion of these topics may aid students in understanding the differences in attitudes between genders and among ethnic groups. Students may learn about the concepts of biology while also learning how to write popular and professional papers (Moore, 1992).

Mitochondrial Eve. The relationship of genes to ethnicity can be best illustrated with an update on the controversy surrounding the "mitochondrial Eve." The basic premise is that genetic relationships between people of different ethnic origins are discoverable by comparing mitochondrial DNA samples. Mitochondrial DNA is maternally inheritable and contains fewer genes than are found in the cell nucleus. Many scientists consider evidence from mitochondrial DNA to be more accurate than anatomical comparisons of human fossils. The genetic analysis seems to support the Noah's Ark hypothesis, which maintains that modern humans (*Homo sapiens*) evolved within a small African population and spread across Asia and Europe replacing the previous human species, *Homo erectus*. By building ancestral trees based on the DNA, researchers can trace the branches backward until they reach the last common ancestor from whom modern humans evolved (Gibbons, 1992). The derived phylogenetic tree traces modern humans to a woman (or small group) living in Africa between 140,000 and 280,000 years ago. This claim and the evidence using mitochondrial DNA has been seriously challenged and provides for a lively debate among student groups in a general biology class.

Origin of Sexual Orientation and Sex Differences. Recent studies have identified differences in brain structures between human males and females and between heterosexual and homosexual males. While these findings are extremely controversial, students can learn about brain structure and function, the neural control of sexual behavior, and modern methods of studying the brain by reading and discussing this literature (Becker and others, 1992). Genes substantially influence the development of homosexuality among women and men according to a number of preliminary studies of identical twins and adopted siblings (Bower, 1992). Again, while the topic is very controversial, students can engage in discussions of nature versus nurture and the relative contributions of environment and heredity to behavior.

The Biology of Disease and Ethnicity. Anything that touches on biological differences among ethnic groups is certain to be controversial. However, it is important to determine how different ethnic groups respond to diseases and to treatment for diseases. Equally important are cultural factors that influence patient education, evaluation, care, and use of medical services. There are well-known racial variations in metabolism, as shown by the enzyme deficiency in many Asians that limits their ability to metabolize alcohol (Holden, 1991). African Americans run a risk of high blood pressure twice as great as that of Caucasians.

Hispanic Americans and African Americans have a disproportionately higher risk of contracting AIDS and HIV infection. Tay-Sachs disease occurs primarily in Jews who have emigrated from northeastern Europe. It is a genetic disease that is clinically apparent by five to six months of age and invariably leads to death by age three or four. The disease involves an enzyme deficiency that leads to the deterioration of the nervous system.

Sickle-cell anemia is another famous genetic disorder associated with a recessive gene and is quite common among inhabitants of Africa, India, Arabia, and the Mediterranean area. About 8 percent of African Americans are heterozygous for the sickle-cell trait. Study of the sickle-cell disorder is a classic illustration of basic genetics, natural selection, and the demographics of disease.

Ethnobotany and Herbal Medicine. The chemistry of various medicinal plants can be used to teach students research methods and strategies involving literature searches, interviews, oral and written reports, laboratory experiments, and chromatography extractions. Survey instruments and computer analysis can be made a part of such investigations. Plant taxonomy can include ethnobotanical classifications (Martinez and Ortiz de Montellano, 1988). The amazing wisdom of many cultures' use of herbs and plants can be highlighted here.

Cultural Diversity Around Time and the Calendar. The calendar can be introduced as evidence of cultural diversity in time measurement throughout history. Students will enjoy discovering the impact of changing day length on pineal function and reproduction. The relationship of environmental cues, migratory patterns, and hormones in the reproductive process can be examined from an evolutionary standpoint. The biological clock in the human brain (the suprachiasmatic nucleus) can be a focus of attention, as can seasonal disorders in people living in different climates and different patterns of night and day (Binkley, 1990).

Patterns of Human Sexual and Reproductive Behavior. Comparative studies of human reproductive behavior can effectively illustrate both coherence and cultural diversity at the same time (Goldstein, 1976). The single unifying principle of evolution — organisms are designed by natural selection to maximize reproductive potential — can be shared with an awareness of the enormous diversity of human behavior both within and between cultures (Daly and Wilson, 1978). How do the various patterns of human courtship maximize human reproductive fitness? How do diverse patterns of sexual interaction contribute to reproductive success? What is the evolutionary derivation of the kiss? These questions can be made the focus of studies on natural selection, genetic drift, and the impact of environment on behavior.

Seeking Common Ground

Higher education can respond successfully to the challenges of equity, diversity, and quality by developing curricula that include both common and diverse heritages. In fact, it must do so if we are to counter prejudice and unfair cultural and disciplinary views that restrict the development of our students. Faculty neutrality is not good enough if we are to promote genuine multicentric learning and development of all students. The question is one of balance, integration, and synthesis. A range of cultures can be studied with a global focus or with attention directed to the "tossed salad" in the United States.

All curricular improvements, regardless of culture, must address the vectors of student development (Pascarella and Terenzini, 1991). Students continually experience greater levels of complexity as matriculation proceeds. These vectors include achieving competence, managing emotions, developing autonomy, establishing identity, freeing interpersonal relationships, and developing purpose and integrity (Chickering, 1969). Each student integrates and organizes the learning process into a coherent identity of self. A solid curriculum can contribute to student development along these lines. Variety of instructional styles and modes, student participation in learning, and student outcomes assessment all have a positive impact on learning.

Past research assumed that identity development was the same for ethnic minority students as it was for white students. However, Helms (1990) has defined *ethnic identity* as consisting of three components:

1. Personal identity, including one's understanding of self
2. Ethnic group orientation, including the extent one uses a group to establish the parameters of development
3. Ascribed identity, including an individual's purposeful affiliation with an ethnic group

Ethnic identity derives from the particular weight an individual assigns to these three components. A successful college exposure to a balanced multicultural curriculum can bring about internalization of identity, inner security, satisfaction with self, and a commitment to reformation of the general culture at large (Pascarella and Terenzini, 1991).

Conclusion

The Maasai have a saying: *Metolu lung' elukunya nabo engeno* (One head does not complete the wisdom). The goal of any institution of higher learning is to enhance student appreciation of cultural diversity by providing an appropriate academic program and a supportive campus environment. General education courses taken by students in languages, literature, history, science, and social science should contain works written by authors from diverse cultures. Students can learn to compare and contrast concepts across multiple settings (Western Association of Schools and Colleges, 1992). The transformation of the curriculum to include ethnic and cultural diversity, racial justice, gender analysis, and environmental consciousness requires faculty catalysts for change. Institutions of higher learning tend to gravitate against innovation and real transformation. Each of us must become informed on multicultural information and skilled at helping all students explore the many accomplishments, values, losses, and so on of the different cultures on the planet. To do so, innovations in the curriculum must be consciously designed and defined clearly. Collegiality will be tested to its limits.

References

Airhihenbuwa, C. O., and others. "HIV/AIDS Education and Prevention Among African Americans: A Focus on Culture." *AIDS Education and Prevention,* 1992, *4,* 267–276.

Association of American Colleges. *Integrity in the Curriculum: Report of the Project on Redefining the Meaning and Purpose of Baccalaureate Degrees.* Washington, D.C.: Association of American Colleges, 1985.

Association of American Colleges. *The Year in Preview: Drawing New Curricular Maps.* Washington, D.C.: Association of American Colleges, 1992.

Becker, J., and others (eds.). *Behavioral Endocrinology.* Cambridge, Mass.: MIT Press, 1992.

Binkley, S. *The Clockwork Sparrow — Time, Clocks, and Calendars in Biological Organisms.* Englewood Cliffs, N.J.: Prentice-Hall, 1990.

Blauner, B. "Talking Past Each Other: The Black and White Languages of Race." *The American Prospect,* Summer 1992, pp. 221–225.

Bower, B. "Genetic Clues to Female Homosexuality." *Science News,* 1992, *142,* 117.

Boyer, E. *College.* New York: Carnegie Foundation, 1986.

California State University. *Statistical Abstracts.* Long Beach: California State University, July 1992.

Carnegie Foundation. *Carnegie Commission on Graduation Requirements: Report of the Commission on Graduation Requirements.* Ann Arbor: University of Michigan, 1974.

Carnegie Foundation. *Missions of the College Curriculum.* San Francisco: Jossey-Bass, 1978.

Chickering, A. *Education and Identity.* San Francisco: Jossey-Bass, 1969.

Daly, M., and Wilson, M. *Sex, Evolution, and Behavior.* Boston: Duxbury Press, 1978.

D'Souza, D. "Multiculturalism 101." *Policy Review,* 1991, *56,* 221–231.

Eaton, J. S. "PC or Not PC: Not the Question." *Reports of the Association of Governing Boards of Universities and Colleges,* 1992, *34,* 30–34.

Erickson, B., and Strommer, D. *Teaching College Freshmen.* San Francisco: Jossey-Bass, 1991.

Fayard, P. "Let's Stop Persecuting People Who Don't Think Like Galileo!" *Public Understanding of Science,* 1992, *1,* 15–16.

Forrest, A. "Managing the Flow of Students Through the Higher

Education System." *National Forum: Phi Kappa Phi Journal,* Fall 1987, pp. 39–42.

Fox-Genovese, E. "The Self-Interest of Multiculturalism." *Tikkun,* July/August 1991, pp. 47–48.

Gibbons, A. "Mitochondrial Eve: Wounded But Not Dead Yet." *Science,* 1992, *257,* 873–875.

Goldstein, B. *Human Sexuality.* New York: McGraw-Hill, 1976.

Goldstein, B. "Functional Morphology as a Tool in General Education." *American Zoologist,* 1989, *29,* 353–362.

Grabmeier, J. "The Political Correctness Clash." *Ohio State Quest,* Winter 1991, pp. 6–7.

Helms, J. (ed.). *Black and White Racial Identity: Theory, Research, and Practice.* New York: Greenwood, 1990.

Holden, C. "New Center to Study Therapies and Ethnicity." *Science,* 1991, *25,* 748.

Holeton, R. *Encountering Culture.* Englewood Cliffs, N.J.: Blair Press, 1992.

Hoppe, K. "Geneticists Track Indo-European Languages." *Science News,* 1992, *142,* 117.

Inkeles, A. *Exploring Individual Modernity.* New York: Columbia University Press, 1983.

Kaplan, K. "Family Lawyers Study Linguistic Gender Gap." *San Francisco Chronicle,* Aug. 12, 1992.

Laszlo, E. *Systems Science and World Order.* Elmsford, N.Y.: Pergamon Press, 1983.

Limerick, P. N. "Information Overload Is a Prime Factor in Our Culture Wars." *Point of View, Chronicle of Higher Education,* July 29, 1992, p. A32.

Martinez, D. I., and Ortiz de Montellano, B. R. "Improving the Science and Mathematic Achievement of Mexican American Students Through Culturally Relevant Science." *Mexican American Education ERIC Digest,* March 1988. (EDO-RC 88-07)

Moore, R. *Writing to Learn Biology.* Philadelphia: Saunders, 1992.

Pascarella, E. T., and Terenzini, P. T. *How College Affects Students.* San Francisco: Jossey-Bass, 1991.

Peterson, G., and Hayward, P. "Model Indicators of Student Learning in Undergraduate Biology." In C. Adelmann (ed.),

Signs and Traces. Washington, D.C.: Office of Research, U.S. Department of Education, 1989.

Searle, J. "The Storm over the University." *The New York Review of Books,* December 6, 1990, pp. 85–86.

Tiedt, P., and Tiedt, I. *Multicultural Teaching.* Needham Heights, Mass.: Allyn & Bacon, 1990.

Toombs, W., and Tierney, W. G. "Meeting the Mandate." *ASHE-ERIC Higher Education Reports,* vol. 6, 1991.

Western Association of Schools and Colleges. *Achieving Institutional Effectiveness Through Assessment.* Oakland, Calif.: Western Association of Schools and Colleges, 1992.

Chapter 8

Experiential Approaches to Enhancing Cultural Awareness

Ellen N. Junn

As a nation, we are about to enter an unprecedented period in our history. Population projections continue to show that our nation's traditionally white, middle-class student pool is declining, while the number of nontraditional students representing diversity across virtually every demographic category continues to grow (Levine and Associates, 1989; Schwartz and Exter, 1989; Solmon and Wingard, 1991). In response, growing numbers of educators are now adding their voices to the urgent call to reformulate a new vision incorporating the values and principles of *diversity* (referring to differences of all kinds — cultural, social class, ableness) and *multiculturalism* (referring more specifically to differences in culture) into our educational system (Adams, 1992; Anderson and Adams, 1992; Astin, 1985; Banks, 1993; Banks and Banks, 1989; Brown, 1986).

Not surprisingly, the semantics of such loaded phrases and terms as *educating for diversity* and *multicultural education* continue to be debated in a variety of contexts (Banks, 1989b; Bullivant, 1989; Grant and Sleeter, 1989a; Siegel, 1991), often resulting in intense and sometimes incendiary dialogue (see, for example, Banks, 1993; Howe, 1991; Noll, 1991; Siegel, 1991;

Wong, 1991). For the purposes of this chapter, the phrase *educating for diversity* will be used to refer to a commitment on the part of educational institutions to implement an effective and culturally inclusive educational experience that seeks to maximize or equalize the learning environments and opportunities of all members of a learning community, regardless of ethnicity, race, culture, economic class, gender, age, sexual orientation, or ableness.

To realize such a lofty goal, members of a learning community must be prepared to wrestle with difficult reforms in two fundamental and complex arenas: reforms in curriculum (What constitutes "accepted" academic knowledge?), and reforms in the total school environment (How does the classroom and the campus climate recognize and honor diversity?). With regard to a curriculum that reflects diversity, an institution's formal academic curriculum should represent both mainstream academic knowledge and the more recent "transformative academic knowledge," which consists of "concepts, paradigms, themes, and explanations that challenge mainstream academic knowledge and that expand the historical and literary canon" (Banks, 1993, p. 9). With regard to the second issue, reforms in the total school environment, institutions of higher learning must also commit to changes aimed at fostering an inclusive and sensitive climate for all members of their learning community — be they students, faculty, administrators, or staff (Banks, 1993; Banks and Banks, 1989; Sleeter and Grant, 1987).

Why should educators be interested in dealing with issues of diversity, especially given the fundamental level of institutional change and reform that would be required to meet the objectives of a multicultural education? Border and Van Note Chism (1992a) furnish us with at least five powerful justifications for institutional reform, from the perspectives of moral, demographic, civic, academic, and political responsibilities. Although their arguments are compelling, their justifications are primarily directed at the level of motivating institutional change.

As an individual faculty member, you may be asking yourself, why should I get involved, and what could I possibly do? For me at least, one of the most potent reasons for my involvement is my sincere belief that explicitly asking students to explore and reflect on sometimes complex or controversial diversity issues results in important changes in their ability to think more critically. Whether students are consciously aware of it or not, each brings into the classroom a wealth of unique or personal cultural knowledge that can be tapped as a rich learning resource. In other words, deepening students' multicultural knowledge and awareness affords them the potential of critically viewing the world and themselves from multiple, complex, and interrelated perspectives. It is precisely this heightened sense of self in relation to other, more global contexts that sets the stage for potentially powerful insights and possibilities as these students set out to navigate both their professional and personal worlds. Viewed in this manner, both collectively and individually, we can all play a critical role in promoting enhanced multicultural and diversity understanding.

The Challenge of Meeting Diversity in Higher Education Today

Undeniable change is written in our national demographics. The challenge is thus the difficult and pragmatic task of just how to make the vision of multicultural education a reality. Already, a significant and growing number of universities and colleges are responding to this challenge by implementing a variety of measures and programs designed to improve the quality of education (Magner, 1990; vom Saal, Jefferson, and Morrison, 1992).

Without diminishing the notable efforts of any institution, it is striking that although administrative supports for multicultural efforts do exist (in the form of new programs and allocation of resources), by and large, these programs still tend to be fragmented and to exist at the periphery of the academy. In addition, while increasing numbers of universities are beginning to address campus and classroom climate issues, fewer institutions have tackled the somewhat more volatile issue of curricular and pedagogical change.

Two examples of current reforms aimed at improving sensitivity and climate are the establishment of separate cultural centers (primarily for use by underrepresented students) and the development of new multicultural training programs often directed at very narrow groups, such as dormitory advisers (Border and Van Note Chism, 1992a; Schmitz, Paul, and Greenberg, 1992; vom Saal, Jefferson, and Morrison, 1992). In the area of curricular reform, some institutions now require students to enroll in new courses designed to broaden their understanding of diversity (see, for example, Magner, 1990; Mays, 1989; Romero, 1989), while other institutions are integrating diversity information directly into existing courses (see, for example, Banks, 1989b; Bronstein and Quina, 1989; Schmitz, Paul, and Greenberg, 1992). Still other faculty are working on the important task of reconceptualizing classroom instructional strategies in order to optimize diverse styles of learning (for example, Adams, 1992; Anderson and Adams, 1992; Beyer and Cuseo, 1991; Collett and Serrano, 1992; Maher and Tetreault, 1992; Sadker and Sadker, 1992).

Although efforts such as these are encouraging, it is often the case that any one program on a given campus has little or no communication with other related efforts elsewhere on the same campus. Therefore, while these programs represent significant and laudable steps to filling in gaps and coming closer to a vision of an inclusive educational system, the picture that emerges is one of multiple, independently functioning pockets of "grassroots" change or reform, often spearheaded by small cadres of faculty, administrators, or staff scattered across any given campus. What seems to be missing is an overarching, coherent, carefully crafted institutional master plan that reconceptualizes and comprehensively addresses diversity as it applies to all of the multiple and complex levels of university life. As idealistic as this may sound, as Banks (1989b) has stated, the success of current models of multicultural reform may depend on the degree to which institutions of higher learning view themselves as complex social systems that consist of many highly interrelated components and variables. Based on this social systems perspective, institutions must not only be prepared to face the task of addressing potential reforms in the areas of formalized curriculum and climate but must also be willing to take on the much larger task of comprehensively reevaluating and building meaningful linkages among the multiple interrelated levels of university life as it applies to issues of diversity.

Invoking the concept of a "master plan" often connotes a strictly top-down process for implementing change. However, given the myriad ways that institutions have already begun tackling the issue of multicultural education, it is clear that change can also be affected through bottom-up, grassroots efforts as well. Thus, some combination of both visionary top-down planning coupled with the realism of existing grassroots efforts would be most fruitful in effecting positive and lasting change.

Following are eight suggestions that should be considered in a truly comprehensive institutional plan for educational equity.

1. Most important, clear, proactive directives, advocacy, and leadership must come from across all top administrative levels in support of diversity in education. Administrative commitment must be manifested not only in a central mission statement that strongly supports, validates, and actively encourages multicultural efforts but also in the allocation of resources, as well as in linking and establishing explicit reward systems to encourage current and future efforts on the part of faculty and administrators. Incentive mechanisms might include such things as awards, monetary support, and release time for faculty and others recognizing a variety of diversity-related accomplishments, or regular newsletters or other public forums recognizing and disseminating information regarding diversity-related work.

2. The volatile issue of curricular change must be tackled and multiple strategies developed, at both the institutional and the individual level. For example, issues such as the balance between developing new courses focusing on diversity versus efforts aimed at infusing diversity into existing courses will need to be addressed. How will faculty be supported, recognized, and rewarded for progress in this area?

3. Positive reforms in tacit, as well as implicit, classroom instructional culture, strategies, and practices must be designed to optimize diversity in learning styles. Similarly, innovative

and effective incentive systems must be developed to encourage and maintain instructor interest and use of these new instructional strategies.

4. Issues of campus climate, including the quality of residential life, extracurricular activities, and student support services (learning centers, cultural centers, counseling facilities, financial aid), should be reexamined closely and systematically for potential improvements.

5. Measures designed to diversify the faculty, administration, staff, and students through proactive recruitment and retention efforts must continue.

6. Efforts should be made toward increasing communication and building reasonable connections between a variety of diversity programs and efforts that may share commonalities.

7. Developing more effective networks with community and business agencies for future vocational and employment opportunities for students would assist their transition to the world outside the university.

8. Finally, concerted attempts must be made to document outcomes and conduct program evaluations at all levels.

When viewed in this light, the task of implementing an inclusive education seems almost unreachable, given the many complexities inherent in the unusual structure, multiple functions, and institutional machinations that characterize life in academe. This is no reason to despair, however, as many institutions of higher learning are already beginning to respond to the call. While it is true that a both top-down master plan and bottom-up implementation is probably the ideal approach for change, individual faculty can have an impact on the system even in the absence of a coherent institutional plan. Indeed, as Adams (1992) has aptly stated, "[I]f all roads lead back to the faculty, then the call for multiculturalism—like other fundamental changes in higher education—depends on faculty acceptance and implementation" (p. 7). Armed then with this spirit of grassroots change, individual instructors may begin to make a difference by taking steps to reconceptualize their curricula and pedagogy in furthering the mission of a truly inclusive education.

Clarifying Pedagogical Goals and Teaching
Methods for a Multicultural Classroom

For the instructor who wishes to incorporate a philosophy of
diversity or multicultural education in his or her courses, it is
useful to clearly define course goals or objectives as a first step.
One way to begin is to consider whether one's goals center on
the promotion of cognitive, affective, or behavioral forms of multicultural learning (Gudykunst, Ting-Toomey, and Wiseman,
1991; Spitzberg and Cupach, 1984). The focus of the cognitive
component of learning lies in the intellectual acquisition of more
complex multicultural factual knowledge, as well as enhanced
multicultural understanding and perspective. This approach is
often characterized by, but certainly not limited to, selected readings and a didactic or lecture instructional format. The affective component of learning primarily focuses on tapping students' emotional and motivational understanding and therefore
frequently utilizes a variety of more active, experiential, and
groupwork techniques, such as structured discussions, role playing, and simulations. Finally, emphasis on the behavioral component of learning requires providing students with appropriate experiential contexts in which to develop and practice specific
behavioral skills and abilities crucial to managing successfully
in a multicultural setting. As with affective learning, development of behavioral skills also tends to rely on experiential training and groupwork techniques (Foeman, 1991). Ideally, of
course, efforts to promote diversity understanding should incorporate some measure of all three types of learning and therefore should include some variable combination of didactic, experiential, and groupwork instruction.

For instructors of courses in the social sciences, such as
anthropology, sociology, and political science, the nature of their
disciplines makes existing courses fairly amenable to reformu-
lation in terms of diversity issues. Courses in literature, business management, history, and the arts also lend themselves
quite well to broadened consideration of multicultural issues.
For example, Banks (1993) provides an illustrative case example of how an instructor might modify a history lesson on the

American westward movement to consider the impact of cultural influences. Disciplines that pose more serious challenges include the so-called hard sciences and mathematics. Nonetheless, a number of prominent instructors in the areas of science and math have substantially improved the academic performance of students (especially students from diverse backgrounds) in these subject areas by using innovative teaching strategies, such as cooperative learning structures and other reforms (Tobias, 1990, 1992; Treisman, 1990). In other words, no matter what the discipline, instructors committed to the notion of multicultural education can have an impact on student performance through changes made at the curricular and instructional levels.

Several other investigators (Anderson and Adams, 1992; Smith and Kolb, 1986; Svinicki and Dixon, 1987) provide a different but related conceptualization of various types of learning and instructional strategies. They describe four types of learning (concrete experience, reflective observation, abstract conceptualization, and active experimentation) and cite a number of specific instructional strategies (readings, papers, discussion, simulations) that can be used to facilitate these different types of learning. In short, serious instructors should take care at the outset to define their goals for multicultural education (cognitive, affective, or behavioral learning) in order to select and design appropriate instructional strategies that will meet these goals.

Some Conceptual Models for Teaching Multicultural Education

It may also be useful to review a number of theoretical or conceptual models of multicultural education to further clarify implications for curricular and pedagogical practices. Several researchers (Grant and Sleeter, 1989b; Pusch, 1981; Sleeter and Grant, 1988; Wurzel, 1988; Wurzel and Holt, 1991) have attempted to categorize a variety of teaching philosophies and methodologies into six roughly distinct but interrelated conceptual approaches for teaching courses on multicultural diversity:

1. *Single group or ethnic studies model.* Teaching methodologies

typically rely on lecture and discussion formats using a variety of didactic resources (books, films, case studies).

2. *Human relations training model.* This model often uses experiential activities designed to improve individual attitudes and skills required for reducing intergroup conflicts, with the goal of improving cognitive, affective, and behavioral learning. This approach tends to draw on research and theory from the psychosocial literature and linguistics. Instructional methods focus on active and cooperative learning contexts, such as experiential class exercises, role-playing, games, simulations, and conflict resolution activities.

3. *Social reconstructionist model.* Those using this approach rely on an interdisciplinary examination of power relations in the context of historical and political inequities, with an emphasis on cognitive and affective learning. This model draws on writings from literature, history, political science, and sociology. Teaching methods include readings, historical films, case studies, and some experiential exercises.

4. *Intercultural communication model.* This model involves an interdisciplinary examination of cultural differences in values and assumptions that lead to differences in individual human interaction processes, with an emphasis on behavioral learning, as well as cognitive and affective learning. This approach utilizes information from psychology, anthropology, sociology, and linguistics. Teaching methods are essentially the same as with the human relations model, with a focus on experiential exercises that improve behavioral skills.

5. *Global education model.* This approach focuses on understanding national cultures in the context of an interdependent global world, stressing cognitive and some affective learning. This model draws on history, geography, linguistics, and comparative education and uses instructional strategies such as lecture, readings, and audio-visual resources.

6. *Historical or reflective thinking model.* Those using this approach seek to examine historical and intercultural conflicts for the purpose of identifying human condition universals for greater insight into contemporary contexts to improve cognitive and affective learning. This approach draws heavily on historical case

studies and relies on the use of lecture formats, written and visual aids, case studies, and some experiential activities. A summary of all six models is presented in Table 8.1.

Although these models are presented separately, they are not mutually exclusive, and instructors are encouraged to use several models in combination, depending on course objectives, specific course constraints (class size, length of class meetings), and instructor and student characteristics. Understanding the differences among these models may be especially useful for instructors who are developing brand-new courses on multiculturalism. Fortunately, a number of helpful resources now exist for this purpose (see, for example, Wurzel and Holt, 1991).

Choosing an Experiential Classroom Technique

Whatever the course, experiential exercises, as opposed to strictly lecture formats, are potentially powerful means for promoting student learning. In fact, an ever-increasing body of literature now points to a number of significant benefits, such as increased student interest, improved motivation, enhanced learning and retention, and even improved interracial relations, that accrue as a result of using active learning (Astin, 1985; Cross, 1987), as well as collaborative and cooperative instruction (Belenky, Clinchy, Goldberger, and Tarule, 1986; Cooper and others, 1990; McKeachie, Pintrich, Lin, and Smith, 1986; Millis, 1991; Slavin, 1989/1990). Moreover, using a repertoire of more varied, flexible teaching strategies (role playing, simulations, field work, logs, journals, brainstorming) appears to enrich the learning of all students, with particularly positive outcomes for diverse students who may possess a greater range of nontraditional learning styles and strengths (see, for example, Anderson and Adams, 1992; Condon, 1986; Schmitz, Paul, and Greenberg, 1992; Svinicki and Dixon, 1987).

In short, when used judiciously, experiential multicultural classroom exercises produce beneficial outcomes for all students, not just for the nonmajority ones. Indeed, as Adams (1992) has said, "It has remained possible for students from the dominant

Table 8.1. Six Models of Multicultural Education.

Model	Description	Purpose	Methodologies
Single group or ethnic studies model	Interdisciplinary in-depth study of a specific target group; emphasis on increasing awareness, acceptance, respect	Broaden knowledge about target group Change negative attitudes/practices Validate experiences of target group and enhance self-esteem of members Promote social equality	Mostly lecture format Varied resource materials (books, films, etc.) Case studies Draws on history, literature, anthropology, psychology
Human relations training model	A focus on attitudes, feelings, and psychosocial factors that influence intergroup relations and conflict	Reduce intergroup conflicts Improve individual attitudes and practices Reduce prejudices and biases Promote group identity and harmonious group coexistence	Emphasis on experiential class activities: role playing, games, simulations, cooperative learning, conflict resolution Draws on psychosocial literature and linguistics
Social reconstructionist model	Interdisciplinary examination of race, class, and gender power relations between majority and minority groups in the context of contemporary historical and political inequities	Reduce prejudice and discrimination Reform societies more equitably Enhance critical thinking and social action skills of individuals Mobilize and coalesce groups for increased future success	Case studies Historical films Some experiential activities Draws on literature, history, sociology

Model			
Intercultural communication model	Interdisciplinary examination of cultural differences in values, assumptions, and behaviors that lead to differences in individual human interaction processes	Improve intercultural understanding Improve human relations and intercultural communication skills	Essentially same methods used by human relations model Draws on psychology, anthropology, sociology, linguistics
Global education model	Interdisciplinary approach to understanding national cultures in an interdependent global world	Increase understanding of national cultures Facilitate global interchanges Manage national interchanges within a global context	Lecture format Written and visual materials/aids Draws on history, geography, linguistics, comparative education
Historical or reflective thinking model	Historical examination of intercultural conflict for the purpose of identifying cultural universals and insight into contemporary intercultural conflicts	Increase understanding of historical perspective Increase understanding and management of contemporary intercultural conflict Identify human condition universals Promote self-reflection	Emphasis on written and visual aids, lecture May use experiential activities Draws on historical case studies

Source: Adapted from Grant and Sleeter (1989b) and Wurzel and Holt (1991).

culture to disregard the fact that theirs is also a culture and to regard 'difference' in culture as meaning merely a greater or lesser departure from their norm" (pp. 6–7). In this way, it may be possible for students to learn, sometimes for the first time, that knowledge is constructed within this larger cultural context (Banks, 1993) and therefore that "values," "meanings," "ideas," and even "facts" are culturally bound. The next step involves encouraging students to attempt to identify, understand, and appreciate the underlying factors that may contribute to the similarities and differences found among cultures and to formulate a deepened awareness of diversity that is fundamentally more humane, empathic, relational, and ecological (Broome, 1991).

In the remainder of this section I will briefly describe a variety of experiential classroom techniques primarily designed to enhance multicultural awareness; many of these exercises could be modified to highlight other noncultural diversity issues as well. Instructors are encouraged to consult the references provided for additional details on how to implement a given technique. In addition, since there does not appear to be general consensus on how to categorize or group the various exercises, I have arbitrarily identified five major types of classroom exercises: role playing, simulations, games, exercises for group discussions, and written exercises.

Role-Playing Classroom Exercises

Role-playing techniques are often effective vehicles for enhancing all three types of learning—cognitive, affective, and behavioral—because of their highly engaging nature. This technique is consistent with the goals of the single ethnic group, human relations training, and intercultural communication models. In general, role-playing exercises ask participants to improvise and act out a make-believe script based on a brief scenario or situation. Generally, it is more effective if participants have some fairly solid knowledge or background about the cultural roles they will be asked to play.

Nonverbal Interactions. Barnak (1979b) described a role-playing exercise involving differences in nonverbal communication styles between members of an "American" group and an "unspecified" cultural group. The "unspecified" group member is instructed to discuss a specific topic (for example, a three-minute discussion of how he or she, as a foreign national, is getting along in America) with an American, while simultaneously engaging in a list of ten atypical nonverbal behaviors (such as maintaining a personal distance of only several inches, using the chin to point, wrinkling the nose to ask "What?"). The audience is asked to observe and analyze the resulting interactions, and during the discussion, participants in the role playing also discuss their reactions. Students participating in this exercise gain heightened observational skills and increased appreciation of and practice with differences in cultural communication styles.

Conflicting Goals and Assumptions. Holmes and Guild (1979c) described a role-playing exercise that involved a scenario between two individuals who are each given different assumptions, conflicting goals, and incompatible methods for trying to reach their desired goal. Each role-playing incident takes about fifteen minutes, with another subsequent twenty minutes of discussion by participants and observers. In this particular scenario, a young English-speaking female student and an immigration official from a non-Western country are asked to interact. The young woman is told that she wishes to extend her visa by staying with the family of a male friend and that she is resentful of the time required to cope with what she believes is a highly inefficient bureaucracy in her host country. Meanwhile, the immigration official is informed that he should take his time and that he should be concerned about the possibility that young people from Western countries often use drugs, that they may be bad influences on local customs, and that young women staying in the homes of local men is considered improper.

Holmes and Guild (1979c) also provide information and suggestions for instructors who wish to construct their own role-playing examples. It is hoped that these exercises help students gain additional behavioral skills and an enhanced appreciation of differences and similarities in cultural norms and values.

The Party. Another extremely popular game, called "The Party," has been used on college campuses such as Berkeley, Stanford, and California State University, Fullerton. In this game, labels such as "male African American athlete," "white female sorority woman," "female Hispanic resident assistant," and "male Asian computer science major" are affixed to students' foreheads or backs. Students are not informed of what their label says but are instructed to pretend that they are at a party where they should interact with each other, based on the stereotypes they've heard about these groups. Interaction is very lively, often humorous, and student involvement is high. At the end of the game, students are asked to guess what label they were wearing; this is followed by focused group discussion.

Students' guesses about their tagged identities tend to be remarkably accurate — with judgments correct roughly 90 percent of the time. This exercise helps students experience firsthand what it feels like to be the target of stereotyping and it helps them increase awareness of the problems and disadvantages associated with stereotyping. (See this chapter's appendix for ordering instructor materials for this game.)

Simulations

Although it is sometimes difficult to distinguish the subtle differences among role playing, simulations, and games, simulations have been defined as a method that immerses students in an operating model of physical or social reality (see, for example, Alley, 1979, for suggestions on how to design your own simulation). As in the case of role playing, simulations can be used to facilitate cognitive, affective, and behavioral learning and are most consistent with the goals of the single ethnic group model, the human relations model, and the intercultural communication model.

BaFa'BaFa'. Perhaps the most widely known and used simulation for intercultural simulation is Shirts's (1977) BaFa'-BaFa'. Participants become members of either the Alpha or Beta culture, each with its own set of fictitious cultural values, expectations, customs, and communication styles (for example,

Alpha culture represents a warm, friendly, patriarchal society, while the Betas are a foreign-speaking task-oriented culture). Members of each group are allowed to visit, observe, and interact with the other group, with the goal of formulating hypotheses about how to interact most effectively with the other culture. After all participants have had a chance to visit the other culture, the instructors debrief them and facilitate a postsimulation group discussion of the experience.

This can be a very powerful and engaging exercise for students (Gillespie, 1979; Gudykunst, Ting-Toomey, and Wiseman, 1991). While a number of important lessons can be learned from this simulation, the most important outcome is a stronger appreciation for how language, stereotyping, and communication styles may influence the interaction between two dissimilar appearing groups. (See the appendix to this chapter for ordering information.)

Survival. Schnapper (1979) describes an interesting intensive ten-day culture "survival" simulation program in which participants are instructed to create a brand-new culture (complete with their own institutions, rules, norms, values, and so on) in order to cope with having survived a crash-landing in one of four environments (desert, swamp, mountain, or lush island). In doing this simulation, some creative groups abolished formal education in favor of informal parent-based tutelage, while other groups dismissed nuclear families and rigid sexual roles. After establishing their own survival culture, groups were brought back into contact with one another, to do a cross-cultural analysis evaluating their own and the other survivor cultures. Following this, "experts" from each culture were dispatched to assist another culture, with the goal of acting as "international aid helpers" to the survivors in that environment. Participants in this simulation were shocked to discover just how strongly ethnocentric they had become—indeed, in every case, each cultural group felt superior to all the others, believing that they alone had evolved the most functionally advanced culture!

Gibbereseans and Nouvellese. Junn (1992) used a class simulation to provide students with the firsthand experience of coping in a classroom situation as a nonnative speaker of a dominant language. Students were randomly assigned to one of two fictional cultures: "Gibbereseans," who represented the dominant culture (they spoke "Gibberish," a made-up language), and "Nouvellese," who were informed only they were members of a nondominant, newly immigrated culture. The Gibberesean students received a handout that includes a detailed description of the class exercise and a "dictionary" of Gibberish vocabulary words and meanings. At the next session, the instructor began by speaking fluent Gibberish sprinkled with the terms that the Gibberesean students understood. All students were given a picture completion task with instructions given in the dominant Gibberesean language. As the exercise progressed, the Gibberesean students successfully followed the Gibberish instructions, while the Nouvellese students floundered and were publicly chastised for their failure to complete the task as specified. At the conclusion of the class simulation, a diversity questions handout (including questions about their own ethnic awareness, ethnic values, positive/negative experiences, and so on) was distributed for students to answer separately, followed by group discussion.

The "Nouvellese" students were stunned at the impact that lack of knowledge of the dominant language had on their learning and motivation in the classroom. In addition, focused group discussions following the simulation were extremely useful for increasing students' appreciation of cross-cultural similarities and differences. Finally, the majority of students reported that the exercise had a positive influence on their appreciation of the challenges that face those from nonmajority backgrounds.

Games

Like simulations, games are often lively, highly engaging, and enjoyable methods for facilitating students' multicultural awareness and understanding. Most often, games can be used to promote cognitive and affective learning. Some of the games described here (such as Star Power) are especially useful when used in conjunction with the social construction, global education, or historical reflective models, but they are also consistent with the goals of the single ethnic group, human relations training, and intercultural communication models.

Star Power. Star Power is a game originally developed by Shirts to explore race and power relations. Participants have the chance to progress from one level of society to another by acquiring wealth through trading chips with other participants in the context of a card game. Once the society has been established, the group with the greatest wealth is permitted to formulate rules for the remainder of the game. The resulting outcome provokes participants to reconsider assumptions regarding the use and abuse of power and privilege in society. (See this chapter's appendix for ordering information.)

Cultural Pursuit. Some instructors have created their own version of Cultural Pursuit, a game analogous to the popular board game Trivial Pursuit. One version of Cultural Pursuit has been developed and used at the University of California, Berkeley. Sample questions include such items as "Has an *Abuela.*" The answer: "*Abuela* is 'grandmother' in Spanish." This game addresses knowledge about diversity (social class, gender) as well as cultures. (See this chapter's appendix for ordering information.)

Power Shuffle. One popular game used by Stanford University's Office of Residential Education to promote multicultural understanding among undergraduate dormitory residents is called Power Shuffle or Cross the Line. A masking-tape line is placed along the floor down the center of the room, and participants are asked to all stand on one side of the line. Then the group facilitator recites a long series of questions, such as: "Is there anyone here who's male? female? Anyone who's a person of color? Anyone who's ever had suicidal thoughts? Anyone who's struggling with their parents? Anyone who's unsure of their career goals?" and so on. Those students who can answer yes, and feel like sharing that information, walk across the line and turn around to face the others for about ten seconds.

Greg Ricks, Stanford University's former multicultural educator, observes that this game has become by far the most powerful program in that it allows students to share who they are, without having to explain or defend themselves. In addition, he states that it allows students to see that their identity is uniquely theirs, that everyone has come through adversity in one form or another. And the exercise gets people talking and listening to one another.

Stand and Declare. In this game, numbers are placed along the wall to represent points along a scale from 1 to 5 (with 1 meaning strongly agree and 5 meaning strongly disagree). The group facilitator reads off a series of questions (such as "The U.S. is the most successful multicultural society of all time") and asks students to decide on their position and walk to that point on the scale. When everyone has made a decision, groups of students at each of the points along the continuum discuss and justify the reasons for their choice to the rest of the class; students are then permitted to change positions if necessary.

Group Discussion Exercises

Focused or structured class discussions on topics involving diversity or culture primarily enhance cognitive and affective learning and would be consistent with all six of the conceptual models of multicultural education. Some suggestions for developing a more effective and inclusive classroom discussion in which all students participate include the following (adapted from Beyer and Cuseo, 1991; Jenkins and Bainer, 1991; Sadker and Sadker, 1992):

- Respond positively to all student efforts to participate.
- Allow sufficient time for student response.
- Encourage students to share culture-specific knowledge if appropriate, but avoid putting them in a spokesperson role for their particular group.
- Pay particular attention to classroom dynamics during the first weeks of class by desegregating student seating and making special efforts to draw on quieter students.
- Reinforce, summarize, probe, prompt, elaborate, and question minority and majority students in similar ways.
- Walk around the room (especially in the far corners and the back) and use effective eye contact, attentive posture, and other nonverbal gestures when listening to student comments.
- Intervene if patterns of interruption are more frequent for minority students.

- Put each student's name on a card, shuffle the cards, then call on each student as his or her name is drawn from the deck.
- Distribute three poker chips to each student, with each chip turned in when the student makes a class contribution. Require students to spend all their chips, but have them refrain from further comments once their chips have been expended.
- Videotape your classroom discussions and analyze it with a more experienced, objective colleague for additional suggestions.

Consideration of these suggestions and the following exercises can effectively stimulate thoughtful small- or large-group discussions.

Critical Incidents Exercises. Participants are presented with a short (five to ten lines) account of an open-ended problem and outcome for a situation that involves a conflict between two cultures' values, standards, or goals. For example:

> "Yesterday I gave a test to the Saudi recruits at my station. Two of the Saudis did very poorly; in fact, one failed completely. When I began to discuss the test results with them, they simply shrugged their shoulders and said, 'In shallah' ('If God wills'). So I said, 'But God didn't answer the test. You did.'"
>
> How did you feel about the way this situation was handled? To what extent do you agree or disagree with what was done or said? Rate your response on the scale below by circling the appropriate number from 1 (completely agree) to 5 (completely disagree) [adapted from Barnak, 1979a].

After participants are asked to rate how much they agree or disagree with the outcome or action taken in the situation, they must identify the underlying cultural values involved and present a more culturally responsive course of action. This is done individually first; then small groups must discuss the issue until arriving at a group consensus. Student outcomes include increased knowledge and sensitivity in identifying and interpreting underlying cultural assumptions that may affect social behavior and improved problem-solving skills in culturally ambiguous situations. (For more information on how to develop your own critical incidents, see Holmes and Guild, 1979b).

Case Studies. A case study is similar to a critical incident but is an in-depth, detailed, extended exploration of a situation that may incorporate multiple characters and multiple points of view. Case studies may or may not have a resolution, and they can be either fictional or real. Case studies should be handed out to participants to read, analyze, and discuss in small groups to arrive at a group consensus (see Holmes and Guild, 1979a; Ross, 1979).

"I" Statements. This exercise consists of simple statements made by students that define or clarify their idea of who they are and where they fit in (for example, "I am Jan, and I am a wife and Italian American"). These statements are useful for initiating discussions (Foeman, 1991) and are helpful in raising the level of cultural consciousness and rapport among participating students.

Difference Activities. In small groups participants share an early life experience during which they first perceived themselves as different. The facilitator can add contextual information, encourage the exchange of new ideas and insights, and raise the implications of being an insider or outsider (Foeman, 1991).

Q and A Sessions. In question-and-answer sessions, members of a group may ask questions of one another regarding cultural attitudes, beliefs, and values, with the added provision that a question may be refused or turned back to the asker to answer. The facilitator monitors and redirects lines of questioning for appropriateness and acknowledges factual information (Foeman, 1991). This exercise can be extremely engaging and eye-opening for students, as it represents a "safe environment" in which to discuss important but rarely openly discussed topics. However, for this very same reason it has the potential of becoming explosive if questions become intrusive, personal attacks. Instructors using this technique must be sensitive and skilled in moderating this type of exchange.

Same-Group Caucuses. This exercise involves assembling individuals from the same group (such as by sex, race, or ethnic group) to discuss the multicultural issues of greatest importance to them, how to further the group's goals, what nongroup members should know about them, or what they like best or find hardest about being a member of the group and why. Groups then reconvene for general class discussion. This can also be a potentially volatile exercise, as discussions can become intense (Foeman, 1991). This exercise can be useful in highlighting interesting levels of diversity among members within a group and for getting individuals within a group to build coalitions with members in different groups on the basis of other shared similarities.

Parables, Axioms, and Proverbs. Hoopes and Ventura's sourcebook (1979) contains short articles on how instructors have used parables, axioms, and proverbs to stimulate cross-cultural understanding and awareness. Parables can be analyzed, interpreted, and discussed by students. Students profit from seeing how popular sayings reflect and reinforce underlying cultural assumptions and values and how individuals transmit this cultural knowledge to subsequent generations through folk tales and other oral traditions.

Films and Videotapes. Using evocative audio and visual material is also an effective way to stimulate group and class discussions. Students may be given a handout containing key questions or issues to attend to, to help guide their viewing. Banks (1991) includes an appendix with an annotated bibliography of videotapes and films on American ethnic groups (see the appendix to this chapter for more sources).

Written Exercises

Written exercises can be used with all six models of multicultural education to further cognitive and affective multicultural or diversity learning. All of the exercises described below involve written assignments for individual students to complete. However, after individuals have done the written portion of these exercises, participants can share their feelings with the rest of a group in classroom discussions as well.

Cultural Assimilators. Although the term is unfamiliar to many, a *cultural assimilator* is simply a paragraph-long description of a cross-cultural incident that requires selection of one correct outcome from among a number of competing alternatives. Evaluative feedback as to the accuracy and reasons supporting the correct choice are provided separately. Such exercises represent a programmed approach to learning more about a given culture's values, beliefs, or customs. Brislin, Cushner, Cherrie, and Young's guide (1986) contains 100 cultural assimilators covering topics such as cross-cultural differences in work, language, roles, attribution, and more. Students can read and analyze the events on their own or work in groups.

Here is an example of a cultural assimilator:

Keiko, a Japanese exchange student, is introduced to her new American classmates. The friendliness of the faculty and students on her first few days impressed Keiko and made her feel at home. As time went on, however, although Keiko earned top grades, she felt that the teachers and students were ignoring her more and more. Few students or teachers talked to her, usually offering no more than a cheery hello or a few casual words in the hallway. She began to wonder if she had offended someone and gradually became withdrawn and isolated.

What do you think has happened? Which of the following four alternatives would you select as most appropriate?

1.   The students resent Keiko's high grades and are showing their jealousy of her.
2.   Americans have a tendency to offer foreigners a special welcome, then refrain from treating them in special ways soon after.
3.   Keiko demands too much attention and has unrealistic expectations.
4.   The students and faculty are obviously insincere in their initial welcomes. They were probably acting on directives from the administration.

Answers and Rationale

1. While jealousy is a possibility, there is no evidence in this scenario for this. Please choose again.
2. Cultures do differ in the amount and duration of attention afforded to foreigners. Visitors to America frequently comment that Americans are polite during initial interaction but then seem much less solicitous or even indifferent at subsequent meetings. Thus, this is the most likely explanation for Keiko's experience. It would be helpful if hosts continue to consider the needs of newly arrived persons and make an effort to involve them in their ongoing social activities.
3. Many sojourners often do have unrealistic expectations. However, Keiko does not appear to be overly demanding. Please choose again.
4. This explanation has no basis in the narrative above. Although their behavior may be causing problems, their motives probably are not. Please choose again.

[adapted from Cushner, McClelland, and Safford, 1992]

Personal Logs or Journals. These writing assignments require students to regularly record, analyze, and reflect on everyday personal experiences and how these experiences relate to issues of culture or diversity. Bond (1989) and Bronstein (1989) both discussed a journal writing option designed for use in psychology courses, while Gudykunst, Ting-Toomey, and Wiseman (1991) describe a log designed to keep track of and later analyze a student's communications with people from other cultures. Tatum (1992) has also described an intriguing psychology of racism course that used a comprehensive journal writing assignment. Because of the highly personalized nature of journals, these assignments are particularly effective vehicles in helping students forge powerful and meaningful connections between their cognitive and affective understanding of diversity issues.

Interview Paper. This written assignment requires students to conduct a semistructured interview with someone from a different cultural or ethnic background. The purpose is to connect and integrate library research and conceptual information with personal experiences (see, for example, Asch, 1989; Bond, 1989; Gudykunst, Ting-Toomey, and Wiseman, 1991). The instructor might also require that students personally respond to the same interview questions they presented to their interviewee.

In a fascinating variation on this method, Tatum (1992) described an innovative technique in which students were required to tape-record an anonymous interview with themselves using a racism questionnaire both at the start and at the end of a course on racism. At the end of the course, students listened to their prerecorded responses and reflected on whether they noted any changes in their attitudes as a function of the course.

Letter-Writing Assignment. Requiring students to write semistructured letters to an imaginary or real audience addressing diversity issues is another innovative assignment with creative potential. (See Junn, 1989, for a letter-writing assignment that could be modified to include cultural or diversity issues.)

Self-Assessment Questionnaires. Several self-assessment surveys are available for student use. For example, Gudykunst (1991) presents approximately twenty self-assessment instruments designed to determine students' attitudes and perceptions of their communicative competence. In addition, the Diversity Awareness Profile (DAP) is a self-scoring instrument designed to increase diversity awareness and help modify behavior primarily in a workplace setting. (See the appendix to this chapter for information on DAP.)

Conclusion: Instructor Characteristics Considered

Although making changes in course content and in instructional methods is necessary in developing a multicultural learning environment, instructor characteristics and style also play an important role in the success of any given course. While a great deal of research and entire texts have been devoted to the topic of effective instructors (for example, McKeachie, 1986), instructor characteristics that have been identified as important include the following:

1. Research on college teaching reveals that effective instructors are rated as being attentive, expressive, enthusiastic, clear, and organized (McKeachie, 1986).

2. Instructors who conduct "student-centered" discussions and who respond positively to student comments, are friendly, are flexible and open, listen attentively, explain clearly, give reasons for criticisms, take a personal interest in students, and are skillful in observing student reactions have been shown to increase their students' motivation and critical thinking skills (McKeachie, Lin, Moffett, and Daugherty, 1978).

3. Instructors who ask thought-provoking questions, rather than presenting statements of fact, increase student learning, interest, and curiosity (McKeachie, 1986).

4. Instructors dealing with diverse students and issues are more effective if they engage in some measure of appropriate self-disclosure in the classroom themselves (Scollon, 1981).

5. Instructors who consciously eliminate stereotypes (Matlin, 1991) and biases (Collett and Serrano, 1992; Gudykunst, Ting-Toomey, and Wiseman, 1991) from their lectures and course content materials are more effective with culturally diverse groups of students.

6. As previously stated, instructors should consider using cooperative and collaborative teaching strategies since these techniques have been shown to have multiple positive benefits on student learning (Anderson and Adams, 1992). (Chapter Five in this volume offers a wealth of suggestions.)

7. Because some of the exercises used in multicultural education may result in inflammatory class discussions and debates, instructors should be open and honest, as well as competent and sensitive in their communication skills in handling such sometimes difficult situations. In general, it is probably wise for the novice instructor to start incorporating multicultural information in increments, all the while seeking assessment information from students on the success of each technique in order to gradually build up to a comprehensive course.

8. Finally, instructors are encouraged to form networks with other colleagues, both within and across departments, to share experiences and expertise. Collegial support and involvement can be invaluable.

Although the dialogue about multicultural issues continues to be a charged one, and the challenges are many, professionals in institutions of higher learning must recognize and commit themselves to the task of developing an inclusive and equitable educational experience for all their students. While we can expect that this type of comprehensive educational reform will take time, effort, and collaboration, the rewards can serve only to strengthen our future. As individuals, we might begin by reevaluating both what we teach and how we teach in order to more meaningfully reach a wider range of students in our classrooms. In so doing, students who come away from our institutions possessing a deepened understanding of culture and diversity will have the potential to view the world and themselves from an enriched global and historical perspective. And from this heightened sense of self in relation to larger contexts springs forth a wealth of powerful future possibilities. For those who accept the call of educating for diversity, the journey promises to be a challenging and rich one indeed.

Appendix: Multicultural and Diversity Resource and Ordering Information

Multicultural Readings and References

Laura L. B. Border and Nancy Van Note Chism provide a comprehensive list of contacts at various institutions as well as a list of print and video resources on multicultural teaching in higher education in their chapter, "The Future Is Now: A Call for Action and List of Resources," in L.L.B. Border and N. Van Note Chism (eds.), *Teaching for Diversity.* New Directions for Teaching and Learning, no. 49. San Francisco: Jossey-Bass, 1992.

J. S. Wurzel and W. Holt provide an excellent and extensive annotated bibliography and a reader with detailed listings of additional information, materials, references, and resources appropriate for each of the six conceptual models of multicultural education in "Teaching Aids for Multicultural Education," *Communication Education,* 1991, *40*(3), 288–291, and in J. S. Wurzel's *Toward Multiculturalism: A Reader in Multicultural Education* (Yarmouth, Maine: Intercultural Press, 1988).

D. S. Hoopes and P. Ventura provide brief but useful information and specific examples for instructors wishing to try role playing, simulations, cultural assimilators, critical incidents, case studies, and parables in their edited *Intercultural Sourcebook: Cross-Cultural Training Methodologies* (Washington, D.C.: Intercultural Network, 1979).

A number of recent books concerning multicultural education and diversity that could be used in undergraduate courses or as resources for instructors are now available. They include:

Cushner, K., McClelland, A., and Safford, P. *Human Diversity in Education: An Integrative Approach.* New York: McGraw-Hill, 1992.

Locke, D. C. *Increasing Multicultural Understanding: A Comprehensive Model.* Newbury Park, Calif.: Sage, 1992.

Gollnick, D., and Chinn, P. *Multicultural Education in a Pluralistic Society.* Columbus, Ohio: Merrill, 1990.

Elliot R. Barkan, along with colleagues Thomas Meisenhelder, Gloria Cowan, Walter Oliver, and Jennifer Randisi, have assembled an extensive bibliography of cross-cultural readings and resources for instructors in the social sciences, psychology, humanities, and English; actual sample course syllabuses are included as well. Copies of this document, titled, "The Combined Bibliographies of the Cross-Cultural Perspectives in the Curriculum Workshops, California State University, San Bernardino, 1985–1986," may be obtained by contacting Elliot Barkan, California State University, San Bernardino, Department of History, 5500 University Parkway, San Bernardino, CA 92407.

For instructors of psychology, Phyllis Bronstein and Kathryn Quina have edited an excellent volume, *Teaching a Psychology of People: Resources for Gender and Sociocultural Awareness* (Washington, D.C.: American Psychological Association, 1989), that is a helpful resource for psychology instructors wishing to address diversity issues in a variety of psychology courses (intro, abnormal, social, developmental, and so on).

Be on the lookout for publishing houses that are expanding their selection of scholarly works addressing issues of ethnic studies, multiculturalism, and diversity. One such publisher is Sage Publications in Newbury Park, California, which has a significant number of titles that deal with more specific multicultural issues. A partial listing includes:

Burlew, A.K.H., Banks, W. C., and McAdoo, H. P. (eds.). *African American Psychology: Theory, Research, and Practice.* 1992.

Gimenez, M. E., Lopez, F. A., and Munoz, C. (eds.). *The Politics of Ethnic Construction: Hispanic, Chicano, Latino?* 1992.

Hecht, M. L., Collier, M. J., and Ribeau, S. A. *African American Communication.* 1993.

Kavanagh, K. H., and Kennedy, P. H. *Promoting Cultural Diversity: Strategies for Health Care Professionals.* 1992.

Locke, D. C. *Increasing Multicultural Understanding: A Comprehensive Model.* 1992.

McAdoo, H. P. (ed.). *Family Ethnicity.* 1993.

Phinney, J. S., and Rotheram, M. J. (eds.). *Children's Ethnic Socialization: Pluralism and Development.* 1987.

Ponterotto, J. G., and Pederson, P. B. *Preventing Prejudice.* 1993.

Riggins, S. H. (ed.). *Ethnic Minority Media: An International Perspective.* 1992.

Root, M.P.P. (ed.). *Racially Mixed People in America.* 1992.

Stanfield, J. H. (ed.). *A History of Race Relations Research: First Generation Recollections.* 1993.

Stanfield, J. H. (ed.). *Race and Ethnicity in Research Methods.* 1993.

Van Dijk, T. A. *Elite Discourse and Racism.* 1993.

Waldinger, R., Aldrich, H., and Ward, R. *Ethnic Entrepreneurs.* 1990.

Multicultural Films and Videotapes

For an excellent and extensive listing of multicultural films on video that focus on different peoples from around the world, consult Films for the Humanities and Sciences, P.O. Box 2053, Princeton, NJ 08543-2053, 800-257-5126.

James A. Banks includes an appendix with an annotated bibliography of videotapes and films on various American ethnic groups in *Teaching Strategies for Ethnic Studies,* 5th ed. (Needham Heights, Mass.: Allyn & Bacon, 1991).

Role Playing

The Party, a game that facilitates understanding of stereotypes, may be purchased as part of a larger packet of diversity training materials for $25 by contacting Edith Ng, University of California, Berkeley, Staff Affirmative Action Office, 2219 Addison Street, Suite 641, Berkeley, CA 94720, 510-643-7464.

Simulations

BaFa'BaFa' can be implemented in two fifty-minute periods with anywhere from twelve to forty participants and two facilitators. The required materials and training manual can be ordered at an educational discount cost of $179 by contacting Simulation Training Systems, P.O. Box 910, Del Mar, CA 92014, 619-792-9743.

RaFa'RaFa' is an analog of BaFa'BaFa' designed for use with fifth- through eighth-grade students. The cost is $89 and is available by contacting Simulation Training Systems.

Games

Star Power can be played in two fifty-minute intervals with anywhere from eighteen to thirty-five participants. The cost is $189. Contact Simulation Training Systems, P.O. Box 910, Del Mar, CA 92014, 619-792-9743 for more information.

Cultural Pursuit is similar in principle to the popular board game Trivial Pursuit. It may be purchased as part of the larger packet of diversity training materials from the University of California, Berkeley, mentioned under "Role Playing Games."

Self-Assessment Instruments

The Diversity Awareness Profile (DAP) by Karen Grote (1991) is a forty-item self-administered instrument designed to increase awareness and behavioral skills among individuals (particularly employees). Another DAP exists that is designed specifically for use by managers. Both are available at a cost of $3.95 for each questionnaire by contacting Order Department ARJ, Pfeiffer and Company, 8517 Production Avenue, San Diego, CA 92121-2280, 619-578-5900.

References

Adams, M. "Cultural Inclusion in the American Classroom." In L.L.B. Border and N. Van Note Chism (eds.), *Teaching for Diversity.* New Directions for Teaching and Learning, no. 49. San Francisco: Jossey-Bass, 1992.

Alley, R. "Simulation Development." In D. S. Hoopes and P. Ventura (eds.), *Intercultural Sourcebook: Cross-Cultural Training Methodologies.* Washington, D.C.: Intercultural Network, 1979.

Anderson, J. A., and Adams, M. "Acknowledging the Learning Styles of Diverse Student Populations: Implications for Instructional Design." In L.L.B. Border and N. Van Note Chism (eds.), *Teaching for Diversity.* New Directions for Teaching and Learning, no. 49. San Francisco: Jossey-Bass, 1992.

Asch, A. "Disability: Its Place in the Curriculum." In P. Bronstein and K. Quina (eds.), *Teaching a Psychology of People: Resources for Gender and Sociocultural Awareness.* Washington, D.C.: American Psychological Association, 1989.

Astin, A. W. *Achieving Educational Excellence.* San Francisco: Jossey-Bass, 1985.

Banks, J. A. "Integrating the Curriculum with Ethnic Content: Approaches and Guidelines." In J. A. Banks and C.A.M. Banks (eds.), *Multicultural Education: Issues and Perspectives.* Needham Heights, Mass.: Allyn & Bacon, 1989a.

Banks, J. A. "Multicultural Education: Characteristics and Goals." In J. A. Banks and C.A.M. Banks (eds.), *Multicultural Education: Issues and Perspectives.* Needham Heights, Mass.: Allyn & Bacon, 1989b.

Banks, J. A. *Teaching Strategies for Ethnic Studies.* (5th ed.) Needham Heights, Mass.: Allyn & Bacon, 1991.

Banks, J. A. "The Canon Debate, Knowledge Construction, and Multicultural Education." *Educational Researcher,* 1993, *22*(5), 4–14.

Banks, J. A., and Banks, C.A.M. (eds.). *Multicultural Education: Issues and Perspectives.* Needham Heights, Mass.: Allyn & Bacon, 1989.

Barnak, P. "Critical Incidents Exercise." In D. S. Hoopes and P. Ventura (eds.), *Intercultural Sourcebook: Cross-Cultural Training Methodologies.* Washington, D.C.: Intercultural Network, 1979a.

Barnak, P. "Role-Playing." In D. S. Hoopes and P. Ventura (eds.), *Intercultural Sourcebook: Cross-Cultural Training Methodologies.* Washington, D.C.: Intercultural Network, 1979b.

Belenky, M. F., Clinchy, B. M., Goldberger, N. R., and Tarule, J. M. *Women's Ways of Knowing: The Development of Self, Body, and Mind.* New York: Basic Books, 1986.

Beyer, V. P., and Cuseo, J. B. "Promoting Minority Student Involvement at the University: Collegial Coaching Support." *Journal on Excellence in College Teaching,* 1991, *2,* 101–114.

Bond, L. A. "Teaching Developmental Psychology." In P. Bronstein and K. Quina (eds.), *Teaching a Psychology of People: Resources for Gender and Sociocultural Awareness.* Washington, D.C.: American Psychological Association, 1989.

Border, L.L.B., and Van Note Chism, N. "The Future Is Now: A Call for Action and List of Resources." In L.L.B. Border and N. Van Note Chism (eds.), *Teaching for Diversity.* New Directions for Teaching and Learning, no. 49. San Francisco: Jossey-Bass, 1992a.

Border, L.L.B., and Van Note Chism, N. (eds.). *Teaching for Diversity.* New Directions for Teaching and Learning, no. 49. San Francisco: Jossey-Bass, 1992b.

Brislin, R. W. "Intercultural Communication Training." In M. Asante and W. Gudykunst (eds.), *Handbook of International and Intercultural Communication.* Newbury Park, Calif.: Sage, 1986.

Brislin, R. W., Cushner, K., Cherrie, C., and Young, M. *Intercultural Interactions: A Practical Guide.* Newbury Park, Calif.: Sage, 1986.

Bronstein, P. "Personality from a Sociocultural Perspective." In P. Bronstein and K. Quina (eds.), *Teaching a Psychology of People: Resources for Gender and Sociocultural Awareness.* Washington, D.C.: American Psychological Association, 1989.

Bronstein, P., and Quina, K. (eds.). *Teaching a Psychology of People: Resources for Gender and Sociocultural Awareness.* Washington, D.C.: American Psychological Association, 1989.

Broome, B. J. "Building Shared Meaning: Implications of a Relational Approach to Empathy for Teaching Intercultural Communication." *Communication Education,* 1991, *40*(3), 235–249.

Brown, T. J. *Teaching Minorities More Effectively: A Model for Educators.* New York: University Press of America, 1986.

Bullivant, B. M. "Culture: Its Nature and Meaning for Educators." In J. A. Banks and C. A. Banks (eds.), *Multicultural Education: Issues and Perspectives.* Needham Heights, Mass.: Allyn & Bacon, 1989.

Collett, J., and Serrano, B. "Stirring It Up: The Inclusive Classroom." In L.L.B. Border and N. Van Note Chism (eds.), *Teaching for Diversity.* New Directions for Teaching and Learning, no. 49. San Francisco: Jossey-Bass, 1992.

Condon, J. C. "The Ethnographic Classroom." In J. M. Civikly (ed.), *Communicating in College Classrooms.* New Directions for Teaching and Learning, no. 26. San Francisco: Jossey-Bass, 1986.

Cooper, J. L., and others. *Cooperative Learning and College Instruction: Effective Use of Student Learning Teams.* Long Beach, Calif.: Institute of Teaching and Learning, 1990.

Cross, P. *Adults as Learners: Increasing Participation and Facilitating Learning.* San Francisco: Jossey-Bass, 1987.

Cushner, K., McClelland, A., and Safford, P. *Human Diversity in Education: An Integrative Approach.* New York: McGraw-Hill, 1992.

Foeman, A. K. "Managing Multiracial Institutions: Goals and Approaches for Race-Relations Training." *Communications Education,* 1991, *40*(3), 255–266.

Gillespie, A. "Using Bafa Bafa." In D. S. Hoopes and P. Ventura (eds.), *Intercultural Sourcebook: Cross-Cultural Training Methodologies.* Washington, D.C.: Intercultural Network, 1979.

Grant, C. A., and Sleeter, C. E. "Race, Class, Gender, Exceptionality, and Educational Reform." In J. A. Banks and C.A.M. Banks (eds.), *Multicultural Education: Issues and Perspectives.* Needham Heights, Mass.: Allyn & Bacon, 1989a.

Grant, C. A., and Sleeter, C. E. *Turning on Learning: Five Approaches for Multicultural Teaching Plans for Race, Class, Gender, and Disability.* Columbus, Ohio: Merrill, 1989b.

Grote, K. *Diversity Awareness Profile, DAP.* San Diego: Pfeiffer, 1991.

Gudykunst, W. B. *Bridging Differences: Effective Intergroup Communication.* Newbury Park, Calif.: Sage, 1991.

Gudykunst, W. B., Ting-Toomey, S., and Wiseman, R. L. "Taming the Beast: Designing a Course on Intercultural Communication." *Communication Education,* 1991, *40*(3), 272–285.

Holmes, H., and Guild, S. "Case Study." In D. S. Hoopes and P. Ventura (eds.), *Intercultural Sourcebook: Cross-Cultural Training Methodologies.* Washington, D.C.: Intercultural Network, 1979a.

Holmes, H., and Guild, S. "Critical Incidents." In D. S. Hoopes and P. Ventura (eds.), *Intercultural Sourcebook: Cross-Cultural Training Methodologies.* Washington, D.C.: Intercultural Network, 1979b.

Holmes, H., and Guild, S. "Role-Plays." In D. S. Hoopes and P. Ventura (eds.), *Intercultural Sourcebook: Cross-Cultural Training Methodologies.* Washington, D.C.: Intercultural Network, 1979c.

Hoopes, D. S., and Ventura, P. (eds.). *Intercultural Sourcebook: Cross-Cultural Training Methodologies.* Washington, D.C.: Intercultural Network, 1979.

Howe, I. "The Value of the Canon." *The New Republic,* Feb. 18, 1991, pp. 40–44, 46–47.

Jenkins, C. A., and Bainer, D. L. "Common Instructional Problems in the Multicultural Classroom." *Journal on Excellence in College Teaching,* 1991, *2,* 77–88.

Junn, E. "'Dear Mom and Dad': Using Personal Letters to Enhance Students' Understanding of Developmental Issues." *Teaching of Psychology,* 1989, *16*(3), 135–139.

Junn, E. "Making Multicultural Awareness Come Alive in the Classroom: An Innovative Classroom Exercise." Poster presented at the annual meeting of California State University Institute for Teaching and Learning Exchange, Los Angeles, March 1992.

Levine, A., and Associates. *Shaping Higher Education's Future: Demographic Realities and Opportunities, 1990–2000.* San Francisco: Jossey-Bass, 1989.

McKeachie, W. J. *Teaching Tips: A Guide for the Beginning College Teacher.* (8th ed.) Lexington, Mass.: Heath, 1986.

McKeachie, W. J., Lin, Y., Moffett, M., and Daugherty, M. "Effective Teaching and Facilitative Versus Directive Style." *Teaching of Psychology,* 1978, *5,* 193–194.

McKeachie, W. J., Pintrich, P. R., Lin, Y., and Smith, D. A. *Teaching and Learning in the College Classroom: A Review of the Research Literature.* Ann Arbor: University of Michigan, 1986.

Magner, D. K. "Difficult Questions Face Colleges That Require Students to Take Courses That Explore Issues Related to Race." *The Chronicle of Higher Education,* March 28, 1990, A19–A21.

Maher, F., and Tetreault, M. K. "Inside Feminist Classrooms: An Ethnographic Approach." In L.L.B. Border and N. Van Note Chism (eds.), *Teaching for Diversity.* New Directions for Teaching and Learning, no. 49. San Francisco: Jossey-Bass, 1992.

Matlin, M. W. "The Social Cognition Approach to Stereotypes and Its Application to Teaching." *Journal on Excellence in College Teaching,* 1991, *2,* 9–24.

Mays, V. M. "The Integration of Ethnicity and Gender into Clinical Training: The UCLA Model." In P. Bronstein and K. Quina (eds.), *Teaching a Psychology of People: Resources for Gender and Sociocultural Awareness.* Washington, D.C.: American Psychological Association, 1989.

Millis, B. J. "Fulfilling the Promise of the 'Seven Principles' Through Cooperative Learning: An Action Agenda for the University Classroom." *Journal of Excellence in College Teaching,* 1991, *2,* 139–144.

Noll, J. W. "Issue 3: Should Curricula Emphasize Commonality Over Multiculturalism? Yes: Richard Rodriguez, No: Alba A. Rosenbaum." In J. W. Noll (ed.), *Taking Sides: Clashing Views on Controversial Educational Issues.* (6th ed.) Guilford, Conn.: Dushkin, 1991.

Pusch, M. D. (ed.). *Multicultural Education: A Cross-Cultural Training Approach.* Yarmouth, Maine: International Press, 1981.

Romero, D. "Teaching Ethnic Psychology to Undergraduates: A Specialized Course." In P. Bronstein and K. Quina (eds.), *Teaching a Psychology of People: Resources for Gender and Sociocultural Awareness.* Washington, D.C.: American Psychological Association, 1989.

Ross, R. "Case Study Method." In D. S. Hoopes and P. Ventura (eds.), *Intercultural Sourcebook: Cross-Cultural Training Methodologies.* Washington, D.C.: Intercultural Network, 1979.

Sadker, M., and Sadker, D. "Ensuring Equitable Participation in College Classrooms." In L.L.B. Border and N. Van Note Chism (eds.), *Teaching for Diversity.* New Directions for Teaching and Learning, no. 49. San Francisco: Jossey-Bass, 1992.

Schmitz, B., Paul, S. P., and Greenberg, J. D. "Creating Multicultural Classrooms: An Experience-Derived Faculty Development Program." In L.L.B. Border and N. Van Note Chism (eds.), *Teaching for Diversity.* New Directions for Teaching and Learning, no. 49. San Francisco: Jossey-Bass, 1992.

Schnapper, M. "Culture Simulation as a Training Tool." In D. S. Hoopes and P. Ventura (eds.). *Intercultural Sourcebook: Cross-Cultural Training Methodologies.* Washington, D.C.: Intercultural Network, 1979.

Schwartz, J., and Exter, T. "All Our Children." *American Demographics,* May 1989, pp. 34–37.

Scollon, R. *Teachers' Questions About Alaska Native Education.* Fairbanks: University of Alaska Center for Cross Cultural Studies, 1981. (ED 238 661)

Shirts, G. *BaFa'BaFa': A Cross-Cultural Simulation.* Del Mar, Calif.: Simulation Training Assistance, 1977.

Siegel, F. "The Cult of Multiculturalism." *The New Republic,* Feb. 18, 1991, pp. 34–39.

Slavin, R. "Research on Cooperative Learning: Consensus and Controversy." *Educational Leadership,* 1989/1990, *47*(4), 52–55.

Sleeter, C. E., and Grant, C. A. "An Analysis of Multicultural Education in the United States." *Harvard Educational Review,* 1987, *57,* 421–444.

Sleeter, C. E., and Grant, C. A. *Making Choices for Multicultural Education: Five Approaches to Race, Class, and Gender.* Columbus, Ohio: Merrill, 1988.

Smith, D. M., and Kolb, D. A. *User's Guide for the Learning Style Inventor: A Manual for Teachers and Trainers*. Boston: McBer, 1986.

Solmon, L., and Wingard, T. L. "The Changing Demographics: Problems and Opportunities." In P. G. Altbach and K. Lomotey (eds.), *The Racial Crisis in American Higher Education*. Albany: State University of New York Press, 1991.

Spitzberg, B., and Cupach, W. *Interpersonal Communication Competence*. Newbury Park, Calif.: Sage, 1984.

Svinicki, M. D., and Dixon, N. M. "The Kolb Model Modified for Classroom Activities." *College Teaching*, 1987, *35*(4), 141–146.

Tatum, B. "Talking About Race, Learning About Racism: The Application of Racial Identity Development Theory in the Classroom." *Harvard Educational Review*, 1992, *62*(1), 1–24.

Tobias, S. "They're Not Dumb, They're Just Different—Stalking the Second Tier." Tucson, Ariz.: Research Corp, 1990.

Tobias, S. "Science Education Reform: What's Wrong with the Process?" *Change*, 1992, *24*(3), 13–19.

Treisman, P. U. "Mathematics Achievement Among African American Undergraduates at the University of California, Berkeley: An Evaluation of the Mathematics Workshop Program." *Journal of Negro Education*, 1990, *59*(3), 463–478.

vom Saal, D. R., Jefferson, D. J., and Morrison, M.K.C. "Improving the Climate: Eight Universities Meet the Challenges of Diversity." In L.L.B. Border and N. Van Note Chism (eds.), *Teaching for Diversity*. New Directions for Teaching and Learning, no. 49. San Francisco: Jossey-Bass, 1992.

Wong, F. F. "Diversity and Community: Right Objectives and Wrong Arguments." *Change*, 1991, *23*(4), 50–54.

Wurzel, J. S. *Toward Multiculturalism: A Reader in Multicultural Education*. Yarmouth, Maine: Intercultural Press, 1988.

Wurzel, J. S., and Holt, W. "Teaching Aids for Multicultural Education." *Communication Education*, 1991, *40*(3), 288–291.

Chapter 9

Unmasking the Myths of Racism

Gale S. Auletta, Terry Jones

As college students are becoming more culturally and racially diverse, our ability to communicate equitably with them across racial and ethnic lines lags embarrassingly behind. Classroom discussions about students' personal experiences with perceived racism are so uncomfortable and painful that most faculty do their best to avoid discussions on the topic. But even though faculty may never openly address the issue, our classrooms, our curriculum, our teaching methods, and yes, we, the faculty, are often perceived by our students to be contributing to their exclusion because of our racism. These beliefs and perceptions when silenced, ignored, or rejected create hazards to learning and contribute to feelings of alienation and hostility.

Deeply saddened and angered by the social distance between students of color and European American faculty on campuses across the country, we (an African American male and an European American female) have sought, for the last ten years, to understand the dynamics that create and perpetuate that distance, whether it is real or perceived as real. We feel fortunate that our teaching and administrative assignments have allowed us to listen to, observe, and converse in formal and informal contexts with hundreds of students, faculty, and administrators about their experiences with diversity. We want to share the voices of the conflicting perspectives we have heard, offer a synthesis of our thinking, and suggest a method for engaging issues of racism and perceptions of racism. Our focus for this chapter is on racism, but we believe that while the particulars may change, the themes and the model also apply to other forms of exclusion based on race, gender, and sexual preference.

We operate on the assumption that while racism is one of society's most serious problems, perceptions of racism are almost as problematic. In this chapter we introduce a language for discussing issues of race and racism. Making a distinction between myths and realities of racism provides one way to think and teach about the perceptions and communication of racism. We need to bring our individual and collective consciousness to all of our daily and taken-for-granted assumptions about ourselves and others. In order to do so, we must break the silence around issues of race and racism.

Educational institutions have become proficient in recognizing and dealing with extreme, individual acts of overt racism, but the less extreme, more pervasive, and more subtle acts of cultural and institutional racism are better disguised and, when detected, more difficult to remedy. We will share several major myths and realities about racism that we see embedded in U.S. higher education. To varying degrees, European Americans and people of color alike have grown up with a combination of these myths and realities. However, how each of us experiences these myths on any given occasion depends on whether we are the perceived victim or the perpetuator of the myth. This framework has served us well as a common language for unpacking and discussing the complexities of racial perceptions in interracial dialogue. We suggest, of course, that you read many of the sources listed in the reference section to deepen your familiarity and thus comfort level with the concepts we present.

Myths of Racism

Myriad myths about racism have grown out of various cultural experiences. These "myths" or beliefs define for each of us those actions or attitudes that constitute racism, which people are racist, and the way in which racism plays out in our institutional and personal experiences. These beliefs about who and what is racist have profound effects on individual and group perceptions about racism. Here are some of the most common myths:

1. *Racism is an on/off phenomenon.* This is the conviction that a person categorically is or is not a racist. According to this belief, a person cannot be "a little bit" of a racist—racism is an all-or-none phenomenon.

2. *Racism is curable.* Even though someone may have been brought up in a household of racists, or may have lived in a society dominated by institutional racism, many people believe that a 100 percent cure is just a seminar, college degree, or revelation away. Thus, racism is seen as not only completely curable but as easily curable with an appropriate educational experience.

3. *Racism is KKK/overt acts.* For a behavior to count as racist, it must be as hostile or blatant as most Ku Klux Klan activities. Many people believe that overt discriminatory acts, such as obvious racial slurs or race-based aggression, are what defines racism. According to this belief, hiring decisions based on "merit" where "merit" has a distinct racial bias couldn't possibly be defined as racist.

4. *Racism must be conscious.* According to this belief, only conscious and intentional thoughts or actions about the superiority and inferiority of people based on their race signify racism.

5. *Racism must be mean-spirited.* This assumption most often surfaces as, "If I am well intentioned and care about people, I can't possibly be racist."

6. *Racism happens in isolated instances.* Individual acts of racism are viewed as separate from their context, and the context that nurtures the seeds for racist behavior is ignored. According to this view, racism is an isolated, simple, and easily identified behavior performed by lone and misguided individuals.

7. *I can't be racist if I have friends of other races.* Having friends and colleagues of different races is seen as an immunization against racism. This belief is similar to the idea that well-intentioned people cannot be racist.

8. *Reverse discrimination is a form of racism.* This belief about

racism is often voiced in response to affirmative action policies. We hear this myth as "Two wrongs do not make a right," "I didn't discriminate against anyone so why single me out for punishment?" or "Those reaping the rewards of affirmative action haven't been slaves, so why reward them?" Such opinions ignore the historical and current context in which racism and its power continue to operate.

These beliefs define racism for many people; they are deeply embedded in the hearts and minds of students and faculty, European Americans and people of color alike. However, these beliefs affect each group differently. These myths are perpetuated on college campuses, in part, because few college faculty know or teach about the huge literature of racism. Ironically, faculty use their own erroneous beliefs about racism to justify their conclusion that there is no need to teach about it. After all, why study racism if you believe that a racist or a racist act is easily identifiable, that a racist can be easily cured, and that racism is perpetuated by lone individuals in isolated situations? A phenomenon as simple as this one supposedly is would not be worthy of college-level instruction.

Realities of Racism

The extensive literature on the realities of racism dispels these eight common myths. It is more accurate to think about racism in terms of five statements that reflect the reality of racism. Faculty who are interested in openly discussing racism in their classrooms could structure a lesson plan in which the commonly believed myths are compared with the following findings from our own research on racism.

1. *Racism occurs on multiple levels: personal, institutional, and cultural.* Racism can be personal, institutional, and social (Blauner, 1972; Carmichael and Hamilton, 1967; Jones, 1972; Knowles and Prewitt, 1969; Takaki, 1990). *Personal racism* involves the belief that certain physical traits are the determinants of social, moral, and intellectual character so that skin color, for example, would signal inferior moral character. *Institutional racism* is an extension of individual racism and includes those institutional

practices that operate to restrict groups of individuals. *Cultural racism* combines elements of individual and institutional racism to perpetuate the belief of cultural superiority of one race and cultural inferiority for all others.

2. *Racism occurs on a continuum.*

Conscious . . . Unconscious
Overt . . . Covert
Little impact . . . Great impact
Agreed upon by one . . . Agreed upon by many
Agreed upon by the victim . . . Agreed upon by the perpetuator
Mean-spirited . . . Well intentioned

Viewing racism on a continuum anchored at one end by acts that are conscious and overt and the other by acts that are unconscious and covert allows us to think about perceived racism from both the victim's and the perpetuator's point of view. It also means that simple, clear-cut decisions about which actions or people are racist are much more difficult than with categorical models, because many acts will not fall neatly near either end. Furthermore, the victim and perpetuator probably will not agree about where on the continuum a specific act should be placed. To what degree is an act of racism perceived to be conscious and overt from the perpetuator's point of view? To what degree does the potential victim interpret the same action to be conscious and intentional? These are important questions for understanding when and why an action is classified as racist by one individual and not racist by another.

3. *Personal racism can be perpetuated by all individuals and groups of people within the United States, but European Americans, because of their institutional power, can and do perpetuate the greatest harm.* This reality takes into consideration the difference between an individual's personal racist beliefs and behaviors to influence a few and the institutional and cultural power of European Americans to influence many. Because so much power in the United States is held by European Americans, the actions of this group are responsible for the greatest harm.

4. *Racism can be reduced, but it cannot be eliminated in our life-*

time. This statement is our professional opinion based on years of research. Racism is so intricately woven into our personal and collective unconscious that only constant vigilance will reduce it in our lifetime. The metaphor we've used is that of diabetes or alcoholism. One can work diligently to reduce its impact, but it will always need to be contained.

5. *Racism always occurs within a context.* All individuals are inextricably bound to a complex web of influences. Racism is perpetuated because it is allowed and nurtured within the context in which it occurs.

The realities of racism are diametrically opposed to the commonly held myths of racism, and for this reason, a tension exists between beliefs and reality. Differences in perception about what constitutes racism can explain some portion of the racial uneasiness that is felt on many college campuses.

Contextual Lenses: Seeing the Campus from Other Perspectives

In our classrooms, students of color are more likely than European American students to notice the racial and gender identity of classmates, faculty, administrators, and those in positions of power both in the college and in society. Consciously or unconsciously, being the only one or one among a few people of color creates a perspective very different from that of being one among many. Students of color, much more so than European Americans, are likely to notice that the only people of color they see on their campus are groundskeepers, secretaries, assistants to assistants, and those in charge of "minority affairs."

Slogans about being an "affirmative action employer" do not necessarily put a student of color at ease. In fact, such promises without action lead to greater feelings of uneasiness. When students feel different, they look for visible signs of an invitation and a sense of acceptance. Surveying the landscape and seeing no one who looks like them in positions of authority, seeing too few who look like them in the classroom, and seeing no written or visual evidence that their history, culture, and legacy are a valued part of the curriculum, students of color can become suspicious, resentful, defensive, alienated and anxiety ridden, or cynical. Worse yet, students can accept that their experiences, their culture, their his-story or her-story doesn't really matter, doesn't count as "education."

When viewed from this perspective, it is easy to see how many students of color perceive a campus environment as racist, while the faculty of European American background do not understand this perception.

Experiences in the Classroom:
The Double Bind

Many of our students of color come from environments in which racism and knowledge of racism are prevalent. Racism and discussions of who is racist, how racist a person or institution might be, how to spot a racist, and how one deals with racists and racism are day-in and day-out realities for many people of color. Awareness of racism and its real and perceived effects is often openly accepted as a necessary survival mechanism for people of color. Those hurt and brutalized by racist acts and perceived racist acts often fall back on the support systems of their communities and families for sustenance and healing. The content of the message they send each other sometimes sound like this: "You damn right that was racist, and if it happens again I think you ought to call the FEPC"; "Yeah, I know him, he is so racist. He was probably George Wallace's speech writer"; "They just don't know, their racism is so thin, we can see right through it. They'd put Rosa Parks in jail again if they had the chance"; "These white folks are so damned dumb and arrogant they don't even know how I play them."

Whether the content of such statements is true is not the issue. Those who rally around the offended individual are sending a strong relational message of support: "We know the hurt you feel. We've been there. What is happening to you is both real and wrong." Such support and validation goes a long way in providing strength, confidence, dignity, and hope to those victimized by racism and perceptions of racism. Such support systems often make the difference between giving up or going back and giving it another try.

In contrast, most European American faculty and students rarely discuss racism in private homogeneous groups, and when they do, they see themselves as the victims of affirmative action and "reverse discrimination." Van Dijk's extensive study of the communication of racism (1987) illustrates the everyday conversations by dominant group members who persuasively communicate their attitudes to other Europeans and European Americans. These messages are transmitted through European American storytelling in which tales of experiences with people of color become "tales of complaint, accusations, self-pity, and resentment." We heard an example just the other day: "With all my qualifications, I got passed over for an affirmative action candidate." Van Dijk identifies *semantic moves* as those messages that show the communicators' attempt to distance themselves from being perceived as racist: "I am not prejudiced, but . . . "; "We also do bad things to . . . "; "They also have good ones among them"; "I don't mind but others do . . . " (p. 383).

In public or interracial groups, European Americans are less likely to raise any discussions about race, and when they do, they are more likely to speak in code, using such terms as "best qualified," "maintaining standards," "the best schools," and so on. So, what we have are students of color and European Americans both sending messages about being the victim of the other when they are within the safe boundaries of their own groups. In interracial settings, European American faculty and students tend to ignore and deny that (1) exclusionary practices of people of color are pervasive or exist at all in the college, and (2) they might in any way be perpetuating that exclusion.

When we apply these principles to college classrooms, we find that students of color are placed at double risk — they have the same low status and lack of control as other students, but they also have to be vigilant for racial tensions, especially when the professor is of European American descent. Students of color frequently report that they wonder: "Why did the professor use that tone when he spoke to me? He didn't use it with the white students" or "I raised my hand and have been raising it now for two class sessions but the professor has not called on me yet. Is it because I'm black?" or "I notice that there is always a group of white students gathered around the professor before and after class and they really appear to be hitting it off, yet when I approach him he seems so cold, so distant, and in so much of a hurry."

How does the student of color handle such feelings and perceptions? To raise such questions to the professor in or out of the classroom disrupts the flow of "comfortable civility" and in so doing can open the door to real or imagined penalties. Being publicly belittled, put down, or ignored, being perceived as a troublemaker by the other students and the professor, and having their grade lowered are very real possibilities in the minds of students of color who contemplate speaking up. Yet not to speak up to the professor, or worse yet, not to have a sympathetic support group to talk with, leaves the student of color suppressing these questions and concerns, wondering whether he or she is being "overly sensitive." In any event, the student is left struggling with the mounting anger, pain, and blame.

Meanwhile, the European American faculty member prepares and teaches the course curriculum, assignments, and evaluations adhering to the disciplinary guidelines for what constitutes a particular course and what is likely to "look good" to the other professors in his or her department and professional organization. Most often, this means approaching courses from the traditional Eurocentric perspective. This method tends to ignore other cultural experiences, especially those involving oppression, or to see them through the European American lens of analysis. Often there is nothing said openly to give the impression of racism, yet students of color frequently report that they are uncomfortable and are marginalized in the classroom. They feel that the professor is ignoring or minimizing the history, legacy, or contributions of all people of color. They hear the topic of institutional or cultural racism as it applies to the particular course of study silenced and denied. And the double bind goes on. Students of color see, hear, and feel their difference in the classroom as well as their professors' discomfort and silence on racial issues.

Conclusion

Racism is real and alive in the United States, and it is flourishing on our college campuses. We cannot afford the luxury of sitting in our ivory towers ignoring or refusing to discuss issues of racism while the towers' bases are being threatened by racial fires. We strongly urge that those responsible for higher education provide leadership in charting a course for more intelligently discussing and working on issues of racism.

References

Blauner, R. *Racial Oppression in America.* New York: Harper-Collins, 1972.

Carmichael, S., and Hamilton, C. V. *Black Power: The Politics of Liberation in America.* New York: Vintage, 1967.

Jones, J. *Prejudice and Racism.* Reading, Mass.: Addison-Wesley, 1972.

Knowles, L. L., and Prewitt, K. *Institutional Racism in America.* Englewood Cliffs, N.J.: Prentice-Hall, 1969.

Takaki, R. *Iron Cages: Race and Culture in Nineteenth-Century America.* New York: Oxford University Press, 1990.

van Dijk, T. *The Communication of Racism: Ethnic Prejudice in Thought and Talk.* Newbury Park, Calif.: Sage, 1987.

Chapter 10

Strategies for Teaching in a Multicultural Environment

Elliott Robert Barkan

Twenty-one years ago, I presented my first conference paper. It was titled "Incorporating Multiculturalism into the General Education Curriculum." Today not only does that task remain incomplete, but the issues have become far more sweeping, far more pressing. The urgency arises from the unmistakable trends in the population as we move toward a "majority minority" in several states by the end of the first decade of the twenty-first century. It arises, as well, from the persistent resistance on many levels — academic and societal — to the changes required if we are to prepare our students to function most effectively in a truly multicultural, multiethnic, multiracial environment, whatever those students' occupations might be. The inescapable fact is that our imminent future is one in which the legitimacy of such diversity will have an even greater certainty, not to be given mere lip ser-

My thanks to David Mauk and Gregory Wuesthoff, of the English Institute, University of Trondheim, Norway, for their comments on an earlier draft of this paper. Thanks are also owed to John Higham and Sidney Stahl Weinberg for their comments and suggestions.

175

vice, treated off-handedly and with disdain (or fear), or simply consigned to others to be dealt with (whomever they might be).

What is now most apparent is that revisions in the curriculum alone are not sufficient; simultaneously, significant attitudinal and institutional changes must be made among professors, administrators, and staff in our universities if the curriculum changes are to have the desired impact on the values, attitudes, and actions of our students. I do not pretend that such an observation has never been uttered or written; I do maintain it has been soft-pedaled and frequently ignored. I would also argue that the challenge has become qualitatively more complicated by those among the ethnic studies faculty who have, in their quest for legitimacy and institutional security, promoted sometimes strident and uncompromising strategies that have alienated the allies they need if they are to achieve their objectives. In fact, it sometimes appears that their actions actually generate a backlash among segments of the general public that seriously compounds the problem of securing ethnic and multicultural education.

Thus, it should be immediately clear that the whole issue of multicultural teaching cannot be divorced from very profound academic political issues. I would divide those political issues into three spheres: those concerning curriculum reform (both general education and in specific programs); those posed by the competing (and sometimes strident) demands of some of the more vocal supporters and opponents of ethnic studies; and those involving the attitudes and actions of instructors, administrators, and staff. This brief chapter, based on more than twenty years of involvement in ethnic studies instruction and curricular reform, will attempt to address what I believe are some of the important aspects of these three spheres, for they underlie the basic question of how we effectively address multiculturalism in the education of our university students. Building on that discussion, I will then focus on a set of strategies that I believe ought to be practiced by all who teach courses involving any of the aspects of multicultural education, for our pressing task is to enable our students to overcome multicultural illiteracy (to borrow Ronald Takaki's phrase) and, even more, multicultural indifference and insensitivity.

Curricular Reform

Overwhelmingly, the architects, builders, and transmitters of American culture — the boundary makers and boundary protectors — have been predominantly white, European in origin (Waspish if not actually WASP), and male . . . if we bear in mind that most white women were not themselves challenging — and perhaps most still do not — the racial, ethnic, and gender norms, values, and practices that tolerated and nourished ethnic and gender degradation. Only someone who has never been a victim, who has never confronted the frustration of experiencing the invisibility that comes with the omission of recognition and respect, could fail to see the long overdue need for an academic revolution paralleling the broader civil rights one. In many disciplines "boundary hunters" have emerged to challenge the old canons, the old definitions, the old curricula. Their work is still largely unnoticed or ignored by many in higher education.

The objective of such curricular reform is not really "mainstreaming," for that implies merely an additive process to a fundamentally unaltered core curriculum. What is needed, as Marilyn Boxer noted nearly a decade ago and as Paul Lauter and others have repeatedly advocated, is the rechanneling of the streams, a willingness to go back and candidly and forthrightly reevaluate the canons of our disciplines that we inherited from our professors, who in turn inherited them from theirs. Those who resist such reassessments and changes are by now more atavistic than academic, medieval in their notions that our bodies of knowledge have been defined for all time in a country whose one constant has been change.

Nonetheless, we do need to address several fundamental aspects of such changes, for they go to the heart of the fears of those who shun the changes and those who, as a consequence, see them as precarious and always vulnerable to backlash:

1. How do we alter the canons of instruction while preserving academic and intellectual coherence — that is, how do we dismantle the old WASP orthodoxy without succumbing to balkanization as the means of satisfying every demand by every group — a splintering that could readily subvert comprehensive learning? (See Chapter Seven for a related discussion.)

2. How do we convey the fact that myriad ethnic communities in America have, for our entire history, been sources of the nation's strength — not weakness — without needing to reject the whole core culture and the forces and traditions that have united us in order to make that point?

3. How do we ensure the legitimacy of ethnic studies and multicultural instruction without substituting a new exclusiveness for the old one, without sanctioning an academic Europhobia in our courses and campus environment?

4. How do we go about rethinking and reexamining and then restructuring our history (and the content of other disciplines), as well as our methodologies, teaching strategies, and whole university environment, without confounding our students?

While this chapter cannot address these issues in depth, one central point can be made quite clear: all faculty and administrators must be consistent throughout, for if mixed messages and misinformation are what we leave our students with, they will continue to misunderstand that which we Americans have shared in common and that has defined our society and civilization — both for good and for ill. And worse, they will go forth with confusion redoubled, with bitter sentiments reinforced, and with stereotypes reaffirmed.

Now, undoubtedly, this academic struggle will be perceived by its critics as having political dimensions. So be it. We must compel the old boundary builders to acknowledge that academia has *always* been a political arena, for, during much of this century, the choices of inclusion and exclusion have consistently been political, reflecting the biases and realities of the larger American society. This was perfectly captured in the observation by a renowned historian who authored a leading survey text during the 1960s concerning the omission of minorities and women: "We didn't think they were important."

If the education revolution is unsettling to some, we must remind them of how long it has been unsettling and frustrating for those so long invisible, and we must convince them that we will all gain from the changes, for our expanded knowledge and perspectives will give our nation a greater strength and unity, "a higher viewpoint" it has been said. They will enlarge our understanding of ourselves as a people who are of one nation but representative of the nations of the world. The fact that all this will take effort, and the labor of revising lecture notes and syllabuses, ought not to be masked by unrelated rationalizations for inaction. In an era of vastly expanding bodies of information, of multitudes of new writers and researchers of all hues and backgrounds, of global media and worldwide exchanges of knowledge and technology, of peoples and products, it is sheer folly for anyone, or any discipline, to insist on an intellectual or academic status quo.

Such fundamental rechanneling must be done by the faculty and be supported by administrators and staff; we simply cannot wait for entrenched obstructionists to retire. By doing so we violate our mandate, our mission to train our students for what we clearly see is coming (and, indeed, what already is here), and in so doing we reaffirm the fears, anxieties, and even not-so-latent anger of those who have long been demanding such reforms.

Ethnic Studies

The ethnic studies faculty are not without their own share of complexities and difficulties, for some among them pose critical problems for our pursuit of effective multicultural education. A phenomenon has been taking place in California and other states with diverse student populations that has confounded many and has expressed one side of the wretched and mischievous controversy over "political correctness."

On the positive side, those of us long in the field of ethnic studies have been deeply concerned about securing the incorporation of ethnic and gender studies and issues into the general education curriculum and into various majors. We have been striving to attain the legitimacy of ethnic studies so that "multiculturalism," as an umbrella approach, is *not* seized upon as a guise for subverting specialized ethnic studies programs by those only lukewarm to change or superficial in their understanding of the issues. The faculty in such programs are vital for providing many of the multicultural courses as well as contributing to the in-depth programs and the scholarly approach essential for integrating ethnic studies into the university curriculum. Multiculturalism without ethnic studies programs would be a Pyrrhic victory at best.

On the other hand, the quest for ethnic studies programs, departments, and schools has prompted some of those involved in teaching the most long-excluded subject areas, concerning racial ethnic groups, to espouse a definition of ethnic studies that substitutes a new exclusiveness for the old one. Not infrequently, that generates a Europhobia in their courses and campus environments, in which all Caucasians are thrown together in the undifferentiate category of "whites" in the same manner that the dominant society so unjustifiably used to deal with African Americans, Native Americans, Latinos, and Asians as monolithic entities (and, not infrequently, still does).

Those who find it fashionable or expedient to lump persons of European extraction into an all-encompassing category of "Euro-Americans" (or "European Americans") overlook the ongoing ethnic vitality of the nation's Armenians, Italians, Russians, Serbs, Croatians, Greeks, Irish, English, Poles, Hungarians, Norwegians, and Swedes—to mention but a few of those who make up important segments of the American community.

There is a political expediency underlying the exclusive emphasis on people of color in the curriculum, for, on one level, it expresses the bitter belief that whites have had the privileges of their color, the option of most easily assimilating, and a wealth of opportunities relatively unobstructed by the barrier of their skin color—or of being prejudged by their appearances (although this was certainly not true in many cases where European immigrants—the first generation—clearly were visible, not only by their physical appearance but also by their language, customs, dress, religion, and sometimes even their occupation). On another level, however, that perspective emerges as culturally, socially, and historically misleading inasmuch as it ignores the struggles of many European ethnic peoples, including those who are second and third (or later) generations, to gain acceptance and respectability in America. It submerges the ongoing arrival of such immigrants, who must replicate the processes of integration. It obscures the differences among white ethnic groups that have contributed to their continuing sense of community and ethnic distinctiveness, even to the multitude of instances where conflicts have existed among and between them and members of the dominant society. And it masks significant in-group differences due to race, religion, gender, social class, occupation, length of time here, and even legal status. *Virtually no ethnic group in America is homogeneous, much less any collective category of persons.*

Of course this does not mean that all ethnic group experiences have been alike, or that peoples of color have not experienced more persistent and endemic problems throughout our history, or that members of groups that have been particularly victimized do not possess valuable insights and perspectives from which all can learn. It does mean that clouding our understanding of other groups' experiences by invalidating their ethnic reality denies us the comparative perspective needed in order to fully comprehend the character and magnitude of the differences. In the end, it deprives *all* students of a multifaceted perspective about American society and, thereby, accomplishes little toward intergroup understanding or intergroup relations.

The politics of anger are legitimate, as are the demands to be heard, understood, and incorporated on terms of full equality. But when the *academic* application of such anger or such demands continues to be so exclusive and rigid as to be divisive, antagonistic, and polarizing, it becomes counterproductive and undermines the vital, long-term strategy of evoking compassion, understanding, and, *especially,* mutual support among administrators, faculty, staff, and students of all backgrounds.

I firmly believe, and do so teach, that we must present a view of history and contemporary society that illustrates both the travesties and the treasures of various societies. We must, for example, clearly and consistently address the facts that the settlement of America was an invasion, that North America was not vacant land, that Native Americans were crudely and unrelentingly displaced, that Africans were brutally enslaved and degraded, that we engaged in imperialistic behavior toward the Mexicans, that we unfairly singled out the Chinese for exclusion, and that we unconscionably interned American citizens of Japanese descent in concentration camps. In other words, numerous peoples of color have quite repeatedly been harshly, and sometimes almost genocidally, treated and have had to cope with numerous assaults on their cultures, societies, and self-esteem. But we must also point out that the Irish were treated horribly, were subjected to fierce anti-Catholicism (which persists today in muted form), and were regarded as the niggers of the last century. We should discuss the ways that Jews were victimized, as were Italians, French Canadians, and many other immigrants of European extraction. By doing so we do not equate such experiences with those of various nonwhite groups, for they are not equal; we only underscore their reality. Students of all backgrounds continue to be astonished to discover how many groups have been victimized and that not all were peoples of color.

It should be obvious, too, that exposing students to such information will also make them more alert to the bitter and protracted (and sometimes devastating) ethnic struggles in the former Soviet Union, the former Yugoslavia, and the former Czechoslovakia—all "former" in part because of deep-seated ethnic and nationalistic animosities—as well as in India, Iraq, Israel, Rumania, Japan, China, and Indonesia and, in recent decades due to new waves of immigrants, in Great Britain, France, Germany, Italy, Norway, Sweden, and the Netherlands.

Thus, ethnic studies courses and programs focusing on specific peoples must be promoted, preserved, and protected as vital components in the achievement of our multicultural goals. At the same time, such departments must not become enclaves into which ethnic studies faculty retreat, nor vehicles for making monopolistic claims regarding particular course topics or instructors. Valuable in-group insights and experiences can be conveyed to others, who can sensitively appreciate and subsequently disseminate much of their content and meaningfulness. Therefore, group membership ought not to be the principal criteria for conferring the sole rights to teach particular ethnic studies courses.

In fact, membership in one group (a racial ethnic one, for example) does not automatically ensure either knowledge or sensitivity about others, or even necessarily about the whole range of experiences of that same group. Moreover, those who advocate this position are actually denying the abilities and motives of their colleagues. In so doing, they provide ammunition for their opponents, delegitimize their own programs, alienate their colleagues (and the public), and, as noted, thereby fail in the pragmatic politics of building alliances with a broad coalition of colleagues. And such a coalition is vital to the long-term success of ethnic studies and multicultural instruction. As serious, from the standpoint of our multicultural objectives, they unwittingly instill in their students the mistaken belief that they are alone, that only they can understand and articulate their people's experiences. They thereby confess that they also have no right to express the experiences of others, even if they, too, be peoples of color. This perverse logic is unquestionably inimical to the goals of multicultural instruction and learning.

The pursuit of a multiculturally enriched university environment must be achieved without substituting a new dogmatism for the old, or a new homogenization that excludes those who do not fit into some arbitrary definitions of ethnicity. We must not replace the long unchallenged whiteness that for so many years discolored our texts, our perspectives, and our teaching with a new orientation so warped in the opposite direction that we rashly distort reality and fragment our history, culture, society, and educational institutions.

Attitudes and Actions

If our unified objective is to prepare our students to be effective members of an extraordinarily diverse society, how ought that be achieved? What, in the final analysis, must we as teachers be able to do to convey the revised curriculum in the most powerful manner, to foster the most receptive environment for learning and understanding, for self-awareness and intergroup sensitivity, especially if we ourselves are not members of the particular ethnic groups in question? Surely, it is not knowledge alone that we are to convey but a whole set of attitudes and affect. We must help our students to unlearn and relearn, to recenter their knowledge, to see the world through the eyes of others, to recognize the complementarity of groups and the interaction of race, class, gender, religion, and national identities, and to understand and modify previous male, Eurocentric analyses in favor of more gender-free, multicentric perspectives, with a grasp of their consequences in both the public and private sectors.

Transmission of knowledge, or fostering the pursuit of knowledge, is thus but one of our goals as teachers. There must be self-searching along with outward searching; there must be intensity to overcome inertia and passion to overcome apathy. No one, and no group, has a monopoly on this: the heart of my argument here is that what we teachers bring into the classroom as people committed to a genuinely democratic, multicultural, multiperspective, multicentric education is more critical than any specific pieces of knowledge, or our race or ethnic backgrounds. Indeed, that fact may be the most vital knowledge we do convey: that we, as teachers of all ethnic backgrounds, care about the future we are shaping, not just about the past we are preserving.

How, then, can this be done? I would suggest the following sixteen strategies as vital for maximally effective multicultural teaching:

1. We must be able to get mad, to feel angry about the injustices that peoples have suffered, and be willing and able to express that anger to convey a sense of the pain, humiliation, anguish, indignation, frustration, and despair many peoples have felt. This is particularly essential for those who are not members of the specific ethnic group they are discussing. Knowledge brings the power of sight, but affect brings the power of insight: no affect yields no effect.

2. We must, without a doubt, be empathetic, able to reach down deep and feel the experiences, pain, and traumas of others. But, as Carlos Cortés has noted, we must be sensitive without being Sensitive — readily hurt by what others may say or how they may challenge. We cannot be merely academic and distant, or perhaps even really impartial, about such issues.

3. We must be willing to be uncomfortable — uncomfortable with the limited extent of our own knowledge about others

and their experiences. Comprehensiveness is not essential for effectiveness; the learning process is not finite.

4. We must, it follows, understand that the pursuit of the answers to the past and present is ongoing. The alternative is the risk of arrogance and condescension.

5. We must, indeed, be able to recognize that others may have experiences that we may not be able to grasp fully or entirely convey. With our passion must come humility.

6. We must, perforce, be open — open to the experiences of others, especially open to student responses and input. The better we listen, the better we teach.

7. We must likewise acknowledge that many wear the badges of oppression but that they belong to no one exclusively. Some badges may be bigger than others, but that cannot deny the validity of those others.

8. We must, with that awareness, strive for balance between the lived experiences and the shared experiences, recognizing those that some uniquely possess and those that we can all potentially transmit. But the first must not be used to deny the second, for then none may teach the past or learn about themselves from others, and potential allies become illegitimate "border crossers."

9. We must, consequently, deny the right of anyone to a monopoly on knowledge, for none have the right to claim that only they understand a particular group's entire experience or that only they have the right to be angry. Such claims of exclusivity are divisive and, in a perverse manner, perpetuate the chasms of the past.

10. We must, then, understand ethnicity as a phenomenon that many diverse peoples experience within common parameters but for different lengths of time, based on different historical events, and with different degrees of intensity and commitment. Shared characteristics of ethnicity do not mean an equality or sameness of experiences.

11. We must, with these insights, be willing to challenge the status quo, the accepted canons of our disciplines. If we transmit the old givens of learning, we equally imply the transmission of old hierarchies of power and dominance.

12. We must, furthermore, always keep in mind the underlying historical reality that America has never been a real "melting pot," because the components included have only been "white" ones, and such biases carried over into many other branches of learning. Moreover, as John Higham has pointed out, no ethnic group that has established itself in America has ever entirely disappeared, including European ones. Through immigration, expansion, enslavement, and conquest we have, from our earliest beginnings, been a culturally, racially, and socially diverse people; assimilation is the act of individuals, not groups.

13. We must, based on all this, pursue a multicentric approach—not Eurocentric or Afrocentric, or any other specific "centric"—if we are to teach multiculturalism effectively. The arrogance of the single perspective is but a replication of past inaccuracies and distortions, be it in reaction to that past or not.

14. We must, for pragmatic reasons, also foster alliances to strengthen ethnic studies programs as a vital foundation for sound multicultural instruction, a diverse faculty, and a healthy range of instructional perspectives. Building bridges as a step to shared power will more effectively strengthen the program and the unity of the faculty, administrators, and staff.

15. We must realistically keep in mind the "six Ps": the administrative Power as a factor in achieving curriculum change; the ongoing needs and vitality of the Programs; the Personality charactéristics—the attitudes in particular—necessary for effective multicultural instruction; the breadth of the Perspectives that we as teachers bring into the classroom; and the modes of Presentation by which one's impact can be greatest by combining scholarship with Passion. Those who use their power to thwart curricular reforms must continue to be challenged, but the practical politics of ensuring multicultural instruction must not confound the academic integrity of the programs themselves.

16. Finally, we must recognize that the vital goal of a successful multicultural education is promoting and achieving unity with pluralism, inclusiveness not exclusiveness, and that the means to achieving this end must entail institutional as well

as curricula change. One without the other will produce superficial changes, uncertainty, and instability and will convey to our students that in reality the status quo essentially endures.

Conclusion

A key objective for the twenty-first century in terms of teaching strategies is this: as we respond to the demands of those calling for the visibility and inclusion of the many long-overlooked ethnic groups — in whatever sphere or discipline we are teaching — we must strive to define a balanced multiculturalism that incorporates by redefining and clarifying the whole, without shattering it or over narrowly detailing the scope of those multicultural or ethnic studies to the extent of denying the rich variety of peoples who are of African, Asian, Native American, Latino, *and* European descent. By so doing we do not equate their historical experiences, only recognize their legitimate place in the history, culture, economy, and politics of America. At the same time, it is not realistic to believe that every group can be included in a coherent curriculum. To attempt such a goal would be to hopelessly fragment our instruction and seriously obscure our students' understanding of the vital core of society, culture, and polity around which this nation has developed. However, once the process of multicultural instruction has begun and information is being taught and passion transmitted, we shall be instilling in our students the capacity to value and respect *all* peoples, to enrich and be enriched by all.

In the process of this instruction we must also be working to empower students by enhancing their self-esteem and their ethnic group pride as well as their respect for others and their willingness and ability to understand, tolerate, and appreciate ethnic differences. We must make them realize that knowledge instills pride (and sometimes anger) but also awareness; group consciousness but also less fear of others; and greater self-understanding but also a new (or renewed) visibility for those long overlooked.

Hence, our ultimate educational goal in terms of multiculturalism is not a matter of political correctness; it is a matter of social and intellectual justness. It is not a question of academic zero summing (with winners and losers), but a question of academic summing up wherein the gains are for all ethnic groups, and for women as well as men, and none are losers. If we fail in this, we fail our students; we fail the next generation.

If, on the other hand, we can finally summon the will to achieve successful multicultural instruction — and I believe that the sixteen steps I've described would significantly contribute to the attainment of that goal — it will be because faculty members of all hues and disciplines at last recognize the strategic pedagogical value of cooperatively working toward a multicultural education that reflects the broadest realities of the nation past, present, and future. In that manner we can strive to replace multicultural illiteracy, indifference, and insensitivity with multicultural knowledge, insight, and sensitivity.

PART THREE

Teaching With and About New Technologies

The number and range of new technologies are increasing at a dizzying pace. It is apparent that these advances can help us work more quickly and more efficiently than ever before. However, the potential in these new forms of media lies not just in their speed, but in their ability to completely alter the way we think, learn, remember, and communicate information. The chapters in this section go beyond the speed factor and address ways to use new technologies to promote the instructional goals that we have established for college-level education.

In Chapter Eleven, Craig Blurton discusses electronic communication and its uses. In Chapter Twelve, Penelope Semrau and Barbara A. Boyer show how interactive videodisc, along with a mix of other media, can help students think more critically, appreciate human diversity, and work cooperatively. Patricia A. Backer and Joseph K. Yabu (Chapter Thirteen) explain how to use hypermedia and, in the process, reveal a changing view of what constitutes a college classroom. In Chapter Fourteen, the last chapter in this section, Ralph H. Miller, Joyce Kupsh, and Carol Larson Jones address the neglected topic of software ethics and advocate that ethics instruction be part of every course in which software is used. These chapters present a vision of a not-so-distant future in which the lone lecturing professor is accompanied by a host of educational technologies, global information, images, and sound that require active student participation in their own learning.

Chapter 11

Using the Internet for Teaching, Learning, and Research

Craig Blurton

In this chapter I describe the Internet, a wide area computer network, and how it can be used to improve and extend the capabilities of professional educators. I discuss what using the Internet has meant to my ability to do those tasks associated with being a professor. Because I want to share my interest and enthusiasm for these new tools for teaching, learning, and research, and encourage similar feelings in the reader, I'll describe what these tools can be used for — with examples — rather than how to use them, except when it is necessary to do so for clarity.

Wide Area Computer Networking

I became interested in using my desktop computer to communicate with others when I was responsible for working with 400 classroom teachers who attended the Elementary Summer Technology Training Institute (ESTTI) at California State University, San Bernardino, in 1986–87. This inservice teacher education program, funded by the California State Legislature, provided four weeks of intense educational experiences in a residential program. The participants were a cadre of classroom teachers and school district and county office staff development specialists from across California who were taught effective uses of technology across the K-8 curriculum.

If we were to effect change in the participants' classroom practices, we believed it would be necessary to continue to support them during the academic year. To accomplish this goal, we used a variety of methods and media—print, conferences, regional meetings, satellite teleconferences, and wide area computer networking. (A wide area computer network—known as a WAN—consists of the wires, cables, control devices, and software that connects various computers and local area computer networks at geographically distant locations, allowing them to communicate. A local area network—known as a LAN—connects computers in close proximity to each other, for example those within a computer lab or a building.) The WAN proved to be the most effective means to meet our goal of maintaining an inexpensive, timely, ongoing interaction with the ESTTI participants.

As part of the program, each participant received a computer and a modem (a modem is a device that makes it possible for computers to communicate with each other over the telephone system). We also purchased for the participants a membership on MIX, a commercial (now defunct) computer network for educators operated by McGraw-Hill. Using the computer and modem, my staff and I could plug into the telephone system, call a remote computer in Minneapolis, and make use of its software to send and receive messages and carry on professional discussions. We used it successfully throughout the three years of the program. However, in terms of functionality and features, MIX was to wide area computer networking what model airplanes are to a Boeing 747. I didn't know this at the time, but I quickly learned it as I interacted with others on MIX who were more experienced with wide area computer networking than I.

I soon learned of CompuServe, The Source, AppleLink, and other commercial networks that were vastly more powerful and sophisticated than MIX, with far more communications capabilities and information resources as well as a larger pool of participants ("users" in the jargon of computing) with whom to interact. (In my metaphor, these commercial services are the Piper Cubs and even Lear Jets of WANs.) And then I was introduced to the Internet, the Boeing 747 of computer networks. MIX connected a few hundred people to a single computer in Minneapolis that had extremely limited capabilities. Some of the large commercial services connect as many as half a million people from across the country and a few other nations to a bank of perhaps a dozen very powerful computers. But the Internet, which only a few years ago operated in 26 countries, comprised more than 5,000 networks, and supported several million users on more than 300,000 computers in several thousand organizations (Cerf, 1991) is even bigger today and continues to grow. The most recent estimates are that Internet operates in over 125 countries, with five to ten million users.

Although it is not my intent to provide a highly technical description of wide area computer networking, an important distinction to make here is that the "more than 300,000 computers" on the Internet are "host" computers, not the individual desktop computers operated by the "several million users" to access the internet through these hosts. In simple terms, a "host" computer is assigned an Internet address and provides a variety of services, including Internet access, for people who connect to the host from their desktop computers. For example, over 4,500 K–12 teachers using a variety of common desktop computers access the Internet via the California Technology Project's California Online Resources for Education (CORE) host computer. They do so by first using their own desktop computer to connect with the CORE computer and then using software on the CORE computer to send and receive electronic mail, telnet to other computers, and retrieve files by anonymous ftp (these three features of the Internet are described in some detail later in this chapter).

To better understand the Internet, it is also important to understand that it is not a single computer network but rather a collection of over 5,000 interconnected ("interoperating") computer networks that use a common way of sharing information known as the internet protocol (IP). Responsibility for, and control over, the Internet's constituent components and resources is distributed across the organizations and individuals who operate the various host computers and networks, and it is completely decentralized. This is important, as we will see later.

Many, if not most, colleges and universities in the United States have access to the Internet, although many instructors may be unaware of the connection or its potential as a rich resource for teaching, learning, and research. It is a resource well worth tapping. Without exaggeration, when I began to explore the Internet from my desktop computer, I connected to a vast human and information resource unlike any in the history of the world. I had at my fingertips access to millions of professionals across the world from all segments of education, business, industry, nonprofit organizations, and governmental agencies. I could query, address, deliberate, review, debate, discuss, educate, and collaborate with people across the planet at almost the speed of light. I became a member of a "virtual" community of scholars, one that can never meet enmass, face-to-face, but one that can converse electronically.

I now have access to powerful communications tools and huge data bases of text, graphic, and software resources, and I have the capability of making use of software on other computers located anywhere in the world that are connected to the Internet. In comparison to the Internet, to stretch the metaphor further, the library at my campus is a balsawood glider.

Electronic Tools

The Internet offers three basic electronic tools by which professional educators can conduct the business of teaching, learning, and research worldwide: electronic mail (E-mail), telnet, and anonymous file transfer protocol (ftp). I discuss each of these tools briefly, describing what I have used them for during the past several years. I also explain them as simply and clearly as I can in light of their functionality and usefulness and include examples of each application. In addition, I have included a short list of resources at the end of the chapter for those who wish to learn more.

What I describe here is based on my experiences exploring the Internet for several years without a user's manual (no really comprehensive manual exists, although FarWestNet in Bellevue, Washington, has developed an excellent user's guide). My experiences evolved from using my desktop computer and a modem to access the Internet over the telephone to connecting with the Internet from a desktop computer on a local area network without the need for a modem and telephone line. (The latter arrangement is much preferred because it allows for faster communications speeds, which becomes important as the size of the data being sent, received, or retrieved increases. A single graphic, such as a NASA artist's rendering of the space shuttle or a weather satellite photograph, can be very large and take a very long time to send or receive at the speeds most modems are capable of achieving.)

Electronic Mail

Electronic mail, commonly known as "E-mail," is the easiest of the three Internet electronic tools to conceptualize. E-mail allows one person to send an electronic message to another and vice versa. Simply put, one writes a message and sends it over the Internet to someone else's electronic mailbox at another computer. The majority of traffic on the Internet consists of such electronic mail messages. Compared to using the United States Postal Service, E-mail is cheaper, faster, and much more convenient to use. (Access to the Internet for faculty generally is subsidized by the university or college for whom they work; but in terms of actual cost per message, E-mail is cheaper than using the U.S. Postal Service.)

I correspond daily in a way that I wouldn't if I had to put pen to paper (or fingers to keys), the paper in an envelope, and the envelope in the mail. The ease of use, and the speed at which messages can be exchanged, has increased my professional communication — and arguably my productivity. I regularly send and receive messages to colleagues in such diverse locations as Brazil, Japan, Norway, England, other countries, many of the fifty states, and the twenty campuses throughout California that constitute the California State University. I use electronic mail to keep informed of their work, learn about the work of others in our field, share pertinent information about upcoming conferences, conduct cooperative research, and ask for assistance in locating hard-to-find information and resources.

Using E-mail, I have collaboratively developed and disseminated agendas for meetings of statewide organizations, received notification of requests for proposals well before such requests appeared in print, and learned about important grant opportunities well before others who are dependent on the Postal Service. I use electronic mail to collaboratively write articles, chapters, grants, and proposals with colleagues, sending and receiving drafts of manuscripts for comment, critique, additions, and revisions. The range and scope of my ability to collaborate is no longer bound by time or distance. Because of E-mail, my collaborators span the globe and international time zones.

I prefer E-mail to the telephone because it is time independent and has helped me eliminate "telephone tag," one of the least entertaining activities in which I am forced to engage. I need not worry about what time zones my message will cross and whether anyone will be awake and in the office to receive it. Once my message is sent, the recipient will read it when he or she checks the electronic mailbox and can respond whether I am on the telephone, in a meeting, away from my desk, at home, or out of the state or the country.

Because most of the large commercial networks have E-mail "gateways" to the Internet, I can send and receive messages to and from users of commercial services such as CompuServe, AppleLink, The Source, and other academic networks such as BITNET. (BITNET is an academic computer network, with fewer features and users, that is technically less advanced than the Internet.)

Electronic Publications. Electronic mail is also used as a delivery mechanism for a new breed of professional publication — those created and delivered only in electronic form. Refereed and nonrefereed electronic journals and newsletters are now being introduced and disseminated by professional groups over the Internet. These publications are sent to a subscriber's electronic mailbox as an E-mail message, albeit a lengthier one than most. For example, *PSYCOLOQUY* is a refereed electronic journal published at Princeton University for psychology and related fields; the *Bryn Mawr Classical Review* is a nonrefereed review journal of books in Greek and Latin classics; the *Electronic Journal of the Astronomical Society of the Atlantic* focuses on amateur and professional astronomy and space exploration; *NLSNews* is an electronic newsletter for the National Longitudinal Surveys of Labor Market Experience that is issued quarterly by the Center for Human Resource Research at Ohio State University (with funding provided by the U.S. Department of Labor); and *EFFector Online* is a publication of the Electronic Frontier Foundation focusing on issues such as freedom of speech and intellectual property rights related to worldwide computer-based communications networks.

Listserv Conferences. Electronic mail is used for group discussions, also known as "listserv" or computer conferences. A listserv is actually software on a host computer located on the Internet or BITNET that distributes every message it receives to the electronic mailboxes of those individuals on its mailing list, wherever their mailbox may be on either of these two networks. Some listserv conferences are "moderated," which means a human intervenes and may edit, compile, or censor messages before they are sent to the individuals on the mailing list. Others, and in my experience most, listserv conferences are totally automated and function without human intervention or screening of content.

Unlike E-mail between two individuals, listserv conferences are a public process. To participate in a listserv conference, an individual sends a message in a specified format to the host computer requesting to be added to the mailing list. Once on the mailing list, every individual message sent by any of the participants to the host computer is duplicated and sent to every other participant's mailbox. If ten people are on the list, each receives a copy of any message sent to the host computer. If all ten send a message, each participant receives nine messages (ten minus one's own message). The same procedure is followed if 100, 1,000, or 10,000 people are on the mailing list.

Once admitted to the listserv, an individual may read and respond to any of the messages posted by any other individual to the host computer. This results in a kind of "never-ending story" in which one person makes a statement or asks a question, others respond, and others respond to the responses until someone starts a new line of discussion.

One need not be a computer scientist to recognize that this form of computer conferencing is unwieldy and primitive. If a listserv is active and has a large membership, it can generate dozens of E-mail messages daily to each participant's mailbox, making it impossible to keep abreast of the volume of information. Someone who belongs to several active listserv conferences may receive hundreds of messages daily. Listservs also do not provide a mechanism by which a participant may search, sort, or scan information to screen out those messages of little or no interest. (Later, in the section on telnet, I will discuss interactive computer conferencing that, to some degree, overcomes these limitations.)

Although primitive in execution, listservs do provide an easy and convenient way for groups of individuals at widely dispersed geographic locations to use E-mail to interact about topics in which they are interested. For example, I belong to a listserv conference operated by the Consortium for School Networking (CoSN), the members of which discuss topics related to K–12 schools' access to and uses of the Internet. I also belong to a list operated by the Association for the Study of Higher Education (ASHE), where I discuss, or more frequently read others' discussions about, issues related to higher education, such as the applications of total quality management (TQM) principles to institutions of higher education and faculty evaluation processes at postsecondary institutions.

Other listservs meet other professional needs. Listserv conferences exist for almost every academic specialty, from agriculture to zoology. Topics discussed range from the science fiction novel as an art form to politics in Central America to polymer physics. Via electronic mail, superconductivity, commutative algebra, dental amalgam, recycling, laboratory primates, and photosynthesis are discussed among individuals from cultures, countries, institutions, and agencies around the world who are participating in virtual communities of scholarship.

E-Mail File Servers. Another purpose electronic mail can serve is to retrieve information from file servers on the Internet (a *file server* is a host computer and a set of stored electronic files containing information — text, graphics, or software — that can be accessed by others to obtain copies of the files).

The following examples will demonstrate why this is a powerful use of E-mail for academics. The National Science Foundation (NSF) maintains a service on the Internet called the Science and Technology Information System (STIS). By querying STIS with electronic mail messages in the appropriate format, it is possible to receive in one's electronic mailbox the *NSF Bulletin, Guide to Programs,* press releases, program announcements, grants booklets (including forms), NSF job announcements, and descriptions of funded research projects.

"Project Gutenberg" provides E-mail and ftp (which I'll discuss later) access to electronic texts (known as "etexts"). Etexts are entire books, the texts of which are being stored electronically on file servers on the Internet so that they may be copied to the computers of network users. Project Gutenberg has made many complete books available electronically, ranging from *The Federalist Papers* to the *1991 CIA World Factbook.* It is the self-proclaimed goal of Project Gutenberg to give away one trillion etexts over the Internet by December 31, 2001; Project Gutenberg's administrators claim to have disseminated almost nine billion copies of etexts already (Hart, 1992, p. 1).

In summary, E-mail is a deceptively simple but very powerful feature of the Internet, allowing professional educators to send and receive individual messages; participate in group discussions; receive electronic publications such as journals, newsletters, and etexts; and access archives of information on remote file servers. Such activities enhance the ability of professional educators to communicate and collaborate with other academics across the globe and to access important information resources for teaching, learning, and research.

Telnet

Telnet is a feature of the Internet that allows one to use another computer anywhere on the network as though it were directly connected to one's desktop computer and to use it interactively in "real time." Given that there are over 300,000 accessible computers on the Internet, telnet provides entry to a wealth of computing power and software. It turns one's desktop computer into an electronic doorway, transporting keystrokes into commands completed by software on scientific workstations, mini and mainframe computers, and supercomputers at distant locations. It also permits the efficient and economical sharing of powerful and expensive computing resources.

Using telnet, it is possible to interactively and remotely search thousands of data bases, browse through hundreds of library catalogues, participate in dozens of interactive computer conferences, use a supercomputer, check the weather, play a virtual reality adventure game, or use an on-line dictionary and thesaurus.

To use the Internet for these purposes, one must have access to the telnet feature of the Internet and know the "address" of the remote computer. Each computer serving as an Internet host has such an address, expressed as a string of numbers, of letters, or both. For example, the telnet address for the NSF Science and Technology Information System is "stis.nsf.gov" or "128.150.195.40." It is possible to telnet to this system and use it interactively rather than send it E-mail requests for information.

Many computers allow public access and are provided as a free service, but others require a password and are fee-based services. Literally thousands of computers are publicly accessible at no charge. Library catalogues (known as Online Public Access Catalogues, or OPACs) have become ubiquitous on the Internet. For example, you may telnet (31.1.0.1) to the University of California's MELVYL catalogue, which contains bibliographical records describing over 11 million monographs (books, maps, films, musical scores, and sound recordings) and over 1 million periodicals (newspapers, journals, proceedings, magazines, and so on) contained in the holdings of the nine University of California campus libraries, the California State Library, and affiliated libraries. Harvard University's HOLLIS catalogue (128.103.60.31) is accessible over the Internet, as is Michigan State University's catalogue (MAGIC.LIB.MUS.EDU), which contains over 1.3 million bibliographical records. Data Research Associates has made almost 4 million records from the Library of Congress available to researchers via the Internet (192.65.218.43). Library catalogues in other countries, such as Australia, Mexico, and the United Kingdom, are accessible over the Internet.

In addition to accessing library catalogues, telnet can be used to connect with Campus-Wide Information Systems (CWIS) at Princeton (pucc.princeton.edu), Columbia (cal.cc.columbia. edu), Cornell (cuinfo.cornell.edu), and the University of New Mexico (bootes.unm.edu), to name but a few, which provide a variety of campus-specific information resources.

Telnet can also be used to access information services such as NASA Spacelink (spacelink.msfc.nasa.gov) at the Marshall Space Flight Center in Alabama, which provides materials for K–12 teachers concerning NASA space flights, and Oceanic: The Ocean Information Center (128.175.24.1) at the University of Delaware, which provides access to information about current marine research around the world, datasets of oceanic research observations, schedules of research cruises, and an electronic directory of marine studies professionals.

Supercomputer access is available over the Internet as well. For example, the San Diego Supercomputer Center (SDSC) offers access to supercomputer time twenty-four hours a day, seven days a week, to scientists and researchers across the country. Most of the time is allocated at no charge to researchers, but time on the various computer systems available is allocated on the basis of peer review by the SDSC Allocation Committee. High school students working with their teachers and university computer scientists have made use of supercomputers in their studies, accessing the machines over the Internet.

Access via telnet to commercial data bases, including bibliographical and full-text data bases, is available over the

Internet—but for a price. Such systems generally require a sub-scription fee and then charge by connect time, by the number of searches conducted, or by a combination of these. Maxwell Online of McLean, Virginia, for example, provides Internet access to three data bases—ORBIT Search Service, BRS Search Service, and BRS Colleague—that contain scientific, medical, and technical information. InfoEd of Albany, New York, pro-vides Internet access to the Sponsored Programs Information Network (SPIN), which is a data base of funding sources and grants programs in all academic fields.

MERIT, which manages NSFNET, offers a single In-ternet address from which many commercial information ser-vices may be reached that are not directly accessible on the In-ternet. By connecting to hermes.merit.edu, it is possible to access over forty commercial services, including CompuServe, Peace-net, and WestLaw. (NSFNET is the National Science Founda-tion–funded high-speed network that provides the "backbone" of the Internet, interconnecting regional computer networks in the United States.)

Telnet also allows one to access interactive computer con-ferencing software hosted on computers at sites remote from the user. Such computer conferencing software, unlike listserv soft-ware, allows the user a great deal of control over how informa-tion is managed. Using such software, anyone can typically see how many messages are contained within any given topic; se-lect only specific messages to read; search through messages for key words, phrases, or authors' names; sort messages accord-ing to date or topic; and so forth.

These features can cut down on the amount of time users spend reading unrelated or trivial messages, can help them track the various "strands" of a discussion, can help them quickly find specific information within a conference, and can help them review previous messages. However, interactive computer con-ferencing software generally is more difficult to use than E-mail, requiring some training and experience to master, and users must be able to use telnet to reach the host computer on which the software resides.

Such computer conferences exist for a multitude of reasons, some professional and some more frivolous. Many such conferences are created for a specific purpose and are relatively short lived; for example, a discussion of pending national legislation of concern to academicians in a specific discipline may be created. Others, of a more general nature, may exist for months or years, such as a discussion of the teaching of mathematics to undergraduates.

Telnet, the second Internet feature I have described, allows users to connect to remote computers on the Internet and use them interactively. With telnet, users can make use of powerful computer resources, enormous collections of information, and computer conferences worldwide—all from within their office using a desktop computer. Because of space limitations, I've listed only a few of the resources of interest for professional educators. For example, I have not discussed Dartmouth's DANTE Project and the University of Virginia's Electronic Text Center—and a thousand other opportunities to access remote computers and use information resources on the Internet.

The nature of my work has changed because of telnet. I used to search by hand through the card catalogue at my campus library; now I electronically browse through catalogues at the greatest research universities in the world. I used to fill out an interlibrary loan request and wait weeks to receive an article; now I can frequently retrieve the full text of articles I need over the Internet. I used to line up with other faculty to make use of a single PC running a statistical package in the basement of our library; now I electronically access much more powerful packages on remote computers and run my analyses. Telnet has empowered me in ways unimaginable a few short years ago and still unimaginable to many of my colleagues.

Anonymous File Transfer Protocol

Many of the computers accessible via the Internet store archives of information as electronic "files." These files may contain text, graphics, or software. To make use of the information, visual images, or software contained in these files, it is necessary to make a copy of them from the remote computer to the local computer being used. The Internet provides a feature to accomplish the transfer of such files from one computer to another. This feature is anonymous file transfer protocol, referred to by the initials ftp.

When connecting to a remote computer—whether by telnet or ftp—it is usually necessary to provide a user identification code known as a *userid* (pronounced "user I-D"). Most computers allowing public access on the Internet via telnet provide instructions about how to access the system on the first screen that is displayed. The userid may be "guest," "new," "public," or some other logical word. Anonymous ftp is so called because one uses "anonymous" as the userid when accessing remote computers to use file transfer protocol.

Ftp requires that users know the Internet address of the computer storing the files that are to be copied, the same way users must know the address of each computer to which they wish to telnet. Once the remote computer is accessed, a directory listing all of the files available can be displayed, the appropriate file can be identified, and then the file can be copied to the user's computer using ftp commands.

There are hundreds of thousands, if not millions, of files of interest to faculty from various disciplines available via ftp on the Internet. Those teaching courses about American history, law, current events, and related subjects may be interested in using ftp to retrieve files containing U.S. Supreme Court opinions from an archive provided by Project Hermes at Case Western Reserve University (ftp.cwru.edu). The court's opinions—including summaries and concurring and dissenting opinions—are made available immediately after they are issued. Musicians and musicologists may want to use ftp to access the archive of song lyrics and discographies of classical and popular artists being collected at the University of Wisconsin (vacs.uwp.edu). More than 1,000 songs and albums are available. Faculty in engineering and the sciences may be interested in the collection of NASA image files and image-viewing software available via ftp from the Ames NASA file server (ames.arc.nasa.gov). This collection includes images from space missions such as Voyager, as well as views of the space shuttle. In addition, those teaching in disciplines that require an understanding of climatic change may be interested in accessing satellite weather photographs, many of them posted within thirty minutes or less of being transmitted, such as those available from Australia (marlin.jcu.edu.au), Europe (cumulus.met.ed.ac.uk), or the United States (uriacc.uri.edu).

To summarize, anonymous ftp allows Internet users to access and make copies of files of text, images, and software electronically archived on computers across the world. While the quantity of information currently available over the Internet is impressive, the rate at which new resources are being added is equally so. Daily, thousands of new resources for teaching, learning, and research are being made available by faculty and researchers to their peers via anonymous ftp over the Internet.

Barriers to Use

After reading this far, a question that may come to mind is "If the Internet is so rich and varied in resources, why don't more academics make use of it?" In my experience, the most important barriers are lack of access, lack of training, difficulty of use, and the lack of centralized services.

To make use of the Internet, access must be available. Many postsecondary institutions, especially smaller institutions, do not have an Internet connection. And even when an Internet connection exists at a college or university, this fact may not be widely known among faculty from disciplines outside of computer science. Furthermore, faculty members often do not have a desktop computer in their offices, let alone one equipped with a modem or connected to a LAN from which to access the Internet.

For faculty who have access to the Internet and wish to learn to use it, there is a paucity of suitable teachers, instructional materials, and educational opportunities. In my judgment, the most effective instruction is from other faculty members who are skilled in the use of the Internet and who understand the teaching, learning, and research needs of the learner. Currently, most instruction on campuses is conducted by technicians and student assistants with little understanding of the particular needs of faculty.

There is a critical need for instructional materials focused on the uses of the Internet for specific disciplines. Instructional materials should include discipline-specific examples of resources available on the Internet that can be used within a faculty member's body of skills, knowledge, and practice. Most of the instructional materials prepared for classes about the Internet are generic, focusing on the technology, and lack examples and lists of resources that would be useful to faculty in a particular discipline.

Even given a knowledgeable faculty member from one's own discipline as a mentor and excellent instructional materials that include discipline-specific examples and resources, learning how to use the Internet can be confusing and difficult. As I noted earlier in this chapter, the Internet is used in over 125 countries with an estimated five to ten million users and several hundred thousand host computers sharing a common way of transmitting information, the Internet protocol (IP). As I also noted, the responsibility for, and control of, hardware, software, and information resources is distributed among the participating institutions and agencies. While this arrangement (some call it freedom; others call it anarchy) has led to exciting and innovative developments both in technology and applications, it has also led to a bewildering array of software interfaces (a software interface is what you see on the computer screen and what you do to use the software).

There is no agreed-upon set of standards for how to access the information stored by any given computer, or even for how the information should be stored. It's like trying to drive a car with the pedals and gear shift in different positions, or one in which accelerating, stopping, and shifting gears are done with devices other than pedals and a lever. And every time you change vehicles, you need to learn a new procedure to drive. It is not enough to learn how to use one's own local host computer's software on the Internet; one must also become proficient with how to use the software resident on other hosts one wishes to access and use. This may require learning how to use dozens, if not hundreds, of interfaces.

Related to this barrier is the lack of a centralized set of services to assist Internet users. Imagine moving to a new city and having a telephone installed in your home or office, but being told there are no information operators or telephone directories. How would you make use of the telephone? Imagine this telephone system without access to repair personnel knowledgeable enough to help solve your problems no matter where on the telephone network they are occurring. Where would you turn to for help? Such is the state of the Internet at the moment, a multimillion-dollar worldwide telecommunications network connecting millions of people and hundreds of thousands of expensive computers but without the provision of basic centralized services. One cannot yet call "information" to search for another's E-mail address, browse through an electronic "yellow pages" to locate communications and information resources, or call 911 for assistance, although these needs are currently being addressed with technology that is under development.

Until truly comprehensive centralized services are provided, making use of the Internet will continue to require a pioneering spirit and a good deal of patience. At the moment, using the Internet is fundamentally a trial-and-error process, although the National Science Foundation has taken the lead in funding projects to establish network information services. In my experience, there are many Internet users who are eager to assist novices as well as many computer conferences devoted to teaching individuals how to navigate through this electronic community. Also, once users are able to communicate over the Internet, their mentors need not be in close proximity to provide tutoring and assistance.

The barriers presented by the multiplicity of software interfaces on the Internet and the decentralization of information services are being addressed by the development of "metasearch" software such as Gopher, WAIS, and Archie. With a simple software interface, these tools allow for the automatic inspection of multiple file servers at remote locations on the Internet from a single desktop computer, thereby making it easier for the nontechnical user to find relevant information. Using one of these metasearch tools, it is possible to issue a single set of commands that will result in an automated search of hundreds of information archives and deliver to the user's computer a list of pertinent items and their locations. These tools can greatly simplify the task of using the Internet to locate and retrieve information.

The Future

The National Research and Education Network (NREN) represents the next step toward what Michael Roberts, EDUCOM's vice president for networking, has called the "National Information Infrastructure (NII)" (Roberts, 1991, p. 11). To revisit my aviation metaphor, the NREN, when it is completed, will be the Concorde of WANs, and someday in the next century the NII will be the space shuttle of WANs.

In terms of sheer speed, the NREN is projected to transmit information 100 times faster than the Internet. Currently, the Internet's "backbone," NSFNET, uses "T-3" technology capable of transmitting at sixty-seven million words a minute (the equivalent of sending an entire encyclopedia coast to coast in sixty seconds). "Broadband network architecture," making use of fiber optics, is currently under development for the NREN that will allow for the same transmission in six-tenths of a second, at gigabit speeds. "Terabit" technologies (another hundredfold speed increase) are on the drawing board.

But the real excitement is not in the development of the technology but rather in the development of the applications the technology is helping to stimulate. For example, at the speeds currently available over the Internet, it is ponderously slow and difficult to transmit video images, requiring sluggish viewing rates and compression routines that degrade the image quality. The speeds at which the NREN will operate will allow the transmission of full-motion video. This will open the door for multimedia applications to be transmitted from remote locations to the classroom.

Faculty and students will be able to access and use instructional materials and information resources that include audio, full-motion video, computer software, single images, computer graphics, and formatted textual materials — not just the unformatted text materials that make up the bulk of information currently available over the Internet. Virtual reality simulations, in which one will be able to swivel one's head to observe a three-dimensional scene from different perspectives and *feel* and *manipulate* components of a scene by means of electronically controlled gloves, will be accessible over the NREN. Newspapers, journals, and textbooks that can be customized by the instructor and students of a course are being developed and will be delivered over the NREN. How we interact with our students, how we teach, how we learn, how we attend meetings, how we conduct research, and more will be influenced by such technological advances.

What I have been describing — the NREN and applications like networkable multimedia, virtual reality, and personalized publications — are all under development as I write. In a sense, although not yet widely available, they represent the present, not the future. As for the more distant future and the development of a true National Information Infrastructure, one can only speculate. Michael Roberts of MIT has written, "The vision I have is of an information infrastructure that would make it easy for computers in every home, office, school, and factory to interconnect . . . creating a new kind of free market for information services" (Dertouzos, 1991, p. 29). How we will use this market and what the implications are for instruction is not yet clear.

A few visionaries, such as John Kountz of Library Services at the California State University Chancellor's Office, are already foreseeing a time when "the individual library becomes a service agency within a community that makes available useful intellectual materials to that community. In these terms, a building full of books is questionable . . . paper is going to be replaced with electronic media" (Kountz, 1992, pp. 39–40). Kountz has also made a strong argument that the "annual operating costs for traditional libraries can be shown to be greater than the cost of distributing a portable computer and related sources of electronic information to each library user in the academic environment" (Kountz, 1992, p. 39).

In my informal discussions with Kountz, he has described his vision of a time when each student will receive a Personal Electronic Learning Kit (PERK) and syllabuses, class schedules, and reading materials stored electronically on computer "flash cards" when enrolling in courses. In addition to the PERK and flash cards, each student would receive an account to access NREN (or its successor) for electronic communications, information retrieval, and research. These students would interact with their instructors and other students, view videos, search data bases, and use computer simulations via wide area computer networks.

With the advent of the microcomputer a little over a decade ago, we were debating the role of computers in the classroom, but now advances in technology are making it possible to debate the role of the classroom in education.

Conclusion

The Internet is an important source of communications and information resources, one that provides powerful new electronic tools for teaching, learning, and research to academics in all disciplines. My intent in writing this chapter is to reach out to faculty at postsecondary institutions who have not heard of or know little about the Internet, and to inform them of the significant opportunities it offers to improve and extend professional capabilities. I have tried to convey enough information about the Internet so that they might ask intelligent questions within their campus community as the first step to becoming a member of the phenomenal global community of scholars engendered by the Internet.

I have also tried to convey some of my personal enthusiasm for the Internet and for the planned National Research and Education Network (NREN). I trust that by explaining how my use of the Internet has altered my job, improving my ability to perform it, I will have motivated at least a few faculty and other readers to take those first steps to overcome the difficulties along the path to accessing and using the Internet. If so inspired, I believe they will find the journey to be worthwhile. I look forward to "seeing" you on the Internet.

Appendix: Resources

Directory of Electronic Journals, Newsletters and Academic Discussion Lists
Association of Research Libraries
Office of Scientific and Academic Publishing
1527 New Hampshire Avenue, NW
Washington, DC 20036

Directory of Periodicals Online: News, Law, & Business
Info Globe
444 Front Street West
Toronto, Ontario M5V 2S9
Canada

Internet-Accessible Library Catalogs and Databases
University of New Mexico
CIRT
Attn: Dr. Art St. George
2701 Campus Boulevard, NE
Albuquerque, NM 87131
Send E-mail requests to "stgeorge@bootes.unm.edu"

Internet Society News
1895 Preston White Drive, Suite 100
Reston, VA 22091

Internet World
Meckler Corporation
11 Ferry Lane West
Westport, CT 06880

New User's Guide to Useful and Unique Resources on the Internet
NYSERNet, Inc.
111 College Place
Syracuse, NY 13244-4100

NorthWestNet's User Services Internet Resource Guide
15400 SE 30th Place, Suite 202
Bellevue, WA 98007

References

Cerf, V. G. "Networks." *Scientific American,* 1991, *265,* 42–51.

Dertouzos, M. "Building the Information Marketplace." *Technology Review,* 1991, *94,* 29–40.

Hart, M. S. (ed.). *Project Gutenberg Newsletter* (electronic journal, for information contact hart@vmd.cso.uiuc.edu), August 1992.

Kountz, J. "Tomorrow's Libraries: More than a Modular Telephone Jack; Less than a Complete Revolution." *Library Hi Tech,* 1992, *10,* 39–50.

Roberts, M. M. "Positioning the National Research and Education Network." *EDUCOM Review,* 1991, *26,* 11–13.

Chapter 12

Enhancing Learning with Interactive Video

Penelope Semrau, Barbara A. Boyer

Higher education seeks to motivate students to develop their critical thinking skills and to prepare them for life and work in the twenty-first century. One technique for increasing motivation and learning in the classroom is to use interactive video. With this technology, students can more actively explore ideas, develop critical thinking skills, and acquire awareness of cultural and gender diversity.

All of the chapters in this section suggest ways in which new technologies can be used in college classrooms to save time, make students active learners, and increase the amount and type of information that is available. Interactive video technology has the additional benefit of helping to increase students' understanding of their own and other cultures. "Cultural literacy" is the ability to critique one's own cultural assumptions as well as the cultural values, attitudes, and beliefs of others. Interactive video can enhance cultural literacy skills by requiring students to describe, analyze, interpret, and evaluate ideas and cultural assumptions embedded in visual imagery (Boyer and Semrau, 1991–92). As described in Chapters Seven through Ten, the development of cultural understanding in students is a significant educational goal. This goal can be facilitated by interactive video.

How Technology Is Used in the Classroom

The intelligent use of interactive video can help educators realize many of their goals. In this section, we will focus on ways to enhance our students' skills in cultural literacy, critical thinking, and cooperative learning by designing learning experiences around interactive video.

Cultural Literacy

Bowers (1988) identified computers as major transmitters of culture and not simply as neutral storage and retrieval devices. Considering the power that technology has had in changing American culture, we were surprised to find a void in the research examining the effect of technology on sociocultural issues. Although a number of studies have investigated female attitudes toward computers (Fetler, 1985; Johnson and Swoope, 1987; Wilder, Mackie, and Cooper, 1985) and the cultural stereotyping of computer use by various ethnic groups (Demetrulias and Rosenthal, 1985; Faflick, 1985; Lepper, 1985), there has been virtually no research examining technology — specifically, interactive video — for transmitting cultural messages or biases. Additionally, few curricular materials are available in which interactive video is used to teach critical thinking in conjunction with cultural literacy.

   The nature of the multicultural classroom today necessitates that students be culturally literate — that is, critically aware of and sensitive to their own culture and the cultures of others (Boyer, 1987). Unfortunately, cultural literacy is not a concept that has been widely promoted at the college level. Nadaner (1983) found that educators, in general, were ill prepared to understand people whose worldviews were different from their own. Nadaner exposed some of the major problems of education, noting how it has fostered gender inequities and encouraged stereotypes of cultures. The 1992 report by the American Association of University Women (AAUW) Educational Foundation reinforced Nadaner's analysis: "Curriculum delivers the central messages of education. It can strengthen or decrease student motivation for engagement, effort, growth, and development through the images it gives to students about themselves and the world. When the curriculum does not reflect the diversity of students' lives and cultures, it delivers an incomplete message" (p. 5).

In our research (Boyer and Semrau, 1991–92), we discovered that most instructional software contained explicit biases in the visual representation of females and of such ethnic groups as African Americans, Latinos, and Asians. In some instances, the software did not include these groups at all. Studies by Ragsdale (1988) and Brownell and McConnaughy (1990) found a majority of the educational software products to be directed and marketed directly to the male user. An investigation conducted by Digranes and Digranes (1989) found that educational software designed for diverse cultural groups is practically nonexistent. The AAUW Educational Foundation confirmed the fact that education in general continually ignores the contributions and experiences of women and girls: "Girls continue to be left out of the debate [in education] despite the fact that for more than two decades researchers have identified gender bias as a major problem at all levels of schooling" (1992, p. 3). Because of these deficiencies, there is an even greater need to use technology for cultural understanding and gender equality to counter the current stereotyping inherent in the technology.

Critical Thinking

Research investigating the use of instructional software for developing critical thinking skills has focused on the ways in which curricular materials could be developed to teach critical thinking. For example, Hunter (1985) who worked with data bases, delineated various student objectives for teaching critical thinking, including discovering commonalities and differences among groups of things, analyzing relationships, looking for trends, organizing and sharing information, and arranging information in more useful ways. Along similar lines, Pon (1984) noted that the way in which students use a data base determines the level of intellectual skill involved. Searching within a data base is a lower-level skill, while interpretation, seeking trends, and evaluation of the data involve higher-level cognitive skills. Thus, a point made in Chapters Two and Six is confirmed here — it's what the students are asked to do with the material that determines the type of thinking in which they engage. Thoughtfully designed interactive video makes demands on users that require critical thinking skills.

Cooperative Learning

Traditional work with computers has been perceived as an independent learning experience, with one student working at one computer. Recently, educators have become interested in using cooperative learning strategies with computer-based instruction. As defined in Chapter Five, cooperative learning involves small teams of students collaborating and pursuing common goals. Studies indicate that cooperative learning teams working with computers show an increase in achievement over those students engaged in competitive work or individualized learning involving computers (Male, 1988).

Hunt (1992), a proponent of computer-based cooperative learning, has criticized the traditional narrow views of students using computers: "Today, with the advent of more powerful machines and far better software, computers are being used for a wider range of activities. . . . However, the most common use of computers in education remains focused on individual students (or pairs of students taking turns) using software which drills on basic skills. This practice lessens interaction among students and between students and teachers and does little to promote the development of higher order thinking skills" (p. 456).

There is also evidence that competition in the classroom may not help to enhance learning. Female students, for example, have demonstrated higher achievement with computers when in a cooperative setting (Male, 1988). The AAUW Educational Foundation Report stressed the importance of cooperative learning for students: "Teaching methods that foster competition are still standard, although a considerable body of research has demonstrated that girls and many boys as well learn better when they undertake projects and activities cooperatively rather than competitively" (1992, p. 2).

Incorporating Interactive
Video into the Curriculum

In the following section we provide three pedagogical examples for incorporating interactive video in the classroom. In each example, the following learning objectives are stressed: (1) thinking critically, (2) developing cultural literacy, and (3) using cooperative learning strategies in the classroom. These three themes are repeated throughout this volume, and interested readers are referred to earlier sections in which these three goals are defined and discussed more fully.

After reviewing videodiscs in art and science, such as the National Gallery of Art videodisc and Vincent Van Gogh Revisited (both by the Voyager Company) and Bio Sci II (by Videodiscovery), we developed materials designed to achieve the three educational objectives we've identified.

Getting Started

Based on our experiences using interactive video at the college level, we offer several suggestions for professors who would like to incorporate this technology into their classrooms. Integrating interactive video into a classroom learning experience requires the use of a Pioneer LD-V2400 or LD-V4200 or Sony MDP-1450 videodisc player, a Sony Trinitron color monitor, and, if desired, a handheld remote control or barcode reader. Of course, other brands are available and the hardware is changing rapidly, so prospective users should shop around.

Greater control can be gained by using a supplementary software product, such as the Vincent van Gogh Revisited Videodisc Companion software for use on the Macintosh IIsi (Mac). Videodisc Companion gives the user access to the images contained on the Vincent van Gogh Revisited videodisc in a manner similar to accessing information from a data base. Students can select images from the videodisc searching for particular periods in art history, themes, art techniques, or influences. Once the software has found all the artworks matching the desired categories, the student may simply click through the individual images displayed on the color video monitor. Videodisc images displayed on the monitor are synchronized to the software screens on the Mac, which are called "cards." The cards provide additional content information related to the videodisc images. For instance, a card may display a map of Paris showing where van Gogh lived while the video monitor plays a full-motion video of those Paris streets. This synchronizing of audio, video, and text makes learning and discovering very exciting for students. Cards can also display text describing a work of art, van Gogh's artistic influences (such as Millet's work), or excerpts from his letters to his brother, Theo. Students have the ability to summon such data as the title of the work, date, period, theme, medium, museum where it is exhibited, museum identification number, and keywords for obtaining additional information. Figure 12.1 depicts a card from the Vincent van Gogh Revisited Videodisc Companion displaying some of the categories mentioned here.

With Videodisc Companion, students can selectively view specific stills from the videodisc, such as all nineteenth-century paintings and sculptures with images of females. Such interactive video capabilities enhance research and promote discovery learning. Full-motion video segments complete with audio can also be selected. A unique feature in most of the supplementary software accompanying videodiscs is allowing students to create their own customized multimedia shows of selected stills and full-motion video segments from the videodisc. These multimedia shows can be saved for playback at a later date. Individual teams of students can arrange the order of showing as well as delete and add selected images. In addition, they can use the software to overlay text on images displayed on the video monitor, such as for displaying titles, definitions, and keywords.

Another positive feature of videodiscs is the ability to show high-quality images. This is because the resolution of a videodisc is higher than that of a videotape. Also, the color of the images on a videodisc will not fade or show deterioration over

Figure 12.1. Category Descriptions
from a Card Displayed on the Macintosh's Screen.

vincent catalog

Head of an Old Peasant Woman

☑ Memo

Date   February 1885
Period   Dutch
             Nuenen
Theme   Portrait

Medium Oil on canvas, 37.5 x 28 cm.

In   Rijksmuseum Kröller-Müller, Otterlo,
               The Netherlands
I.D.   F74, H83, JH648
               Letters: 394, 395

More   Cap, head, peasant
Keywords

From December 1884 through March of
1885 Vincent was engaged in painting
peasant heads "which come straight out
of a cottage with a moss-covered
thatched roof."

In a letter to Theo, Vincent described the
type of models he sought during this
period: "rough, flat faces with low
foreheads and thick lips, not sharp, but
full and Millet-like and with those very
same clothes."

SLIDE/VIDEO LIST	FIND:	Period	Theme	Date	Type In	NOTES • INDEXES
🏠 ◇	Search Criteria:	Millet			Find Next	BROWSE ← →

Source: From the Vincent van Gogh Revisited Videodisc Companion software. Used by permission of the Voyager Company, Inc., Santa Monica, Calif.

the years as do slides and videotapes. And unlike with a traditional slide show, one need not be concerned about slides being shown upside down, getting warped, or stuck in the slide projector.

Cooperative Learning with Interactive Video

The pedagogical examples that we have developed for working with interactive video stress the importance of critical thinking as well as students' learning about their own culture and the cultures of other people. An excellent way to encourage students to get to know each others' culture is to provide opportunities for them to work in cooperative learning groups.

One way to use interactive video is to divide the class into cooperative learning teams. The number of students on each team will depend on class size, availability of equipment, and other variables that are beyond the professor's control. Whenever group work is required, instructors should help students reflect on the social skills they need in order to work together as a team. Cooperative learning teams work well if each team has specific objectives and each team member has a particular role and responsibility. For example, each student can be given a specific responsibility, such as group facilitator in discussions and research, recorder, class reporter, software manager, or librarian/media organizer. Then, each team can be assigned to investigate a specific period in Vincent van Gogh's life, focusing on the influences, themes, culture, and people who lived during that time. Identification of the culture and people of van Gogh's time can then be used to determine differences between or similarities to today's culture and people. Learning experiences with interactive video should stress the excitement of searching for and discovering new material, ideas, and information.

Example One:
The National Gallery of Art Videodisc

Classroom materials we developed for the National Gallery of Art videodisc take a critical issues approach to examining works of art. Students critique changing sociocultural values depicted in paintings. In particular, they focus on how women were depicted. This task allows for an interdisciplinary learning experience that includes art, history, and sociology. Transitions in art styles and social attitudes can be compared and discussed by the various cooperative learning teams. The major objective is to develop skills in cultural literacy using critical thinking.

Objectives to be accomplished by having the cooperative learning teams interact with the National Gallery of Art videodisc include (1) classify paintings by styles and periods in art history; (2) identify the specific roles of women depicted in artworks by examining the visual elements and symbols in the paintings and sculptures; (3) interpret and contrast various artists' depictions of women in the past with images of women in contemporary art and the roles of women in today's culture; (4) create a multimedia presentation on a related sociocultural issue, such as how men's and women 's roles differ in different cultures, or how people's roles are determined by economic status.

Each cooperative team selected a specific period and culture in art history, such as the sixteenth-century French period. Then they began to collect information about the roles of women during that time. Figure 12.2 illustrates how these descriptors were entered into the Videodisc Companion software. Once entered, the software program searched the National Gallery of Art videodisc, selecting images matching the descriptors. Students then clicked through the selected images.

**Figure 12.2. Entering Keywords into the
National Gallery of Art Videodisc Companion Software.**

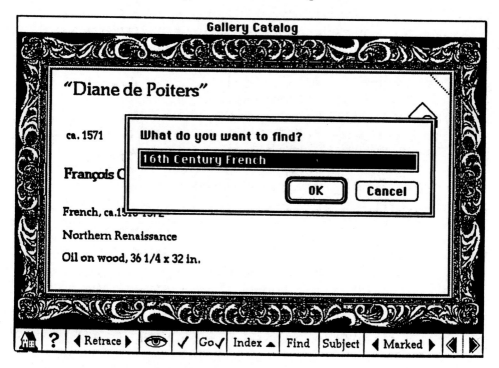

Source: From the National Gallery of Art Videodisc Companion software. Used by permission of the Voyager Company, Inc., Santa Monica, Calif.

Teams then compare this information to information they have collected about their own culture and the artwork currently being produced. As can be seen through this example, exploring is a significant way for students to work with interactive video. However, even though much can be gained through spontaneity, discovery, and nonlinear approaches to learning, guidelines are needed for structuring the students' research so that they will get the most out of the videodisc. For instance, each team is given a checklist of categories for examining the paintings in their research area, such as the artist, cultural group, title, date, style, theme, compositional properties, symbols, expressive properties, and cultural values and attitudes for that time period. Students are then asked to discuss and write about comparisons to their own particular culture and contemporary period. For each category, specific questions are to be answered. For example, questions relating to "expressive properties" include: What particular mood or feeling do you get from the painting? How do your feelings about the painting relate to the values or attitudes portrayed by the artist and the culture that he or she lived in? Are the artist's values or attitudes different from or similar to yours?

Library research, including art history and social science books and journals, is necessary for incorporating a more in-depth knowledge base for each team's subject area. The team's findings from the videodisc and the library research can then be presented to the whole class as a creative multimedia show. Critical dialogue by the class may revolve around the similarities and differences between the various styles and cultural beliefs in the artworks, as presented by the various teams in their multimedia shows.

Example Two:
Vincent van Gogh Revisited Videodisc

In this second example, we integrated critical thinking skills, art criticism, and literature related to the students' own feelings and cultural attitudes. For example, because of the capabilities of interactive video, students could observe the relationship between van Gogh's paintings and his writings to his brother, Theo, in which he discussed his paintings. One area that can be focused on is van Gogh's expressive use of color and how the culture of his time influenced his perceptions of color. Other themes can be developed around his portraits of people, his self-portraits, or his feelings toward nature.

Objectives for students using the Vincent van Gogh Revisited videodisc included (1) analyzing other artists' works and explaining how these artworks influenced van Gogh's paintings and his use of color; (2) critiquing the expressive qualities in van Gogh's writing; (3) demonstrating a relationship between his writing and the expressive style in his painting; (4) identifying and analyzing a particular color scheme he used; (5) comparing van Gogh's use of color with how other cultures use color; (6) discussing how students' own cultural attitudes toward color are similar to or different from van Gogh's; and (7) writing about their own feelings in relation to van Gogh's paintings.

Each cooperative learning team can be assigned a specific period in van Gogh's life to research, focusing on cultural influences, colors emphasized, and subject matter. Providing teams with worksheets and guidelines reflecting the intent of the learning objectives keeps the students on task and focused.

The content in the Vincent van Gogh Revisited videodisc and ancillary Videodisc Companion is rich. The software cards contain an abundance of text material. Figure 12.3 illustrates a card from the Videodisc Companion.

One audio track from the videodisc contains narration by Leonard Nimoy, while the other plays excerpts read from van Gogh's letters. Students can complement this material with library research. They may also refer to other artists who have written about their work, such as Picasso or O'Keefe, and examine these artists' works in relation to their written expression and cultural influences. Students can write about their feelings regarding a specific artist's work or can create a work of their own on a topic they have studied and write a short essay about it.

Example Three: The Bio Sci II Videodisc

The Bio Sci II videodisc is correlated to college biology textbooks and contains over 7,000 stills, 400 diagrams, and 25 minutes of full-motion video, including 3D computer animations.

Figure 12.3. One Card Displayed on the Macintosh Screen.

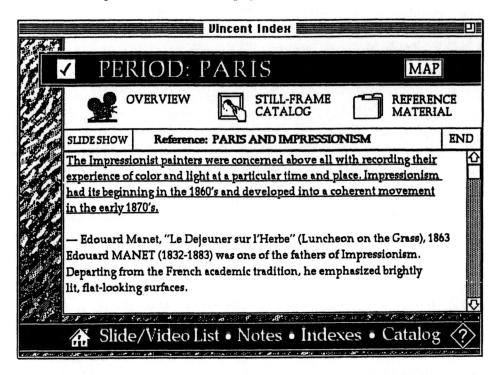

Source: From the Vincent van Gogh Revisited Videodisc Companion software. Used by permission of the Voyager Company, Inc., Santa Monica, Calif.

The videodisc is divided into twenty-two chapters that cover everything from dissecting frogs to using a microscope, from blood circulation to plant structures. Our example concentrates on the biome section of the Bio Sci II videodisc. Figure 12.4 shows a biome card from the software. Data such as rainfall, temperature, elevation, and latitude can be accessed from the videodisc with the software. Typical terrains, plants, and animals can be viewed on the video monitor for each biome. Using software, instructors and students can produce their own multimedia shows with the "Slide Show" and "Notebook" features.

Objectives accomplished by students working with the Bio Sci II videodisc include (1) identifying and describing

Figure 12.4. The Desert Biome Card.

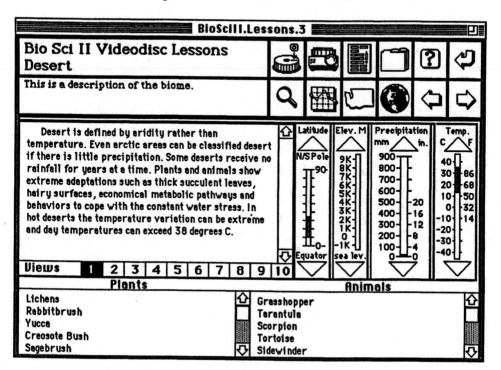

Source: From the Bio Sci II software. Reprinted by permission of Videodiscovery, Inc., Seattle, Wash.

the physical conditions of a particular biome (desert, rain forest), as well as the plants and animals that inhabit it, (2) designing a simple shelter that would allow people to live in a particular biome all year round, and (3) examining how people in the same type of biome in different parts of the world adapt to their environment through their shelter, clothing, foods, and rituals.

Cooperative teams identify and analyze the physical conditions of a particular biome and the plants and animals that inhabit it. At a higher level of thinking, students go beyond collecting and analyzing data to solving problems and creating new scenarios. After thoroughly researching the geographical conditions of their particular biome, each cooperative team can investigate the various groups of people living in that biome. They can then research a specific group's language, dress, food, shelter, music, art, and rituals. They may identify how the biome's conditions have affected the cultural behaviors and beliefs of that group.

The team can also engage in creative problem solving, such as designing a shelter appropriate for living in their particular biome using materials predominant in the biome. A major consideration of the design should be sensitivity to the environment, plants, and animal life.

Knowledge about biomes is important for people attempting to adapt to living on this earth. Students can research plays, novels, and films related to biomes and human adaptation. In addition, they can develop their own stories or plays related to people's struggles and solutions to living within certain biomes.

Benefits for Teaching and Learning

There are many advantages to using interactive video in the classroom. As an archive, a videodisc such as the Vincent van Gogh Revisited videodisc may contain 54,000 stills, thirty minutes of full-motion video, or a combination of stills and video. Each of the 54,000 frames can be accessed and displayed on the monitor within seconds. By comparison, imagine trying to find a specific slide out of 54,000. The opportunity for students to have access to artworks, maps, and videos as well as to be able to observe the relationships across categories and influences from other artists all from one videodisc is, indeed, exciting. Plus, features inherent in working with interactive video, such as the learner's opportunity to select the content, the order of the presentation of the content, and the pace of the program, help meet the needs and multiple learning styles of more students.

Students can be highly motivated to analyze, interpret, and evaluate their own cultural assumptions related to a multitude of visual images from different sources — all contained on the same videodisc. Students can use interactive video to explore and discover visual images from specific cultural groups. Then, through directed research using books, films, newspapers, and magazines, they can compare familiar images and ideas in their own culture to those of other cultures. Through class discussions and multimedia presentations, students can develop their own evaluations and individual conclusions. With ancillary software, like the Vincent van Gogh Revisited Videodisc Companion, students can interact with the videodisc and be in control of the technology instead of simply being passive viewers (Semrau and Boyer, 1991–92).

Conclusions and Recommendations

The number of students coming from various cultural backgrounds is increasing. Yet most videodiscs used in education have not accommodated the needs of the multicultural student population. The National Gallery of Art, Vincent van Gogh Revisited, and The Louvre are all videodiscs for major museum collections primarily focused on white European cultures. Therefore, we have been developing supplemental classroom materials integrating cultural literacy (Semrau and Boyer, 1991–92). The ways in which we use interactive video emphasizes the following cultural literacy tasks: (1) describing specific values, attitudes, and beliefs centering on a sociocultural topic, such as expected roles of women or environmental attitudes; (2) analyzing and contrasting attitudes of one's own culture with those discovered in investigating the interactive video program; (3) interpreting the meanings and assumptions reflected in visual images and revealed through cultural and historical changes; and (4) evaluating and expanding on new solutions related to the information in the interactive video program.

We believe that companies producing educational videodiscs need to focus more on multicultural objectives. The AAUW Educational Foundation underlined the significance of alerting the public to cultural and gender inequities: "A critical step in correcting educational inequities is identifying them publicly" (1992, p. 3). Instructors need to critically evaluate the visual images and implicit cultural and gender messages embedded in the software they are using in the classroom (Boyer and Semrau, 1990; Semrau and Lu, 1992). Nichols (1989) found that few educators examine the ways educational technology reproduces culture.

Software developers have neglected cultural and gender issues. They need encouragement to create educational software free of bias that can be used by men and women of all races, ages, and cultures.

References

American Association of University Women Educational Foundation. *How Schools Shortchange Girls — Executive Summary.* Washington, D.C.: American Association of University Women Educational Foundation, 1992.

Bowers, C. A. *The Cultural Dimensions of Educational Computing: Understanding the Nonneutrality of Technology.* New York: Teachers College Press, 1988.

Boyer, B. A. "Cultural Literacy in Art: Developing Conscious Aesthetic Choices in Art Education. In D. Blandy and K. Congdon (eds.), *Art in a Democracy.* New York: Teachers College Press, 1987.

Boyer, B. A., and Semrau, P. "Gender and Ethnic Imagery in Interactive Video." In P. Taylor (ed.), *Art with a Capital A.* Sacramento, Calif.: California Art Education Association, 1990.

Boyer, B. A., and Semrau, P. "Critiquing Cultural Assumptions in Educational Software. *Humanities Journal,* 1991–92, 26–29.

Brownell, G., and McConnaughy, K. "The Representation of Females and Minorities in Computer Clip Art." *Journal of Computer Science Education,* 1990, *5,* 7–11.

Demetrulias, D. M., and Rosenthal, N. R. "Discrimination Against Females and Minorities in Microcomputer Advertising." *Computers and the Social Sciences,* 1985, *1,* 91–95.

Digranes, J. L., and Digranes, S. H. "Adapting Computer Applications for Multicultural Teaching." *The Computing Teacher,* 1989, *17,* 20–23.

Faflick, P. "Peering into the Poverty Gap." In D. G. Johnson and J. W. Snapper (eds.), *Ethical Issues in the Use of Computers.* Belmont, Calif.: Wadsworth, 1985.

Fetler, M. "Sex Differences on the California Statewide Assessment of Computer Literacy." *Sex Roles,* 1985, *13,* 181–191.

Hunt, N. "Lesson 5: Planning for Computer-Based Cooperative Learning." In E. Murdock and P. Desberg (eds.), *Computers in the Curriculum*. Long Beach: California State University Foundation, 1992.

Hunter, B. "Problem Solving with Data Bases." *The Computing Teacher*, May 1985, pp. 20–27.

Johnson, C. S., and Swoope, K. F. "Boys' and Girls' Interest in Using Computers: Implications for the Classroom." *Arithmetic Teacher*, 1987, pp. 14–16.

Lepper, M. R. "Microcomputers in Education: Motivational and Social Issues." *American Psychologist*, 1985, *40*, 1–18.

Male, M. *Special Magic: Computers, Classroom Strategies and Exceptional Students*. Mountain View, Calif.: Mayfield, 1988.

Nadaner, D. "On Art and Social Understanding: Lessons from Alfred Schutz." *Journal of Multi-Cultural and Cross-Cultural Research in Art Education*, 1983, *1*, 15–22.

Nichols, R. G. "A Critique of Educational Technology." *AECT-RTD Newsletter*, 1989, *13*(3), 11–20.

Pon, K. "Databasing in the Elementary and Secondary Classroom." *The Computing Teacher*, Nov. 1984, pp. 28–31.

Ragsdale, R. G. *Permissible Computing in Education*. New York: Praeger, 1988.

Semrau, P., and Boyer, B. A. "Using Interactive Video to Examine Cultural Issues in Art." *The Computing Teacher*, Dec./Jan. 1991–92, *19*, 24–26.

Semrau, P., and Lu, M. "Design Issues and Trends in Creating Hypermedia." *Journal of Hypermedia and Multimedia Studies*, 1992, *2*, 8–17.

Videodiscovery. *Bio Sci II* (videodisc). Seattle, Wash.: Videodiscovery, 1983–1990.

Voyager Company. The National Gallery of Art Videodisc Companion. Santa Monica, Calif.: Voyager Company, 1987–1991.

Voyager Company. Vincent van Gogh Revisited (videodisc). Santa Monica, Calif.: Voyager Company, 1988–1991.

Wilder, G., Mackie, D., and Cooper, J. "Gender and Computers: Two Surveys of Computer-Related Activities." *Sex Roles*, 1985, *13*, 215–228.

Chapter 13

Hypermedia as an Instructional Resource

Patricia A. Backer, Joseph K. Yabu

The concept of hypertext originated in a classic article by Vannevar Bush (1945) titled "As We May Think." Bush hypothesized a future tool that would enhance human memory and thinking and allow people to access information from a computer in the same way that they access information from human memory. Over the next two decades, Bush's vision remained a theoretical concept, because of the lack of computing power. But in 1963 Engelbart at the Stanford Research Institute regenerated Bush's ideas by developing working models of hypertext systems on large-scale computers. This model evolved over the years into a system called Augment, now marketed by McDonnell-Douglas (Smith, 1988). Also, while early models of hypertext were being developed, the concept of nonsequential writing was introduced and was labeled "hypertext" by Theodore Nelson (1974). Through the 1970s and early 1980s, hypertext environments were developed on a variety of large-scale computers. In 1987 Apple introduced, bundled free with the purchase of each Macintosh computer, a hypertext environment for the personal computer called HyperCard. This development brought hypertext into mass accessibility.

Since Nelson's first coining of the word *hypertext,* the nature of hypertext has evolved. The first hypertext systems consisted solely of words that could be manipulated. Hypertext has since evolved to include still graphics, audio, video, and interactive links with other users. Because of this change, the term *hypertext* is being superseded by the term *hypermedia*. Gaines and Vickers's definition of a hypermedia system is "one that uses the most advanced technology practically available to facilitate those significant activities that result from increasing the effectiveness of interaction between people and materials relating to knowledge" (1988, p. 6). This definition, in their words, allows for various interpretations of hypermedia. Three different concepts of hypermedia are currently in use. The *strict hypermedia* definition sees it as integrating some components of information technology and modern graphic and videodisc media. The *growing hypermedia* concept is more general, seeing it as using information technology to extend all existing media. The *generalized hypermedia* definition sees it as a knowledge support system that integrates human knowledge transfer processes with information technology, instrumentation and control technology, and the full range of media. Currently, there is no consensus in the field about the best definition. As hypermedia itself changes drastically in its applications day to day, so does the definition of what it is.

In defining hypermedia, it helps to compare it with traditional text or instructional media. Traditional text is sequential — that is, a set linear sequence defines the order of pages. Similarly, in most instruction, there is a set order of content coverage. Hypermedia, however, is nonsequential. There is no single order that determines the sequence in which the information is to be read or processed. The user controls the flow of information. Hypermedia presents several options to the user, who determines which of them to follow at the time of interaction with the document.

As mentioned before, hypermedia consists of still graphics, audio, video, and interactive links with other users; these interlinked pieces of information are called *nodes*. Whatever the piece of information is, it is connected to other pieces of information (nodes) by *links*. This linkage allows the computer user to access any or all of the stored information in an appropriate sequence. Some nodes are related to many other nodes, but others serve as destinations for links and have no outgoing links. There are actually two types of links in hypermedia documents: referential and organizational. Referential links simply connect two nodes, while organizational links portray the relationship between the two nodes (Conklin, 1987; Nielsen, 1990a). In sum, hypermedia is a tool that allows nonlinear, associational linkage of information stored in a variety of media (Stevens, 1989).

Most of the early hypermedia systems were based on workstations like Sun (the hypermedia interactive learning environment, Intermedia, and its uses are discussed in detail in Landow, 1992), Symbolics, or Xerox (Notecards — see Irish and Trigg, 1989). However, the use of hypermedia was limited to those who had access to these computers. When Apple began providing the program HyperCard with the purchase of a Macintosh computer in 1987, hypermedia was thrust into common usage. Since that time, hypermedia programs have been developed for the Macintosh (SuperCard) and the IBM PC (Toolbook, Linkway, Hyperpad, Hyperties), or for both (Guide, Plus). All these programs have in common the concepts of nodes, links, and controllability by the user.

Theoretical Basis of Hypermedia Instruction

The use of hypermedia as an instructional strategy is based on its offering of easy access to large bodies of information, its ability to be an interactive environment for the user, and the fact that end users are able to modify hypermedia systems. Nelson (1974, 1981), the originator of the term *hypertext,* believed that a writer's structuring of knowledge may be arbitrary and therefore counterproductive to individual readers. Because each person's knowledge structure is unique, the ways that each would prefer to access, interact with, and interrelate knowledge are also distinct and based on individual needs. Hypermedia has the potential to meet those needs.

Hypermedia requires a macro-level instructional design to fully utilize its capabilities as an extensive and generalized information environment. The learner must be allowed to create associations and follow related pathways and ideas while remaining within a framework that guides and structures the learner's progress. This requires finding a balance between instruction and exploration (Rezabek and Ragan, 1989).

A promising approach to establishing this balance is the elaborated resources theory, which has its basis in web learning. According to the web theory, new information is integrated into the structure of knowledge by means of associations and is integrated into prior knowledge by means of a weblike structure rather than in a linear fashion (Norman, 1973). Elaboration resources theory, built on the web theory, utilizes a general-to-detailed sequence of instruction with a great amount of learner control (Reigeluth, 1979). It facilitates the design of hypermedia environments that can serve as tutor, tool, and tutee, enhancing both instruction and learner exploration (Rezabek and Ragan, 1989).

Other theories have been proposed as the basis for hypermedia instruction, a significant one being the schema theory (Jonassen, 1988). According to this theory, learning is a reorganization of *knowledge structures* (groups of ideas) in semantic memory, which is memory for facts and procedures. A schema for an object, event, or idea is composed of a set of *attributes,* which are the associations that an individual forms around an idea. In this theory, learning consists of building new structures by constructing new schemata (nodes) and interrelating them (linking) with existing schemata and with each other (Norman, 1976). Because hypermedia is designed to mimic a semantic network, it encourages the building of new structures of knowledge.

Constructivism has been used as the basis of another theory, the cognitive flexibility theory. In the constructivist view, learners don't merely incorporate new knowledge into existing knowledge structures; they actually construct new internal representations of information based on what they already know. This theory allows a way of thinking about the design of hypermedia that is "sensitive to and dependent upon the cognitive characteristics necessary for advanced knowledge in ill-structured domains" (Spiro, Feltovich, Jacobson, and Coulson, 1991, p.32).

The theory links learning in ill-defined knowledge areas (such as medicine, history, and literary interpretation) to the need for cognitive flexibility, which results from learning information in a variety of ways and contexts. Hypermedia systems are well suited to the presentation of such learning.

Issues in Hypermedia

Hypermedia offers exciting new models for teaching and learning. These models are based on the latest cognitive theories of how people learn, retrieve, and use information. Thus, hypermedia has great potential for improving teaching and learning. But there are also new problems associated with its use.

The Potential of Hypermedia

Marchionini (1988) identified three main characteristics of hypermedia systems that have great potential for the learning environment. First, hypermedia allows huge collections of information in a variety of media to be stored in a compact form and to be accessed rapidly. Second, hypermedia is an enabling rather than a directive environment, offering high levels of user control. Third, hypermedia offers the potential to alter the roles of teachers and learners and the interactions between them.

Specifically, Jonassen (1986) notes that hypertext breaks traditional sequential processing and permits text presentation to be modified by the user to meet individual needs. Because of this feature, users can break out of traditional sequential processing and modify the presentation of material to be most meaningful to them (Stanton and Stammers, 1989). The advent of hypertext allows the design of courseware without any predetermined structure, making the designer's task easier, and allows greater flexibility for learners to structure the learning environment to suit their own needs. In this way, hypertext supports nonlinear access to information and learning (Happ and Stanners, 1991).

Instructional designers traditionally developed computer-based instruction by creating learning environments that promoted individual learning of a body of information (Merrill, 1983). Hypermedia provides learners with the ability to browse through information spaces, acquiring knowledge and information on their journey (Byers, 1987). Geske (1991) has argued that the ability to access, organize, manipulate, and comprehend information may be the most important feature of hypermedia. According to Hooper (1990), director of Apple Computer's Multimedia Lab, the entire investigation of knowledge representation emphasizes the interlinking of conceptual materials, something that is a major focus of hypermedia.

Problems with Hypermedia Instruction

Jonassen (1991) described three major problems that occur with hypermedia instruction: navigation difficulty (users get lost in the document), difficulty in integrating the presented information into personal knowledge structures, and cognitive overload. In addition, a learner's interactions with hypermedia are not predictable and are less deterministic than with other modes of instruction. Other researchers (Beeman and others, 1987) have noted that the successful use of hypermedia requires nonlinear thinking, which may not be successful for all users.

Gray (1990) investigated the problem of navigation by analyzing protocols and model drawings from ten users of a hypermedia document on violent crime. She found that the problem of navigation occurs when the linear expectations of naive users are violated by the hypermedia. In addition, she found that users were persistent in attempting to work within a linear model despite its inapplicability.

Marchionini (1988) pointed out that the use of hypermedia on a widespread basis as an instructional delivery system might require teaching new reading and writing strategies. In addition, he discussed a set of instructional problems with hypermedia, including lack of authoring principles and methods and problems with managing learning in electronic environments, creating assignments and activities, and evaluating materials and learning. Locatis, Letourneau, and Banvard (1990) found that the few existing guidelines for authoring hypermedia focus on hypertext (hypermedia documents with text-only nodes); no guidelines exist for other forms of hypermedia (see also Tucker and Dempsey, 1991).

Westland (1991) examined the economic barriers to hypermedia design and found that production costs can differ depending on the hypermedia strategy used. In addition, there are other constraints to authoring. A three-year project at the University of South Alabama attempted to train faculty in its College of Education to incorporate hypermedia into their curricula (Tucker and others, 1990). Results of the program evaluation revealed that the early adopters of HyperCard had prior training and that the biggest need cited was time to practice.

Use and Instructional Strategies

Conklin (1987) divides the use of hypermedia as an instructional tool into four categories. *Browsing systems* are hypermedia documents in which the user does not collaborate with others, nor does the user add to the knowledge base. Tutorials would generally fall in this category. *Problem exploration tools* are work-related systems that enable group (or project-related) work. Examples are CASE, which is a software engineering system (Bigelow, 1988), and the Writing Environment (Smith, Weiss, and Ferguson, 1987). *Macro-literary systems* are a collection of materials linked together by the hypertext. An example is Beyond Einstein, developed in WNET's Learning Laboratory in New York (Osborn, 1990). This hypermedia system comprises approximately 200 modules of video or audio, text, simulations, and graphics structured in a thematic way. *General-purpose hypermedia* are information systems that can be tailored for individual needs. An example of this type of system is Notecards, developed at Xerox PARC (Palo Alto Research Center), which helps people write and read notes connected by links (Halasz, Moran, and Trigg, 1987).

Schools today use hypermedia most often as a presentation and reporting tool for teachers and students. Hypermedia used in this way enhances delivery of a lecture or presentation of a term paper. Hypermedia is also used as a simple index/data base tool. Students and teachers find that they can organize their information easily without all the restrictions of a typical computer data base. Last, hypermedia is also used for two types of instructional programs: commercial drill and practice exercises and self-written tutorials. Lengel and Collins (1990) categorized these instructional usages as the lowest level: the Drill Stage. They found few schools to be using the higher levels of computer usage (problem exploration and student-initiated hypermedia).

Hypermedia Applications

In this section we offer examples of hypermedia applications currently in use today. Our discussion is not exhaustive, nor does it cover all the applications available. We emphasize the use of hypermedia in education, ranging from kindergarten to on-the-job training. The applications are divided by content area.

Engineering and Technology

Technical education uses hypermedia quite extensively, because of the necessity for employees to be able to understand and apply information contained in technical manuals. Harrison and colleagues (1990) developed a technical literacy test to identify level of familiarity with or likely aptitude for work using a computer. The information yielded by such a test not only determines an individual's current computer literacy, as measured by industry standards, but also serves as a diagnostic tool for identifying further training needs. To teach the disk operating system (DOS) to adult learners with different backgrounds, Blanchard (1990) developed a hypertext computer-assisted instruction program and found that, in spite of the students' apprehension and anxieties about computer use, more passed a DOS proficiency test after eight weeks using the computer-assisted instruction method than did those using the traditional training method. Student attitudes also improved.

At the school of Engineering at Vanderbilt University, new learning environments based on a combination of artificial intelligence-based instructional methods, qualitative simulation, and intelligent hypertext are used to augment and enhance undergraduate engineering education (Peters, Bourne, and Kawamura, 1990). This combination of methodologies is termed *intelligent hypertutoring.* The goal is to provide virtual laboratory experiences for undergraduate engineering students; this approach not only offers individualized learning but also significantly reduces the cost of laboratory instruction. Another system, HyperCOSTOC, was developed by Huber, Makedon, and Maurer (1989). This advanced computer-assisted instruction system retrieves and processes, in a nonlinear fashion, structured molecules of instruction or information material networked together. HyperCOSTOC is based on hypertext concepts and includes a data base of lessons called COSTOC.

At an Alcoa plant, hypertext systems are used for troubleshooting and maintaining complex manufacturing equipment (Hill and Roehl, 1988). Alcoa's system, called EGADS (Electronics Guidance and Documentation Systems), provides utilities for building and maintaining very large documentation data bases (tens of thousands of pages) and knowledge representation mechanisms for creating a variety of "viewpoints" of the data base. These viewpoints represent strategies for helping manufacturing personnel navigate through a documentation data base to solve problems associated with equipment malfunctions and maintenance.

Hypermedia is also used as an instructional medium to teach content areas in engineering and technology. Backer and Yabu (in press) developed a self-paced hypertext tutorial on introductory concepts of manufacturing and engineering drawings for use in a required class on the product development life cycle in a manufacturing organization. Cwiakala (1990) used hypermedia to develop a user-friendly interface for a computer-assisted drafting program, to increase students' understanding and use of the drawing package. In addition, at the University of California, Berkeley, Hsi and Agogino (Agogino, 1992) developed a hypermedia application to help students link theoretical and analytical aspects of engineering and design with more practical real-world counterparts. Using a collection of Hyper-

Card stacks, students evaluate the design strategies of a human-powered vehicle design on the computer, visualize vehicle parts, and produce designs on CAD equipment.

Medical Professions

Development and use of hypermedia systems by the medical professions is expanding. Quentin-Baxter and Dewhurst (1990) described a hypermedia program that uses text, graphics, sound, and animation with associative information linking techniques to teach functional anatomy. The program includes a nonintimidating tutor to minimize computer anxieties in students. Murray (1989) described the use of a hypertext environment to facilitate teaching of introductory pharmacokinetics to sophomore medical students. This environment promises to ease the instructor's task of developing lecture material and provides a novel way for students to view the subject matter from several perspectives. The system combines a graphic windowing environment (Windows), a feature called Guide, and a custom glossary program, used to process text and graphics created with off-the-shelf programs.

An interesting application of hypermedia in medical instruction was discussed by Stensaas and Sorensen (1988) who described a neuroanatomy course being taught with a combination of lectures, videotapes, hypermedia, and videodiscs. The hypermedia application, called HyperBrain, is used by medical students at multiple stages in their neuroscience training and includes a laboratory syllabus with digitized figures, glossary, quizzes, laboratory examinations, clinical case studies, and atlases.

Other programs have been developed for prescription-based problems in pharmacy education (Cotter and Gumtow, 1991), for lab exercises in pathology (Sideli and Lefkowitch, 1988), and to teach cardiovascular imaging (Klingler, Leighton, and Andrews, 1988).

Biological Sciences

One of the first hypermedia systems to be developed was Intermedia, used to design a course on microbiology at Brown

University (Landow, 1988). Since then many other applications have been developed. For example, Hall and colleagues (1989) describe an interactive hypermedia environment used to teach cell biology to undergraduate students.

Physical Sciences

One of the most comprehensive programs developed, called Beyond Einstein, was created in 1986 in WNET's Learning Laboratory in New York (Osborn, 1990). The subject of this program was quantum physics, and it was designed as a massive knowledge base with video, audio, text, and simulations. Another hypermedia application was developed by Cole, Krull, and Sweitzer (1990) to build intuition and visualization skills in students of physics electromagnetics courses. The purpose was to use upper-division students in physics to help generate solutions and, in the process, teach those students how to write numerical code and display the results. The Diagnoser, a HyperCard tutorial construction system for physics concepts, assesses students' concepts in a given domain and gives them a course of action (Levidow, Hunt, and McKee, 1991).

Writing and Literature

Hypermedia is used extensively for instruction in writing. Nelson (1981) developed a large-scale hypermedia environment, called Xanadu, that provides on-line libraries to which people can add their own links and annotations on others' work as well as on their own. Another program is Notes (Neuwirth and others, 1987) which investigates the effects of computers in the writing process and provides tools to support the decisions writers make while acquiring and structuring knowledge from sources. Another system, referred to as Roundtable (Goodrum and Knuth, 1991), supports the following processes in a social, interactive environment: comprehension, idea generation, analysis, composition, reflection, and communication.

Yet another use of hypermedia is found in Project Jefferson, an innovative hypermedia project developed at the University of Southern California (Kinnell and Richards, 1988). It assists freshman writers in acquiring the skills necessary to create research papers on ethical issues raised by the U.S. Constitution. May (1990) developed a hypermedia program aimed at faculty who teach college-level English education courses and those who are planning a course on the use of technology in the English classroom. The program provides access not only to the text of the short story but also to concepts and patterns throughout the story.

Foreign Languages

The Army Research Institute has done extensive work in the applicability of hypermedia to foreign language instruction (Psotka and others, 1988). The programs developed the cognitive skills that underlie foreign language competence by using linguistic models and semantic networks built into hypermedia systems. A second application was developed by Paulsell (1989), who designed a HyperCard program for use in a third-year college business German class. This interactive and flexible program consists of seven HyperCard stacks, providing user-driven instruction on Germany's business environment and language. Another program is Grammateiuon (Pierce, 1990), a hypertext system developed to simplify the use of ancient language symbols in scholarly work by providing basic grammatical and lexical information about the Greek language. All of these programs allow teachers to spend more time interacting with students and also allow students to work with original texts.

Psychology

At Stanford, Dougherty (1990, 1992) developed a hypermedia application for lecture and self-paced study of perception. This program, called Contour, teaches introductory psychology students about principles of visual perception using subjective contour illusions. The program allows users to make notes to themselves and to search the subjective contour literature for relevant articles and save this information in their own text file. Another program in psychology presents and illustrates concepts in person perception and attribution theory for undergraduate students (Petty and Rosen, 1991).

Library Science

Bourne (1990), among others (such as Farmer, 1991), discussed the use of computer-assisted instruction and its improvement through the use of hypertext and hypermedia for bibliographic instruction programs in libraries. Also, Thomas (1990) introduced CatTutor, an interactive tutorial for training catalogers in the descriptive cataloging of computer files. The program consists of a tutorial that allows the novice cataloger to build bibliographic records and is linked through hypertext to key reference tools. Originally developed on the Macintosh and utilizing HyperCard, CatTutor is now exported to the DOS environment.

Statistics

Hypermedia is also used for information management. Halavin and Sommer (1990) described hypermedia as a powerful authoring tool for allowing statistics teachers to develop documents to assist students in an algorithmic (step-by-step) approach. Cognitive scientists use HyperCard software in designing software that analyzes student solutions to standard problems by inferring a student's intentions from the details of his or her solution and then offering diagnostic assistance (Dolbear, 1988). Programs such as Stat Helper for the Macintosh allow students to interact with the computer in solving a variety of problems. For instance, students can learn about regressions better through hands-on experience on personal or mainframe computers.

Computer Science

Hypermedia has been used not only to teach courses in the humanities and medicine but also to teach a survey course in computer science (Decker and Hirshfield, 1990). This course was distinctive in three ways. First, it presented a comprehensive disciplinary survey of the field. Second, it used a foundational approach by emphasizing liberal education as opposed to technical training. Last, it used a hands-on approach to learning with hypermedia.

Hypermedia and Individual Student Differences

Most of the work in hypermedia has focused on developing programs or applications. Little work has been done in the evaluation of this media as an instructional tool or on its efficacy with differing student populations. In addition, minimal research has been done on the characteristics of hypermedia instruction and how these characteristics affect learning. In one study comparing performance differences in structured and unstructured environments, Stanton and Stammers (1989) found that the ability of students to function in an unstructured learning environment depends on their individual learning styles. For example, Campagnoni and Ehrlich (1989) found that individuals with better spatial visualization skills were faster in retrieving information in a hypertext-based help system than those with poorer visualization skills. In addition, the Campagnoni and Ehrlich study highlighted another important feature of hypertext: the structure of hypertext seems to cause new strategies in learning material by browsing rather than by employing indices or predetermined menus. To compensate for differing characteristics of users, Eck (1989) designed his hypermedia document to allow users to choose how to use the tutorial. For instance, a learner who wanted to read in a linear fashion could, and a learner who wanted to skim could do that as well. Another hypermedia learning environment strategy was developed by Smith and Hahn (1989) to teach medical decision making. In their application, the environment allows total learner control until the learner demonstrates a need for guidance.

Related to the efficacy of hypermedia instruction, Higgins and Boone (1990) conducted two studies to field-test hypertext computer study guides with forty ninth-grade students (ten with learning disabilities, fifteen remedial, and fifteen regular education). Their findings indicated that the hypertext treatment was as effective as the lecture method, with posttest scores higher for the computer study group.

As noted earlier, Backer and Yabu (in press) investigated the effects of a self-paced hypertext tutorial on student learning of introductory concepts of manufacturing and engineering drawing, compared to a control group taught by the traditional lecture method. Scores on a pretest/posttest examination were analyzed. Students who used the HyperCard tutorial ($n = 31$) had significantly higher posttest scores ($p < 0.001$) when compared to students instructed by the traditional lecture method ($n = 19$). The effectiveness of hypermedia instruction over traditional methods was verified in a study by Petty and Rosen (1991), who tested sixty undergraduates on concepts in person perception and attribution theory. They found that students using HyperCard materials scored significantly better on a test than those using traditional text materials after two hours of exposure to the material. Also, the HyperCard group expressed positive reactions to the experience, whereas the text group found the instruction boring.

In a study of twenty adults, including electrical engineers, stockboys, secretaries, graduate students, and teachers, Stone and Hutson (1984) found that hypertext instruction was effective in assisting people in completing complex assembly tasks. The tutorial explained how to assemble a miniature loading cart. Task performance was better than that of subjects in previous studies employing the same task. This finding of increased performance using hypertext versus traditional text has also been verified by other researchers (Egan and others, 1989a, 1989b).

Challenges in Developing Hypermedia

Stotts and Furuta (1989) recommend that hypermedia documents be written so that different classes of readers can be allowed or denied access to various portions of the document; this would allow for more guidance for inexperienced or naive users. Nielsen (1990b), after studying the usability of various hypermedia interfaces, stated (1) that it is important to do some usability testing; (2) that to help users navigate, designers must help them understand their current location and their relation to the universe; and (3) that a backtrack facility is an important navigation feature for novice users.

Most authors agree that developing a hypermedia document for the first time is time consuming. In particular, new authors have a tendency to overdesign or include too much information. In addition, authors need to address the common problems of users: navigation, difficulty in integrating the presented information into personal knowledge structures, and cognitive overload. Although these problems are prevalent, they can be mitigated by designing the document to allow the users to know where they are in relation to the rest of the document and to reduce the amount of information that must be navigated. A key to building a hypermedia document is to find a balance between instruction and exploration. For instance, "A framework must be created to guide and structure the learner's progress, but the learner must also be allowed to create associations and follow related pathways and ideas. Hypermedia-based instruction needs to provide both structure and freedom" (Rezabek and Ragan, 1989, p. 6).

Conclusion: Future Implications

The true potential of hypermedia may not be as an information delivery vehicle. Jonassen (1989) thinks its real potential may lie in its capacity as a study aid or cognitive learning tool that fosters or facilitates a deeper or more meaningful level of information processing in learners. According to him, having students create their own hypermedia documents may provide them with the most powerful learning aid yet.

Hofmeister (1990) feels that in the future, "School will be the place where students come after they have had excellent presentations and where they will, with their teachers, investigate the meaning, implications, and relationships of their presentations. School will be the place where knowledge is integrated, synthesized, and tested instead of a place where knowledge is transmitted from those who know to those who don't" (p. 221).

However, this freedom and flexibility places new responsibility on users and learners. Unlike users of traditional computer-based instruction, "[H]ypermedia users must be mentally active while interacting with the information" (Jonassen and Grabinger, 1990, p. 7). They further point out that the way in which hypermedia works "will place more responsibility on the learner for accessing, sequencing, and deriving meaning from the information" (p. 4). As with any learning environment, it is unclear, at this point, which students are most likely to benefit from this type of instructional medium.

References

Agogino, A. "Multimedia on Campus." *Syllabus,* No. 22, Apr./May, 1992, p. 18.

Backer, P. R., and Yabu, J. K. "Hypercard Tutorial as an Instructional Strategy: A Comparative Study." *The Journal of Industrial Technology,* in press.

Beeman, W. O., and others. "Hypertext and Nonlinear Thinking." In *Proceedings of Hypertext '87.* Chapel Hill: University of North Carolina, 1987.

Bigelow, J. "Hypertext and CASE." *IEEE Software,* Mar. 1988, pp. 23–27.

Blanchard, D. D. *A Hypertext Computer-Assisted Instruction (CAI) Program: Teaching the Disk Operating System (DOS) to Community College Students.* Master's Practicum, Nova University, 1990. (ED 331 491)

Bourne, D. F. "Computer-Assisted Instruction, Learning Theory, and Hypermedia: An Associative Linkage." *Research Strategies,* 1990, *8*(4), 160–171.

Bush, V. "As We May Think." *Atlantic Monthly,* July 1945, pp. 101–108.

Byers, T. J. "Built by Association." *PC World,* Apr. 1987, pp. 245–251.

Campagnoni, F. R., and Ehrlich, K. "Information Retrieval Using a Hypertext-Based Help System. *ACM Transactions of Office Information Systems,* 1989, *7*(3), 271–291.

Cole, R., Krull, D., and Sweitzer, M. "Visual Electromagnetics Using Mathemica and HyperCard." *Antennas and Propagation Society International Symposium Digest,* 1990, *4,* 1671–1674.

Conklin, J. "Hypertext: An Introduction and Survey." *Computer,* 1987, *20*(9), 17–41.

Cotter, P. M., and Gumtow, R. H. "A Computer Program for the Management of Prescription-Based Problems." *American Journal of Pharmaceutical Education,* 1991, *55*(2), 134–138.

Cwiakala, M. "Using Hypermedia Concepts to Enhance CAD." In *Computers in Engineering 1990 — Proceedings of the ASME International Computers in Engineering Conference and Exposition.* Boston: American Society of Civil Engineers, Boston Society of Civil Engineers, 1990.

Decker, R. W., and Hirshfield, S. H. "Survey Course in Computer Science Using HyperCard." *SIGCSE Bulletin,* 1990, *22*(1), 229–235.

Dolbear, F. T. "Software for Economics Statistics Courses." Paper presented at the annual convention of the Eastern Economic Association, Boston, Mar. 10–12, 1988. (ED 309 128)

Dougherty, T. J. "Contour: A Hypermedia Environment for Teaching About Subjective Contours and Other Visual Illusions." *Behavior Research Methods, Instruments, and Computers,* 1990, *22*(2), 223–227.

Dougherty, T. J. "Multimedia on Campus." *Syllabus,* No. 22, Apr./May 1992, p. 17.

Eck, M. K. "Hypercard Tutorial That Accommodates Different Learning Styles." *ACM SIGUCCS User Services Conference XVII 1989.* New York: ACM, 1989.

Egan, D. E., and others. "Acquiring Information in Books and Superbooks." Paper presented at the annual meeting of the American Educational Research Association, San Francisco, 1989a.

Egan, D. E., and others. "Behavioral Evaluation and Analysis of a Hypertext Browser." In *Proceedings of the ACM CHI'89 Conference on Human Factors in Computing Systems.* Washington, D.C.: ACM, 1989b.

Engelbart, D. C. "A Conceptual Framework for the Augmentation of Man's Intellect." In P. W. Howerton and D. C.

Weeks (eds.), *Vista in Information Handling.* Washington, D.C.: Thompson, 1963.

Farmer, L.S.J. "Hyperlearning: Library Instruction Through HyperCard." *Journal of Youth Services in Libraries,* 1991, *4*(4), 393–395.

Gaines, B. R., and Vickers, J. N. "Design Considerations for Hypermedia Systems." *Microcomputers for Information Management,* 1988, *5*(1), 1–27.

Geske, J. "HyperCard—Another Computer Tool." *Communication: Journalism Education Today,* 1991, *24*(4), 14–17.

Goodrum, D. A., and Knuth, R. A. "Supporting Learning with Process Tools." In E. Hansen (ed.), *Collaborative Learning in Higher Education. Proceedings of the Teaching Conference.* Bloomington, Ind.: Bloomington Division of Development and Special Projects, 1991. (ED 335 984)

Gray, S. H. "Using Protocol Analyses and Drawings to Study Mental Model Construction During Hypertext Navigation." *International Journal of Human Computer Interaction,* 1990, *2*(4), 359–378.

Halasz, F. G., Moran, T. P., and Trigg, R. H. "Notecards in a Nutshell." In *Proceedings of the 1987 ACM Conference on Human Factors in Computer Systems.* Toronto, Apr. 5–9, 1987.

Halavin, J., and Sommer, C. "Using Hypertext to Develop an Algorithmic Approach to Teaching Statistics." 1990. (ED 334 195)

Hall, W., and others. "Using HyperCard and Interactive Video in Education: An Application in Cell Biology." *Educational and Training Technology International,* 1989, *26*(3), 207–214.

Happ, A. J., and Stanners, S. L. "Effects of Hypertext Cue Presentation on Knowledge Representation." In *Proceedings of the Human Factors Society* (35th annual meeting), 1991.

Harrison, C., and others. "The Technical Literacy Project: A Comparison of Computer Literacy Skills Among School Students and Employees in Industry." Paper presented to the annual conference of the British Educational Research Association, Aug. 30–Sept. 1, 1990. (ED 330 308)

Higgins, K., and Boone, R. "Hypertext Computer Study Guides and the Social Studies Achievement of Students with Learning

Disabilities, Remedial Students, and Regular Education Students." *Journal of Learning Disabilities,* 1990, *23*(9), 529–540.

Hill, C. R., and Roehl, E. A. "Hypertext System for Troubleshooting and Maintaining Complex Manufacturing Equipment." In *Computers in Engineering 1988 — Proceedings.* New York: American Society for Mechanical Engineering, 1988.

Hofmeister, J. F. "The Birth of HyperSchool." In S. Ambron and K. Hooper (eds.), *Learning with Interactive Multimedia.* Redmond, Wash.: Microsoft Press, 1990.

Hooper, K. "HyperCard: A Key to Educational Computing." In S. Ambron and K. Hooper (eds.), *Learning with Interactive Multimedia.* Redmond, Wash.: Microsoft Press, 1990.

Huber, F., Makedon, F., and Maurer, H. "HyperCOSTOC: A Comprehensive Computer-Based Teaching Support System." *Journal of Microcomputer Applications,* 1989, *12*(4), 293–317.

Irish, P. M., and Trigg, R. H. "Supporting Collaboration in Hypermedia: Issues and Experiences." In E. Barrett (ed.), *The Society of Text: Hypertext, Hypermedia, and the Social Construction of Information.* Cambridge, Mass.: MIT Press, 1989.

Jonassen, D. H. "Hypertext Principles for Text and Courseware Design." *Educational Psychologist,* 1986, *21*(4), 269–292.

Jonassen, D. H. "Designing Structured Hypertext and Structuring Access to Hypertext." *Educational Technology,* 1988, *28*(11), 13–16.

Jonassen, D. H. *Hypertext/Hypermedia.* Englewood Cliffs, N.J.: Educational Technology Publications, 1989.

Jonassen, D. H. "Hypertext as Instructional Design." *Educational Technology, Research, and Development,* 1991, *39*(1), 83–92.

Jonassen, D. H., and Grabinger, R. S. "Problems and Issues in Designing Hypertext/Hypermedia for Learning." In D. H. Jonassen and H. Mandl (eds.), *Designing Hypertext/Hypermedia for Learning.* Heidelberg: Springer-Verlag, 1990.

Kinnell, S. K., and Richards, T. "Online Interface Within a Hypertext System: Project Jefferson's Electronic Notebook." *Online,* 1988, *13*(4), 33–38.

Klingler, J. W., Leighton, R. F., and Andrews, L. T. "Using Hypermedia to Teach Cardiovascular Imaging: A Prototype

System." In *Computers in Cardiology 1988*. Piscataway, N.J.: IEEE Service Center, 1988.

Landow, G. *Hypertext in Literary Education, Criticism, and Scholarship*. Providence, R.I.: Brown University, Institute for Research in Information and Scholarship, 1988.

Landow, G. *Hypertext*. Baltimore, Md.: Johns Hopkins University Press, 1992.

Lengel, J. G., and Collins, S. "HyperCard in Education: The Potential." In S. Ambron and K. Hooper (eds.), *Learning with Interactive Multimedia*. Redmond, Wash.: Microsoft Press, 1990.

Levidow, B. B., Hunt, E., and McKee, C. "The Diagnoser: A HyperCard Tool for Building Theoretically Based Tutorials." *Behavior Research Methods, Instruments, and Computers*, 1991, *23*(2), 249–252.

Locatis, C., Letourneau, G., and Banvard, R. "Hypermedia and Instruction." *Educational Technology, Research, and Development*, *37*(4), 1990, 65–77.

Marchionini, G. "Hypermedia and Learning: Freedom and Chaos." *Educational Technology*, 1988, *28*(11), 8–12.

May, C. *The American Short Story: From Poe to O'Henry. A Hyper-Card Application*. 1990. (ED 330 315)

Merrill, M. D. "Component Display Theory." In C. M. Reigeluth (ed.), *Instructional Design Theories and Models: An Overview of Their Current Status*. Hillsdale, N.J.: Erlbaum, 1983.

Murray, R. B. "Pharmacokinetics Guide: A Hypertext Teaching Assistant." In *Proceedings of the Annual Symposium on Computer Applications in Medical Care*. Piscataway, N.J.: IEEE Service Center, 1989.

Nelson, T. *Dream Machine*. South Bend, Ind.: The Distributors, 1974.

Nelson, T. *Literary Machines*. Swarthmore, Penn.: T. Nelson, 1981.

Neuwirth, C. M., and others. *The Notes Program: A Hypertext Application for Writing from Source Texts*. Pittsburgh, Penn.: Carnegie Mellon University, Center for Educational Computing in English, 1987. (ED 308 499)

Nielsen, J. *Hypertext and Hypermedia*. New York: Academic Press, 1990a.

Nielsen, J. "Through Hypertext." *Communications of the ACM,* 1990b, *33*(3), 298–310.

Norman, D. A. "Memory, Knowledge, and Answering of Questions." In R. L. Solso (ed.), *Contemporary Issues in Cognitive Psychology: The Loyola Symposium.* Washington, D.C.: Winston, 1973.

Norman, D. A. *Studies in Learning and Self-Contained Education Systems.* Washington, D.C.: Office of Naval Research, Advanced Projects Agency, 1976. (ED 121 786)

Osborn, H. "Media Computers, Motivation, and Informal Education: Gutenberg 2000?" In S. Ambron and K. Hooper (eds.), *Learning with Interactive Multimedia.* Redmond, Wash.: Microsoft Press, 1990.

Paulsell, P. R. "A HyperCard Program for Business German." *Proceedings of the Annual Eastern Michigan University Conference on Language and Communication for World Business and the Professions,* 1989. (ED 324 932)

Peters, A., Bourne, J., and Kawamura, K. "The Use of Intelligent Hypertutoring Systems Technology for Engineering Education." *Antennas and Propagation Society International Symposium Digest,* 1990, *4,* 1681–1683.

Petty, L. C., and Rosen, E. F. "Using HyperCard to Teach Person Perception and Attribution Concepts." *Behavior Research Methods, Instruments, and Computers,* 1991, *23*(2), 247–248.

Pierce, R. H. "Hypertext: Grammateion." *Bulletin of the American Society for Information Science,* 1990, *16*(3), 23–24.

Psotka, J., and others. "Cognitive Models of Students' Language Structure: The View from Intelligent Computer-Assisted Instruction." Paper presented at the Interagency Language Roundtable Invitational Symposium on Language Aptitude, Rosslyn, Va., Sept. 14–16, 1988. (ED 308 693)

Quentin-Baxter, M., and Dewhurst, D. "A Computer-Based Atlas of a Rat Dissection." *Humane Innnovations and Alternatives in Animal Experimentation: A Notebook,* 1990, *4,* 147–150.

Reigeluth, C. M. "In Search of a Better Way to Organize Instruction: The Elaboration Theory." *Journal of Instructional Development,* 1979, *2*(3), 8–15.

Rezabek, R. H., and Ragan, T. J. "Elaborated Resources: An

Instructional Design Strategy for Hypermedia." Paper presented at the annual meeting of the Association for Educational Communications and Technology, Dallas, Tex., Feb. 1–4, 1989. (ED 316 175)

Sideli, R. V., and Lefkowitch, J. L. "Integrated Hypertext and Expert System in Pathology Laboratory." In *Proceedings of the Annual Symposium on Computer Applications in Medical Care.* Piscataway, N.J.: IEEE Service Center, 1988.

Smith, J., Weiss, S. F., and Ferguson, G. J. "A Hypertext Writing Environment and Its Cognitive Basis." In *Proceedings of Hypertext '87.* Chapel Hill: University of North Carolina, 1987.

Smith, K. E. "Hypertext — Linking to the Future." *Online,* 1988, *12,* 32–40.

Smith, W. R., and Hahn, J. S. "Hypermedia or Hyperchaos: Using HyperCard to Teach Medical Decision Making." In *Proceedings of the Annual Symposium on Computer Applications in Medical Care.* Piscataway, N.J.: IEEE Service Center, 1989.

Spiro, R. J., Feltovich, P. J., Jacobson, M. J., and Coulson, R. L. "Cognitive Flexibility, Constructivism, and Hypertext: Random Access Instruction for Advanced Knowledge Acquisition in Ill-Structured Domains." *Educational Technology,* 1991, *31*(5), 24–33.

Stanton, N. A., and Stammers, R. B. "Comparison of Structured and Unstructured Navigation Through a CBT Package." *Computers and Education,* 1989, *15*(1–3), 159–163.

Stensaas, S., and Sorensen, D. K. "'Hyperbrain' and 'Slice of Life': An Interactive HyperCard and Videodisc Core Curriculum for Neuroscience." In *Proceedings of the Annual Symposium on Computer Applications in Medical Care.* Piscataway, N.J.: IEEE Service Center, 1988.

Stevens, G. H. "Applying Hypermedia for Performance Improvement." *Performance and Instruction,* 1989, *28*(6), 42–50.

Stone, D. E., and Hutson, B. A. "Computer-Based Job Aiding: Problem Solving at Work. Ithaca, N.Y.: Cornell University Department of Education, 1984. (ED 244 613)

Stotts, P. D., and Furuta, R. "Access Control and Verification in a Petri-Net-Based Hyperdocument." In *Proceedings of the Fourth Annual Conference on Computer Assurance: Systems Integrity,*

Software Safety and Process Security. Piscataway, N.J.: IEEE Service Center, 1989.

Thomas, S. E. "CatTutor: A Hypertext Tool for Catalogers." Paper presented at the annual conference of the Society for Applied Learning Technology, Orlando, Fl., Feb. 1990. (ED 329 265)

Tucker, S. A., and Dempsey, J. V. "Semiotic Criteria for Evaluating Instructional Hypermedia." Paper presented at the annual meeting of the American Educational Research Association, Chicago, Ill., Apr. 3–7, 1991. (ED 337 155)

Tucker, S. A., and others. "Training University Faculty to Integrate Hypermedia into the Teacher Training Curriculum." Paper presented at the International Conference on Technology and Education, Brussels, Belgium, Mar. 20–22, 1990. (ED 327 162)

Westland, J. C. "Economic Constraints in Hypertext." *Journal of the American Society for Information Science,* 1991, *42*(3), 178–184.

Chapter 14

Software Ethics: Teaching by Example

Ralph H. Miller,
Joyce Kupsh, Carol Larson Jones

New technologies permit educators and businesses to become more effective and productive. For example, the advent of the copying machine brought new capabilities to the educational and business worlds. Documents no longer needed to be typed and retyped, or duplicated with blurry carbon paper. Photocopiers offered speed, convenience, and quality at low cost. Today's students cannot even imagine doing library research without a photocopier. They would have to take notes, use typewriters, or use word processing software programs on computers to record information. These methods are now considered primitive and painstakingly slow.

Technological advancement can have drawbacks, however. The ease with which documents can be reproduced creates the possibility of copyright violation, which is a form of theft. Such violations have resulted in criminal prosecutions by publishers to protect themselves and their authors from those who illegally copy and distribute copyrighted materials without paying royalties (DeLoughry, 1987).

Education involving the use of new technology, such as

copiers, videotape recorders/duplicators, computers, and scanners, must therefore be accompanied by instruction on ethics. Without such education, students might be unaware of the legal and ethical issues involved in copying a book passage, recording a television program, making a copy of a computer program, or using a scanner to digitize the work of a famous artist. Most students would never dream of taking money from their mother's purse or taking merchandise from a store, yet they will blithely "steal" printed materials or computer software.

Laws and social mores have established what is appropriate and ethical behavior as people go about the business of their daily lives. But when a new technology is introduced, rules or laws regarding its use are often nonexistent. These laws must be created, disseminated, and integrated into the culture at large, which may take time. During this period, vast numbers of people may be unaware of the regulations that govern the new technology.

To compound this matter, we, as educators, may not always practice completely ethical methods. We may argue that as teachers we must acquire and use all the latest software within our discipline area. We may rationalize that since our schools have budget problems and we already spend too much of our own funds for school purposes, we are justified in using illegal copies of computer software (Sacks, 1985). To make matters even worse, students may become aware of the practices followed by their teachers. Because teachers are role models, students may do whatever they see or know their teachers do, such as copying a software program for use elsewhere.

The Need for Teaching Computer Software Ethics

Many authors have addressed the subject of computer software ethics. In addition, research findings support the need for including computer software ethics in the curriculum. Both educators and business people have been surveyed to determine student and employee attitudes on this vital issue. A brief summary of these findings is included in the following sections.

Educational Settings

Gagne (1977) divided computer ethics into two parts: rules and attitudes. Each is taught differently, and each must be learned. According to Gagne, the preferred method for teaching ethical rules is the lecture approach, whereas the teaching of ethical attitudes must be done via the modeling method, with the teacher as a model. Thus, educators must use computers ethically, as they are being watched and imitated.

In a study conducted by Simpson, Simpson, Willis, and Huston (1990), high school students enrolled in computer literacy and computer science classes were asked to complete a questionnaire, with guaranteed anonymity, at the beginning and end of the course. The premeasure found that most of the respondents realized that software piracy is wrong and had not engaged in such activity. However, after using computers and software, and discussions of ethics, fewer students believed that software piracy is wrong. Perhaps using the software convinced students of the need to obtain the software, even illegally. The key motivating factor contributing to software piracy was identified as lack of money (Simpson and others, 1990).

In a study of students' attitudes on copying software, an anonymous seven-item questionnaire was administered to 159 graduate and undergraduate management students (Oz, 1990). The results led to a discouraging conclusion: young professionals have no scruples about copying software illegally. According to the findings, this attitude starts in college and does not change with time. Furthermore, ethics courses do not seem to alter this attitude. Therefore, it seems clear that educators and the software industry must find more effective ways to minimize software piracy.

To further explain this problem, Grever (1989) surveyed 1,424 Illinois students. The survey sample consisted of 703 high school students, 403 community college students, and 318 university students. One major finding was that students were far more likely to copy software to help the teacher. Grever also found that high school students were more likely to copy than university or community college students.

A modified replication of the Grever study was conducted at California State Polytechnic University, Pomona, in 1990 (Jones, Miller, and Kupsh, 1992). This survey included a sample of students ($n = 905$), faculty ($n = 145$), staff ($n = 117$), and administrators ($n = 27$) from the colleges and schools within the university. Overall, the students were significantly less ethical than the faculty, staff, and administrators, who did not differ from each other. Further analysis revealed that males were less ethical than females and that lower-division students were less ethical than upper division, but that computer ownership was not a factor. When comparing what they themselves would do to what others would do in a given situation, respondents consistently saw themselves as more ethical than others. Finally, a comparison of hypothetical ethics scenarios revealed that ethical behavior is a function of the situation (see Exhibit 14.1). Apparently, the social and emotional appeal of a request from a best friend is enough to override strictures against unethical behavior. Likewise, if someone in a position of authority (such as a professor) directs it, unethical behavior is more likely to occur.

Business Environment

The lack of computer software ethics in schools may be carried over to the business environment. At least one study appears to confirm this statement.

During September 1988, 500 practicing managers, members of The Institute of Management Science (TIMS), were randomly selected for a study regarding their practices and beliefs about copying software (Shim and Taylor, 1989). The TIMS managers were used because they were interdisciplinary and were interested in computer-related issues. They were from a variety of organizations and held a variety of management positions; 80 percent were male, and 50 percent were age twenty-five or under. The return rate was 40.6 percent. The results indicated that 93 percent purchased their software, while 4 percent copied copyrighted software. Although 88 percent felt copying software was unethical, 61 percent stated they did not understand the law.

Exhibit 14.1. Ethics Scenarios.

1. Last semester you were having some difficulty in a math course, and Sarah, who was also in the course, gave you a lot of help so that you could get a good grade in the course. This semester Sarah is taking a computer course, and she is having difficulty learning one of the software packages being taught. She has a part-time job, and she is unable to go to the lab to get extra help because of her work. She has a computer at home, but she does not have the software. She has talked with you about her dilemma several times. You feel obligated to help her in return, but the only way to help her is to make a copy of the software used in class.

I would
( ) Make a copy for Sarah.
( ) Not offer to make a copy.
( ) Undecided.

I believe this activity is

Extremely Unethical	Probably Unethical	Undecided	Ethical But with Reservation	Highly Ethical

Others would
( )
( )
( )

2. Jay West, an accounting teacher at your school, has been doing a good job teaching students how to use the computer for accounting. He has been wanting the school to purchase an updated software package, but the school could purchase only half as many copies as are needed. Since you often help Mr. West around the classroom, he asked if you would come to the classroom an hour early and make copies of the software so there would be a software disk for each computer.

I would
( ) Help Mr. West make copies of the software.
( ) Tell Mr. West that you would prefer not to make copies.
( ) Undecided.

I believe this activity is

Extremely Unethical	Probably Unethical	Undecided	Ethical But with Reservation	Highly Ethical

Others would
( )
( )
( )

3. Your dad just purchased a new computer for his work. He told you that you could also use it to catch up on your computer course, but you do not have any of the software used in your class at school. You would like to use it, and you realize that while you are doing assignments in the computer lab at school you could probably make a copy of the software, since the lab attendant generally remains at the desk unless a student asks for help.

I would
( ) Make a copy of the software.
( ) Continue on as you have been without a copy.
( ) Undecided.

I believe this activity is

Extremely Unethical	Probably Unethical	Undecided	Ethical But with Reservation	Highly Ethical

Others would
( )
( )
( )

4. You are in charge of the computer lab room at your school for two hours three days a week. Students use the lab to complete assignments and projects. You are responsible for checking the software out to the students and for seeing that only students who have permission to do so work in the lab. Two of the students are rather loudly working together at one of the computers. As you walk over to tell them to work quietly, you notice that they are making copies of the software checked out to them.

I would
( ) Ignore what the students are doing.
( ) Stop students from making copies.
( ) Undecided.

I believe this activity is

Extremely Unethical	Probably Unethical	Undecided	Ethical But with Reservation	Highly Ethical

Others would
( )

( )
( )

---

5. Bill, a good friend of yours, is in three of your classes, and computers are used in one of the classes. Students have been told that assigned work on the computer will not be accepted late. Bill is a star basketball player and misses classes when the team plays out-of-town games. He has a computer at home, and he could do the assignments there, but he does not have the software needed to do the work. Bill is behind in his assignments, and if his work isn't turned in on time, he is faced with getting a D in the class. He will be suspended from the team and his team is likely to lose out on their bid for the tournament. As a good friend, Bill has asked you to make a copy of the software so that he can do his assignment at home and pass the course.

I would
( ) Make a copy for Bill.
( ) Tell Bill you prefer not to make a copy.
( ) Undecided.

I believe this activity is

Extremely Unethical	Probably Unethical	Undecided	Ethical But with Reservation	Highly Ethical

Others would
( )

( )

( )

---

6. Your good friend Julie goes to school at a near-by university and works part time for a computer software company. Julie has explained to you that she and two others work as a team and write software programs. Part of Julie's salary comes from the sale of the software programs she and her teammates write. Julie is dependent upon her salary to pay her way through school. Both of you have known Bob for a long time, and Bob knows you like the computer game Snafu. Yesterday Bob offered to make a copyy of his Snafu game and sell it to you at a bargain price. You know this game is a program that Julie helped write.

I would
( ) Buy the copy from your friend Bob.
( ) Tell Bob you will buy your own copy at the store.
( ) Undecided.

I believe this activity is

Extremely Unethical	Probably Unethical	Undecided	Ethical But with Reservation	Highly Ethical

Others would
( )

( )

( )

Exhibit 14.1. Ethics Scenarios, Cont'd.

7. Your school has a local chapter of the PBL/FBLA Business Club, and Dave has just been elected treasurer of the state organization. The state organization has a computer, and Dave is to use an updated data base software for the records. The software has been ordered, but it has not arrived. Dave has to have time to get the records set up before the state convention—which is three weeks away. You know that your dad uses this new updated software for his business and allows you to use it at the office, and Dave has asked you if he can have a copy of the software to use for several weeks until his software arrives. He promises to give the copy back to you when his software arrives.

I would
( ) Tell Dave you will make a copy for him.

( ) Tell Dave you will not make a copy for him.

( ) Undecided.

I believe this activity is

Extremely Unethical	Probably Unethical	Undecided	Ethical But with Reservation	Highly Ethical

Others would
( )

( )

( )

8. You own a small lawn-care business that you have developed over the past four summers. As your business has picked up, it becomes more difficult to keep track of the records. When visiting a friend in another city who does similar work, you tell him that you want to put your records on the computer, but the software for doing this is too expensive. Your friend then tells you that you can take the software he uses for his records and make a copy for your use.

I would
( ) Make a copy of the software.

( ) Thank your friend for the offer but not make a copy.

( ) Undecided.

I believe this activity is

Extremely Unethical	Probably Unethical	Undecided	Ethical But with Reservation	Highly Ethical

Others would
( )

( )

( )

9. Beth Montell is your best friend at school, where you both belong to the Business Computer Club. The software used by the club is purchased by the school for classroom use and it is not to be taken from the room. At one of the club meetings, you accidentally put a software disk in your folder and take it home. When you discovered this and told Beth, she asked you to let her make a copy of the software before you return it. She said that if you were really her friend, you would let her do it.

I would
( ) Let Beth make a copy.

( ) Not let Beth make a copy.

( ) Undecided.

I believe this activity is

Extremely Unethical	Probably Unethical	Undecided	Ethical But with Reservation	Highly Ethical

Others would
( )

( )

( )

10. You and your friends have been having a lot of fun playing the Zork computer game at the local computer store. Knowing that you enjoy the game, your parents buy you the software game for your birthday. When your friends find out that you have the software, several ask you to make them a copy so that they can play the game on their own computers.

I would
( ) Make a copy for your friends.
( ) Tell them you prefer not to make a copy.

( ) Undecided.

I believe this activity is

Extremely Unethical	Probably Unethical	Undecided	Ethical But with Reservation	Highly Ethical

Others would
( )
( )

( )

11. You own the software of a very popular computer game called WhizzyWhig. You want to buy another computer game, but find it costs more than you can afford to pay. Bill tells you that if you will make a copy of your WhizzyWhig for him for half price, you will then have money to purchase the new game.

I would
( ) Sell a copy to Bill.
( ) Tell Bill you can't sell him a copy.

( ) Undecided.

I believe this activity is

Extremely Unethical	Probably Unethical	Undecided	Ethical But with Reservation	Highly Ethical

Others would
( )
( )
( )

( )

12. For a long time you have been wanting to join a very popular club at your school, but you can't join unless you are "invited" to join. This club is a computer club to which several of your good friends and other popular students in school belong. You are invited to join. You are told, however, that to become a member, you must make a copy of some software program and donate it to the club.

I would
( ) Join the club and take a copy of a software program.

( ) Tell them you are sorry, but that you cannot join the club.

( ) Undecided.

I believe this activity is

Extremely Unethical	Probably Unethical	Undecided	Ethical But with Reservation	Highly Ethical

Others would
( )

( )

( )

Source: Jean Grever, Illinois State University, Normal, Ill. Reprinted with permission.

From these results it is apparent that both education and industry need to provide more information regarding software acquisition and use to their respective constituencies. This is the subject to which we now turn.

Topics to Include in the Curriculum

With the emergence of new technology, the curriculum must be amended. The debate always arises as to whether the subject matter warrants a whole new course or whether it should be integrated into already existing courses. We believe that computer software ethics should be a part of each and every course about or using computers. The topic may also be appropriate for some classes not using software, such as courses in philosophy, business, and psychology. Obviously, the subject is of vital importance for the future honesty and integrity of workers, and for the welfare of the software industry.

After determining that ethics will be included in the curriculum of numerous classes, the next subject for educators to address is what should be covered. A first step is to make students aware of the license or limited warranty agreements that accompany software. Next, instruction needs to be given on the terminology of computer software ethics. Sample scenarios or case studies can be used to help students understand the problems. Finally, since the issue is not simply black or white but frequently involves some gray areas, we offer a set of ethics guidelines for educators.

Software License

Software developers, manufacturers, and sellers are in business to make a profit. If software is used by a hundred people but only one copy was actually purchased, the developers, manufacturers, and sellers are not only being deprived of a profit on their investment, they may not last long in business.

Most newly purchased software packages contain a license agreement. Such agreements should be read, reviewed, and discussed thoroughly with the students, who may not be aware that

they are actually buying a license rather than the software disk
or disks enclosed in the package.

Terminology

As with any subject area, defining specialized terms will provide students with a basic foundation in the topic. The following terms are useful for students to understand and internalize
as part of their education in software ethics:

> *Copy protection.* A method originated by software de-
> velopers to prevent a disk from being copied.
>
> *Copyright.* The legal right granted to an author, com-
> puter user, playwright, publisher, or distributor to
> exclusive publication, production, sale, or distribu-
> tion of a literary, musical, dramatic, or artistic
> work.
>
> *Ethics.* A system of moral principles.
>
> *Freeware.* Software programs—usually written for fun
> by a hobbyist—offered for use free of charge.
>
> *Legal.* Permitted by law.
>
> *License.* An agreement between the vendor and the
> purchaser of software.
>
> *Piracy.* The copying or duplicating of computer soft-
> ware without proper authorization.
>
> *Public domain software.* Software available to anyone at
> no cost, or at a limited cost to cover the expense of
> the disk and the copying service.
>
> *Shareware.* Software available for free trial use. If users
> like the product, they are requested to submit a
> registration fee.
>
> *Softlifting.* The process of making illegal copies for
> personal use or for friends.

Scenarios/Case Studies

Everyone can understand a rule or a law in theory. However,
when confronted with a scenario or case study, people tend to

identify with the characters and their situation and may lose sight of ethical and legal principles, just as they do in real life. Such cases are extremely helpful, therefore, in providing the basis for a discussion of the problems and issues involved in software ethics.

Scenarios developed by Grever (1989) have been used in her study of Illinois students and in the Cal State Poly (Leick, 1990) study. These scenarios recognize and address the idea that gray areas do exist. Each scenario asks respondents to indicate the action they would take rather than the response they believe is right. Next, they are asked to mark what they believe most students would do. Finally, they are asked to indicate along a continuum the degree to which they believe the behavior described is ethical or unethical. Examples of these scenarios are provided in Exhibit 14.1. These examples may provide educators and industrial trainers with the material they need to explore and present the ethical dilemmas surrounding the use of copyrighted computer software.

Guidelines

As educators, we can develop guidelines for students rather than taking the perhaps unrealistic stand of saying they should *never* copy software. In general, copying a licensed software program is illegal, but there are instances when one can ethically and legally copy software. Both sides of the situation should be adequately represented, rather than offering quickly rationalized reasons such as "One little copy won't hurt a big company." As a class activity, students can develop guidelines.

We suggest the following list of guidelines for educators:

1. *Obtain legal copies of any software installed in classrooms or laboratories.* Educators must be role models.

2. *Contact vendors for educational site licenses or laboratory package discounts.* Most vendors are aware of educational needs and may offer special educational discounts. Some "lab packs" are available that will provide ten or fifteen copies with one or two manuals at a price equal to one or two legal packages. Vendors realize that providing affordable software for students is a good

investment for the future. For instance, workers will buy or encourage their employers to buy software with which they are familiar.

3. *Make a single backup copy to protect the purchased software, and store it safely in a secure location.* This practice is legal and strongly recommended by vendors. A disk can go bad; a hard disk can crash. Thus, protection is needed to assure that what has been legally purchased can, indeed, be used.

4. *Let students know that the software you're using is legal and that it is illegal for them to copy it.* Simply avoiding teaching students how to copy software is not satisfactory. Copying computer documents is a task that they need to know how to do, and it is closely related to copying a copyrighted software program. Even if you avoid teaching this step, someone will know the procedure or will figure it out. Students must be instructed to buy their own legal copies of the software they use. Many vendors supply very good student and educational discounts on software purchased at the campus bookstore.

5. *Request demonstration copies from a vendor.* Often vendors have a demonstration copy that they will be glad to send you. Some of the disks have a label on them that reads "Demo Disk — Copy freely and share as much as you like." Frequently, demo copies are limited versions of the full program. They may be missing vital elements, such as the dictionary or printing capabilities. For example, the limited version may allow a word processing program to turn out documents with only a few pages, or may permit a data base or speadsheet program to operate with limited storage capability.

6. *Buy any software that is actively used in your work on your own personal computer system.* As a teacher, you may tend to rationalize and say that you need to secure (legally or illegally) all the software you can so that you are knowledgeable and can compare or discuss the software in your classes. Request a complimentary copy for your own use from the vendor. Vendors frequently understand this need. They also recognize that you have the potential to influence hundreds, maybe even thousands, of students on both current and future purchases.

7. *Visit computer shows and exhibitions to get a demonstration*

and to try out software. Rather than pirating or softlifting and then having to learn software without the proper documentation, why not have an expert demonstrate the software to you? Vendors may even be willing to have a sales representative come to your classroom and demonstrate the software.

8. *Practice the golden rule.* If you were the author, developer, programmer, or vendor, how would you feel if someone copied and distributed, without buying a license, work that you had spent days, months, or even years originating? When confronting the gray areas of computer software ethics, the golden rule is probably a good guideline to keep in mind.

Conclusion

The advent of the microcomputer has brought about exciting new capabilities for both education and business. However, new technologies always create new challenges. In the case of the computer, one of the challenges facing both educators and businesses of today is computer software ethics. Available research has shown that neither students nor workers seem to be aware of or conscientious about following ethical and legal procedures.

As educators, we have a responsibility to follow as well as teach ethical procedures. Students should be introduced to sample license agreements. They need to learn new terminology. Scenarios or case studies are helpful in demonstrating problems and providing a discussion basis for difficult situations. A set of guidelines for teachers that can be shared with students should provide the needed foundation for using and teaching about and with new technologies.

References

DeLoughry, T. J. "Widespread Piracy by Students Frustrates Developers of Computer Software." *Chronicle of Higher Education,* 1987, *33,* 31.

Gagne, R. M. *The Conditions of Learning.* Troy, Mo.: Holt, Rinehart & Winston, 1977.

Grever, J. "Ethics Scenarios." Unpublished manuscript. Illinois State University, Normal, 1989.

Jones, C. L., Miller, R. H., and Kupsh, J. "Computer Software Ethics." *The California Business Teacher,* 5, 1992.

Leick, A. "Statistical Analysis for a Study of Computer Ethics." Unpublished senior project, California State Polytechnic University, Pomona, 1990.

Oz, E. "The Attitude of Managers-to-Be Toward Software Piracy." *Operations Research/Management Science Today,* 1990, *17,* 24–26.

Sacks, J. "To Copy Protect or Not to Copy Protect?" *Popular Computing,* 1985, *4,* 73–75.

Shim, J. P., and Taylor, G. S. "Practicing Managers' Perception/Attitudes Toward Illegal Software Copying." *Operations Research/Management Science Today,* 1989, *16,* 30–33.

Simpson, P., Simpson, C., Willis, T. H., and Huston, C. R. "Teaching Software Ethics: An Experiment in a High School Classroom." *Western Decision Sciences Institute Proceedings,* Lihue, Kauai, Hawaii, Mar. 1990.

PART FOUR

Assessing Teaching Effectiveness and Learning Outcomes

Numerous suggestions have been made throughout this text for improving college-level instruction. If faculty and administrators concerned about improving undergraduate education were to adopt the changes that the chapter authors have advocated, that would be a good start. But a critical step would still be missing — assessing the effect of the changes on student learning. Has making the curriculum multicentric really changed the worldviews of students? Did the cooperative exercises make them more likely to work well together? Are the students thinking more clearly, more critically, because faculty have changed what and how they teach? What is the effect of using new technologies? Have we improved the quality or reduced the cost of higher education? Countless questions could be asked to determine whether the changes have had the intended effect. A meaningful assessment of learner outcomes is the only way of answering these questions — it is the only way to determine what works in higher education.

In Chapter Fifteen, Ralph A. Wolff and Olita D. Harris explain why we need to develop a "culture of evidence" to examine the effect of college instruction on students. The information gained from assessment can be used to make data-based decisions about what works on college campuses. In Chapter Sixteen, Susan G. Nummedal presents many methods that can be used by individual faculty members to determine whether their students are learning what the instructors had intended for them to learn. The methods for classroom assessment are quick ways of obtaining feedback about a particular class or segment of material. In Chapter Seventeen, Mary Kay Crouch and Sheryl I. Fontaine discuss another method of assessment, student portfolios, that can be used by individual instructors in any discipline. Crouch and Fontaine explain how they use porfolios in a writing program, with examples that can be easily adapted for use with any course or program. Finally, in Chapter Eighteen, James L. Ratcliff focuses on the assessment of general education — those core courses that constitute the breadth requirement on virtually every college campus.

Chapter 15

Using Assessment to Develop a Culture of Evidence

Ralph A. Wolff, Olita D. Harris

Overheard recently in a faculty office was a comment similar to the following:

> Assessment? I am not sure what all this emphasis is about, but we do lots of assessment here. I grade my students, they evaluate me after each course, and every five or six years my department gets reviewed. Isn't that enough? Why are people asking for more?

Such attitudes reflect the growing challenge of learning about and responding to a variety of assessment initiatives that are under way in American higher education.

Why the Current Emphasis on Assessment?

All institutions engage in assessment of student learning through the grading process and other forms of evaluation. Nonetheless, a national "assessment movement" has developed in the past decade as a result of two major forces—one external and the other internal to the academy. While overlapping, they have not been entirely complementary.

Externally, demands have been growing over the past decade for greater accountability of American higher education, which has increasingly become viewed as a strategic resource in the struggle to regain American competitiveness globally. In addition, higher education is no longer viewed as a privilege and instead has become fundamentally linked to the education and training of the new American work force. As a result, support for higher education is seen as an investment in the future of the country. In an era of limited resources, pressure increases for such investments to yield demonstrable results, especially in comparison to other competing demands on public resources (Ewell, 1991).

The need for higher education to support national goals has arisen at a time when many have questioned the quality and integrity of higher-education institutions. Public concerns over large tuition increases, the failure of higher education to recruit and graduate significant numbers of minority students, scandals concerning the academic performance of athletes, large student loan defaults, cost overruns in the overhead charges for federal research grants, and campus crime have undermined confidence in American higher education. The public no longer sees colleges and universities as having the will or the ability to address these problems internally. As a result of these concerns, a majority of states have enacted legislation requiring increased assessment of student learning.

Meanwhile, an internal drive for reform has undergirded the assessment movement. Spurred by several national reports on the need to reform undergraduate learning, increasing attention has been placed on the effects or outcomes of the learning experience as a means of improving program and institutional quality and effectiveness. The American Association for Higher Education has both stimulated and shaped these efforts through its annual Assessment Forum and publications. The literature and research on assessment have also grown substantially, giving emphasis to classroom research and assessment (Cross and Angelo, 1988; Nummedal, this volume); faculty organized assessment, such as the Harvard Assessment Seminars (Light, 1992); assessment of diversity issues such as campus climate; and the use of assessment in institutional planning and accreditation self-study (California Postsecondary Education Commission, 1989, 1992a, 1992b; Ewell and Lisensky, 1988).

The accreditation process has been one arena in which these external and internal forces have converged. In the past several years, all six regional accreditating associations have revised their standards to place greater emphasis on assessment and now require greater attention to student learning issues in the self-study. In several regions, assessment has become a significant focus of the self-study and institutional visit process (Wolff, 1992). Thus, whether by state mandate or by accreditation review, all institutions will need to demonstrate more evidence of student learning and of program and institutional effectiveness.

Who Is Assessment *Really* For?

Notwithstanding these mandates for assessment, capturing institutional attention and genuine commitment to assessment has been difficult. Often this problem is a result of the perception that assessment is primarily something required externally to prove the value of higher education to constituencies that may not understand the complexity of learning or be judicious in using assessment results. Under such circumstances, resistance to assessment is understandable. The primary goal of assessment, however, is to improve institutional quality; thus, the real beneficiaries are faculty, staff, and students.

Whether the impetus of assessment is perceived to be external or internal can have a critical impact on whether a real commitment to assessment can be achieved within an institution. As Table 15.1 indicates, there are significant differences in approaching assessment if the goal is to establish accountability to an external authority than if it is to stimulate internal improvements through better data collection and analysis.

Assessment generated by external mandate is typically directed toward establishing accountability through summative measures, such as testing at graduation or at different stages. It focuses heavily on individual performance or achievement;

Table 15.1. Comparison of Assessment Sources.

Source of Mandate	External	Internal
Goal	Accountability	Improvement
Mode of evaluation	Summative	Formative
Type of evaluation	Assesses individual student performance	Evaluates patterns and trends
Use of results	Results compared publicly	Results linked to improvement
Focus	Focuses primarily on results	Focuses equally on questions

as such, results can be compared publicly. When improvement is the motivation for assessment, formative evaluations can be valuable, with evidence grouped into patterns and trends rather than focused on individual performance. With an internal emphasis, results can be applied toward improving institutional effectiveness.

Moreover, when assessment is directed by an institutional desire to improve, participation becomes easier to achieve. Accountability can be established by demonstrating that the institution is asking probing questions of itself, gathering data, and undertaking improvement. Under such a scenario, the institution determines the type and scope of questions asked, as well as the distribution of data. This is clearly a situation preferable to any form of external control. Paradoxically, when institutions refuse or fail to demonstrate that such internal forces are engaged within the institution, pressures mount for external mandates.

What Is Assessment, Anyway?

Once an institution begins to undertake assessment, it must recognize that assessment means different things to different audiences. Our language about assessment is a source of great confusion. Assessment refers to both the *process* of gathering data and the *product* of the data collection, such as when we speak of assessment data. Moreover, assessment is intended to be a *means* to institutional improvement, but all too often becomes an *end* in itself. Particularly when institutions attempt to respond to external audiences, the act of gathering data can be mistaken for real improvements in student learning or programs.

Much of the language and attention of assessment is focused on *student learning outcomes*, yet the habits of thinking and methodologies developed in the assessment movement can and should be applied throughout the institution, such as to student services, campus climate, and teaching effectiveness. In addition, different types of assessment activities are typically conducted simultaneously at different levels of an institution. For example, individual faculty members might be incorporating classroom assessment techniques into their courses, while the department is undertaking a program review and considering an alumni survey, and the school is reviewing transcripts to track the sequence of courses students take to fulfill general education requirements. At the same time, the university might be undertaking a major review of writing across the institution and conducting focus group meetings and student satisfaction surveys on the effectiveness of student services and campus climate.

In light of this confusing array of definitions and activities, what should be the organizing basis for assessment activities? We suggest that institutions strive to develop "a culture of evidence," an environment in which evidence about important issues is routinely gathered and discussed. A culture of evidence needs to be supported by an attitude of open inquiry, where questions are routinely asked about the effectiveness of the courses, programs, and patterns of established practices.

How Can an Institution Build a Culture of Evidence?

Ironically, all institutions gather far more data than can effectively be used, yet many important decisions throughout the institution are not supported by meaningful information and data (qualitative and quantitative). The goal of building a "culture of evidence" is not intended to cause significantly more data to be collected. Indeed, one of the greatest problems with many institutions' responses to the recent increase in emphasis on assessment is the generation of new data collection, added to existing workloads but still disconnected from the issues considered most important to faculty and others.

A culture of evidence is best built by honoring a number of principles, regardless of the size or type of institution:

1. A culture of evidence is as much a set of attitudes as a set of activities. When assertions are made about the quality or effectiveness of a course, a department, a school, or the institution at large, an immediate question should be, "What is our source of evidence for that assertion?" We must be willing to probe beyond comfortable assertions to learn whether they are supported and what assumptions underlie them.

2. Assessment activities should be embedded in the existing infrastructure of an institution and not built into a separate set of structures and activities. For example, most institutions engage in periodic program reviews of academic and nonacademic departments. Incorporating questions addressing evidence of student learning, departmental climate, and program effectiveness into such an existing process can go a long way toward building assessment into the institutional culture. Similarly, committee chairs might be asked about what data they commonly receive to discharge committee functions, and what data would be most helpful. This is particularly relevant for curriculum committees.

3. Assessment should start with the institution or department's current situation. A census of what data have already collected and how they are disseminated and used can reveal a great deal. Possibly some information routinely collected will be eliminated or recast in more useful patterns. New data collection should be undertaken with knowledge of existing data use.

4. The process should begin with questions that will be of greatest interest to faculty or staff. Global agendas rarely capture the interest of faculty or others. Efforts should be made to identify those questions that will provide insight into the issues being addressed. For example, a question about the effective-

ness of writing instruction could lead to a comprehensive review of the writing program. An institution might start, however, with just one or two questions, with further research directed by those responses. For example, the institution might try to learn how much students actually write while attending the institution, or what types of writing support students have found most valuable.

5. Institutions should start small and build. Comprehensive assessment efforts require a great deal of expertise as well as resources. In some cases, such efforts are valuable; in others, small pilot projects are a better place to begin. For example, rather than attempting to assess all the goals of the general education program, an institution might assess the status of just one or two goals. Not only is such an approach more cost-efficient, but it can also yield valuable insight into the effectiveness of available methodologies.

6. Entrepreneurship about assessment should be promoted within the institution. A culture of evidence involves everyone, not just a director of institutional research, in the process and culture of asking questions. Different types of projects should be encouraged as a basis for involving more members of the institutional community and fostering greater creativity, and ultimately application of evidence gathered for program improvement.

What Stages Will Our Institution Go Through?

Institutions fall along a continuum of engagement in assessment. Knowing where the institution rests along that continuum helps direct both internal and external attention to appropriate expectations about assessment activities and the progress being made toward the development of a culture of evidence. There are a number of perspectives from which to view this phenomenon. However, two perspectives, organizational renewal and death and dying, seem to be the most helpful in explaining what happens in organizations, such as universities, when faced with the need to launch an initiative such as assessment. This process has much in common with the reorganization of social, emotional, and intellectual content that accompanies a death or any event that requires a reordering of everyday thoughts and actions that have become ritualized. The stages of reorganization are attempts to reestablish equilibrium, or a state in which stress is manageable and coping skills are adequate to the everyday events and tasks.

The major authors whose writings and research were drawn on to inform this discussion about the changes that take place in a university are Marris (1975), Becker (1964, 1971), Bowlby (1973), Hersey and Blanchard (1988), and Kübler-Ross (1969). The authors, with the exception of Hersey and Blanchard, are usually associated with the concepts of loss, change, death, and dying. The initiation of assessment does represent a death of sorts — a death of the usual way things are done, cherished, and known, if not comfortable. A pattern is disturbed, a rip occurs in the fabric of daily routine. Research tells us that the prospect of change almost always results in resistance. The university is no exception. In fact, university faculty have perfected the art of resistance to change and have taken it to new heights in attempts to preserve cherished and traditional ways of conducting postsecondary education.

The two notions of change are important in attempting to explain what happens as people try to adjust to an alteration in their usual patterns of managing their daily lives and responsibilities. These patterns become "programs" or imperatives that are more or less automatically engaged when a familiar or usual event occurs. When the events are outside of the usual or the expected, other mechanisms are mobilized in an attempt to regain the status quo. Whether this happens at an individual or an organizational level, similar processes can serve to explain the stages of adjustment. Much depends on how fundamental the change is and on the centrality of the change to the belief system. The more central the changes, the more complex the processes. At the social and emotional levels, change is characterized by grief and looking back at what was lost. At the organizational level, organizational renewal is an opportunity to move the entire system forward.

Models of Change

Kübler-Ross (1969) and others characterize the stages of grief reaction as denial and isolation, anger, bargaining, depression, and acceptance. French and Bell (1978) use the term *organizational renewal* to encompass such processes as organizational problem solving and organizational change. Lippitt (1969) and others characterize organizational renewal as the process of vitalizing, energizing, initiating, creating, and confronting needed changes and adapting to new conditions through technical and human resources.

Change also includes processes associated with making the results of change congruent with the stated purposes. One of the consequences of these processes is the development of an organizational culture, which French and Bell (1978) define as the prevailing patterns of activities, interactions, norms, sentiments (including feelings), beliefs, attitudes, values, and products, including technology. They further describe these patterns as forming "the covert part of the organizational iceberg, the nine-tenths that is largely unseen" (p. 15). The part of the iceberg that is overt or seen includes such aspects of the organization as goals, technology structure, policies and procedures, and financial resources. In other words, the formal aspects of what happens in an organization largely rest on the informal aspects and are sustained by them.

Hersey and Blanchard (1988), on the other hand, present the levels of organizational change over time in terms of knowledge changes, attitudinal changes, behavioral changes, and group changes. According to Hersey and Blanchard, knowledge changes are the easiest to make. They may simply result from reading a book or news article or hearing a speech made by a respected person. Attitude structures carry with them an emotional charge, positive or negative, never neutral. The emotional charge, however, makes them more difficult to change. Changes in individual behavior seem to be considerably more difficult to make than those in knowledge or attitudes.

Complications and complexity increase when change is initiated within groups or organizations. When participative change is wed with these levels of change, a potentially effective process is initiated. This type of change takes place when individuals or groups are directly involved in selecting or formalizing new methods for reaching desired goals. Hersey and Blanchard (1988) point out that translation of commitment into behavior is an important feature of this process. Further, identification and support of informal and formal leaders in work groups can facilitate the desired organizational changes. Finally, persuading others to duplicate the strategies and behaviors in other parts of the organization introduces the notion of incipient group norms and subsequent institutionalization.

Note that the two notions of change have differing emphases. The Kübler-Ross/Bowlby/Marris/Becker models pay close attention to social and emotional content and adjustments. The French and Bell/Hersey and Blanchard models of change focus primarily on the progression of change through levels from individuals to institutions and from the overt to the covert and the manner in which these serve to undergird the mandated activities of the organization. Both refer to the social constructions surrounding the realities associated with any change, personal or organizational. However, both conceptualizations are needed to help explain what happens with the advent of assessment in institutions such as a university. Given these frameworks, the great emotional impact and initial resistance associated with changes in the university when assessment is introduced might be anticipated.

Stages of Change

Organizational change, however characterized, is often presented as a linear process. However, it is almost never linear, and it is not always (seemingly) logical and rational, because of the emotions, values, established ways of doing things, perceived "sacred cows," level of comfort, and the like, of the people involved.

The continuum of attitudes, feelings, and behavior and the resultant organizational structures can be explicated and used to facilitate understanding about what may be occurring as any significant organizational change is proposed and carried out. We will be presenting such a schema here. However, while the schema may *appear* linear, it is for purposes of illustration only. The reality is that several stages may be displayed at the same time, depending on the unit of the university that may be under consideration. The idea is to attempt to pinpoint the *predominant* stage, to see how far the institution has come and where it needs to go. After all, the process can be as important as the product. In other words, the journey can be as important (and as gratifying) as reaching the destination.

There usually are few clues to follow in making judgments about the status of assessment in an institution or determining the ways in which an institution pays attention to institutional effectiveness. This is especially so when an institution is in the throes of a commitment crisis — that is, deciding whether to pay serious attention to assessment or develop a culture of evidence. Internal reports or even the institutions' self-study may also be of little help. Self-studies and other reports omit a number of the activities that might legitimately be termed assessment but have not been identified as such by the institution.

The following schema was developed to assist the institution as well as external evaluators in determining the stage of institutional engagement in assessment, the behavior to expect, the feelings expressed, the organizational structure in place to facilitate the development of an assessment venture, and the level of involvement and differential leadership roles of faculty and administration. This schema has practical value because it is based on observations made during accreditation site visits in both large public institutions and small private ones.

Assessment is usually introduced by a faculty member or administrator who has attended a conference where assessment was either mentioned or the dominant feature. In many states, assessment has simply been imposed by the legislature. Whatever the mode of introduction, the process presented here is typical of what occurs when institutions begin developing a culture of evidence.

The following schema presents the engagement of assessment from the initial introduction to institutionalization and involvement by the entire faculty and administration. The schema describes, in addition to the stage of development, the apparent mode of adjustment/behavior, the climate of opinion, organizational structures that support the growth of assessment, and level of involvement and leadership roles assumed both by administration and faculty. While the schema is not intended to be exhaustive, it is meant to be illustrative and illuminating. We will discuss each stage in turn. Table 15.2 summarizes the schema.

Denial. The first stage in the development of a culture of evidence is the denial stage, based on the Kübler-Ross grief model. This stage is characterized by denial that there is anything to be concerned about. Emphasis is on maintaining stability and the status quo. The mode of adjustment and behavior is governed by a social version of the second law of thermodynamics (an object in motion will tend to remain in motion unless acted on by an outside force; conversely, an object at rest will remain at rest . . . and so on). This dynamic, called *inertia,* is easily identified in an institution. Faculty and administrators continue to act as they always have and to ignore assessment as much as possible. Vague feelings of uneasiness and ambivalence will be experienced by faculty and administrators alike. The typical sentiment expressed is, "If we wait long enough, maybe assessment will go away." At this point, there does not tend to be an existing organizational structure on campus available to tackle the issue. The level of involvement and leadership roles of administrators run the gamut from advocate ("That sounds good — in theory") to adversary ("You can't make me"). Faculty are usually not involved or are involved only minimally.

Resistance. The second stage, resistance (subtitled "fussing and fuming") continues the Kübler-Ross terminology. At this point there is a great deal of wheelspinning and threshing about. Any initial efforts toward change tend to be unorganized. There will be some risk taking through beginning innovations and questioning. Such questions as "What do our students know, what can they do, and how do we know it?" become dominant features.

A great deal of energy is often generated at the resistance

Table 15.2. Stages of Assessment Development.

Stage	Mode of Adjustment/Behavior	Climate of Opinion	Organizational Structures	Level of Involvement	
				Administration	Faculty
Denial	Status quo Ritualism	Vague feelings of uneasiness		Advocate Adversary	
Resistance (fussing and fuming)	Unorganized efforts Beginning innovation	Diffuse anxiety Perceived threat "No time, money"	Conversations Ad hoc committees	Adversary Advocate	Contestant Questioner
Understanding (ah hah!)	Limited organized efforts Assessment defined Census of existing efforts/ data collection	"Show me" "Let's talk"	Ad hoc committees	Promoter Planner	Promoter
Campaign (demonstrations)	Planned efforts Assessment principles/ guidelines developed	Limited endorsements	Task groups Ad hoc committees Standing committees	Enabler Facilitator Convener	Guide Catalyst Mediator
Collaboration	Assessment goals and objectives Implementation/utilization of data Feedback and revision	"This can work" Broad engagement	Standing committees	Enabler Facilitator Convener	Consultant Coordinator
Institutionalization	Refining efforts	Consensus	Standing committees	Promoter Enabler Supporter	Advocate Enabler Facilitator Convener

stage. However, it is primarily felt as diffuse, unfocused anxiety precipitated by a perceived threat and anger at having to examine the status quo, most often expressed in terms of not having the time or the resources to engage in assessment activities or to generate a culture of evidence. This is the point at which institutions begin referring to assessment as "the A word," which is rarely meant kindly or in jest. The reference is clearly pejorative and derisive. The organizational structure takes the form of conversations and ad hoc committees. The level of involvement of and leadership roles taken by administrators continue from the first stage and are those of adversary and advocate. Faculty become contestants ("Why should I?") and questioners ("What's in it for me?" "Who is behind this, anyway?"). This is the point at which the process can stall if a critical mass of faculty and administrators cannot channel the energy of resistance in a positive and affirming direction. A level of trust, a "we-ness," must be created to enable stage three to begin.

Understanding. The third stage begins genuine understanding of the potential of developing a culture of evidence. Following the Kübler-Ross model, a certain amount of bargaining takes place at this stage. Many express having an "ah hah!" experience. This may be called the therapeutic or teachable moment. It is a pivotal stage — one at which the aggravation (distrust and anger) of maintaining the status quo is greater and more difficult than the anxiety associated with the change. The fulcrum allows the balance to be weighted on the side of the culture of evidence. Limited organized efforts in the form of pilot projects are initiated. A beginning effort is made in defining assessment for the institution — what it does and does not mean.

At this point, campuses often conduct a census of existing efforts and data collections. The climate of opinion still tends to be somewhat skeptical, but pockets of faculty seem to be more positively predisposed toward assessment and developing a culture of evidence. Organizational structures continue to be dominated by ad hoc committees. The level of involvement and leadership roles among administrators are those of promoter and planner. If administrators are not "cheerleaders" and advocates, sustained efforts simply will not occur. Almost every instance of successful assessment initiative is accompanied by administrative support and by faculty-driven and student-focused activities. Faculty roles clearly fall into the area of promoter. At this juncture, an institution can really begin to talk with some conviction and coherence about an identifiable culture of evidence. It becomes a tangible product of ongoing processes that are "owned" by ever-wider groups of faculty.

Campaign. Stage four begins the campaign or demonstrations. Following the Kübler-Ross paradigm, "letting go of the past" occurs in an attempt to get on with life. In a similar vein, assessment and building a culture of evidence are beginning to become priorities for the institution. The campus efforts are diverse and planned for more purposeful data collections. Assessment guidelines and principles are developed and widely circulated. The climate of opinion is that of limited endorsements and commitments. "Cautious but steady" might be used to characterize the progress. Task groups, ad hoc committees, and standing committees are all organizational structures that would facilitate the beginning of sustained efforts.

The level of involvement and leadership roles become more complex. The multiple faculty roles of guide, catalyst, and mediator indicate the importance of this stage. The catalyst role implies that the faculty member is a change agent who is committed to and intimately involved in moving the organization to the next stage. The change agent often does more pushing than guiding. The guide role is a more benign one. It implies that people agree on the destination—they just need help in getting there in the most efficacious manner. The mediator's domain is the middle ground between conflicting groups—that is, those who want to move ahead with assessment and those who continue to be reluctant and unsure and who lag at an earlier stage. The administration also takes multiple roles: enabler, facilitator, and convener. The enabler assists faculty with the resources, knowledge, opportunity, and sanctions necessary to activate assessment activities. The facilitator removes obstacles and generally eases the path for faculty who desire to begin assessment projects. The convener makes it possible for interested

groups of faculty to come together for assessment conferences
or workshops or even for informal gatherings, such as brown
bag lunches. Underlying all these administrative roles is a supporting function that is crucial for the continuation of assessment activities by faculty.

Collaboration. The fifth, or collaboration, stage is what
Kübler-Ross termed as acceptance. This stage is characterized
by a more pervasive assessment presence. An institutional plan
for assessment has been established; assessment goals and objectives are in place. Analysis of assessment data and a plan for
utilization of that data have been organized. Feedback for curriculum or program revision is a reality. The climate of opinion is one of confidence that assessment can work for the good
of the organization. There is broad engagement by faculty and
administration. Administrative roles continue from the previous stage—enabler, facilitator, and convener. Faculty roles have
broadened to include those of consultant and coordinator. The
faculty consultant is usually invited to other departments to assist in getting conversations started, identifying existing practices that can easily be reframed to reflect genuine assessment
activities, and determining where the gaps might be. The coordinator works with the administrative convener to bring together
groups of faculty to plan initiatives involving more than one
department or in broad curriculum areas, such as general education or undergraduate studies.

Institutionalization. The last stage is institutionalization.
Behavioral efforts are directed at refinement. Assessment and
developing a culture of evidence have achieved the level of
legitimacy characterized by the status quo. The climate of opinion is that of consensus. The organizational structures that support this stage are standing committees. Administrative roles
become those of promotor, enabler, and supporter. The promoter furthers assessment at ever higher levels of decision making, secures resources that cannot be obtained in other ways,
and in general advances the aims of assessment. The supporter
essentially lends strength to assessment endeavors and, like the
promotor, supplies resources or other necessities. The supporter
is a champion of assessment. The result is the empowerment
of the faculty, who at this stage have taken on many of the roles

formerly relegated to and assumed by administration, such as advocate, enabler, facilitator, and convener.

In attempting to use this schema to locate the predominant stage of assessment development, it is important to listen to the conversations. Who is involved (faculty or administration)? Who initiates the conversations? At what levels are the activities taking place? The answers, to some degree, structure the subsequent conversations. In the initial stages, the administration tends to take the lead. At later stages, faculty are more prominent. However, we look to the institution to define the discussion and the level at which assessment conversations takes place. This schema simply suggests points of departure for examining an organization. All organizations will differ; it is incumbent upon the examiner to keep in mind that there can be as much variation within an institution as between institutions. Therefore, all institutions must be individualized to some extent. Therein lies the attraction of this schema: it allows for variations yet captures the commonalities.

Conclusion

Although externally and internally mandated assessments have somewhat different goals, they both provide evidence about how well an institution is fulfilling its mission. Assessment brings various departments of the university together to discuss what the goals should be and the best ways to achieve them. Institutions that begin assessment with a few goals and a plan for determining how well they are being accomplished are off to a good start.

The process of change often proceeds through a series of stages, and an assessment program is no exception. If the participants can understand the process of change, then an assessment program will proceed more smoothly, and the institution will realize the benefits of the "culture of evidence" that is at the heart of programmatic assessment.

References

Becker, E. *Revolution in Psychiatry*. New York: Free Press, 1964.
Becker, E. *Birth and Death of Meaning*. New York: Free Press, 1971.

Bowlby, J. *Separation, Anxiety and Anger*. New York: Basic Books, 1973.

California Postsecondary Education Commission. *Building a Multiracial, Multicultural University Community*. Palo Alto, Calif.: Stanford University, 1989.

California Postsecondary Education Commission. *Resource Guide to Assessing Campus Climate*. Sacramento: California Postsecondary Education Commission, 1992a.

California Postsecondary Education Commission. *Toward an Understanding of Campus Climate.* Sacramento: California Postsecondary Education Commission, 1992b.

Cross, P., and Angelo, T. *Classroom Assessment Techniques*. Ann Arbor, Mich.: National Center for Research to Improve Postsecondary Teaching and Learning, 1988.

Ewell, P. "Back to the Future." *Change*, Nov./Dec. 1991, pp. 12–17.

Ewell, P., and Lisensky, R. *Assessing Institutional Effectiveness: Redirecting the Self-Study Process*. Washington, D.C.: Consortium for the Advancement of Private Higher Education, 1988.

French, W., and Bell, C. H. *Organizational Development*. (2nd ed.) Englewood Cliffs, N.J.: Prentice-Hall, 1978.

Hersey, P., and Blanchard, K. H. *Management of Organizational Behavior*. (5th ed.) Englewood Cliffs, N.J.: Prentice-Hall, 1988.

Kübler-Ross, E. *On Death and Dying*. New York: Macmillan, 1969.

Light, R. *The Harvard Assessment Seminars: Second Report*. Cambridge, Mass.: Harvard University, 1992.

Lippitt, G. *Organizational Renewal*. New York: Appleton-Century-Crofts, 1969.

Marris, P. *Loss and Change*. New York: Anchor Books, 1975.

Wolff, R. *Incorporating Assessment into the Practice of Accreditation: A Preliminary Report on Accreditation, Assessment and Institutional Effectiveness*. Washington, D.C.: Council on Postsecondary Accreditation, 1992.

Chapter 16

How Classroom Assessment Can Improve Teaching and Learning

Susan G. Nummedal

During the past decade, concern has been growing over the quality of undergraduate education offered by our institutions of higher learning. Appeals from within the academy to reconsider the "priorities of the professorate" (Boyer, 1990) and calls for accountability from elected officials and the public at large (Ewell, 1991) make it clear that this concern is felt by both those within higher education and those being served by it. Nowhere within the community of higher education has this concern been more clearly expressed than at the 1992 annual conference of the American Association for Higher Education, a conference dedicated to the theme of "Reclaiming the Public Trust."

In his keynote address to the conference, Bok (1992) echoed the concerns of many in this country who believe that "our institutions are not making the education of students a top priority" (p. 15). He argued that one of the reasons the public doubts our commitment to quality undergraduate education is that universities for the most part have not come forward with a "compelling vision" of what it is they are trying to help their

289

students accomplish. Bok believes that catalogues and bulletins listing course offerings do not provide meaningful answers to the questions most on the minds of the public, including questions such as "How is this institution going to help my child think more clearly, be a more moral human being, find some compelling vocation in life, or embrace values that will help [him or her] make intelligent choices?" (p. 16). He could well have included additional questions, such as "How is this institution going to help my child be more sensitive to human diversity, develop both the confidence and competence to work with emerging technologies, or more generally make the connection between what is taught in the classroom and the realities of the world in which they live?"

This volume is dedicated to helping shape a "compelling vision" of undergraduate education for the twenty-first century. It addresses questions such as those just posed and offers some answers. It is important to note that these answers are not relevant only to educational practice in the next century. In the most fundamental sense, they are just as relevant to what we do today. The volume's unifying theme is that turning this vision into educational practice will require some significant changes in our college classrooms, that we must rethink the assumptions on which we build our undergraduate educational programs, and that we must rethink the ways that both faculty and students approach the teaching and learning process. In so doing, all those engaged in the teaching/learning process face what Knefelkamp (1992) has so aptly described as "stunning new challenges," not only in *what* is taught and learned but also in *how*, with *whom*, and *where* that teaching and learning takes place.

College teachers are being challenged to examine their basic beliefs and assumptions about the nature of the teaching/learning process, to examine their basic practices as instructors, and to revisit questions of both *what* and *how* they teach. In addition, they are being challenged to pay particular attention to *whom* they teach. They need to develop instructional strategies that are responsive to the voices of an increasingly diverse student population that brings to the classroom an ever-broader range of learning styles and ways of perceiving information (Jenkins and Bainer, 1991). And they are being challenged to reconsider *where* they teach, striving to create a more appropriate match between instructional setting, on the one hand, and desired student outcomes on the other (Appleberry, 1992).

Students are being challenged to become active partners in the learning process rather than passive recipients of information. They are being challenged to understand the unique perspectives voiced in a classroom populated by students who differ from them in a variety of ways. They are being challenged to take responsibility for their own learning. They are being challenged to assess their own learning process and outcomes. In doing so, they are being challenged to develop those attitudes and abilities that will enable them to become lifelong learners.

As necessary as it may be to respond to these challenges by changing college classrooms in the ways described in this volume, it is not sufficient. For, in the process of creating change, it is also necessary to assess the impact of these changes on the teaching and learning process. Higher education has a long history of failure with respect to providing evidence about the effectiveness of various instructional innovations on the improvement of student learning. Because of this failure, "[W]e do not have any process of enlightened trial and error by which to improve our methods of instruction" (Bok, 1992, pp. 16, 18).

Launching a movement for change in the absence of what Wolff (1991) calls a "culture of evidence" (relevant information about existing institutional performance) may be hazardous. Yet even in the absence of a strong body of empirical evidence, it is possible to argue, as has been argued throughout this volume, that a variety of signs point to the need for change in the ways we approach higher education. To launch such a movement for change without a well-thought-out plan for the ongoing assessment of the effects of the proposed instructional innovations on student learning simply will not do.

The public will continue to demand answers to questions about the effectiveness of this "new and improved" undergraduate education. No longer will they accept a system that can only report degrees earned by graduates without also reporting the actual accomplishments of those graduates (Appleberry, 1992). While the public continues to demand assessment for accountability, those within higher education must not lose sight of the fundamental purpose of assessment: to improve the teaching/learning process. As Wolff and Harris put forth the case in Chapter Fifteen, efforts to change the college classroom must be accompanied by efforts to ask a broad range of critical questions about the impact of those changes—and to provide answers to those questions.

    This chapter focuses on one of the critical questions, the question that Cross (1990) has urged all faculty interested in improving student learning to ask: "What are *my* students learning in *my* classroom as a result of *my* instruction?" (p. 12). When faculty seek answers to this question, by assessing student learning *while that learning is in progress,* they are engaging in what Cross (1986) has described as classroom assessment. In what follows, the case for classroom assessment is set forth. Included are a discussion of the purpose and process of classroom assessment, a presentation of the evidence available on its effectiveness in improving student learning, and a discussion of the implications for educating students for the twenty-first century.

The Purpose of Classroom Assessment

The purpose of classroom assessment is twofold. First, as Angelo (1990) has argued, "Classroom assessment . . . makes use of assessment to improve the effectiveness of higher education where it matters most: in the college classroom" (p. 72). Through this kind of assessment, faculty introducing instructional innovations will be able to find out *early* what is—and what is not—working in the changing classrooms they create. By obtaining feedback on how and how well students are learning what they are being taught, faculty will be able to make appropriate modifications in their teaching while student learning is taking place.

    For example, at the end of a class session, an instructor might use the popular classroom assessment technique known as the "muddiest" point (Mosteller, 1989) to obtain feedback from students about what was least clear in the class session. The instructor can then use this feedback to shape the next class session. Depending on the feedback received, the response could involve simply repeating some of the points covered during the previous class, expanding and elaborating on the points, or perhaps even devising completely new ways of presenting them.

Second, classroom assessment is not just an assessment tool. It is also a teaching tool, an instructional innovation in its own right. When teachers ask students to provide feedback on a particular class session, such as by using the muddiest point technique, they are asking students to reflect on what they do and do not understand about the material under consideration. This requires students to engage in the metacognitive processes of monitoring and assessing their own learning. If faculty make *frequent* use of such classroom assessment techniques, they are providing an opportunity for students to develop these metacognitive abilities. When teachers share the feedback obtained with their students, it helps students "improve their learning strategies and study habits in order to become more independent, successful learners" (Angelo, 1991b, p. 17). It is precisely this quality of independent, successful learning that lies at the heart of educating students. Through the process of classroom assessment, students can become partners in the teaching/learning process, sharing responsibility for it and reaping its benefits.

It is important to realize that classroom assessments differ from other forms of in-class assessment (Angelo, 1991a). They are not like the usual classroom assignments, papers, quizzes, or examinations. Typically, they are not graded, nor are the responses of individual students identifiable. In fact, most teachers conduct classroom assessments *before* graded assessments as a way to improve both the teaching and the learning processes as they take place. Thus, classroom assessments are designed as an intervention at various phases of the typical teaching/learning cycle of teach→study/learn→test/apply. They can be inserted between any of the phases of this cycle (between the teaching and studying phases, the studying and testing phases, and even the testing and teaching phases). Their value is that they provide feedback to both teacher and students about the teaching/learning process.

The Process of Classroom Assessment

Classroom assessment has been described as "a straightforward, learner-centered, teacher-directed approach" to assessment (Angelo, 1990, p. 72). It is one element in a more comprehensive approach to conducting research in the college classroom, an approach Cross (1990) has named classroom research. Most often, it represents the first step taken by faculty interested in improving the teacher/learning process.

As college teachers move from wanting to find out more about a specific class session to developing assessment goals for an entire course, classroom assessments become part of larger classroom research projects. For example, Olmsted (1991) reports using a variety of classroom assessment strategies as part of a semester-long classroom research project designed to improve student success rates and increase student satisfaction in a large lecture, general chemistry course. This project has moved well beyond asking a single question about a specific class to becoming a prototypical classroom research project, one that Cross (1990) has described as "a continuous, ongoing study of teaching and learning in the everyday classroom" (p. 14). I describe some classroom research projects later in conjunction with a discussion of the evidence on the effects of classroom assessment.

To conduct a meaningful classroom assessment, college teachers need to begin by developing a clear formulation of their teaching and learning goals. When teachers are unclear about what it is they want to assess and why, the feedback received from classroom assessments cannot serve the intended purpose. The Teaching Goals Inventory developed by Angelo and Cross (1993) can be used to assist teachers in the goal formulation process. This inventory consists of fifty-two goal statements representing six goal clusters: higher-order thinking skills, basic academic success skills, discipline-specific knowledge and skills, liberal arts and academic values, work and career preparation, and personal development. Inventory instructions ask college teachers to focus on a specific course, then rate the importance of each goal statement on a five-point scale, ranging from "not applicable" to "essential." With the aid of a self-scoring work-sheet (Angelo and Cross, 1993), the inventory can help college teachers "become more aware of what they want to accomplish in individual courses" (p. 20) and, hence, what they need to assess. Angelo and Cross have also provided a table that indexes the goal clusters by specific classroom assessment techniques, thus enabling college teachers to link their teaching goals to particular classroom assessments.

One additional point regarding goals should be noted. Formulating teaching and learning goals is not necessarily just the teacher's responsibility. Students can also be invited to contribute to these goals. The classroom assessment technique called *goal ranking and matching* (Angelo and Cross, 1993; formerly called the student goals ranking, Cross and Angelo, 1988) provides one way to bring students into the process. By asking students to list their individual goals for a course and then rank them for importance in their lives, college teachers can discover the "match" between their goals and those of their students, students can begin to think about the ways in which their personal goals might be met in the course, and both the teacher and students have an opportunity to create shared goals.

Once a clear statement of teaching and learning goals has been formulated, the next step is to generate a *simple* question to ask—one that will enable the teacher to obtain feedback about the progress the *class as a whole* (not a specific individual) is making toward a particular goal. Students answer the question anonymously. Their responses are not graded. The teacher summarizes the feedback and shares it with the entire class. The feedback then becomes the basis for improving the quality of both teaching and learning. This two-way feedback process—from students to teacher and teacher to students—opens up the dialogue between them. It also opens up the dialogue among students as they learn not only about their own learning but also about that of others in the classroom. As such, the process creates a partnership in learning among all members of the classroom.

The most complete description of classroom assessment techniques is contained in *Classroom Assessment Techniques: A Handbook for College Teachers* (Angelo and Cross, 1993). This handbook describes some fifty different techniques. The book provides a wealth of information about each technique, including estimations of ease of use for both faculty and students; information about its purpose and associated teaching goals that can be assessed with its use; suggestions for use, including actual examples; step-by-step procedures for use; suggestions for analyzing and summarizing the feedback collected; ideas for adapting and extending its use, as well as arguments (both pro and con) regarding its use; and, last but not least, "caveats." To assist in the selection of appropriate techniques, the authors index them by discipline-specific examples and Teaching Goals Inventory clusters. Users can adapt the classroom assessment techniques for their own purposes.

Evidence for Effectiveness
of Classroom Assessment

Cross (1991) reports that as of the summer of 1991, more than 5,000 teachers and administrators nationwide had participated in workshops on classroom assessment. The results of some of the emerging classroom assessment projects are just beginning to make their way into the literature. The best evidence on these projects can be found in *Classroom Research: Early Lessons from Success*, edited by Angelo (1991a). (Also see Angelo and Cross, 1993, for a "lessons learned" as adapted from Angelo, 1991a.) It contains examples of classroom assessment projects covering fifteen different disciplines, conducted in settings that vary from a small English composition course to a large introductory science class of over 100 students, and using more than twenty-five different classroom assessment techniques adapted from those presented in the first edition of the Cross and Angelo (1988) handbook. What follows is description of projects bearing directly on four of the core issues raised in this volume: (1) turning passive students into active learners, (2) improving students' critical thinking and problem-solving abilities, (3) enhancing student learning through cooperative learning, and (4) educating students from increasingly varied backgrounds to become more sensitive to human diversity.

Active Learning

Actively involving students in the teaching/learning process has been described throughout this volume as a necessary condition for successfully educating students for the twenty-first century. While it can be argued that classroom assessments by their very nature change passive students into active ones, some classroom assessment projects have been designed specifically to assess how well this goal is achieved.

For example, Olmsted (1991) used a wide variety of classroom assessment techniques in a large lecture course to assess and promote active learning. In-class questionnaires were used at the beginning and end of the course to assess students' perceptions of the most valuable components of the course. Mid-lecture assessments were used to determine how the teaching/learning process was going during particular class sessions. Furthermore, self-analysis of homework assignments was incorporated into the course to help students reflect on what and how they were learning from these assignments.

Using several indices, Olmsted assessed for changes in active learning over the semester. The results showed that students made increased use of office hours, that the addition of various classroom assessment techniques made the course a more productive one for them (compared to a traditional course), and that the use of these techniques were more effective as an instructional strategy than "encouraging student questions, frequent homework assignments, and presentation of 'real-life' applications" (p. 63). Overall, Olmsted reported an increase in student involvement in the course, an improvement both he and his students associated with the use of classroom assessments. This improvement in active student learning was also associated with other measures of increased student satisfaction with the course.

Critical Thinking

Several classroom assessment projects have been designed to assess the effectiveness of instructional interventions on specific aspects of critical thinking and, at the same time, to help students develop these critical thinking abilities. In particular, these projects have focused on specific higher-order thinking and problem-solving abilities.

Angelo (1991b) describes a number of classroom assessment projects that have targeted the kinds of learning at the heart of instruction designed to improve higher-order thinking abilities. These projects focus on student learning that goes well beyond the acquisition of simple declarative knowledge (the learning of facts and principles). Instead, they focus on the kinds of learning that are necessary if students are going to be able to relate what they have learned in college to the world in which they live and work. As characterized by Angelo, these projects include classroom assessments of (1) procedural learning (knowing *how* to apply what has been learned), (2) conditional learning (knowing *when* and *where* to apply what has been learned), and (3) reflective learning (knowing how to reflect on the values, beliefs, and motivations so as to understand *why* they as well as others think and act as they do).

According to Angelo (1991b), classroom assessment projects in English literature, clinical nursing, and mathematics have been conducted to improve the procedural learning of students. These projects have used classroom assessment techniques such as the *directed paraphrase* (students are directed to summarize or restate important information or concepts for a specific purpose and audience) and *documented problem-set solution* (students document their problem-solving process), as well as adapted versions of a technique known in writing across the curriculum programs as the *one-word journal* (students generate one word to best summarize a particular reading). In these projects, results of the classroom assessments have enabled both the faculty and the students to better understand the difficulties faced when attempting to apply concepts in new situations. With repeated assessments and subsequent modifications in the teaching/learning process, notable improvements in procedural knowledge have been found to occur.

For example, in an English literature course, students were asked to produce a one-word journal summarizing a particular reading and to justify the choice of that word. After several experiences with this assessment, the students developed not only improved summarizing skills but also improved abilities to explain and justify their word choice.

Similar classroom assessment projects designed for improvement in the areas of conditional and reflective learning have been described by Angelo. Faculty in business management and social work have used the "What's the Principle?" and student-generated minicases assessment techniques to further improve both the teaching and learning of conditional knowledge (Angelo and Cross, 1993). "What's the principle?" is a technique that assesses students' ability to "associate specific problems with the general principles used to solve them" (p. 218). The student-generated minicases technique asks students to write a minicase that might follow from the application of principles or concepts to specific situations. Angelo and Cross report improvement in the ability of students to evaluate the conditions under which the application of specific strategies and principles might lead to successful outcomes. And faculty in physical education and physics have found ways to improve reflective learning through the use of the student goals ranking technique and the informal attitude surveys designed to assess how students view particular issues.

Nakaji (1991) describes a more comprehensive classroom research project designed to improve students' problem-solving abilities. The project began with a classroom assessment technique designed by Nakaji to assess the role of visualization in solving physics problems. Students were asked "to draw the pictures or images they were 'seeing' in their minds as they were choosing the most appropriate frame of reference" for solving a particular physics problem (p. 80).

As is often the case with a first attempt at classroom assessment, Nakaji found this assessment raised more questions than it answered. He reports that while he did learn something about the effect his teaching was having on the ways in which students visualized problems, he also discovered that many students had considerable difficulty even completing the assessment. The images they eventually produced were affected by several factors, including the inability to self-monitor the problem-solving process, the effects of the process of drawing on the mental representation of the image itself, and concern about how well they were drawing.

These observations led Nakaji to develop two more comprehensive, long-term classroom research projects on the relationship between visualization and problem solving in physics. In the first, classroom assessments of students' problem solving yielded important information about the difficulties students had in changing mental representations during the problem-solving process, the importance of the quality (versus quantity) of the visualization, and the uses students made of their visualizations. The second follow-up project allowed Nakaji to probe more deeply into a broader range of processes students use while solving physics problems. His classroom assessments led to a better understanding for both him and his students of the ways in which a variety of mental images used during different phases of the solution process affected the final outcome.

Cooperative Learning

Cooper (see Chapter Five in this volume) has documented many of the positive outcomes associated with the instructional strategy of cooperative learning. Much of this documentation comes from evaluation studies designed to determine the overall effect on student outcomes of courses in which cooperative learning groups have been used. While these summative evaluation results are important, it is only through a formative evaluation process, such as classroom assessment, that instructors can monitor and modify the cooperative learning process as it unfolds.

Many have found a "natural" fit between cooperative learning strategies and classroom assessment. For example, Cottell (1991) reports using two classroom assessment techniques in an ongoing assessment of the effectiveness of the cooperative learning group process in an accounting course. He began with the quality control circle, adapted from the classroom assessment quality circles described in Cross and Angelo (1988). With this technique, he was able to get regular feedback about how the cooperative learning groups functioned when assigned the task of reviewing homework. The members of the quality control circle soon alerted him to an all-too-familiar problem associated with group work—that is, the problem of "hitchhikers" (group members who are underprepared, are unprepared, or fail to attend class). The circle members then helped design a classroom assessment that would deal with the problem. They adapted the Cross and Angelo (1988) teacher-designed evaluation miniforms. The resulting assessment strategy, the cooperative learning peer evaluation, allowed members of each cooperative learning group to perform individual evaluations of group members' participation. The results gave both the instructor and the students ways to resolve the problem of group hitchhikers.

Obler, Arnold, Sigala, and Umbdenstock (1991) also document a series of classroom research projects that make use of classroom assessment to increase the effectiveness of cooperative learning groups. The more than sixty classroom researchers adapted some classroom assessment techniques and created others to improve student learning within a "pro-diversity" curriculum. It is this curriculum and its relationship to classroom assessment that will be discussed next.

Multicultural Education

The Obler and colleagues classroom research projects provide an excellent example of how classroom assessment can be used to both monitor, at the classroom level, the implementation of cultural diversity in the curriculum and to improve the learning of an increasingly diverse student population. These authors describe the curriculum at their college as a "pro-diversity" curriculum. By this, they mean a curriculum that "promotes the use of teaching and learning methods and materials that meaningfully include as many underrepresented groups as possible" (p. 107). Using a number of classroom assessment techniques, not only were instructors able to improve the effectiveness of student cooperative learning groups, they were able to "increase students' awareness, skills, and applications of course content to a diverse, multicultural society" (p. 106). For example, focused listing (Cross and Angelo, 1988) was used in a U.S. history class to help students recognize and understand the ways in which perceptions of minority group members may or may not have changed by specifically asking them to list negative images that had not changed over a particular period of history. Another classroom assessment technique was used in a political science class in conjunction with a cooperative learning exercise to help students understand the differences in the composition of U.S. ethnic/racial groups represented in prison populations. Specifically, in an adaptation of the one-minute paper technique, students were asked to respond to an article they had discussed by describing one *clear* idea and one *fuzzy* idea.

Conclusion: Implications for Educating Students for the Twenty-First Century

Evidence from the classroom assessment projects I have described serves to illustrate the ways in which faculty from a broad range of disciplines have gathered evidence on student learning using classroom assessment techniques, providing support for the proposition that classroom assessment is one assessment strategy that can help faculty find out early what is — and what is not — working to improve the teaching/learning process. For faculty seeking to make fundamental changes in the process of educating students for the twenty-first century, classroom assessment would seem to be a critical component of the instructional innovation process.

In a concluding chapter for their handbook, Angelo and Cross (1993) address the question of whether classroom assessment actually increases student learning. They summarize evidence from a broader range of projects than have been described here, describe results from these projects that show both improvement and no change in student learning, and present an analysis of why it is so difficult to provide a definitive answer to the question. While acknowledging that it is possible that classroom assessment actually doesn't improve student learning, they also suggest methodological problems that may be contributing to the mixed results, including (1) the problems associated with using class grades as indicators of student learning, (2) the possible mismatch between the knowledge tapped by classroom assessments and that tapped by tests, and (3) the fact that the time frame within which improvement is measured may not be sensitive to changes associated with long-term retention or depth of understanding that may derive from the use of classroom assessments. They conclude by calling for more carefully planned and well-controlled experiments or quasi-experiments to document these effects.

In addition to its promise as a way to improve student learning, classroom assessment is significant as an approach to developing teaching expertise. By providing feedback about the teaching/learning process, classroom assessments can enable faculty to establish what Shulman (1988) has described as "pedagogically meaningful relationships" with students. In his research on the assessment of teachers, Shulman has found consistent evidence that teaching expertise rests on what he has termed *pedagogical content knowledge*. This knowledge goes beyond knowledge of generic teaching skills on the one hand and subject matter expertise on the other.

According to Shulman (1988), pedagogical content knowledge includes, but is not limited to, (1) knowledge of how to develop optimal ways of selecting and sequencing subject matter so as to ensure future understanding of material; (2) knowledge of where in the subject matter sequence students are likely to encounter the greatest difficulties and the ability to design appropriate instructional interventions to overcome these difficulties; (3) knowledge of the kinds of preconceptions and misconceptions that interfere with student learning and ways to assist students in overcoming them; and (4) knowledge of the kinds of representations of ideas and concepts that enable students to learn more effectively. Clearly, this is not the kind of knowledge teachers possess when they enter their first college classroom. Nor is it necessarily the kind of knowledge they possess when launching new instructional innovations. Classroom assessment is a procedure that can assist teachers in developing such expertise.

Improving student learning and teaching expertise will

be necessary if the challenge of educating students for the twenty-first century is to be met. As the college classroom changes, we have an opportunity to closely monitor and modify the teaching/learning process within that classroom. Classroom assessment provides a compelling model for realizing this opportunity. By systematically finding out what students are learning in specific classes as a function of specific instructional interventions, classroom teachers can also make a real contribution to the "culture of evidence" so clearly demanded by those both within the academy and those served by it.

References

Angelo, T. A. "Classroom Assessment: Improving Learning Quality Where It Matters Most." In M. D. Svinicki (ed.), *The Changing Face of College Teaching.* New Directions for Teaching and Learning, No. 42. San Francisco: Jossey-Bass, 1990.

Angelo, T. A. (ed.). *Classroom Research: Early Lessons from Success.* San Francisco: Jossey-Bass, 1991a.

Angelo, T. A. "Ten Easy Pieces: Assessing Higher Learning in Four Dimensions." In T. A. Angelo (ed.), *Classroom Research: Early Lessons from Success.* San Francisco: Jossey-Bass, 1991b.

Angelo, T. A., and Cross, K. P. *Classroom Assessment Techniques: A Handbook for College Teachers.* San Francisco: Jossey-Bass, 1993.

Appleberry, J. B. "Change in Our Future: How Will We Cope?" Invited Convocation Address, California State University, Long Beach, Sept. 1992.

Bok, D. "Reclaiming the Public Trust." *Change,* 1992, *24*(4), 13–19.

Boyer, E. L. *Scholarship Reconsidered: Priorities of the Professorate.* Princeton, N.J.: Carnegie Foundation for the Advancement of Teaching, 1990.

Cottell, P. G. "Classroom Research in Accounting: Assessing for Learning." In T. A. Angelo (ed.), *Classroom Research: Early Lessons from Success.* San Francisco: Jossey Bass, 1991.

Cross, K. P. "Using Assessment to Improve Instruction." Paper presented at the 47th ETS Invitational Conference, New York City, Oct. 1986.

Cross, K. P. "Teaching to Improve Learning." *Journal on Excellence in College Teaching,* 1990, *1,* 9–22.

Cross, K. P. "What Next for Classroom Research?" Paper presented at the 3rd annual Workshop on Classroom Research, University of California, Berkeley, Aug. 1991.

Cross, K. P., and Angelo, T. A. *Classroom Assessment Techniques: A Handbook for Faculty.* Ann Arbor, Mich.: National Center for Research to Improve Postsecondary Teaching and Learning, 1988.

Ewell, P. T. "Assessment and Public Accountability: Back to the Future." *Change,* 1991, *23,* 12–17.

Jenkins, C. A., and Bainer, D. L. "Common Instructional Problems in the Multicultural Classroom." *Journal on Excellence in College Teaching,* 2, 1991, 77–88.

Knefelkamp, L. L. "The Multicultural Curriculum and Communities of Peace." *Liberal Education,* 1992, *78*(2), 26–35.

Mosteller, F. "The 'Muddiest Point in the Lecture' as a Feedback Device." *On Teaching and Learning: The Journal of the Harvard-Danforth Center,* 1989, *3,* 10–21.

Nakaji, D. M. "Classroom Research in Physics: Gaining Insights into Visualization and Problem Solving." In T. A. Angelo (ed.), *Classroom Research: Early Lessons from Success.* San Francisco: Jossey-Bass, 1991.

Obler, S., Arnold, V., Sigala, C., and Umbdenstock, L. "Using Cooperative Learning and Classroom Research with Culturally Diverse Students." In T. A. Angelo (ed.), *Classroom Research: Early Lessons from Success.* San Francisco: Jossey-Bass, 1991.

Olmsted, J. "Using Classroom Research in a Large Introductory Science Class." In T. A. Angelo (ed.), *Classroom Research: Early Lessons from Success.* San Francisco: Jossey-Bass, 1991.

Shulman, L. S. "A Union of Insufficiencies: Strategies for Teacher Assessment in a Period of Educational Reform." *Educational Leadership,* 1988, *46,* 36–41.

Wolff, R. A. *Assessment and Accreditation: A Shotgun Marriage?* Washington, D.C.: American Association for Higher Education, 1991.

Chapter 17

Student Portfolios
as an Assessment Tool

Mary Kay Crouch, Sheryl I. Fontaine

The use of portfolios for purposes of assessment represents a major change in the way a profession thinks about evaluation. Rather than looking only for the end results of learning, professionals who choose portfolio evaluation want to understand the activities and the kinds of performance that went into the pieces assembled in a portfolio. In other words, they seek to put their assessment practices in context.

The term *portfolio* is defined as a selection of assignments that a student has consciously assembled from a number of pieces produced over a semester or some other period of time. Larson (1991) notes that a portfolio can be used for various purposes. It may determine students' final evaluation for a course or program. Or, if the essays are placed in chronological order, the portfolio can show students' development or demonstrate accomplishments that allow them to enter or exit a university or

We acknowledge Beth Harnick-Shapiro, Patricia Watson, Gerald Gordon, and Kathleen Brooks, who served on the panel that provided the original idea for this chapter. Our thanks to Patricia Watson for helping to compile information on CSUF students.

receive a degree in one of its majors. Although a portfolio should be "ordered and purposeful, it can also be flexible—a tool of value in bringing elements, steps, or parallel tracks in a student's academic career together for examination at the same time by a single reader or group of readers" (Larson, 1991, p. 138). Currently, portfolios are being used for these purposes in university courses as diverse as technical writing, biology, business communication, and mathematics, and in the evaluation of teaching development (see, for example, Boyer, 1990; Millis, 1991; Seldin, 1991).

As writing specialists, we draw our example of portfolio assessment from the writing program and writing center in which we work. We both feel strongly that responsibility for the teaching of writing extends beyond English departments and that a system of portfolio assessment could offer faculty from other departments a way to integrate into their courses attention to writing content and writing quality. But aside from our contention that *all* teachers are teachers of writing, by illustrating the evolution and impact of portfolio assessment in one particular educational support network, we hope to offer a starting point from which other educators might develop their own systems within the context of their own institutions, programs, and courses. To this end, our discussion concludes with lists of what we believe to be the components of any system of portfolio assessment and the positive consequences that portfolio assessment can have for all instructors and students.

Principles of Portfolio Evaluations

When writing-program administrators make decisions about what constitutes growth or improvement in writing—*what* will be measured, *how* it will be measured, and *when* it will be measured—they are also revealing what they assume to value most in student writing and in the teaching of writing. In determining the possible educational appeal and impact that any particular form of writing assessment will have for teachers and students, we must examine these assumptions theoretically and practically. If they are to effect lasting change, they must be at once theoretically sound enough to extend beyond any individual classroom and adaptable enough to adjust to the idiosyncratic teaching styles of particular instructors.

Within the context of a whole writing program, portfolio assessment assumes that if we are to improve student writing, we must change the *way* students write. Improving students' editorial skills or teaching them essay structures may give poor writing the appearance of having changed for the better, but such changes are, at best, useful only in the context of the classroom and, at worst, relatively superficial. The semester-long process of creating a writing portfolio moves students beyond making mere surface changes to affecting the way they think about and produce writing. Portfolio assessment promotes the belief that good writing takes time; it includes thinking and planning, rethinking and revising. Good writing is seldom produced in isolation — no matter that ultimately the writer usually writes alone — but rather is the result of interactions between and among people that occur in social contexts. It benefits from the writer talking and sharing, listening and responding, and it meets the needs and expectations of different audiences. Finally, it is the result of the writer's acting on successful intuition and taking responsibility for the writing.

Portfolios, of necessity, require some metacognitive work: in writing classes, for example, students have to consider their composing processes and their development as writers over time. In this way, students become self-reflective about their writing; they can look longitudinally at their writing, begin to recognize change, and grow in their knowledge of who they are as writers. Yancey (1992) points out that through portfolios students are able to view their individual essays as a whole rather than as a series of unrelated pieces: they see the writings "separately and then together, in context" (p. 104). Further, rather than viewing each piece as finished at the time of its composing, student writers know they are not bound by the text as it stands at a particular moment in time. They come to regard revision as an integral part of their writing because portfolio assessment requires them to include the writing that represents the best work they can produce over a semester.

Portfolios also highlight the *performance,* or active process, of the learner in a particular area, much as art portfolios demonstrate the artistic act of the painter or sculptor, whether novice or professional. Because writing can be traced through preliminary drafts, it is comparable to an artist's preliminary sketchbook drawings of a painting or a sculpture that are available even after the final project is completed. These drawings may also contain added information (comments, sketches) contributed by an instructor, peers, or friends. Since writing, too, is a performance art, collaboration with others is an important element for the performer in compiling a portfolio. In the case of student writers, they themselves can take advantage of their preliminary drafts and peer reviews to more effectively evaluate the growth of their own skills, since learning of any kind, looked at developmentally, must allow for errors and spurts of growth, as well as for regression as learners attempt new skills. The semester-long effect of assembling portfolio pieces permits all of these normal processes to take place naturally, rather than pushing students to turn in "perfect" work at a time when they are still developing and testing their skills.

Assembling a finished portfolio—thus meeting institutional requirements for evaluation—lets both teacher and student see the pieces included from a dual perspective. On the one hand, they can view the development of skills through drafts of papers and their revisions (taking "skills" here in its broadest possible sense); on the other hand, they can see and measure the finished pieces that represent the student's level of success at a skillful performance. In all of these processes, the students realize that they can take charge of their own learning under the guidance of their teachers and peers. The learning is interactive and socially based.

Increasingly, portfolios are being used for assessment in writing classes and programs (see Belanoff and Dickson, 1991; Yancey, 1992) because they provide both the student and the teacher with important information. Lucas (1988), for example, argues that the attractiveness of portfolios for assessment purposes is their "ecological validity: the extent to which a text reflects (and hence reports results from) the whole writing environment of the learner, and the extent to which it impacts that environment in positive rather than negative ways" (p. 12). The environment situates real writers writing real texts, not mere writing exercises. Further, when evaluation is ecologically valid, teachers and students get more information that is of a higher quality and usefulness than they would from a timed test or a single sample. In other words, portfolios allow both learners and instructors to observe longer-term learning processes, rather than simply to prepare for one specific test or learning task.

One of the best features of assessment by portfolio rests on the contextual nature that such evaluation allows. Here *context* is used in two senses. First, the term refers to the ways in which a portfolio can be constructed. As we have already suggested, an instructor can develop portfolios to fit a particular class or program; he or she is not bound to follow exactly the procedures of another instructor or program. In this way, portfolios are very flexible and make possible a consideration of the needs of a particular institution and of particular students in developing assessment to meet those requirements. Second, *context* is used in our discussion to describe the broad areas of assistance that are available—from classroom instructors, graduate assistants, and writing center tutors—as students prepare for their portfolio assessment specifically in the Developmental Writing Program at California State University, Fullerton (CSUF).

A Model of Writing-Portfolio
Assessment in the Classroom

Our personal knowledge of portfolio assessment comes mainly from its application in writing classes: one of the authors (Crouch) began using them in her freshman writing sections and initiated them as a tool for assessment in the Developmental Writing Program at CSUF; the other author (Fontaine) has used portfolios in the freshman writing program at an East Coast university and in the basic writing program at CSUF and applies their principles to tutor training. While we will take the CSUF Developmental Writing Program as the primary example of successful portfolio assessment, we hope to suggest through our model how portfolios can be used for a broader range of disciplines and courses, not only those in which writing is the sole focus.

The portfolio assessment procedures used in the Developmental Writing Program have been in effect since 1988; however, they are not static. They have evolved over that time and will continue to be modified as program coordinators, instructors, graduate assistants, and tutors learn from our changing population of students, from others who use portfolio evaluation, and from our attempt to discover our own preferences for pieces to be included in the portfolio to provide us with valid evaluation. Most important, because of its flexibility to meet the needs of our students, all involved in the portfolio evaluation find it a highly satisfactory means of assessment.

As we have already noted, portfolios are adaptable to various contexts. To set the stage for what we do at CSUF, we will describe the broad context for our particular use of portfolios for assessment: the student population in the Developmental Writing Program, the network to which students have access for assistance, the specifics of portfolio construction, and the actual evaluation of the portfolios, which we use as a criterion for exiting the course.

The Students in the Writing Program

The students who are required to take developmental writing, a noncredit-bearing prebaccalaureate course, generally are first-generation college students who lack role models for what college students do. Most are in their first year of college; many enter as part of a program for low-income students or an intensive learning program designed for students who score in the lowest quartile of the English Placement Test given throughout the California State University system. The students at CSUF make up a diverse ethnic population with 28 percent ethnic minorities. (Orange County, the site of CSUF, is home to the largest population of Vietnamese outside of Vietnam.) The Developmental Writing Program serves a population of about 70 percent minority students. For many of our students, English is a second language or, if they are Latino, a second dialect. Often they report that they have low self-esteem as writers, or they have high self-esteem (many took advanced placement classes in high school) but low productivity and an inability to produce academic writing.

The Assistance Network for Students

Figure 17.1 shows the context of the rich, interactive writing network that students become part of when they take the developmental writing course. Writing instructors serve as co-constructors of our teaching and assessment philosophy as well as teaching the course. They act as mentors for the graduate students (referred to as graduate assistants, or GAs) who assist in their classes and are the primary liaisons between the classroom and the Writing Center, where the GAs tutor. This center is staffed by both the GAs and undergraduate tutors (known as student assistants, or SAs).

As part of their course work, students in developmental writing are required to make at least four appointments to visit the Writing Center for help with their papers. Through this requirement, students experience another part of the contextual network of writing and come to understand the support both the program and the center provide through that network. Also, it further strengthens the idea of the collaborative nature of writing, extending out from classroom activities to the center. GAs and SAs are familiar with the nature of the assessment required of the students and tailor their tutoring to meet the special needs of the students. We also hope that through these visits students will continue to be users of this center throughout their academic lives at Fullerton.

Creating and Responding to the Portfolio

The portfolio process, then, becomes thoroughly integrated into all facets of the student writer's experience with the course be-

Figure 17.1. Contextual Elements Contributing to Portfolio Evaluation.

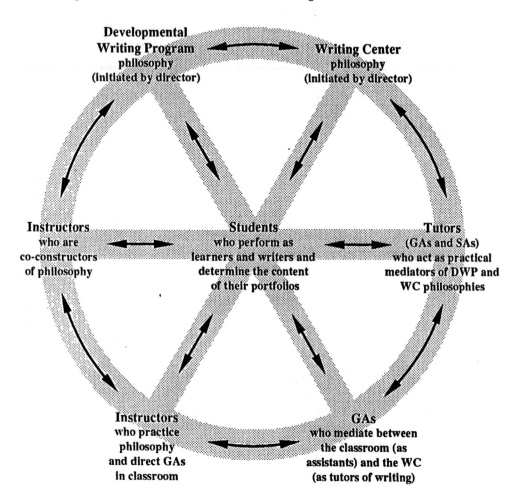

cause all participants — students, instructors, GAs, SAs — work toward preparing students for constructing their portfolios at the end of the term. This compilation of essays will determine whether students complete the course in one term or will need a second term of basic writing before moving into the bacca-laureate course. In helping students prepare their portfolio, each person who interacts with them plays the role of coach rather than grader, thus providing a great deal of formative evaluation. That is, various readers *respond to* the writing, rather than giving it a summative, or grade-based, evaluation. In this way, students see their writing from the reader's standpoint; the writing is treated as "real" writing that the reader is attempting to get meaning from rather than one more writing exercise to be graded and then cast aside. (For the notion of the teacher as coach, see Belanoff and Elbow, 1991. For responding to drafts rather than final products, see Sommers, 1982.)

Responses to writing are more effective than grades, for they allow instructors to indicate what is effective about a piece as well as where the writing fails when the reader cannot understand what the writer is trying to argue, analyze, narrate, and so on. Rather than evaluating texts as if they were truly finished, instructors can ask questions of and give encouragement to the writers as part of their critique (for example, "I'm not sure what argument you're trying to make here." "What do you mean by this term? How are you defining it?" "Good point!"). Student writers begin to understand the concept of revision, of "reseeing" their work, the process that "real" writers go through.

Writing for a particular assignment often begins in the classroom, with everyone participating in generating ideas. Other classroom activities are carried out in small groups under the direction of the instructor and the GA. In these peer groups, students read and respond to each other's papers, thus extending the collaborative nature of writing and thereby teaching students in a very immediate and active way about how others read their writing. Through their experience of reading the essays of their peers, writers also learn how others will read their portfolio papers, since portfolios are evaluated by two instructors other than the student's own. In addition, the instructor and the GA continually reinforce the tutoring possibilities in the Writing Center, where yet another audience can be called on for response, thus offering students many audiences and much feedback for what they write.

For their portfolio, students are required to turn in three papers, two of which are finished (in the sense that they have been extensively revised and the final drafts are typed) and one that has been written in class under time constraints. Students do a great deal of writing during the semester, but through selecting essays that they will make part of their portfolios, they learn something about what writers really do. They understand that not every piece they turn in needs to be finished or revised. They learn that some writing will be tentative, something on the way to a final piece but in need of much change before it can be called polished. They also learn about writing under time constraints, as the third essay in the portfolio is written in class. (Instructors are encouraged to assign two essays of this latter type so that students have a choice of in-class timed writings to put into the portfolio.)

Here is the procedure we use for this type of essay. The in-class essay is written over the period of a week and collected each day at the end of the class. Students may receive help from the instructor and GA during the class. At the end of the week, the instructor places these essays in a file until the end of the term. On the last day of class, students are given forty-five minutes to make final revisions on the essay before placing it in their portfolio.

A timed writing piece is included in the portfolio for valid reasons. First, we know that students are required to write under pressure of time in other courses; we are, therefore, preparing them for this kind of writing task. Second, timed writings provide some check on the possibility of plagiarism, an issue for portfolio evaluation because students are encouraged to get as much reader response to their papers as they can to assist with revision. However, because this is a writing course and teachers see drafts of papers as they are being produced, spotting plagiarism in student writing is relatively easy, and it is rarely an issue in the assessment process.

Finally, the timed writing provides a check on the language skills of the large number of nonnative English-speaking students who take the course. While we teach several English-as-a-second-language (ESL) sections each term, staffed by instructors specially trained in this area, ESL students are enrolled in all sections of the course. When we began using portfolios, the ESL instructors contended that without timed writings we would have no way of assessing the ESL students' writing abilities. They also argued that ESL students might resort to plagiarism or even have others completely rewrite their papers to eliminate the kinds of errors nonnative speakers make that might keep them from passing the course. By exerting more control over the writing—that is, watching it actually being produced in class—we could control for plagiarism, and we would also be able to better assess the students' writing skills. Thus far, the timed writing adequately addresses these concerns.

Critical Role of the Instructors

What transpired in the discussions about evaluating ESL students' portfolios—a debate that continued among instructors over three semesters as we all became comfortable with portfolio evaluation—highlights an important aspect of this kind of assessment: the involvement and commitment needed from those who participate in it. Lucas (1988) asserts quite rightly that successful evaluation "requires a continuing commitment to team-assessment, to continual sharing and reshaping of assessment purposes, processes, tasks, . . . scoring criteria and methods of analyzing writing samples" (p. 16). Evaluation by portfolio is not a process that can simply be imposed on instructors if it is to be used successfully by a whole program. In the Developmental Writing Program, instructors truly have become co-constructors of our philosophy and practice, because they determine the rationale behind the types of papers that are included and they help construct the standards for evaluation, the rubric.

Instructors must "buy into" and believe in portfolios, and they have, in a number of ways. First, they had to agree to try this type of evaluation, knowing that they would have to adapt their teaching to the preparation of the portfolio. They had to understand that greater demands would be made on their time at the end of the term in respect to grading. For example, with our previous evaluation, in one long afternoon instructors could train for and score holistically the timed essays collected from 400 students, because students wrote on a common topic and their essays were relatively short, about three or four handwritten pages. Portfolios have tripled our essay reading, for now we read three essays on various topics from each student. (This is one of the pragmatic reasons for requiring students to type the two extensively revised essays. They are simply easier and faster to read.)

Portfolios, as we evaluate them, require about ninety minutes of training and two grading sessions because each portfolio is read twice. The first reading takes place over a weekend, with individual instructors scoring the portfolios as Pass or No Pass. Depending on the instructor's experience and the number of students who are taking the course, this grading can take from three to six hours. The second reading is carried out in small groups, usually made up of four instructors, once they have met and reminded themselves of the norms for Pass/No Pass. This grading session usually takes about three to four hours. Then individual instructors look at the scores and determine whether students will exit the course or take it for a second term. If, for example, a portfolio receives two passing scores, clearly the student will pass. However, if there is a split score, the student's instructor reads the portfolio and determines whether the writing merits passing or not.

Instructor investment and belief in this kind of evaluation has been strengthened in another way. With the guidance of the program director, instructors have determined the general criteria by which portfolios will be judged. Because most instructors were already familiar with holistic scoring of timed essays when we began portfolio evaluation, we decided to score the portfolios holistically. We do so in two senses: (1) we read the papers themselves holistically, focusing attention on values of coherence, voice, and audience awareness over correctnesss of grammar and punctuation; (2) we score the portfolio as a whole — that is, rather than scoring each of the three essays individually and then arriving at a final evaluation through averaging the scores, we look at the quality of each portfolio as a whole and assign either Pass or No Pass. By reading sample portfolios submitted at the end of the term and matching them to our set of criteria, we can make informed judgments about portfolios that pass or fail. We look for *general,* not absolute, agreement among the evaluators, since portfolios do not lend themselves to absolute judgments in the way that timed writings often can, especially when we are looking at two finished papers as well as one written under time constraints and that is, therefore, less polished.

Involving Faculty and Students
in Assessment and Feedback

As part of the sharing process among teachers that Lucas (1988) refers to, program instructors talk both formally (in meetings) and informally (in offices, hallways, at the copy machine) about their students and the portfolios. Thus far, two practices have arisen from this sharing of information. The first is to exchange topic ideas for the timed writings, those that have been effective in eliciting good writing from the students. A second, and more elaborate, practice was developed by several instructors. The assignment is designed to help students get a sense of an unknown audience for their writing, much like that for the portfolio grading. A paper exchange takes place between two classes toward the end of the term, a time when we feel students are most familiar with the critiquing and revision processes and the standards by which they will be judged. Students are asked to read one paper from another class set and write a reader's response to it. This response is attached to the paper and returned to the student writer in the other class. Through this practice, the context of the portfolio assessment extends further into the program.

Instructors involved in this latter process train their students to respond constructively to the papers from the other class. Students have their own teacher's past comments on their papers to use as a model for responding to a peer's paper. Through the exchange, students see themselves in a concrete way as both producers of writing and as readers of the writing produced by others. The students often decide to include this particular paper as part of the portfolio because the exchange is usually a pivotal experience for them. They understand what "audience" means in yet another way. When the student reader writes in her critique, "I don't know exactly what bilingual education is.

How does it work? If you explained that, I would understand your essay better," the writer understands that his writing teacher is not the only who needs clarification. The student learns that the instructor is not so idiosyncratic a reader after all. Further, the student readers, like the instructor readers of the portfolio, have no idea what the other instructor's assignment was and therefore respond as real readers to what the writers have to say. The student readers can judge only the writing, not the writer. Students generally take this critique very seriously—as they should—and are better prepared to revise their papers for the unknown audience of other instructors, those who will determine whether they pass the course or remain in it for a second term.

Instructors also help determine future directions for portfolio evaluation. For example, our portfolio now requires two "finished" essays, but we are considering the possibility of including an essay that demonstrates the student is attempting a new skill, or a journal entry that illustrates the formation of ideas for a finished essay. These might be accompanied by the student's description of what this kind of writing shows about the writer and what he or she learned about writing from producing it. Whether to include pieces of these types and, if so, the ways in which they will be evaluated will be decided by the instructors with guidance from the program coordinator. Naturally, decisions like these influence classroom activities and cannot be made unilaterally. Their effect touches too many instructors and students.

It should be noted that, with only one or two exceptions, the instructors we refer to here are all part-time lecturers. Their schedules often do not allow them the luxury of the extended collegial conversations one might find taking place among full-time faculty. Yet a great deal of conversation occurs as a result of this kind of evaluation. Again, we believe it occurs because the instructors are pleased with the type of evaluation used and with the support network of GAs and writing tutors they and their students have available to them throughout the whole process. Here is the great advantage of several people, if not a whole program, using this kind of assessment: the support network engenders new and often innovative practices and provides a sounding board for overcoming the problems encountered when instituting and continuing such an assessment method.

As instructors of the same course, they also appreciate having common standards for evaluation that they have an investment in, since they helped develop the standards. Sharing the standards with their students allows the instructors to demonstrate the criteria that guide the evaluation of *all* students taking the course, no matter who their instructor is. Students do not feel that their passing or not passing is left to the grading whims of an individual teacher. Common standards also add to the feeling of cohesiveness among the instructors in the program, especially because some of them never see one another until the regular meetings before, during, and at the end of the term. Yet the adaptable nature of the portfolio allows individual instructors to teach according to the style that suits them best; it is not necessary to impose a common syllabus for the course. What they all have in common are the standards. Even in a large program, then, portfolios are flexible enough to fit individuals.

Extending the Model to the Writing Center

The context for learning and teaching writing at CSUF includes the Writing Center, a student facility that acts as an extension of the classroom. The job of any university or college writing center is to provide students with one-on-one tutorial assistance that is either an adjunct to or, in some instances, a replacement for classroom writing experiences. Beyond this common definition, writing centers vary widely: tutors may be undergraduate or graduate students, full-time or part-time faculty; tutor training courses can last from one weekend to one semester; tutors may provide a diagnostic/testing service or oral response to essays tutees have written for various classes; available resource materials might include grammar exercises, handbooks, computers, or simply the tutors' expertise; the center itself may be a small converted office or a space designed specifically for the purpose of tutoring. However it is structured and whatever tutoring strategies it advocates, a writing center implies a particular set of assumptions about what it means to write, to learn to write, and to help others learn to write.

Because students in our developmental writing classes are required to visit the Writing Center, and because graduate student tutors also assist with sections of this course, it is especially important that our tutors understand what the portfolio implies about writing and the learning of writing and that their tutoring reinforce these implications. Moreover, if the assumptions and philosophy supporting the use of portfolio assessment are as institutionally contextualized as we believe, they should be integrated throughout the entire writing instructional network — from the classroom to the Writing Center. For the tutors and the tutees, the center should come to represent the same philosophy of writing that underlies portfolio assessment, a philosophy in which writing is produced slowly, in rich rhetorical contexts, with the help of others, but always with the writer in control.

As with the classroom instructor who concentrates students' attention on drafting the essays that may be included in their portfolios, our Writing Center tutors ask students to bring their earliest drafts to their half-hour tutorial sessions. Knowing that the portfolio will not be assembled until the end of the semester, tutors can focus on providing students with formative responses to their writing and on encouraging students to revise. Since the final "due date" is weeks or months away, students have the unfamiliar luxury of really working through a piece of writing, and tutors have the responsibility of helping students postpone the final revision and understand that creating better pieces of writing requires that they change the way they write as much as it does *what* they write.

One common misperception that students hold about writing centers is that they are "fix-it shops" staffed by individuals who will repair broken sentences and ensure passing grades. Surely this image doesn't fit with the philosophy of writing espoused by the portfolio — a philosophy in which the writer takes control and good writing takes time and revision. But until students understand the nature of revision — that it occurs in response to unresolved questions raised by the text — they will be hesitant to let go of their fix-it shop profile of the Writing Center. One way of bringing students to this understanding is for tutors to emulate the kinds of open-ended, facilitative writing response used in the classroom. Rather than supplying students with the fixes or gold stars for which they eagerly wait, tutors must play the role of readers, asking questions that lead to revisions.

For example, while reading an essay draft aloud, the tutor finds the focus of the piece to be unclear. Rather than writing "unclear focus" on the draft or rewriting the sentences, the tutor asks the writer about the purpose of the essay or about the contradictions that grow from the garbled ideas. In another instance, the tutor may come across an especially disorganized paragraph and stop to ask the writer questions that may arise in a reader's mind because the events or propositions are out of order. In this way, the tutor becomes an audience, and the student writer comes to understand the consequences of a poorly focused or disorganized essay in terms of the reader's experience. Students learn that, like their instructor and their final portfolio readers, this audience reads first, evaluates next.

If we turn back the clock on any teacher's evaluation, we see that it originated in a reader's reaction. And by focusing on reader response, the real source of any evaluation, tutors — like instructors — help students learn to become their own readers, to understand the process of drafting and revising that will improve their writing and strengthen their portfolio.

In the Writing Center, even editing for the portfolio becomes a matter of audience response. Spelling, usage, and grammar are important because they aid or impede the reader's understanding of the writer's meaning. Their importance becomes especially visible when a student actually sees a tutor's furrowed brow or quizzical expression as the tutor pauses or struggles over a misspelled word or an incorrect sentence construction. Students who experience this moment in the Writing Center may be more eager to edit their portfolio pieces, knowing that "correctness" is not a white glove that teachers carry but an integral element of communication, one on which the success of a portfolio may rely.

Finally, tutoring sessions in the Writing Center both support and enlarge on the social context for writing that begins with students' instructors and peers in the classroom, may include students in other classes, and ends with the portfolio reading. When students come into the center for their first tutorial, they are introduced to a situation much like the portfolio reading: a stranger, someone more expert than they, but someone other than their instructor, will be reading their essays. This situation, like the portfolio reading, usually proves to be both frightening and frustrating for students. Few of them have had readers outside the familiar structure of the classroom or the reassuring circle of family and friends. But as portfolio assessment emphasizes, writers must often be prepared to meet the needs and expectations of audiences with whom they have no previous or current history. It is common for students to shrug off tutors' queries with a "Well, you know." But a tutor—or a portfolio reader—who knows nothing more about the writer or the prompt than what is provided in the text, does not know. Once the student writers recognize the limitations of their readers' perspective, most will write more specifically, with fewer unclear sentences or references. Meeting with tutors, they may overcome—or at least reduce—their fear of such an audience. Listening to the tutors' questions about their drafts, they may learn how to predict where readers would be troubled, where revising might take place.

Most important to each of these tutoring strategies is the student writer's own sense of responsibility and control. If we are to affect the way our students write, we must affect the way they feel about themselves as writers. Developmental writers are frequently insecure either because they have been labeled as failures for so long or because they have so little experience with written English. Portfolio assessment seeks to strengthen writers' self-concepts by helping them make effective rhetorical decisions. Indeed, success in these decisions results in a successful portfolio. At the end of the semester, students must select and submit the essays that they perceive most likely to contribute to a passing portfolio. Because insecure students may fervently resist making this choice, feeling inadequate to the task, our goal in the center is to make this choice easier by having students make comparable choices all semester. In asking questions and offering responses, being a reader rather than an evaluator, the tutor continually hands control back to the writer. If tutors were to make judgments about what is good or bad in a piece of student writing, prescribing changes for it, any resistance students raise against selecting essays for a portfolio might be warranted. But we hope that students' classroom experiences, reinforced by the experiences they have in the Writing Center, prepare them to accept the responsibility of becoming a writer.

So far we have described ways in which tutoring strategies in the Writing Center reinforce for developmental writing students the general philosophy implied by our means of portfolio assessment. For these strategies to be used successfully, for this philosophy to emerge and have a significant impact, the undergraduate and graduate students who tutor in the Writing Center must not only learn about the assumptions supporting this philosophy, they must have experienced them. Just as the instructors must be committed to the philosophy if it is to work, so, too, must the tutors.

As in any tutor-training course, our tutors read about how to conduct tutorial sessions, what the writing process is, and what special problems they may encounter in the center. They must also understand portfolio assessment in relation to other forms of writing assessment and to their responsibilities as tutors. To this end, they read descriptive articles about using and understanding writing portfolios in the context of a writing program (see, for example, Belanoff and Elbow, 1991).

Because they will focus tutees' attention on revising, tutors themselves must understand the difference between evaluating writing and responding to writing: evaluation assumes the writing is complete and ready to be awarded a degree of merit; responding assumes the writing is still being revised and deserves a reader's reaction. In the course of their own learning, most students have become quite familiar with having their writing evaluated, "slashed" with the red pen, or terminally judged with a letter grade. Few students have much experience with responses to their writing, with reader questions and observations.

When they have received such responses, many have been unsure of their significance, looking around to find the grade. So, in the tutor-training course, we look at essays that the tutors themselves have written and to which they have received an evaluation or a response. We ask tutors to read one another's essays, to "translate" the instructors' responses for one another. What does it really mean when a sentence is labeled "awkward" or "wordy"? What makes a reader stumble over a clause or get lost in a description? In effect, we treat these responses as a language that tutors must learn—not only because they will be expected to perform such translations for tutees but also because they will have to develop their own language for responding to student writing.

Beyond learning *about* a philosophy of writing and tutoring writing that is consistent with the one evoked by portfolio assessment, the tutors-in-training *experience* such a philosophy. The course creates for them the same emphasis on drafting and revising, the same unfamiliar audience experience that their tutees experience with the portfolio. From the first day of the semester, tutors are aware that they will have to submit an essay on any topic they choose related to tutoring. Apart from being used to evaluate tutors' performance in the training course, these essays become part of an anthology that will be used in the following semester's training class and will also serve as a reference book in the Writing Center. Early on, tutors must bring their topic proposals to class; they then read and respond to one another's drafts. Similarly, the instructor responds to drafts, asking the kinds of questions and making the kinds of observations that the tutors will be expected to make of student writing in the Writing Center. On the last day of class, the essays are arranged and, with the instructor's introduction, taken to a copy center where they are printed into textbooks for the next semester. By the time tutors have completed the project, they have experienced the same process of drafting, responding, revising, and editing that their tutees are experiencing. And, like their tutees, they will have experienced this process in the context of a fairly complicated and intimidating rhetorical situation—writing for both familiar and unfamiliar, novice and expert audiences.

Finally, like the students who will be submitting writing portfolios, the tutors are encouraged to establish their own diverse social contexts for writing, a community other than the classroom into which they can take writing for conversation and response. In addition to the peer response provided in the training class, several other situations can be established for this context and can exist after tutors complete the class. For example, we "built" a tutor lounge by arranging some tables and room dividers where off-duty tutors can share their own writing and their tutoring stories. We have encouraged tutors to conduct student workshops on various writing concerns — workshops that their peer tutors help plan and often attend. Tutors who are socially connected writers themselves, who regularly seek response to their own writing, will conduct themselves in the Writing Center with greater commitment to and understanding of its purpose in relation to the portfolio.

Conclusion

The greatest strength of portfolio evaluation is that it embodies a set of consistent elements and assumptions about teaching and learning, while it is adaptable to many different kinds of classes, programs, and schools. The portfolio assessment procedures we use at the Developmental Writing Program and the Writing Center at CSUF is in some ways idiosyncratic to the structure and requirements of our English department and university. However the portfolio is used for assessment, certain elements remain the same:

1. Portfolios represent work assembled over time and draw on the continual learning of the student over that period of time. A portfolio must be an "ordered" and "deliberate compilation, gathered according to some plan, for use by an identified reader or readers for specific needs or purposes" (Larson, 1991, p. 138).
2. Portfolio evaluation does not penalize students for poor skills with which they may enter a course. It allows them to develop skills over time.

3. Portfolios stress reworking, rethinking, and revising.
4. Portfolios allow students to work toward expert or mastery level of a subject or skill by engaging them in the kinds of activities experts carry out.

Finally, no matter how portfolio assessment is adapted, it has important consequences for instructors and students:

1. Instructors get a better sense of what is working and what is not working in the classroom. Because pieces are not judged summatively until the end of the semester, both students and instructor can discuss assignments as trials for a final product.
2. In programmatic use of portfolios, instructors collaboratively design the evaluation rubric and learn from one another practices that enhance both teaching and learning.
3. Students learn that they cannot expect everything they produce to be of equal quality but that they have *time* to bring pieces up to some standard. They also learn how to judge their own work and develop their own standards, rather than waiting for someone to impose standards on them.
4. If students choose a limited number of pieces for the portfolio, they also learn they can abandon work that they are not interested in or that is not—and may never be—successful.
5. Students have the opportunity to show what they have learned about writing, not simply what they have learned for a midterm or final exam.
6. Students have the pleasure of putting together something truly "finished" for a course because they have time to do so.

The extent to which writing portfolio assessment can be adapted to a variety of institutional contexts and to which it effects changes in the way students write and think about writing suggests the profound impact this form of assessment has had on the teaching and evaluating of writing. As more instructors and programs replace traditional forms of assessment with the portfolio, making it fit their particular needs and requirements, using it in ways that have yet to be tried, the value of portfolio assessment will continue to be revealed.

References

Belanoff, P., and Dickson, M. (eds.). *Portfolios: Process and Product.* Portsmouth, N.H.: Boynton/Cook, Heinemann, 1991.

Belanoff, P., and Elbow, P. "Using Portfolios to Increase Collaboration and Community in a Writing Program." In P. Belanoff and M. Dickson (eds.), *Portfolios: Process and Product.* Portsmouth, N.H.: Boynton/Cook, Heinemann, 1991.

Boyer, E. *Scholarship Reconsidered: Priorities of the Professorate.* Princeton, N.J.: The Carnegie Foundation, 1990.

Larson, R. (1991) "Using Portfolios in the Assessment of Writing in the Academic Disciplines." In P. Belanoff and M. Dickison (eds.), *Portfolios: Process and Product.* Portsmouth, N.H.: Boynton/Cook, Heinemann, 1991.

Lucas, C. "Toward Ecological Evaluation." *The Quarterly,* 1988, *10,* 1–3, 12–17.

Millis, B. "Putting the Teaching Portfolio in Context." *To Improve the Academy,* 1991, *10,* 215–232.

Seldin, P. *The Teaching Portfolio: A Practical Guide to Improved Performance and Promotion/Tenure Decisions.* Bolton, Mass.: Anker Publishing, 1991.

Sommers, N. "Responding to Student Writing." *College Composition and Communication,* 1982, *33,* 148–156.

Yancey, K. "Portfolios in the Writing Classroom: A Final Reflection." In *Portfolios in the Writing Classroom: An Introduction.* Urbana, Ill.: NCTE, 1992.

Chapter 18

Assessment's Role in Strengthening the Core Curriculum

James L. Ratcliff

Assessment can be seen as a threat or as an opportunity for changing college classrooms. As a threat, it may be seen as the long arm of some superordinate body (the accrediting agency, the legislature, the higher education system office, or "the administration") placing its ugly hands on the faculty's sacred domain, the classroom. Assessment may also be seen as an additional chore that a faculty member has to do, such as compile student portfolios or read and grade student essays. For some, assessment has become an end in itself. Some colleges wish to say that they "do assessment" in hope that those superordinate forces will leave them alone; they settle for making broad statements about how they are meeting public demands for greater accountability.

Assessment can be a powerful and much needed tool in the reform of general education curricula. In the coming decade, we need to envision general education as more than a smorgasbord of courses from which to choose to fulfill degree requirements. Similarly, assessment in the 1990s can go beyond meeting the expectations of external agencies, providing usual feedback to students, or being an add-on activity seen as an end in itself. Assessment can help guide targeted and meaningful change in college classrooms.

Assessment clearly means different things to different people. That ambiguity alone contributes to some of the confusion, anxiety, and resistance to using assessment information to reform college curricula and classrooms. First, assessment means the kind of evaluation activity in which faculty have always engaged: determining the extent of student learning that has occurred in their classrooms. That activity has been the basis for student grading and for individual faculty revisions of what they teach and how they teach it. This level and form of assessment is clearly the domain and responsibility of the individual faculty member, and probably there is no comprehensive assessment program administered at the end of one, two, or four years of collegiate study that will describe more accurately what students have learned in individual classes.

Some of the fear faculty feel toward assessment is that it will serve as a test of how well they conduct their classes. While instructors must be accountable for their professional conduct in teaching, no known assessment program currently does or promises to evaluate the adequacy and performance of individual teachers. The closest we come to such an assessment is the use of Student Evaluations of Teaching (SETs). While some institutions regularly collect end-of-class evaluations of the effectiveness of individual instructor's teaching performance, no clear link has been established between the items on a SET form and *long-term learning* of students. While SETs may indicate how clearly the instructor of an introductory macroeconomics course communicated key concepts, SETs will not tell us how well the microeconomics and macroeconomics courses worked together to produce the intended learning outcomes of the discipline. Also, SETs tend to assess the *process* of teaching rather than its *effects*. In short, faculty fears about assessment as a tool in evaluation, promotion, or tenure decisions is misplaced.

Institutional assessment of student outcomes has a different purpose than assessment within the individual classroom, determining the net and cumulative effects of the collegiate experience. Our college catalogues state that certain types of learning result from the general education curriculum. Do they? Catalogues frequently also claim that study in specific fields and majors prepares individuals for graduate education, specific jobs, and careers and that it imparts certain specialized knowledge. Does it? These questions regarding the effectiveness of general education, major curricula, and minor curricula ask about *the cumulative effect* of taking a series or combination of courses intended to produce the desired effect on student learning. Assessment's role here is to determine the extent to which students fulfilling the requirements for these curricula actually acquire the desired and intended knowledge, skills, and abilities the programs purport to provide.

Accurate assessment of such knowledge, skills, and abilities requires consideration of the contribution and role of individual faculty and single courses. However, they need not (and to date cannot) be empirically evaluated individually or in isolation relative to the overall general and liberal learning goals of an institution. An education is more than the sum of its parts. We already know that if a student acquires the prerequisite number of credits in courses where he or she made passing marks, then that student has met the requirements for the degree. The sad circumstance about our credit system (and there are many merits to it as well) is that we have no clear indicators as to whether the curriculum has succeeded in accomplishing its aims.

Rethinking Assessment and the Curriculum

For assessment truly and positively to affect curricular change, the notion of what composes a curriculum must be viewed differently in the 1990s. Faculty and academic leaders must embrace a few maxims emerging from the research of the 1980s to reframe how we view and use assessment information. First among these is that the variety of what students learn in college is far greater *within* institutions than *between* them (Baird, 1988; Pascarella and Terenzini, 1991; Ratcliff, 1992b). Assessments have usually been based on uniform criteria applied to all students regardless of their ability or the curriculum they select; assessments of general education have been grounded on the supposition that all students experience some common collegiate experience that can be readily described, measured, or in some other way evaluated. Research confirms what common sense tells us: that students who study different subjects and take different courses learn different things (Ratcliff, 1992b). An entering first-year student at even a modest-sized college or university has one to three *thousand* courses from which to choose. By the time that student has earned a bachelor's degree, he or she will have selected only thirty-five to forty-five of those courses. A first assessment question asks what the effect is of these courses on the student; faculty use exams, papers, projects, and grades to make such determinations. A second and equally important question is *what the cumulative effect is of the particular combination of courses* that compose the student's degree. Answers to this second question hold the key to improving curricula and instruction in the coming decade. This is the important question that assessment can answer and that will guide the reform of collegiate curricula.

Most colleges and universities have distributional general education degree requirements (Toombs, Fairweather, Amey, and Chen, 1989). Table 18.1 shows coursework of graduating seniors at four institutions (Ratcliff, 1990). Examining the transcripts of the students produces lists of thousands of courses, even at the liberal arts college. When counting individual courses only once, eliminating duplication, the vastness of curricula choices is still apparent; the 105 seniors at the research university chose 1,445 separate courses to complete their degree requirements. In only 303 of these courses did more than 5 of the 105 students enroll. In three of the four institutions, a graduating senior would have from 16 to 21 percent of his or her coursework in common with 5 other students out of 100. In the comprehensive college, the professional curricula in business, health, and journalism dictate greater uniformity in course selection (35.6 percent). Simply put, students at these institutions took different courses and learned different things.

While general education on average makes up from 35 to 38 percent of the credits required for the baccalaureate, few students experience the same coursework (Boyer and Ahlgren, 1987; Ratcliff, 1990). Students in the same graduating class may

Table 18.1. Coursework Appearing on the Transcripts
of Graduating Seniors at Four Institutions of Higher Education.

Parameters	Doctoral-Granting University	Comprehensive College	Liberal Arts College	Research University
Number of student transcripts	134	146	62	105
College calendar	Quarters	Semesters	Semesters	Quarters
Total number of courses on student transcripts	6,183	6,249	2,844	5,541
Average number of courses taken by students to graduate	46.14	42.80	45.87	52.77
Unduplicated courses per 100 students	1,358	1,136	990	1,445
Number of unduplicated courses taken by 5 or more students	282	405	157	303
Percent of courses taken by 5 or more of each 100 students	20.8%	35.7%	15.9%	21.0%
Unduplicated courses taken by 5 or more of each 100 students	210	277	253	289

Note: Unduplicated courses are courses that are counted only once even though they were taken by more than one student.

have few courses in common that they have all taken. "General education requirements" have little common or coherent meaning under such a system. While the Association of American Colleges (1985) and the directors of the National Endowment for the Humanities under presidents Reagan (Bennett, 1984) and Bush (Cheney, 1989), and others (Zemsky, 1988) have lamented the lack of a core curriculum of limited "essential" subjects in general education, there is reason to believe that an expansive curriculum is needed to fully represent the diversity of student backgrounds and interests and the mushrooming of knowledge and fields of study that represent higher learning and the educated individual (Becher, 1989; Ratcliff, 1992a; Squires, 1990). Still, with such diversity in the formal educational program, is it any wonder that the differences in learning are greater within institutions than between them? In reality it is the students who select their educational program. The program that appears on the student's transcript is the most accurate representation of those parts of the college curriculum that are most relevant to gains in that student's general and liberal learning. Those combinations and sequences of courses, rather than all those from which the student had to choose, have direct bearing on that individual's formal academic experience.

College curricula are built on the assumption that enrollment in certain sequences and combinations of courses produces certain differential effects in student learning (Ratcliff, 1990). Since 1986 I have examined over 72,000 courses appearing on the transcripts of some 1,600 seniors in college. These seniors reflected a cross section of majors, academic abilities, and backgrounds; collectively they had attended every major type of higher-education institution. From these analyses comes a model for linking what courses students take as undergraduates with what they learn. The Coursework Cluster Analysis Model (CCAM) was developed for use in institutions with distributional general education requirements; broad curricular offerings; extensive diversity of entering student abilities, interests, and achievement; and multiple measures and methods of assessing general and liberal learning. Given the complexity of variation in student abilities, curricular and extracurricular effects, and student outcomes, the CCAM is complex. The conceptual framework and practical applications of CCAM are presented in *Assessment and Curricular Reform* (Ratcliff, 1992b). Plans and procedures for getting started using CCAM are described in the *Handbook on Linking Assessment and General Education* (Ratcliff, Jones, and Hoffman, 1992). From this research comes some basic steps in linking student learning with the courses students take.

Linking General Education Coursework with Assessments of Student Learning

The Coursework Cluster Analysis Model allows an assessment program to use multiple measures of general and liberal learning, to preserve and strengthen the coursework contained in the distributional requirements, to test new measures of student learning, and to provide a meaningful basis for the improvement of faculty development activities, curricular reform, and academic advisement. The CCAM is admittedly complex, and the specific steps to be taken in implementing it have been profiled elsewhere (Ratcliff, Jones, and Hoffman, 1992; Ratcliff, 1992b). However, certain basic points and principles emerge from this research that are applicable to using any general education assessment program to revise, reform, and revitalize the undergraduate curriculum.

1. *Check to ensure that your curricular goals match your general education requirements.* For many institutions, it is a long leap from the lofty proclamations of general education goals to the requirements for degree completion. Not uncommonly, colleges and universities require students to complete twenty credits of coursework in mathematics and sciences without stating what such a requirement is designed to accomplish. How does such an oversight affect the students in your classroom? Consider Sue, who recently completed a series of outcomes assessments; she showed large gains in math and science reasoning from the time she entered college to when she completed her baccalaureate. Consider also Joe, a second student, who showed few gains. From the CCAM analyses of transcripts, we typically find that Sue fulfilled her general education requirements by completing a *curricular sequence,* such as Chemistry 31 (Chemical Principles), Chemistry 33 (Structure and Reactivity), and Chemistry 35 (Organic Compounds). Typically, Sue attained grades of B or better in these classes. Joe also began with Chemistry 31 but received a grade of D. He next enrolled in Biology 31 (Molecular and Cell Biology), the first course in a three-course introductory sequence to the biological sciences; here he earned a C. Having low grades and a relatively unsuccessful encounter with the first two sciences, Joe elects to complete the general education sequence with the first course in a third science, physics. In sum, Joe completed the general education degree requirements without gaining the cumulative effect in science knowledge and reasoning intended by any one of three introductory science sequences. The requirements were met, but the general education

goal of deep learning in scientific inquiry was not achieved. Such deep learning is rare in general education (Adelman, 1992).

The coursework patterns of high-achieving and low-achieving students are significantly different. One predominant characteristic of low-achieving students is the high probability that they will enroll in courses not matched to their prior academic ability. Students of low ability relative to the student population of the institution they are attending have a one in seven chance of enrolling in coursework attuned to their abilities. Students showing high achievement have better than a 50 percent chance of enrolling in courses matched to their abilities and prior achievement (Ratcliff, 1990; Ratcliff, Jones, Guthrie, and Oehler, 1991). Underprepared students limit faculty's ability to teach effectively. Mismatches between student abilities and learning environment lead to nominal completion of general education requirements without concomitant attainment of general education goals. Ensuring that general education goals and requirements match is a first step to general curricular coherence as well as to linking what courses students take with what they actually learn.

2. *Make sure the general education goals are assessable.* To some, this point may seem overly simple, easy, and obvious. To others, it may seem impossible and reductionistic. Why set goals if you have no way of determining whether you have attained them? Accrediting associations and state legislatures want to hold colleges and universities accountable for general education and liberal learning. Does an institution really want to claim to develop "the whole student" if it must somehow show that it has indeed done so? Consider as another example the distributional general education requirement that students must complete twenty credits of humanities and fine arts courses. You cannot easily measure student attainment of perspective in a figure drawing class, performance in an orchestral class, or appreciation in an art history class. Yet, can you describe the difference between students who have successfully completed these courses and those who have not?

Assessment involves more than measurement; it calls for judgment. To link what students take with what they learn, faculty must develop means of describing the learning that takes place in the courses included in each component of the general education requirement. Means and methods for making general education goals requiring performance assessable are described in *Performance and Judgment* (Adelman, 1988). No matter whether the general education goals are to develop the students' cognitive abilities, content knowledge, or values and attitudes toward learning, they become valuable goals when they are assessable goals.

3. *Determine one or more assessment criteria, measures, or indicators for each general education goal.* Because learning at the collegiate level is multifaceted, multiple measures of student learning better portray student achievement than do single means. Assessment of general education and liberal learning entails describing student achievement in content learning, cognitive development, values and attitudes toward learning, and progress, persistence, and performance toward degree attainment (Terenzini, 1989). Normally, assessments of content learning entail knowledge, skills, and abilities in mathematics and the sciences, the humanities and fine arts, and the social sciences. Assessments of cognitive development may range from basic skills in oral and written communication to higher-order abilities, such as critical thinking and problem solving.

Colleges and universities have been less eager to overtly state the values and attitudes they intend to impart to students. Nevertheless, faculty acknowledge that they seek to teach more than the content and modes of inquiry in such fields as nursing, economics, or nuclear physics; they also want their students to acquire the values and attitudes attendant to substantive and ethical content in these fields. General education seeks to affect students' cultural, aesthetic, and intellectual attitudes and educational and occupational values and to help them develop a sense of social, political, and civic responsibilities.

Finally, how well students do in their classes (performance), how rapidly they move ahead in their program of studies (progress), and whether they complete their degree program (persistence) are important factors in assessing student learning. To illustrate the importance of persistence, I examined the transcripts of students graduating from a doctoral-granting institution and found that those who enrolled in an introductory accounting class consistently showed large gains in their mathematics, data interpretation, and quantitative reasoning abilities. However, when I looked at the transcripts of these students, I found many with low grades in the class; several had failed the class and had reenrolled in a later term. While the transcript analysis was limited to students who had completed the accounting class (graduating seniors), linking transcripts and assessment results placed the spotlight on the course for further examination. Registration records for the class showed that many students dropped out of the university during the term when they were enrolled in this class. So, while the survivors of this course showed large gains in math-related knowledge and skills, there were many casualties along the way. Without examining what students took (transcripts) as well as how much they learned (assessments), one could not discern positive from negative learning environments. How content learning, cognitive development, values and attitudes, and persistence have been monitored and measured in students is described extensively in Pascarella and Terenzini's *How College Affects Students* (1991).

4. *Determine the extent to which the assessment criteria accurately describe the variety of students and student learning.* This is an important point and represents a major hurdle in implementing a general education assessment program. Faculty assessment committees frequently become embroiled in debate over what constitute valid measures of student learning. Often the assessment program becomes stymied because of lack of agreement on what measures to use. Several factors contribute to the problem. First, these assessment scores will reflect positively or negatively on the college and on their work — they do not want to embarrass or to misrepresent the institution or themselves. There is real pressure to select only measures with the highest credibility and validity. Second, assessment programs are viewed mechanistically rather than dynamically. Faculty believe that once assessment measures and methods have been selected, they will be bound to use them from now to eternity. Third, little allowance is given for variation in the curriculum and student learning;

hence, faculty committees feel pressured to choose the one best measure for a given general education goal. These three related problems contribute to a major hurdle in the conduct of a program to assess student learning in general and liberal education.

Rethinking the nature of assessment on campus can help overcome this obstacle. If the assessment program is viewed as dynamic — subject to continuous change and improvement — rather than as static and mechanistic, faculty members may feel freer to experiment with different measures of general student learning. If the committee or office charged with the oversight of assessment reviews and revises the assessment program annually, then experimentation in curriculum and instruction is encouraged rather than discouraged. Such annual review of methods and measures does not mean that a completely new set of assessment tools will be selected every year; rather, it allows a college to retain those measures that tell the most about student learning at that institution and to jettison those that are less useful.

Just as commercial testing services incorporate experimental items on their instruments as part of their efforts to update, enhance, and renew, a college or university can track student learning through reliable and authentic measures while augmenting and enhancing the portrait of student learning through a dynamic program of experimentation and renewal. A dynamic assessment program incorporating the principles of continuous improvement allows for the assessment criteria (and hence the general education curriculum) to change and evolve. If assessment is developed with an atmosphere of experimentation, review, and revision, the pressure on the assessment committee to find and permanently adopt the one best measure or criteria is reduced. Such a system also allows for the use of multiple measures of student learning.

If faculty members disagree on what might be the most appropriate measure of student learning, a flexible assessment program can provide data to assist in their selection. Two or three measures or methods of assessing might be proposed. For example, one faculty member may be an advocate of the Watson Glaser Critical Thinking Test, while another may feel that the module in the ACT College Academic Assessment Program (CAAP) may better measure general student learning. Examining the results of a pilot study of both tests can determine (1) the extent to which each test explains the variance in student learning at your campus, and (2) the extent to which these tests measure similar or different types of learning. If there is an 80 percent correlation between scores ($r^2 = .80$), both tests may be measuring comparable learning. If a substantial number of students are achieving near perfect scores on one of the tests, then it may not accurately reflect the level and extent of student learning on the campus.

Commercially produced and locally developed means, methods, and measures of assessment offer alternate avenues to evaluate specific types and levels of learning. The assessment program should be built on a set of multiple measures to afford a broad enough window on student learning to profile the extent to which the students are attaining the general education goals of the institution. This leads us to the next step in linking assessment with general education curricular reform.

5. *Determine the distribution of student scores or performance on the assessment criteria.* Coming from the research of college effects on students is the concept of subenvironments (Pascarella, 1985). Because the variation in student learning is greater within institutions than between them, it follows that there are more productive and less productive learning subenvironments. *Productive* is defined here as improved student learning relative to one or more assessment criteria for a specific group of students. A subenvironment consists of the students' curricular and extracurricular experiences. Assessment can help identify what is a productive learning subenvironment, and formal coursework serves as a beacon in such investigations. When students first enroll, they may have few friends, little familiarity with the campus environment, and a vague notion of what they want to study. With each successive term, they meet new friends, develop new social and study habits, become more immersed in campus life, and make curricular choices based on ever clearer notions of their interests and abilities. From this perspective, enrollment in an institution with a distributional requirement

is a term-by-term set of choices of friends, living arrangements, and curricular and extracurricular activities that constitute the subenvironment to which the student belongs. To find these subenvironments, we must first discover how student learning varies according to each assessment measure or criteria employed. So a preliminary task in linking assessment results to curricular change is to determine the salient student background, achievement, and curricular characteristics that make for a productive learning experience.

6. *Determine which students have shown the greatest improvement.* Again, this may seem like a simple task, but if you take into account different student subenvironments, multiple measures of general and liberal learning, and a curriculum of several thousand courses from which students may choose, the complexity rises exponentially. While the CCAM allows an institution to monitor and measure student learning within such complexity, it is also possible to begin simply. For each general education criteria and assessment measure, determine which students showed the strongest performance. If you are assessing change from the time they entered college to when they graduated, that performance can be expressed in terms of talent developed or value added by the college experience (Astin, 1991). Using student transcripts (and a computer), you can then identify courses taken by the students who showed large gains, those taken by students showing little gains, and those taken by both groups. Focus only on those courses taken by students showing large improvement. Coursework taken by those showing little improvement are not "bad" courses; the students enrolling in them may be showing large gains in other areas of learning, such as another general education assessment criteria or learning in a major. The task is to identify which courses were taken by students showing the largest improvement. Because these students will have taken thirty-five to forty-five such courses each, simple frequency counts will identify those courses most often selected by such students.

Course sequences and combinations will emerge from such analysis, permitting comparisons between student groups. Such comparisons will allow you to identify which students are completing the planned course sequences in the sciences. It will allow you to identify good matches between student ability and a challenging curriculum in key skills such as reading, writing, and mathematics, and it will identify the extent to which the courses listed in the general education requirement are also associated with improvement in student learning in general and liberal education (Ratcliff, 1992b; Ratcliff, Jones, Guthrie and Oehler, 1991; Ratcliff, Jones and Hoffman, 1992).

7. *Determine why certain coursework patterns are associated with large gains in learning.* It is important to remember that the relationships established by linking what students take with what they learn are merely *associational;* they are not cause and effect. If a student enrolls in a math class and subsequently shows large improvement in math skills, it is temptingly easy to claim that that math class *caused* that learning. Furthermore, it is a small but highly dangerous leap from saying that the class caused the learning to saying that the instructor who taught the class caused the learning. Both assumptions cast learning and instruction in too simplistic terms. First, the math class may have helped with the development of math skills because it was taken concurrently or sequentially with an accounting class, a statistics class, a test and measurement class in education, or any of a number of other quantitatively oriented courses in the undergraduate curriculum. Second, we know that classroom learning is facilitated by many factors other than the instructor alone. Just a few of these include the instructor's qualifications; the instructional methods used; the texts and materials selected; the role and place of the course in the student's program of study; the time of day, schedule, and calendar of the course; the student's prior achievement and ability in the subject studied; and the student's interest and motivation to learn.

Once you have identified courses associated with improvement in student learning, you can interview the students and the faculty to determine the factors that may have contributed to student learning. In examining the coursework of some high-achieving engineering students, I noticed a lone music course (Orchestral Band) among a long list of science, math, and engineering coursework. In an interview, the instructor of this course indicated that the majority of students enrolling were in a "high-pressure, high achievement-oriented" curriculum, had learned some musical instrument in high school, and had enrolled in the band course to let off steam associated with their other studies. On further investigation, we discovered that these students lived mostly in the same residence hall together and also took the same physical education class, crew rowing, together. Courses are where students often meet other students for the first time. They form groups to study but discover other interests. Those associations that stick, last a lifetime. That is the essence of student subenvironments. Linking coursework to student assessment scores can lead to the identification of such subenvironments.

The seven steps outlined here will lead to identification of productive learning environments within the growing diversity of students and within the general education curriculum on our campuses. Each step requires some precision in execution, to be sure. Nevertheless, it will lead to the identification of how the curriculum and the extracurriculum work together to foster student learning.

Insights Offered by Assessment

What do we know about teaching and learning from assessment? First, we know that faculty are far more concerned with knowledge acquisition, student comprehension of basic concepts, ideas, and terms, and the application of this basic knowledge than they say they are. Faculty purport to be engendering analysis, synthesis, and evaluative skills in students. Because they labor within institutions of higher learning, perhaps they believe this means they are stimulating students to think critically and to enhance their analytic capacities. Our examination of course syllabuses and exams and our interviews with faculty failed to bear this out. There is a significant gap between good faculty's intentions and reality that needs to be closed (Ratcliff, Jones, Guthrie, and Oehler, 1991).

We also know that faculty think they are far more evocative than they are. They continue to prefer didactic modes of instruction. They use mediated instruction when it supports their role as information giver, rather than viewing it as a potential partner in the instructional process. Once again, we have a gap here between intentions and reality. Faculty think that they engage students in the learning process. Curriculum guides, syllabuses, course assignments, and examinations suggest differently. Students are rarely used to set course goals, as peers or collaborators in the learning process, or as evaluators of the learning that has occurred. Once again, until we use assessment to highlight the gap between wishful thinking and reality, progress is not likely.

Conclusion: Making a Difference in Student Learning

We should care for and use information derived from assessments of undergraduate student learning. The future improvement of the undergraduate curriculum rests to a large degree on our ability to link courses in which students enroll with the learning they evidence. As faculty, we devote great energy to the design and delivery of our individual teaching assignments. We carefully plan and implement instructional strategies, study and reflect on the interactions and dynamics they produce among students, and often spend hours grading and evaluating student exams, papers, and projects. All this effort is given in the name of effective teaching and learning. Yet, to date we have limited information on the *cumulative* effect of the courses in which students enroll, and the picture is not very positive.

Assessment information is properly concerned with the progressive and cumulative effects of student learning in college (Ratcliff, 1992b). This is most obvious and often the most accepted when we examine student learning within a program or major field. Nevertheless, the cumulative effect of student learning is also embedded in the concept of general education. It is implicit in so-call "depth" requirements in general education. It is also embedded in the cognitive and personal development goals found in many general education goals. While we regularly gather information on the nature and extent of student learning in individual courses, we rarely attempt to determine whether the curricular goals and required coursework produce the results we claim.

Although broad concerns exist about the quality of teaching and learning at the classroom level, larger issues of the effectiveness of the undergraduate educational experience have gone unaddressed for over a decade. It's true that the strident calls of the 1980s to improve undergraduate education did stimulate action (Association of American Colleges, 1985, 1989; Bennett, 1984; Cheney, 1989; National Institute of Education, 1984). During the past decade more than 90 percent of colleges and universities engaged in some kind of revision or reform of their undergraduate curriculum (Gaff, 1989). Over the same time period, nearly 80 percent of colleges and universities implemented some kind of assessment of student learning. The American Council on Education repeatedly reported in *Campus Trends* that most colleges and universities were engaged in curricular reform. Yet, from a negative point of view, "[O]ne can point to little in the way of completed curricular modifications or, more important, changes in student performance that . . . emerged . . . as the 1980s ended" (Eaton, 1991, p. 61).

We have yet to make a meaningful connection between undergraduate curricular content and improved student learning. What little evidence we have shows that the curriculum is still in disarray after a full decade of reform. No wonder scholars on the subject, such as Astin (1991), are urging curriculum reformers to give up on tinkering with the general education requirements and to start building on meaningful student-faculty interaction outside the classroom and improving the campus climate and extracurricular experiences of students.

We should not give up on improving the general education curriculum. Discernable long-term effects can guide us in reforming the curriculum. The focus of our effort should be on identifying productive learning subenvironments on campus. Assessment can tell us how courses work together with the related extracurricular activities to produce the desired effect on students. Meaningful ways exist to assess the curriculum that can guide reforms so as to maximize the impact of general education on students. Assessment so conceptualized can be the beacon of revision, reform, and transformation in the coming decade.

References

Adelman, C. (ed.). *Performance and Judgment: Essays on Principles and Practices in the Assessment of College Student Learning.* Washington, D.C.: U.S. Department of Education, Office of Educational Research and Improvement, 1988.

Adelman, C. *Tourists in Our Own Land: Cultural Literacies and the College Curriculum.* Washington, D.C.: U.S. Department of Education, Office of Educational Research and Improvement, 1992.

Association of American Colleges. *Integrity in the College Curriculum: A Report to the Academic Community.* Washington, D.C.: Association of American Colleges, 1985.

Association of American Colleges. *A New Vitality in General Education.* Washington, D.C.: Association of American Colleges, 1989.

Astin, A. *Assessment for Excellence: The Philosophy and Practice of Assessment and Evaluation in Higher Education.* San Francisco: Jossey-Bass, 1991.

Baird, L. "The College Environment Revisited: A Review of Research and Theory." In J. Smart (ed.), *Handbook of Theory and Research in Higher Education,* Vol. 4. New York: Agathon Press, 1988.

Becher, T. *Academic Tribes and Territories: Intellectual Enquiry and the Cultures of Disciplines.* Bristol, Penn.: Open University Press, 1989.

Bennett, W. *To Reclaim a Legacy.* Washington, D.C.: National Endowment for the Humanities, 1984.

Boyer, C. M., and Ahlgren, A. "Assessing Undergraduates' Patterns of Credit Distribution: Amount and Specialization." *Journal of Higher Education,* 1987, *58,* 430–442.

Cheney, L. *50 Hours: A Core Curriculum for College Students.* Washington, D.C.: National Endowment for the Humanities, 1989.

Eaton, J. S. *The Unfinished Agenda: Higher Education and the 1980s.* New York: Macmillan, 1991.

El-Khawas, E. *Campus Trends, 1990.* Washington, D.C.: American Council on Education, 1990.

Gaff, J. "General Education at the Decade's End: The Need for a Second Wave of Reform." *Change,* 1989, *21,* 11–19.

Jones, E. A., and Ratcliff, J. L. "Which General Education Curriculum Is Better: Core Curriculum or the Distributional Requirement?" *Journal of General Education,* 1991, *40,* 69–101.

National Institute of Education, Study Group on the Conditions of Excellence in American Higher Education. *Involvement in Learning: Realizing the Potential of American Higher Education.* Washington, D.C.: U.S. Department of Education, 1984.

Pascarella, E. T. "College Environmental Influences on Learning and Cognitive Development: A Critical Review and Synthesis." In J. Smart (ed.), *Higher Education: Handbook of Theory and Research,* Vol. 1. New York: Agathon Press, 1985.

Pascarella, E. T., and Terenzini, P. T. *How College Affects Students: Findings and Insights from Twenty Years of Research.* San Francisco: Jossey-Bass, 1991.

Ratcliff, J. L. *Development and Testing of a Cluster-Analytic Model for Identifying Coursework Patterns Associated with General Learned Abilities of College Students: Final Report, May 1990.* University Park: Center for the Study of Higher Education, Pennsylvania State University, 1990.

Ratcliff, J. L. "Undergraduate Education." In B. R. Clark and G. Neave (eds.), *The Encyclopedia of Higher Education.* New York: Pergamon Press, 1992a.

Ratcliff, J. L. (ed.). *Assessment and Curriculum Reform.* New Directions for Higher Education, no. 80. San Francisco: Jossey-Bass, 1992b.

Ratcliff, J. L., Jones, E. A., Guthrie, D. S., and Oehler, D. *The Effect of Coursework Patterns, Advisement, and Course Selection on the Development and General Learned Abilities of College Graduates: Final Report.* University Park: Center for the Study of Higher Education, Pennsylvania State University, 1991.

Ratcliff, J. L., Jones, E. A., and Hoffman, S. *Handbook on Linking Assessment and General Education.* University Park, Penn.: National Center on Postsecondary Teaching, Learning, and Assessment, 1992.

Squires, G. *First Degree: The Undergraduate Curriculum.* Bristol, Penn.: Open University Press, 1990.

Terenzini, P. T. "Assessment with Open Eyes: Pitfalls in Studying Student Outcomes." *Journal of Higher Education*, 1989, *60*, 644–664.

Toombs, W., Fairweather, J., Amey, M., and Chen, A. *Open to View: Practice and Purpose in General Education, 1989*. University Park, Penn.: Center for the Study of Higher Education, 1989.

Zemsky, R. *Structure and Coherence: Measuring the Undergraduate Curriculum*. Washington, D.C.: American Association of Colleges, 1988.

Chapter 19

Closing Thoughts:
Creating a New Scholarship
of College Teaching

Diane F. Halpern

The pace of change is rapidly accelerating in every area of human endeavor. Scientific literature is being generated at a dizzying rate, political structures seemingly change overnight, and technologies tackle problems few of us ever imagined, with advances occurring in every academic field of study, including the addition of new disciplines that did not exist a few years ago. It is the job of college professors to prepare the future leaders and the most educated of the citizenry for a future about which we know very little. The theme of change and preparing our students for change runs throughout all of the chapters in this volume. It is the thread that ties higher education together—it is the reason why we need colleges where teaching and learning are valued.

A variety of pressures have come together at this time to create a renewed emphasis on college-level teaching. Perhaps the greatest impetus for making teaching and learning a priority is the current economic situation. As colleges throughout North America face the belt-tightening measures caused by a prolonged recession, class sizes are bulging, faculty and staff salaries are stagnating, building maintenance is being deferred, and morale is dropping. The financially driven crisis has caused the participants in higher education to prioritize the many activities that occur on college campuses, including the traditional components of faculty life—teaching, research, and service to the institution and the broader community. Fortunately, for an increasingly large number of colleges, student learning has emerged as the reason for higher education and is being recognized as the primary mission of faculty. The chapters in this volume offer a variety of ways to improve student learning and to provide students with the knowledge, skills, and abilities they will need for the next six or more decades in which many of them will live.

Although the emphasis of this volume is on the teaching and learning process, it was not the intent of the chapter authors to denigrate the importance of research in college and university life. College faculty have, as one of their tasks, the generation of new knowledge—a task that must be carried out if we are to progress as a society. But, as Boyer (1990) recently argued, scholarship is multidimensional, and the application, integration, and teaching of knowledge are also part of its newly expanded definition. The old dichotomy of "publish or perish" is no longer meaningful, as scholarship connotes more than churning out pages of text. The scholarship of teaching is emerging as the most valid and valuable scholarly activity. It is the one that taxpayers, legislators, parents, and students believe that they are paying for. It is the best way to ensure that we survive and thrive through the next millennium and beyond.

The broader view of scholarship will revitalize college classrooms because it is now permissible to "care about" teaching. Students, faculty, and the rest of society will benefit from the pro-teaching movement, with its emphasis on the enhancement of thinking skills, working cooperatively, understanding and appreciating diversity, and using new technologies to obtain these and other worthy goals in a cost- and time-efficient manner. This is an exciting time to be in higher education, a time when faculty who care can truly change the future.

References

Boyer, E. L. *Scholarship Reconsidered: Priorities of the Professorate.* Princeton, N.J.: The Carnegie Foundation, 1990.

Name Index

A

Aburdene, P., 13
Adams, M., 128, 131, 133, 135, 137, 153
Adelman, C., 336, 337
Agogino, A., 238
Ahlgren, A., 332
Allen, R., 33
Alley, R., 142
Amabile, T. M., 65, 67
American Association of University Women (AAUW) Educational Foundation, 214–215, 216–217, 227
American Council on Education, 345
American Psychological Association, 11
Amey, M., 332
Anderson, J. A., 128, 131, 135, 137, 153
Andrews, L. T., 239
Angelo, T. A., 43, 51, 272, 292, 293, 294, 295–296, 298, 299, 300, 301, 302
Appleberry, J. B., 291, 292
Arnold, V., 301
Asch, A., 152
Aschner, M. J., 95
Association of American Colleges, 86, 112, 113, 333, 345

Astin, A. W., 79, 128, 137, 341, 345
Auletta, G. S., 108

B

Backer, P. A., 189
Backer, P. R., 238, 244
Bainer, D. L., 146, 291
Baird, L., 331
Banks, C.A.M., 128, 129
Banks, J. A., 128, 129, 131, 140, 149
Banvard, R., 235
Bargh, J. A., 29
Barkan, E. R., 108
Barnak, P., 141, 147
Baron, J., 19
Bearison, D. J., 30
Becher, T., 333
Becker, E., 278, 280
Becker, J., 121
Beeman, W. O., 235
Belanoff, P., 309, 314, 324
Belenky, M. F., 137
Bell, C. H., 279, 280
Bempechat, J., 20
Bennett, W., 333, 345
Berliner, D. C., 30
Beyer, B., 18
Beyer, V. P., 131, 146
Bigelow, J., 236

353

Binkley, S., 122
Blanchard, D. D., 237
Blanchard, K. H., 278, 279, 280
Blauner, B., 120
Blauner, R., 168
Bloom, B. S., 23, 95
Blosser, P. E., 95
Blurton, C., 189
Bok, D., 86, 289–290, 291
Bond, L. A., 151, 152
Boone, R., 243
Border, L.L.B., 129, 131
Borg, W., 94
Bourne, D. F., 242
Bourne, J., 238
Bower, B., 121
Bowers, C. A., 214
Bowlby, J., 278
Boxer, M., 177
Boyer, B. A., 189, 213, 214, 215, 227
Boyer, C. M., 332
Boyer, E. L., 6, 86, 112, 289, 307, 350
Bransford, J. D., 16, 22
Brislin, R. W., 150
Bronstein, P., 131, 151
Broome, B. J., 140
Brophy, J., 94, 98
Brown, A. L., 16, 22
Brown, T. J., 128
Brownell, G., 215
Bullivant, B. M., 128
Bush, V., 230
Bushey, B., 34
Byers, T. J., 235

C

Caine, G., 65–66
Caine, R., 65–66
California Postsecondary Education
    Commission, 273
California State University, 110
Calvino, I., 61
Campagnoni, F. R., 243
Campione, J. C., 16, 22
Carmichael, S., 168
Carnegie Foundation, 111
Cerf, V. G., 193
Chen, A., 332
Cheney, L., 333, 345
Cherrie, C., 150
Chickering, A., 123

Clegg, A., 94
Clinchy, B. M., 137
Cobb, P., 26, 30
Cole, R., 240
Collett, J., 131, 153
Collins, S., 237
Condon, J. C., 137
Conklin, J., 232, 236
Conrad, J., 78
Cooper, J. L., 12, 78, 83, 84, 87, 100,
    137, 214, 300
Cortés, C., 184
Cottell, P. G., 300
Cotter, P. M., 239
Coulson, R. L., 233
Crick, F.H.C., 61
Cross, K. P., 43, 51, 137, 272, 292,
    294, 295–296, 299, 300, 301,
    302
Crouch, M. K., 270
Cupach, W., 134
Cuseo, J. B., 131, 146
Cushner, K., 150, 151
Cwiakala, M., 238

D

Daines, D., 95
Daly, M., 119, 123
Dantonio, M., 94, 98
Daugherty, M., 153
deCharms, R., 14
Decker, R. W., 242
Decyk, B. N., 11–12, 66
DeLoughry, T. J., 254
Demetrulias, D. M., 214
Dempsey, J. V., 236
Dennett, D. C., 60
Dertouzos, M., 209
Deutsch, M., 77
Dewey, J., 77
Dewhurst, D., 239
Dickson, M., 309
Digranes, J. L., 215
Digranes, S. H., 215
Dillon, J. T., 18, 22
Dixon, N. M., 135, 137
Doise, W., 26, 30
Dolbear, F. T., 242
Dougherty, T. J., 241
D'Souza, D., 116
Dweck, C. S., 20

E

Eaton, J. S., 116, 345
Eck, M. K., 243
Egan, D. E., 244
Ehrenberg, L. M., 98
Ehrenberg, S. D., 98
Ehrlich, K., 243
Einstein, A., 61
Elbow, P., 314, 324
Elmer-Dewitt, P., 14
Engelbart, D. C., 230
Ennis, R. H., 19
Erickson, B., 110
Ewell, P. T., 272, 273, 289
Exter, T., 128

F

Faflick, P., 214
Fairweather, J., 332
Faraday, M., 34
Farmer, L.S.J., 242
Feltovich, P. J., 233
Ferguson, G. J., 236
Ferrara, R. A., 16, 22
Fetler, M., 214
Flammer, A., 22
Flavell, J. H., 21, 22
Foeman, A. K., 134, 148, 149
Fontaine, S. I., 270, 310
Forrest, A., 110
Fox-Genovese, E., 115
French, P. A., 60
French, W., 279, 280
Frierson, H. T., 78
Furuta, R., 244

G

Gaff, J., 345
Gage, N. L., 30
Gagne, R. M., 256
Gaines, B. R., 231
Gall, M. D., 94, 95
Gallagher, J. J., 95
Geske, J., 235
Gibbons, A., 121
Gillespie, A., 143
Goldberger, N. R., 137
Goldstein, B., 107, 117, 122
Good, T., 94, 98
Goodrum, D. A., 240
Grabinger, R. S., 246

Grabmeier, J., 114
Grant, C. A., 128, 129, 135
Gray, S. H., 235
Greenberg, J. D., 131, 137
Grever, J., 256, 264
Gudykunst, W. B., 134, 143, 151–153
Guenter, C. E., 12
Guild, S., 141, 148
Gumtow, R. H., 239
Guthrie, D. S., 336, 342, 343

H

Hafner, J., 33
Hahn, J. S., 243
Halasz, F. G., 236
Halavin, J., 242
Hall, W., 240
Hamilton, C. V., 168
Hansen, C. B., 12
Happ, A. J., 234
Harris, O. D., 269, 292
Harrison, C., 237
Hart, M. S., 199
Hayes, J. R., 64–65
Hayward, P., 117
Helms, J., 123
Hersey, P., 278, 279, 280
Higgins, K., 243
Higham, J., 186
Hill, C. R., 238
Hirshfield, S. H., 242
Hoffman, S., 334, 335, 342
Hofmeister, J. F., 245
Holden, C., 121
Holeton, R., 119
Holmes, H., 141, 148
Holt, W., 135, 137
Hooper, K., 235
Hoopes, D. S., 149
Hoppe, K., 120
Howe, I., 128
Huber, F., 238
Hunt, E., 240
Hunt, N., 216
Hunter, B., 215
Huston, C. R., 256
Hutson, B. A., 244

I

Inkeles, A., 119
Irish, P. M., 232

J

Jacobson, M. J., 233
Jefferson, D. J., 130, 131
Jenkins, C. A., 146, 291
Johnson, C. S., 214
Johnson, D. W., 76, 77, 78, 81, 85, 87
Johnson, R. T., 76, 77, 78, 81, 85, 87
Jonassen, D. H., 233, 234, 235, 245, 246
Jones, C. L., 189, 257
Jones, E. A., 334, 335, 336, 342, 343
Jones, J., 168
Jones, T., 108
Junn, E. N., 108, 143, 152

K

Kagan, S., 79, 81
Kaplan, K., 120
Karp, D., 84
Kawamura, K., 238
Kekulé von Stradonitz, F. A., 61
Kennedy, M., 17
Kerry, T., 18, 22
Khatena, J., 69
King, A., 11, 17, 22-23, 25, 28-29, 30, 32, 94, 95
King, S., 44, 48
Kinnell, S. K., 241
Klingler, J. W., 239
Knefelkamp, L. L., 290
Knowles, L. L., 168
Knuth, R. A., 240
Kolb, D. A., 135
Kountz, J., 209-210
Krull, D., 240
Kübler-Ross, E., 278, 279, 280
Kupsh, J., 189, 257

L

Landow, G., 232, 240
Langer, E. J., 19
Larson, R., 306, 307, 326
Laszlo, E., 118, 119
Lauter, P., 177
Lefkowitch, J. L., 239
Leick, A., 264
Leighton, R. F., 239
Lengel, J. G., 237
Lepper, M. R., 214
Letourneau, G., 235

Levidow, B. B., 240
Levine, A., 128
Lewin, K., 77
Light, R., 272
Lightman, A., 61
Limerick, P. N., 115
Lin, Y., 137, 153
Lippitt, G., 279
Lisensky, R., 273
Locatis, C., 235
Lu, M., 227
Lucas, C., 309-310, 316, 318

M

McClelland, A., 151
McConnaughy, K., 215
MacGregor, J., 87
McKeachie, W. J., 137, 152, 153
McKee, C., 240
Mackie, D., 214
McKinney, M., 12, 100
Magner, D. K., 130, 131
Maher, F., 131
Makedon, F., 238
Male, M., 216
Mandelbrot, B. B., 61
Marchionini, G., 234, 235
Marris, P., 278, 280
Martinez, D. I., 118, 122
Matlin, M. W., 153
Maurer, H., 238
May, C., 241
Mayer, R. E., 16, 26
Mays, V. M., 131
Merrill, M. D., 235
Miller, R. H., 189, 257
Millis, B. J., 137, 307
Miltz, R. J., 30
Moffett, M., 153
Moore, R., 120
Moran, T. P., 236
Morrison, M.K.C., 130, 131
Mosteller, F., 292
Mueck, R., 78
Mugny, G., 26, 30
Murray, R. B., 239

N

Nadaner, D., 214
Naisbett, J., 13
Nakaji, D. M., 299-300

National Center on Postsecondary Teaching, Learning, and Assessment, 6
National Institute of Education, 86, 345
National Science Foundation, 3
Nelson, T., 230, 232, 240
Neuwirth, C. M., 240
Nichols, R. G., 227
Nielsen, J., 232, 244
Noel, M., 87
Noll, J. W., 128
Norman, D. A., 233
Nummedal, S. G., 270, 272

O

Obler, S., 301
Oehler, D., 336, 342, 343
Olmsted, J., 294, 297
Ortiz de Montellano, B. R., 118, 122
Osborn, H., 236, 240
Osborne, A. F., 66
Oz, E., 256

P

Paradise, L. V., 94
Parnes, S. J., 67
Pascarella, E. T., 123, 124, 331, 338, 340
Paul, R., 21
Paul, S. P., 131, 137
Paulsell, P. R., 241
Perez, S., 101
Perkins, D. N., 19, 21, 32, 33, 34
Peters, A., 238
Peterson, G., 117
Petty, L. C., 242, 244
Pierce, R. H., 241
Pintrich, P. R., 137
Pon, K., 215
Prescott, S., 81, 82
Pressley, M., 16
Prewitt, K., 168
Psotka, J., 241
Pusch, M. D., 135

Q

Quentin-Baxter, M., 239
Quina, K., 131

R

Rabi, I., 18
Ragan, T. J., 233, 245

Ragsdale, R. G., 215
Ratcliff, J. L., 270, 331, 332, 334, 335, 336, 342, 343, 344
Reigeluth, C. M., 233
Resnick, L., 15
Rezabek, R. H., 233, 245
Richards, T., 241
Ricks, G., 145
Roberts, M. M., 208, 209
Robinson, P., 12, 100
Roehl, E. A., 238
Rohwer, W. D., 16
Romero, D., 131
Rosch, E., 42-43
Rosen, E. F., 242, 244
Rosenshine, B. V., 30
Rosenthal, N. R., 214
Ross, R., 148
Rowe, M. B., 20
Rutter, R. A., 15

S

Sacks, J., 255
Sadker, D., 131, 146
Sadker, M., 131, 146
Safford, P., 151
Salomon, G., 32
Schmitz, B., 131, 137
Schnapper, M., 143
Schul, Y., 29
Schwartz, J., 128
Scollon, R., 153
Scutnik, L., 47
Searle, J., 116
Seldin, P., 307
Semrau, P., 189, 213, 215, 227
Serrano, B., 131, 153
Sharan, S., 77
Shim, J. P., 257
Shirts, G., 142, 145
Shoenfeld, A. H., 19
Shulman, L. S., 303
Sideli, R. V., 239
Siegel, F., 128
Sigala, C., 301
Simpson, C., 256
Simpson, P., 256
Slavin, R. E., 75, 77, 78, 137
Sleeter, C. E., 128, 129, 135
Smith, B. L., 87
Smith, D. A., 137

Smith, D. M., 135
Smith, J., 236
Smith, K. A., 78, 81, 87
Smith, K. E., 230
Smith, W. R., 243
Socrates, 44, 45, 50
Solmon, L., 128
Sommer, C., 242
Sommers, N., 314
Sorensen, D. K., 239
Spiro, R. J., 233
Spitzberg, B., 134
Squires, G., 333
Stammers, R. B., 234, 243
Stanners, S. L., 234
Stanton, N. A., 234, 243
Stensaas, S., 239
Sternberg, R. J., 5
Stevens, G. H., 232
Stone, D. E., 244
Stotts, P. D., 244
Strickland, E., 101
Strommer, D., 110
Svinicki, M. D., 135, 137
Sweitzer, M., 240
Swoope, K. F., 214

T

Taba, H., 98
Takaki, R., 168, 176
Tarule, J. M., 137
Tatum, B., 151, 152
Taylor, G. S., 257
Terenzini, P. T., 123, 124, 331, 337,
　338
Tetreault, M. K., 131
Thomas, J. W., 16
Thomas, S. E., 242
Thurber, J., 93
Tiedt, I., 109, 110, 116
Tiedt, P., 109, 110, 116
Tierney, W. G., 111, 112
Ting-Toomey, S., 134, 143, 151, 152,
　153
Tinto, Z., 87
Tobias, S., 135
Toffler, A., 13, 14

Toombs, W., 111, 112, 332
Treisman, P. U., 78, 135
Trigg, R. H., 232, 236
Tucker, S. A., 236

U

Umbdenstock, L., 301
U.S. Department of Education, 15

V

van Dijk, T., 172
van Gogh, V., 218, 222–223
Van Note Chism, N., 129, 131
Ventura, P., 149
Vickers, J. N., 231
vom Saal, D. R., 130, 131

W

Wagner, R. K., 5
Watson, J. D., 61
Webb, N. M., 29
Wehlage, G. G., 15
Weiss, S. F., 236
Western Association of Schools and
　Colleges, 111, 124
Westland, J. C., 236
Wilder, G., 214
Wilen, W. W., 94
Willis, T. H., 256
Wilson, M., 119, 123
Wingard, T. L., 128
Wiseman, R. L., 134, 143, 151, 152,
　153
Wittgenstein, L., 39, 46, 58
Wittrock, M. C., 16
Wolff, R. A., 269, 273, 291, 292
Wong, F. F., 129
Wurzel, J. S., 135, 137

Y

Yabu, J. K., 189, 238, 244
Yancey, K., 308, 309
Yoels, W., 84
Young, M., 150

Z

Zangwell, I., 109
Zemsky, R., 333

Subject Index

A

Academic freedom, and multiculturalism, 114

Accountability, 272, 273, 289, 291-292, 336

Accreditation, 273, 281

Administrators: and educating for diversity, 132, 133; and institutional assessment, 273, 282, 284-286, 287

Affective learning, 134, 140

American Association for Higher Education, and reform of undergraduate education, 272, 289

Ames NASA file server, 204

Anonymous file transfer protocol (ftp), 193, 194, 203-205

AppleLink (computer network), 192-193, 196

Aschner-Gallagher's classification system, 95

Assessment: and accountability, 272, 273, 289, 291-292, 336; beneficiaries of, 273-274; and culture of evidence, 275-277, 281, 291; data, 275-276; defined, 274-275; of outcomes, 4, 272, 275, 330-331; reasons for, 271-273. *See also* Assessment, classroom; Assessment, institutional; Assessment, learning; Assessment, student; Portfolios, student

Assessment, classroom, 8, 9; and accountability, 289, 291-292; and classroom research, 294, 299-300; and cooperative learning, 300-301; and critical thinking, 297-300; effectiveness, 296-302; feedback in, 9, 292-293, 295; and learning, 291, 293, 295, 297-303; vs. learning assessment, 330-331; and multicultural education, 153, 301-302; process, 294-296; purpose of, 292-293; research on, 302-303; and students, 291, 293, 295, 297, 330; and teaching, 290-291, 292-293, 294-296, 302, 303; techniques, 295-296

Assessment, institutional: and accountability, 272, 273, 289; and accreditation, 273, 281; beneficiaries of, 273-274; and change models, 279-280; and change stages, 277-278, 280-287; continuum, 277, 280-281; and culture of evidence, 275-277, 281, 291; defined, 274-275; external and internal, 271-274; reasons for, 271-273; schema, 280-282

Assessment, learning, 4, 272, 275, 329–331; and assessable goals, 336–337; vs. classroom assessment, 330–331; and Coursework Cluster Analysis Model (CCAM), 334; and coursework patterns, 342–343; criteria selection for, 338–340; and cumulative effect of courses, 331, 332, 334, 335–336, 344; and curricular goals vs. requirements, 335–336; and curricular reform, 329–331, 344–345; and differences in learning, 331–334, 335–336, 340–341; experimentation in, 339–340; insights from, 343–344; multiple criteria for, 337–338, 340; research, 334–335; and student improvement, 341–342; and subenvironments, 340–341, 343

Assessment, student, 4, 272, 275, 330. *See also* Portfolios, student

Association for the Study of Higher Education (ASHE) listserv conference, 198

Attitudinal changes, 279

Attributes, in schema theory, 233

Augment hypertext system, 230

B

Background Knowledge Probe, 43, 51, 59

BaFa'BaFa' exercise, 142–143, 157

Behavioral changes, 279

Behavioral learning, 134, 140

Beliefs: and organizational culture, 279; and thinking, 19–21

Beyond Einstein hypermedia program, 240

Biases, 153

Bio Sci II videodisc, 217, 223–226

Biological sciences: and hypermedia instruction, 239–240; and multicultural instruction, 117–123

BITNET (computer network), 196

Bloom's taxonomy, 23, 95

Brainstorming examples, 51

Business. *See* Workplace

C

California Online Resources for Education (CORE), 193

California State University, Fullerton (CSUF). *See* Developmental Writing Program

Campaign stage, and change, 285–286

Campus climate: and diversity, 113–115, 133; and learning, 345

Campus-Wide Information Systems (CWIS), 201

CatTutor hypermedia program, 242

Change: continuum, 277, 280–281; and institutional assessment, 277–287; models of, 279–280; and organizational culture, 279; resistance to, 278, 282, 284; stages of, 280–287; in student demographics, 2–3, 110, 128; in teaching and learning, 2, 3–4, 291–292, 349; technological, 1–2; workplace, 2

Cognition, 21

Cognitive learning, 134, 140; cognitive flexibility theory, 233–234

Collaboration in Undergraduate Education (CUE) Collaborative and Cooperative Learning Network, 89

Collaboration stage, and change, 286

Collaborative learning, 74, 75, 137, 153, 314

Communication: feedback, 9, 292–293, 295, 318–320; about racism, 165–166. *See also* Internet

CompuServe (computer network), 192–193, 196, 202

Computers: addresses of, 200, 204; computer science and hypermedia instruction, 242–243; and cooperative learning, 216; and critical thinking, 215–216; and cultural literacy, 214; DOS instruction, 237; host, 193; and hypertext, 230; and modems, 192, 195; software for, 194, 200, 202, 207–208, 217–218, 227–228. *See also* Electronic mail; Hypermedia; Interactive video; Internet; Software ethics; Technology

Conferences, listserv, 197–199

Consortium for School Networking (CoSN), 198

Constructive (structured) controversy, 80

Constructivism, and cognitive flexibility theory, 233
Contour hypermedia program, 241
Cooperative learning: and classroom assessment, 300–301; and collaborative learning, 74, 75; constructive controversy, 80; and creativity, 66; experimenting with, 81–82; features of, 75–76, 81; future of, 86–88; group investigation, 80–81; implementing, 82–84; and individual accountability, 75, 86, 301; and interactive video, 216–217, 219–220; jigsaw, 80; objections to, 84–86; and positive interdependence, 75, 83; research on, 77–79, 86–88, 137, 153; STAD (student teams achievement division), 79–80; types of, 79–81
Cooperative Learning Center, 89–90
Copy protection, 263
Copyright, 254–255, 263
Counterexamples, 46–47
Coursework Cluster Analysis Model (CCAM), 334–335
Creativity: and cooperative learning, 66; environmental factors for, 68; and instructor characteristics, 68; and motivation, 65–66; in problem solving, 64–65; SCAMPER technique, 66–67; stimulating, 66–67; strategies to foster, 69–70
Criterion-referenced grading, 83
Critical epistemology, 33–34
Critical thinking: and choices, 13, 14–15; and classroom assessment, 297–300; defined, 13, 19; and educating for diversity, 130; empowerment through, 14–15, 33–34; and explanations, 29–31; and guided reciprocal peer questioning, 22–29; and interactive video, 215–216; and knowledge construction, 15–16, 26; and languages of thinking, 21; and learning community, 31; and metacognition, 21–22, 27; teaching, 17–22; and thinking dispositions, 19–21; transfer of, 31–33; in workplace, 2, 111
Cultural assimilators, 150–151
Cultural diversity. See Multiculturalism
Cultural lag, 119

Cultural literacy, 213, 214–215, 227–228
Cultural Pursuit game, 145, 157
Cultural universals, 118–119
Culture: of evidence, 275–277, 281, 291; organizational, 279
Curricular coherence, 111–113, 177, 336
Curricular sequence, 335, 341–342
Curriculum: coherence of, 111–113, 177, 336; and diversity, 129, 131, 132; and general education, 331–338; multicultural, 111–113, 115–116, 123–124, 177–179, 214–215, 301–302; reform, 177–179, 329–331, 344–345; software ethics in, 262. See also Assessment, learning; Learning; Teaching

D

Data, assessment, 275–276
Data Research Associates, 201
Denial stage, and change, 282
Developmental Writing Program (CSUF), 310–311; assessment and feedback, 318–320; assistance network, 312, 319–320; faculty, 316–318, 319–320; portfolio process, 312–316; students, 311–312, 318–319; and Writing Center, 312, 320–326
Diagnoser, The, hypermedia program, 240
Discrimination, reverse, 167–168, 172. See also Racism
Discussion format, 84; group, 146–149
Dispositions, thinking, 19–21
Diversity: educating for, 128–130; master plan, 131–133; and multiculturalism, 128. See also Multiculturalism
Diversity Awareness Profile (DAP), 157–158

E

EGADS (Electronics Guidance and Documentation Systems) hypermedia system, 238
Elaboration resources theory, 233
Electronic mail (E-mail), 193, 194, 195–196; electronic publications,

196-197; electronic texts (etexts), 199; file servers, 199, 204-205; listserv conferences, 197-199

Employment. *See* Workplace

Empowerment, 14-15, 33-34

Endowed professorships, 8

Engineering, and hypermedia instruction, 237-239, 244

English as a second language (ESL), 315-316

Entity learning, 20

Equal protection, and multiculturalism, 114

Ethics, defined, 263. *See also* Software ethics

Ethnic gap, 120

Ethnic identity, 123-124

Ethnic studies, 113, 115, 135-136, 178, 179-183

Ethnicity, and disease, 121-122

Ethnobotany, 122

Evaluation. *See* Assessment; Assessment, classroom; Assessment, institutional; Assessment, learning; Assessment, student; Portfolios, student

Examples, teaching with, 39-41; brainstorming, 51; counterexamples, 46-47; example map, 51-53; exercises, 54-57; misinterpreted, 44-45; objections to sequencing, 57-62; paradigmatic, 41-44, 45-46; parameters of, 48-50; sequencing, 47-50; stereotypical, 45; student-generated, 51-57; transfer of, 46; typicality effects, 42-44

Exercises, experiential, 137, 140; games, 144-146; group discussion, 146-149; role-playing, 140-142; simulations, 142-144; written, 149-152

Exercises, sequencing, 54-57

Explanations, student-generated, 29-31

Extracurricular activities, 340-341, 345

F

Faculty: challenges for, 290-291; and classroom assessment, 290-291, 292-293, 294-296, 302, 303; and curricular reform, 178-179; and educating for diversity, 133, 183-187; and institutional assessment, 273, 282, 284, 285, 286-287; and instructor characteristics, 152-154; and learning assessment, 338-340, 343-344; and portfolio assessment, 316-318, 319-320, 327; and racism, 172-173. *See also* Assessment, classroom; Teaching

FarWestNet (computer network), 195

Feedback, 9, 292-293, 295, 318-320

Forced associations, 67

Foreign languages, and hypermedia instruction, 241

Free speech: and computer networks, 197; and multiculturalism, 114

Freeware, 263

Ftp (anonymous file transfer protocol), 193, 194, 203-205

G

Games: concept of, and sequencing examples, 51-53; and creativity, 69; and educating for diversity, 144-146, 157

Gender: equality, 112, 118, 215, 227-228; gap, 120

General education, and curriculum, 331-338

Generic questions, 23

Genetics, and multiculturalism, 119-120, 121-122

Gibbereseans and Nouvellese exercise, 143-144

Goals: general education, 335-338; teaching, 294-295

Grading, 83, 316-318, 320

Graduate students, teaching experience for, 9

Grammateiuon hypermedia program, 241

Grant proposals, 5

Groups: changes in, 279-280; collaborative, 314; and cooperative learning, 75-76, 79-81, 84, 220; and creativity, 66; group discussion, 146-149; group investigation, 80-81, 102-103; group processing, 76; hypermedia tools for, 236; and individual accountability, 75, 86, 301; small-group interactions, 100

H

Harvard Assessment Seminars, 272
Herbal medicine, 122
Hero concept, and sequencing examples, 47–48
Hitchhikers, in groups, 301
HOLLIS catalogue (Harvard University), 201
Homosexuality, 121
HyperBrain instruction program, 239
HyperCard, 230, 232, 236, 240, 241, 242, 244
HyperCOSTOC instruction program, 238
Hypermedia: browsing systems, 236; defined, 231–232; general-purpose, 236; and hypertext, 230–231, 234, 236; and information, 230–235, 245–246; instruction research, 243–244; instructional difficulties with, 235–236, 244–245; instructional theories, 232–234; instructional uses, 236–243; and knowledge, 231, 232–235, 245–246; and learning, 233–234, 243–244; macro-literary systems, 236; nodes and links, 231–232; and nonlinear thinking, 235; potential of, 234–235; problem exploration tools, 236
Hypertext, 230–231, 234, 236

I

Incentives. *See* Rewards
Incremental learning, 20
Individual accountability, and cooperative learning, 57, 86
InfoEd data base, 202
Information: assessment, 275–276, 318–320, 344; feedback, 9, 292–293, 295, 318–320; and hypermedia, 230–235, 245–246; through Internet, 194, 196, 198, 199, 200–203; vs. knowledge, 16; National Information Infrastructure (NII), 208, 209; overload, 114–115; and student portfolios, 309–310, 318–320
Inquiry. *See* Questioning, guided reciprocal peer; Questioning, teaching by
Institutionalization stage, and change, 286–287

Intelligence, practical, 5
Intelligent hypertutoring, 238. *See also* Hypermedia
Interactive video: benefits of, 226–227; Bio Sci II videodisc, 217, 223–226; and cooperative learning, 216–217, 219–220; and critical thinking, 215–216; and cultural literacy, 213, 214–215, 227–228; hardware/software for, 217–219, 227–228; National Gallery of Art videodisc, 217, 220–222; Vincent van Gogh Revisited videodisc, 217, 222–223
Intermedia instruction program, 232, 239–240
Internet (computer network): anonymous file transfer protocol (ftp), 193, 194, 203–205; barriers to, 205–208; conferences, 197–199, 202–203; electronic mail (E-mail), 193, 194, 195–199; electronic publications, 196–197; electronic texts (etexts), 199; file servers, 199, 204–205, 207; and future developments, 208–210; instruction in using, 205–206; listserv conferences, 197–199; local area computer network (LAN), 192, 195; metasearch software, 207–208; NREN, 208–209; protocol (IP), 194, 206; resources, 211; telnet, 193, 194, 200–203; userid, 204; wide area computer network (WAN), 191–194

J

Jigsaw, 80, 102
Journals: electronic, 196–197; student, 69
Judgment, deferred, 67

K

Killer statements, 67
Knowledge: changes, 279; construction, 15–16, 26, 140, 233–234; and hypermedia, 231, 232–235, 245–246; pedagogical content, 303; revolution, 111–112, 115; structures, 233; and teaching, 350; transformative academic, 129

L

Language, and multiculturalism, 119-120
Languages of thinking, 21
Leadership, and change, 280, 282, 284-285, 286
Learning: active, 4, 11, 137, 291, 297; change in, 2, 3-4, 291-292, 349; and classroom assessment, 291, 293, 295, 297-303, 330-331; community, 31; conditional, 298, 299; and curricular reform, 329-331, 344-345; differences in, 331-334, 335-336, 340-341; entity, 20; and explanations, 29-31; factors influencing, 342; forms of, and multicultural education, 134-135, 140; and hypermedia, 233-234, 243-244; incremental, 20; and knowledge construction, 15-16, 26, 233-234; procedural, 298-299; and questioning, 23-27, 94; reflective, 298, 299; student responsibility for, 291, 293, 295, 309; subenvironments, 340-341, 343; teaching and, cycle, 293; theories, 15-16, 233-234; web, 233. *See also* Assessment, learning; Cooperative learning
Lecture format: vs. active learning, 11, 15-16, 17; and cooperative learning, 76, 81-82, 84-85; and knowledge construction, 15-16; and student-generated questions, 28
Library science, and hypermedia instruction, 242
License, software, 262-263, 264-265
Literature, and hypermedia instruction, 240-241
Local area computer network (LAN), 192, 195. *See also* Internet

M

Make-sense epistemology, 33
Maxwell Online data bases, 202
Medical professions, and hypermedia instruction, 239, 243
MELVYL catalogue (University of California), 200-201
Mentors, 312
MERIT (computer network), 202

Metacognition, 21-22, 27, 293, 308
Michigan State University catalogue, 201
Minorities, 2-3, 15, 110, 115, 311-312. *See also* Multiculturalism
Mitochondrial Eve, 120-121
MIX (computer network), 192-193
Mixed concepts, 59
Modems, 192, 195
Monty Python and the Holy Grail, 41, 45, 59
Motivation, 65-66, 137, 153, 213
Multiculturalism, 2-3; attitudes toward, 176, 183-187; and classroom assessment, 153, 301-302; and cultural literacy, 213, 214-215, 227-228; and curricular coherence, 111-113, 177; and curricular outcomes, 115-116, 123-124, 133, 135, 187-188, 214-215, 301-302; and curricular reform, 177-179; and diversity, 128; and educating for diversity, 128-130; ethnic studies, 113, 115, 135-136, 178, 179-183; films and videotapes, 156; and forms of learning, 134-135, 140; and general education requirements, 113; in hard sciences, 116-123, 135; issues of, 113-115; in liberal arts, 116, 134-135; multicultural education, 109-110; 123-124, 134-137; multicultural education models, 135-137; readings and references, 154-156; and student demographics, 2-3, 110, 128. *See also* Diversity

N

NASA: Ames NASA file server, 204; Spacelink information service, 201
National Center for Educational Statistics, study by, 6
National Center on Postsecondary Teaching, Learning, and Assessment, 88
National Gallery of Art videodisc, 217, 220-222
National Information Infrastructure (NII), 208, 209
National Research and Education Network (NREN), 208-209

Network for Cooperative Learning in Higher Education, 88–89
Networks, 133, 153, 312. *See also* Internet
New England Resource Center for Higher Education, 90
Norm-referenced grading, 83
Notes hypermedia program, 240
NSFNET (National Science Foundation network), 202, 208

O

Oceanic: The Ocean Information Center, 201
Online Public Access Catalogues (OPACs), 200–201
Organizational renewal, 279. *See also* Change
Outcomes: assessment of, 4, 272, 275, 330–331; multicultural curriculum, 115–116, 123–124, 133, 135, 187–188, 214–215, 301–302; student, 4, 111–113, 123–124, 272, 275, 331–334. *See also* Assessment, learning; Learning

P

Paired responses, 100
Paradigmatic examples, 41–44, 45–46; parameters of, 48–50
Party, The, 142, 157
Pedagogical content knowledge, 303
Performance assessment, 337, 340–342. *See also* Assessment, learning; Portfolios, student
Performing arts, and creativity, 69–70
Physical sciences, and hypermedia instruction, 240
Piracy, software, 256, 263
Plagiarism, in writing courses, 315, 316
Political correctness, 179, 187
Politics, and curricular reform, 178
Portfolios, student: assessment and feedback, 318–320; assessment model, 310–320; assessment principles, 307–310, 326–327; assessment process, 312–316, 320–326; assistance network, 312, 319–320; contextual nature of, 310, 312, 323, 326; defined, 306–307; Developmental Writing Program (CSUF), 310–320; and

faculty, 316–318, 319–320, 327; grading, 316–318, 320; information provided through, 309–310; and metacognition, 308
Positive interdependence, and cooperative learning, 75, 84
Power Shuffle game, 145
Practical intelligence, 5
Prejudice, 115, 118. *See also* Racism
Probing, 94
Problem solving: and classroom assessment, 299–300; creative, 64–65; face-to-face, 76. *See also* Critical thinking
Project Gutenberg, 199
Project Hermes file server (Case Western Reserve University), 204
Project Jefferson hypermedia program, 240–241
Psychology, and hypermedia instruction, 241–242
Public domain software, 263
Publications, electronic, 196–197
Publishing, 5–6, 8–9, 350

Q

Quality: educational, 6–7; teaching, 8–10
Questioning, guided reciprocal peer, 23–27; and empowerment, 33–34; research on, 27–29, 32; and transfer of thinking skills, 31–33. *See also* Questioning, teaching by
Questioning, teaching by, 17–18, 22–31, 94–104, 153; Aschner-Gallagher's classification system, 95; Bloom's taxonomy, 23, 95; enhancing responses, 101, 104; and explanations, 29–31; interactions, 98–101; and knowledge construction, 26; and learning, 23–27, 94; and metacognition, 27; paired responses, 100; phrasing, 94; probing, 94; processes, 98; research on, 27–29, 32, 94, 98; small-group interactions, 100; student-generated, 22–31; types of, 94–98; whole-class techniques, 101. *See also* Questioning, guided reciprocal peer
Questionnaires: classroom assessment, 297; self-assessment, 152, 157–158

R

Racism: classroom, 172–173; and classroom instruction, 118; communicating about, 165–166; and context, 170; continuum, 169; cultural, 169; and curriculum, 112; and free speech, 114; ineradicable, 169–170; institutional, 168–169; interview exercise, 152; myths of, 166–168; personal, 168, 169; and perspective, 170–171; semantic differences, 120; sensitivity to, 171–172

Relationships, explaining, 30

Release time, 7, 9, 115, 132

Reproductive behavior, and multiculturalism, 122–123

Research: classroom, 294, 299–300; and Internet computer network, 194, 196, 199, 200–203, 204–205; library, and interactive video, 222; National Research and Education Network (NREN), 208–209; and teaching, 6–7, 9–10, 350; universities, 6

Resistance, to change, 278, 282, 284

Rewards: for diversity in education, 132, 133; and teaching quality, 8

Risk taking, and creativity, 68

Role playing, 140–142, 157

Roundtable hypermedia program, 240

S

San Diego Supercomputer Center (SDSC), 201

SCAMPER technique, and creativity, 66–67

Schema theory, 233

Scholarship, 6, 350

Science and Technology Information System (STIS), 199

Self-assessment instruments, 152, 157–158

Semantic moves, and racism, 172

Sexism, 112, 118

Sexual behavior, and multiculturalism, 122–123

Sexual orientation, 121

Shareware, 263

Simulations, 142–144, 157; virtual reality, 209

Situational ethics, 257

Skills: contextbound, 31–32; workplace, 111

Small-group interactions, 100

Softlifting, 263

Software. *See* Computers: software for; Software ethics

Software ethics: attitudes toward, 255–258; and copyright violation, 254–255; guidelines, 264–266; research on, 255–258; scenarios, 258–261, 263–264; and software license, 262–263; teaching, 255, 262–266; terminology, 263. *See also* Computers

Source, The (computer network), 192–193, 196

STAD (student teams achievement division), 79–80

Stand and Declare game, 146

Stanford University, and multiculturalism, 113

Star Power game, 145, 157

Stat Helper hypermedia program, 242

Statistics, and hypermedia instruction, 242

Stereotypes, 115, 116, 118, 119, 153, 214

Student Evaluations of Teaching (SETs), 330

Students: challenges for, 291; changing demographics of, 2–3, 110, 128; and classroom assessment, 291, 293, 295, 297, 330; development of, 123–124; high-/low-achieving, 336; and hypermedia instruction, 234–236, 243–244; motivating, 65–66, 137, 153, 213; outcomes of, 111–113, 123–124, 272, 275, 331–334; persistence of, 337–338; and portfolio assessment, 318–319, 327; responsibility of, for learning, 291, 293, 295, 309, 323–324; and software ethics, 256–257; and subenvironments, 340–341, 343. *See also* Learning; Portfolios, student

Subenvironments, learning, 340–341, 343

Survival exercise, 143

T

Teaching: assessment insights about, 343–344; assistance centers, 8; change in, 2, 3–4, 291–292, 349; expertise, 303; goals, 294–295; importance of, 1, 4, 349–351; improving, 8–10, 292–293; and instructor characteristics, 152–154; and learning cycle, 293; load, 7; multicultural education, 116–123, 135–137, 183–187; prejudice against, 4–7; quality, 8–10; and research, 6–7, 9–10, 350; scholarship of, 350; software ethics, 255, 262–266; technology in, 3–4. *See also* Assessment, classroom; Assessment, learning; Cooperative learning; Creativity; Critical thinking; Examples, teaching with; Exercises, experiential; Hypermedia; Interactive video; Questioning, teaching by

Teaching Goals Inventory, 294–295, 296

Teachism, 7

Teams, cooperative learning, 75–76, 79–81, 84, 220. *See also* Groups

Technology: hypermedia and technical instruction, 237–239; new, 1–2, 254–255, 262; in teaching and learning, 3–4. *See also* Computers; Electronic mail; Hypermedia; Interactive video; Internet; Software ethics

Telnet, 193, 194, 200–203

Time measurement, and multiculturalism, 122

Transfer: of critical thinking, 31–33; of examples, 46

Triads, 102

Trust, and change, 284

Tutors, 312, 320–326

2-4-8: Tell/Retell (small-group interaction strategy), 102

Typicality effects, 42–44

U

Understanding stage, and change, 284–285

Universities: quality of, 6–7; teaching vs. research, 6

University of Wisconsin file server, 204

V

Videodiscs. *See* Interactive video

Videotapes, 147, 149, 156, 218–219

Vincent van Gogh Revisited videodisc, 217, 222–223

Virtual reality simulations, 209

Vision, of undergraduate education, 289–290

Visual arts, and creativity, 69–70

W

Wait time, 20

Washington Center for Improving the Quality of Undergraduate Education, 90–91

Web learning, 233

Whole-class techniques, 101

Wide area computer network (WAN), 191–194. *See also* Internet

Women: and computers, 214, 215, 216; depiction of, in art, 220–221; and linguistic gap, 120; students, 2, 110; studies of, 115

Workplace: change, 2; and critical thinking, 111; networks with, 133; and software ethics, 257

Writing: centers, 312, 320–326; Developmental Writing Program (CSUF), 310–320; grading, 316–318; and hypermedia instruction, 240–241; responding vs. evaluating, 314, 324–325; and student portfolios, 307–310; timed, 315–316

Written exercises, and multiculturalism, 149–152

X

Xanadu hypermedia program, 240

Printed in the United States
37458LVS00001B/181